The

Basics

—— *of* ——

New Testament
Syntax

Other Books by Daniel B. Wallace

Greek Grammar Beyond the Basics

The Abridgment of *Greek Grammar Beyond the Basics*

The
Basics
—— *of* ——
New Testament
Syntax

**AN INTERMEDIATE
GREEK GRAMMAR**

Daniel B.
WALLACE

ZONDERVAN.com/
AUTHOR**TRACKER**
follow your favorite authors

The Basics of New Testament Syntax
Copyright © 2000 by Daniel B. Wallace

Requests for information should be addressed to:

Zondervan, *Grand Rapids, Michigan* 49530

Library of Congress Cataloging-in-Publication Data

Wallace, Daniel B.
    The basics of New Testament syntax: an intermediate Greek grammar / Daniel B. Wallace.
      p. cm.
    "Abridgment of Greek grammar beyond the basics: an exegetical syntax of the
New Testament"—P.1.
    Includes bibliographical references and index.
    ISBN 10: 0-310-23229-5 (hardcover)
    ISBN 13: 978-0-310-23229-2 (hardcover)
    1. Greek language, Biblical—Syntax.   2. Greek language, Biblical—Grammar. 3. Bible. N.T.— Lan-
guage, style. I. Wallace, Daniel B. Greek grammar beyond the basics. II. Title.   PA851.W338 2000
487'.4 – dc   00-029003
                                                                CIP

This edition printed on acid-free paper.

Printed in China

08 09 10 11 12 13 14 15 16 17 18 19 • 21 20 19 18 17 16 15 14 13 12 11 10 9

To Pati

CONTENTS

Illustrations 9
Abbreviations 12
Preface 15
The Language of the New Testament 17

Syntax of Words and Phrases

    Part I: Syntax of Nouns and Nominals

        The Cases

            The Cases: An Introduction 25

            Nominative Case 28

            Vocative Case 38

            Genitive Case 41

            Dative Case 65

            Accusative Case 81

        The Article

            Part I: Origin, Function, Regular Uses, Absence 93

            Part II: Special Uses and Non-Uses of the Article 114

        Adjectives 129

        Pronouns 140

        Prepositions 160

    Part II: Syntax of Verbs and Verbals

        Person and Number 174

        Voice 179

            Active 180

            Middle 182

            Passive 186

        Mood 192

            Indicative 195

            Subjunctive 201

            Optative 209

            Imperative 210

Tense. 213
   The Tenses: An Introduction 213
   Present. 219
   Imperfect 232
   Aorist 239
   Future 244
   Perfect and Pluperfect. 246
  The Infinitive 254
  The Participle 266

Syntax of the Clause

  Introduction to Greek Clauses. 286
  The Role of Conjunctions 293
  Special Studies in the Clauses
   Conditional Sentences. 303
   Volitional Clauses (Commands and Prohibitions) 316

Subject Index/Cheat Sheet 323
Scripture Index. 329

ILLUSTRATIONS

Tables

1. Literary Levels of New Testament Authors 23
2. Five-Case System Vs. Eight-Case System 27
3. The Functions of the Adjective 130
4. Attributive and Predicate Positions of the Adjective 137
5. How Agency is Expressed in the New Testament 187
6. The Semantics of the Moods Compared 193
7. English Tenses in Direct and Indirect Discourse. 199
8. The Semantics of Deliberative Questions 203
9. The Forms of the Periphrastic Participle. 282
10. The Structure of Conditions 309

Charts, Figures, and Diagrams

1. The Multifaceted Nature of New Testament Greek 22
2. Frequency of Case-Forms in the New Testament 25
3. Frequency of Cases in the New Testament (Nominative) 28
4. Semantic Relation of Subject and Predicate Nominative 31
5. Frequency of Cases in the New Testament (Vocative). 38
6. Frequency of Cases in the New Testament (Genitive) 42
7. The Relation of Descriptive Genitive to Various
   Other Genitive Uses. 46
8. The Semantics of the Attributive Genitive 49
9. A Semantic Diagram of the Attributive Genitive and
   Attributed Genitive. 50
10. Genitive of Content Vs. Genitive of Material 51
11. Genitive of Apposition Vs. Genitive in Simple Apposition. 53
12. Diagrams of Subjective and Objective Genitive 58
13. Frequency of Cases in the New Testament (Dative) 66
14. Frequency of Cases in the New Testament (Accusative) 82
15. The Semantics of the Object-Complement Construction 85
16. The Cases for Time 91
17. The Basic Forces of the Article 94
18. Individualizing Vs. Generic Article 101
19. The Semantic Relations of the Individualizing Article 102
20. Flow Chart on the Article with Substantives 103

21. The Semantics of Anarthrous Nouns...........................108
22 The Semantics of Indefinite Nouns............................109
23. The Semantics of Qualitative Nouns..........................109
24. The Semantics of Generic Nouns 109
25. The Semantics of Definite Nouns 110
26. The Different Databases for Colwell's Rule Vs.
      Colwell's Construction 116
27. The Semantic Range of Anarthrous Predicate Nominatives.........117
28. Distinct Groups, though United [TSKS Plural
      Personal Construction]....................................123
29. Overlapping Groups [TSKS Plural Personal Construction].........124
30. First Group Subset of Second [TSKS Plural Personal Construction] . 125
31. Second Group Subset of First [TSKS Plural Personal Construction] . 125
32. Both Groups Identical [TSKS Plural Personal Construction] 126
33. The Semantic Range of the Forms of the Adjective 135
34. Frequency of Pronoun Classes in the New Testament 142
35. Frequency of Pronoun Terms in the New Testament 159
36. Frequencies of Prepositions in the New Testament 161
37. The Spatial Functions of Prepositions........................162
38. Semantic Overlap Between Simple Case and Preposition + Case.....164
39. Overlap in Uses of Ἀντί and Ὑπέρ...........................172
40. The Scope of "We" in the New Testament 175
41. The Direction of the Action in Greek Voices 180
42. Voice Statistics in the New Testament........................181
43. The Moods Viewed in Two Continua 194
44. Mood Frequencies in the New Testament......................194
45. Semantic Overlap of Subjunctive and Optative...................201
46. Relative Frequency of Tenses in the New Testament 214
47. The Force of the Instantaneous Present 221
48. The Force of the Progressive Present 222
49. The Force of the Extending-from-Past Present 223
50. The Force of the Iterative Present............................223
51. The Force of the Customary Present..........................224
52. The Force of the Gnomic Present 225
53. The Force of the Historical Present...........................226
54. The Force of the Perfective Present...........................228
55. The Force of the (True) Conative Present......................228
56. The Force of the Tendential Present 229
57. The Force of the Completely Futuristic Present.................229
58. The Force of the Mostly Futuristic Present.....................230

59. The Basic Force of the Imperfect. 233
60. The Force of the Progressive Imperfect 233
61. The Force of the Ingressive Imperfect. 234
62. The Force of the Iterative Imperfect 235
63. The Force of the Customary Imperfect. 235
64. The Force of the (True) Conative Imperfect. 236
65. The Force of the Tendential Imperfect 237
66. The Force of the Aorist Indicative 239
67. The Force of the Future Tense. 244
68. The Force of the Perfect. 247
69. The Force of the Intensive Perfect. 248
70. The Force of the Extensive Perfect 248
71. The Force of the Dramatic Perfect 249
72. The Perfect with Present Force 250
73. The Aoristic Perfect and Perfect with Present Force Compared 250
74. The Force of the Pluperfect 251
75. The Force of the Intensive Pluperfect 251
76. The Force of the Extensive Pluperfect. 252
77. The Semantic Range of the Infinitive 256
78. Time in Participles 267
79. The Semantic Range of the Participle 269
80. The Tenses of Adverbial Participles 273
81. The Semantic Overlap of Purpose and Result Participles. 279

ABBREVIATIONS

➥	Common categories that all intermediate Greek students must know
†	Abused categories that intermediate Greek students should be aware of
acc.	accusative
Accordance	Macintosh software program that performs sophisticated searches on a morphologically tagged Greek NT (Nestle-Aland[26/27] text) as well as a Hebrew OT (*BHS*). Marketed by the Gramcord Institute, Vancouver, Washington, and programmed by Roy Brown.
BAGD	Bauer, W. *A Greek-English Lexicon of the New Testament and Other Early Christian Literature.* Trans. and rev. W. F. Arndt, F. W. Gingrich, and F. W. Danker. Chicago: University of Chicago Press, 1979.
BDF	Blass, F., and A. Debrunner. *A Greek Grammar of the New Testament and Other Early Christian Literature.* Trans. and rev. R. W. Funk. Chicago: University of Chicago Press, 1961.
Bib	*Biblica*
Brooks-Winbery	Brooks, J. A., and C. L. Winbery. *Syntax of New Testament Greek.* Washington, D.C.: University Press of America, 1979.
Chamberlain, *Exegetical Grammar*	Chamberlain, W. D. *An Exegetical Grammar of the Greek New Testament.* New York: Macmillan, 1941.
Dana-Mantey	Dana, H. E., and J. R. Mantey. *A Manual Grammar of the Greek New Testament.* Toronto: Macmillan, 1927.
dat.	dative
ExSyn	*Exegetical Syntax*
Exegetical Syntax	Wallace, Daniel B. *Greek Grammar Beyond the Basics: An Exegetical Syntax of the Greek New Testament.* Grand Rapids: Zondervan, 1996.
Fanning, *Verbal Aspect*	Fanning, B. M. *Verbal Aspect in New Testament Greek.* Oxford: Clarendon, 1990.
gen.	genitive

Gramcord	Windows software program that performs sophisticated searches on a morphologically tagged Greek NT (Nestle-Aland[26] text) as well as a Hebrew OT (*BHS*). Marketed by the Gramcord Institute, Vancouver, Washington, and programmed by Paul Miller.
GTJ	*Grace Theological Journal*
JB	Jerusalem Bible
KJV	King James Version
LXX	Septuagint
McKay, "Time and Aspect"	McKay, K. L. "Time and Aspect in New Testament Greek," *Novum Testamentum* 34 (1992): 209–28.
Moule, *Idiom Book*	Moule, C. F. D. *An Idiom Book of New Testament Greek*. 2d ed. Cambridge: Cambridge University Press, 1959.
Moulton, *Prolegomena*	Moulton, J. H. *A Grammar of New Testament Greek*. Vol. 1, *Prolegomena*. 3d ed. Edinburgh: T. & T. Clark, 1908.
Mounce, *Basics of Biblical Greek*	Mounce, W. D. *Basics of Biblical Greek*. Grand Rapids: Zondervan, 1993.
MS(S)	manuscript(s)
NASB	New American Standard Bible
NEB	New English Bible
NET	New English Translation
Nestle-Aland[26]	*Novum Testamentum Graece*. Ed. K. Aland, M. Black, C. M. Martini, B. M. Metzger, A. Wikgren. 26th ed. Stuttgart: Deutsche Bibelgesellschaft, 1979.
Nestle-Aland[27]	*Novum Testamentum Graece*. Ed. B. Aland, K. Aland, J. Karavidopoulos, C. M. Martini, B. M. Metzger. 27th ed. Stuttgart: Deutsche Bibelgesellschaft, 1993.
NKJV	New King James Version
NIV	New International Version
nom.	nominative
NovT	*Novum Testamentum*
NRSV	New Revised Standard Version
NT	New Testament
NTS	*New Testament Studies*
OT	Old Testament

Porter, *Idioms*	Porter, S. E. *Idioms of the Greek New Testament*. Sheffield: JSOT Press, 1992.
Robertson, *Grammar*	Robertson, A. T. *A Grammar of the Greek New Testament in the Light of Historical Research*. 4th ed. New York: Hodder & Stoughton, 1923.
RSV	Revised Standard Version
TSKS	Article-Substantive-Καί-Substantive
UBS³	*The Greek New Testament*. Ed. K. Aland, M. Black, C. M. Martini, B. M. Metzger, A. Wikgren. 3d ed., corrected. Stuttgart: United Bible Societies, 1983.
UBS⁴	*The Greek New Testament*. Ed. B. Aland, K. Aland, J. Karavidopoulos, C. M. Martini, B. M. Metzger. 4th ed., corrected. Stuttgart: United Bible Societies, 1994.
Vaughan-Gideon	Vaughan, C., and V. E. Gideon. *A Greek Grammar of the New Testament*. Nashville: Broadman, 1979.
v.l.(l)	textual variant(s)
voc.	vocative
Williams, *Grammar Notes*	Williams, P. R. *Grammar Notes on the Noun and the Verb and Certain Other Items*, rev. ed. Tacoma, Wash.: Northwest Baptist Seminary, 1988.
Young, *Intermediate Greek*	Young, R. A. *Intermediate New Testament Greek: A Linguistic and Exegetical Approach*. Nashville: Broadman, 1994.
Zerwick, *Biblical Greek*	Zerwick, M. *Biblical Greek Illustrated by Examples*. Rome: Pontificii Instituti Biblici, 1963.

PREFACE

This grammar is essentially an abridgment of *Greek Grammar Beyond the Basics: An Exegetical Syntax of the New Testament* (Grand Rapids: Zondervan, 1996). It is systematically cross-referenced to the larger work (referred to as *Exegetical Syntax* or *ExSyn* throughout this book) so that the interested student may be able to find expanded discussions easily.

Because of the size of *Exegetical Syntax* several teachers of intermediate Greek have felt it was unwieldy to use as a one-semester textbook. This book is offered to them in the hope that they will find it more useful. *Basics of New Testament Syntax* is about one third the size of *Exegetical Syntax*. It may be helpful to list the kinds of things that have been omitted:

- The rarest categories of usage
- Most exegetical discussions[1]
- Most of the biblical examples and cited references
- The select bibliographies at the beginning of each chapter
- Virtually all text-critical notes
- Advanced material (e.g., the appendices on verbal aspect and conditional clauses)
- Many of the more detailed discussions of the semantics of a particular syntactical category

What has not been removed or altered are the following:

- Category titles
- "Arrowed" and "daggered" categories, indicating which uses are common and abused, respectively
- The vast bulk of charts and tables

At bottom, this book "majors on the majors." It is designed more for the student whose interests are focused on Greek syntax than for those who desire to see the relevance of syntax for exegesis. Nevertheless, at over 300 pages, one could hardly call this a mere *outline* of Greek syntax! It should be helpful for anyone who wants to learn (or relearn) the basics of New Testament syntax.

Basics of New Testament Syntax was not produced in a vacuum. Thanks are due especially to Chris Bradley, Chad Crammer, and Les Hicks for their help in the summer of 1999. Among other things, Chris keyed in the cross-references to *Exegetical Syntax*, while Chad and Les helped with style and content. Thanks are due, too, to Princeton University for their stipend to Chris, enabling him to work on this project.

---

[1] *Exegetical Syntax* includes over 800 discussions of texts whose interpretation is impacted by the syntax. Only a handful of these have been retained in this work, but most of the discussions are cross-referenced by way of a footnote.

To Pati, my wife of more than a quarter of a century: I am grateful for your impatience with my long-windedness; it is because of you that I understand why a book like this is needed.

I am thankful as well to Zondervan Publishing House for accepting yet another manuscript from me: to Jack Kragt, whose sensitivity to the needs of Greek teachers first prompted me to think about writing this book; to Stan Gundry, for his vision and leadership in Christian academic publishing; and especially to Verlyn Verbrugge, whose encouragement in the editing process made writing this book a light task.

THE LANGUAGE OF THE
NEW TESTAMENT[1]

In this chapter our goal is twofold: (1) to see where NT Greek fits in the history of the Greek language (this is known as a diachronic and external study), and (2) to look at certain issues related to NT Greek per se (this is a synchronic and internal study).

Overview of Chapter

Stages of the Greek Language (Diachronic) 17
   1. Pre-Homeric (up to 1000 BCE). 17
   2. The Age of the Dialects, or the Classical Era
      (1000 BCE–330 BCE) 18
   3. Κοινή Greek (330 BCE–330 CE). 18
   4. Byzantine (or Medieval) Greek (330 CE–1453 CE) 18
   5. Modern Greek (1453 CE to present) 18

Κοινή Greek (Synchronic) 19
   1. Terminology 19
   2. Historical Development. 19
   3. Scope of Κοινή Greek 19
   4. Changes from Classical Greek. 19
   5. Types of Κοινή Greek 20

New Testament Greek 20
   1. The Language Milieu of Palestine. 20
   2. Place of the Language of the New Testament in
      Hellenistic Greek 21

Stages of the Greek Language (Diachronic)   *ExSyn 14–17*

There are five great stages of the Greek language.

1. Pre-Homeric (up to 1000 BCE)

As early as the third millennium BCE, tribes of Indo-European peoples wandered into Greece. Unfortunately, because we lack literary remains, we know little from this period about the Greek language.

---

[1] See *ExSyn*, 12–30.

2. The Age of the Dialects, or the Classical Era (1000 BCE–330 BCE)

Geography and politics (e.g., independent city-states) caused Greek to fracture into several dialects, four of which were predominant: Aeolic, Doric, Ionic, and by far the most influential, Attic. Attic Greek, in fact, was an offspring of Ionic; it was the dialect of Athens, the political and literary center of Greece during the "golden age" of classical Greek (5th–4th centuries BCE). Attic is often equated with classical Greek.

3. Κοινή Greek (330 BCE–330 CE)

The Koine was born out of the conquests of Alexander the Great. First, his troops, which came from Athens as well as other Greek cities and regions, had to speak to one another. This close contact produced a melting-pot Greek that inevitably softened the rough edges of some dialects and lost the subtleties of others. Second, the conquered cities and colonies learned Greek as a second language. By the first century CE, Greek was the lingua franca of the whole Mediterranean region and beyond. Since the majority of Greek speakers learned it as a second language, this further increased its loss of subtleties and moved it toward greater explicitness.

4. Byzantine (or Medieval) Greek (330 CE–1453 CE)

When the Roman Empire split between East and West, Greek lost its *Weltsprache* status. Latin was used in the West (Rome), Greek in the East (Constantinople).

5. Modern Greek (1453 CE to present)

In 1453 the Turks invaded Byzantium, so that Greek was no longer isolated from the rest of the world. The Renaissance was born in the West as scholars fled with copies of Greek classics under their arms; the Reformation developed in northern Europe as Christian scholars (such as Erasmus and Luther) became aware of NT Greek manuscripts. Nevertheless, although Greek got out of the East, Europe did not get in. That is to say, copies of ancient Greek literature finally brought Europe out of the Dark Ages, but Europe had no impact on the living language. The net effect is that "the modern Greek popular speech does not differ materially from the vernacular Byzantine, and thus connects directly with the vernacular κοινή."[2] The Greek language has changed less over three millennia than English has in one.

Today, there are two levels of Greek, *katharevousa* (καθαρεύουσα = "literary language") and *demotic* (δημοτική = "popular language"). The former is not actually a historical development of the language, but is "book Greek," an artificial attempt at resurrecting the Attic dialect in modern times. Since 1977, demotic Greek has been the official language of Greece, tracing its roots directly back to Koine.

---

[2] Robertson, *Grammar*, 44.

Κοινή **Greek (Synchronic)**   ExSyn 17–23

1. Terminology

Κοινή is the feminine adjective of κοινός ("common"). Synonyms of Koine are "common" Greek, or, more frequently, Hellenistic Greek. Both New Testament Greek and Septuagintal Greek are considered substrata of the Koine.

2. Historical Development

The following are some interesting historical facts about Hellenistic Greek:

- The golden age of Greek literature effectively died with Aristotle (322 BCE); Koine was born with Alexander's conquests. The mixture of dialects among his troops produced a *leveling* effect, while the emerging Greek colonies after his conquests gave Greek its *universal* nature.
- Koine Greek grew largely from Attic Greek, as this was Alexander's dialect, but was also influenced by the other dialects of Alexander's soldiers. "Hellenistic Greek is a compromise between the rights of the stronger minority (i.e., Attic) and the weaker majority (other dialects)."[3] As such, it became a more serviceable alloy for the masses.
- Koine Greek became the lingua franca of the whole Roman Empire by the first century CE.

3. Scope of Κοινή Greek

Koine Greek existed roughly from *330 BCE to 330 CE*—that is, from Alexander to Constantine. With the death of Aristotle in 322 BCE, classical Greek as a living language was phasing out. Koine was at its peak in the first century BCE and first century CE.

For the only time in its history, Greek was *universalized*. As colonies were established well past Alexander's day and as the Greeks continued to rule, the Greek language kept on thriving in foreign lands. Even after Rome became the world power in the first century BCE, Greek continued to penetrate distant lands. Even when Rome was in absolute control, Latin was not the *lingua franca*. Greek continued to be a *universal* language until at least the end of the first century. From about the second century on, Latin began to win out in Italy (among the populace), then the West in general, once Constantinople became the capital of the Roman empire. For only a brief period, then, was Greek the universal language.

4. Changes from Classical Greek

In a word, Greek became *simpler*, less subtle. In terms of morphology, the language lost certain aspects, decreased its use of others, and assimilated difficult

---

[3] Moule, *Idiom Book*, 1.

forms into more frequently seen patterns. The language tended toward shorter, simpler sentences. Some of the syntactical subtleties were lost or at least declined. The language replaced the precision and refinement of classical Greek with *greater explicitness*.

5. Types of Κοινή Greek

There are at least three different types of Koine Greek: vernacular, literary, and conversational. A fourth, the Atticistic, is really an artificial and forced attempt at returning to the golden era.

a. Vernacular or vulgar (e.g., papyri, ostraca). This is the language of the streets—colloquial, popular speech. It is found principally in the papyri excavated from Egypt, truly the *lingua franca* of the day.

b. Literary (e.g., Polybius, Josephus, Philo, Diodorus, Strabo, Epictetus, Plutarch). A more polished Koine, this is the language of scholars and littérateurs, of academics and historians. The difference between literary Koine and vulgar Koine is similar to the difference between English spoken on the streets and spoken in places of higher education.

c. Conversational (New Testament, some papyri). Conversational Koine is typically the *spoken* language of educated people. It is grammatically correct for the most part, but not on the same literary level (lacks subtleties, is more explicit, shorter sentences, more parataxis) as literary Koine. By its very nature, one would not expect to find many parallels to this—either in the papyri (usually the language of uneducated people) or among literary authors (for theirs is a written language).

d. Atticistic (e.g., Lucian, Dionysius of Halicarnasus, Dio Chrysostom, Aristides, Phrynichus, Moeris). This is an artificial language revived by littérateurs who did not care for what had become of the language (much like many advocates of the KJV today argue for that version's renderings because it represents English at the height of its glory, during the Shakespearean era).

New Testament Greek   *ExSyn 23–30*

There are two separate though related questions that need to be answered regarding the nature of NT Greek: (1) What were the current languages of first-century Palestine? (2) Where does NT Greek fit into Koine?

1. The Language Milieu of Palestine

Aramaic, Hebrew, and Greek were in use in Palestine in the first century CE. But how commonplace each of these languages was is debated. An increasing number of scholars argue that Greek was the primary language spoken in Palestine in the time of, and perhaps even in the ministry of Jesus. Though still a minority opinion, this view has much to commend it and is gaining adherents.

2. Place of the Language of the New Testament in Hellenistic Greek

In 1863, J. B. Lightfoot anticipated the great discoveries of papyri parallels when he said, "If we could only recover letters that ordinary people wrote to each other without any thought of being literary, we should have the greatest possible help for the understanding of the language of the NT generally."[4]

Thirty-two years later, in 1895, Adolf Deissmann published his *Bibelstudien*—an innocently titled work that was to revolutionize the study of the NT. In this work (later translated into English under the title *Bible Studies*) Deissmann showed that the Greek of the NT was not a language invented by the Holy Spirit (Hermann Cremer had called it "Holy Ghost Greek," largely because 10 percent of its vocabulary had no secular parallels). Rather, Deissmann demonstrated that the bulk of NT vocabulary was to be found in the papyri.

The pragmatic effect of Deissmann's work was to render obsolete virtually all lexica and lexical commentaries written before the turn of the century. (Thayer's lexicon, published in 1886, was outdated shortly after it came off the press—yet, ironically, it is still relied on today by many NT students.) James Hope Moulton took up Deissmann's mantle and demonstrated parallels in syntax and morphology between the NT and the papyri. In essence, *what Deissmann did for lexicography, Moulton did for grammar*. However, his case has not proved as convincing.

There are other ways of looking at the nature of NT Greek. The following considerations offer a complex grid of considerations that need to be addressed when thinking about the nature of the language of the NT.

a. Distinction between style and syntax. A distinction needs to be made between syntax and style: Syntax is something external to an author—the basic linguistic features of a community without which communication would be impossible. Style, on the other hand, is something internal to each writer. For example, the frequency with which an author uses a particular preposition or the coordinating conjunctions (such as καί) is a stylistic matter (the fact that Attic writers used prepositions and coordinating conjunctions less often than Koine writers does not mean the syntax changed).

b. Levels of Koine Greek. As was pointed out earlier, the Greek of the NT is neither on the level of the papyri, nor on the level of literary Koine (for the most part), but is conversational Greek.

c. Multifaceted, not linear. Grammar and style are not the only issues that need to be addressed. Vocabulary is also a crucial matrix. Deissmann has well shown that the lexical stock of NT Greek is largely the lexical stock of vernacular Koine. It is our conviction that *the language of the NT needs to be seen in light of three poles*, not one: style, grammar, vocabulary. To a large degree, the style is Semitic, the syntax is close to literary Koine (the descendant of Attic), and the

---

[4] Cited in Moulton, *Prolegomena*, 242.

vocabulary is vernacular Koine. These cannot be tidily separated at all times, of course. The relationship can be illustrated as follows.

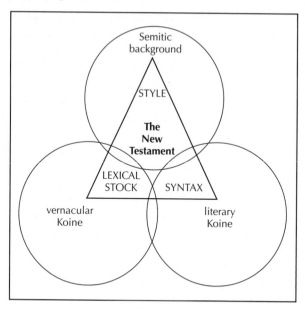

Chart 1
The Multifaceted Nature of New Testament Greek

d. Multiple authorship. One other factor needs to be addressed: the NT was written by several authors. Some (e.g., the author of Hebrews, Luke, sometimes Paul) aspire to literary Koine in their sentence structure; others are on a much lower plane (e.g., Mark, John, Revelation, 2 Peter). *It is consequently impossible to speak of NT Greek in monotone terms.* The language of the NT is not a "unique language" (a cursory comparison of Hebrews and Revelation will reveal this); but it also is not altogether to be put on the same level as the papyri. For some of the NT authors, it does seem that Greek was their native tongue; others grew up with it in a bilingual environment, though probably learning Greek after Aramaic; still others may have learned it as adults.

e. Some conclusions. The issues relating to the Greek of the NT are somewhat complex. We can summarize our view as follows:

- For the most part, the Greek of the NT is *conversational Greek* in its *syntax*—below the refinement and sentence structure of literary Koine, but above the level found in most papyri (though, to be sure, there are Semitic intrusions into the syntax on occasion).
- Its *style*, on the other hand, is largely Semitic—that is, since almost all of the writers of the NT books are Jews, their style of writing is shaped both by their religious heritage and by their linguistic background. Furthermore, the style of the NT is also due to the fact that these writers all share one

thing in common: faith in Jesus Christ. (This is analogous to conversations between two Christians at church and the same two at work: the linguistic style and vocabulary to some extent are different in both places.)

- The NT *vocabulary* stock, however, is largely shared with the ordinary papyrus documents of the day, though heavily influenced at times by the LXX and the Christian experience.
- *Individual authors:* The range of literary levels of the NT authors can be displayed as follows:

Semitic/Vulgar	*Conversational*	*Literary Koine*
Revelation Mark John, 1-3 John 2 Peter	most of Paul Matthew	Hebrews Luke-Acts James Pastorals 1 Peter Jude

Table 1
Literary Levels of New Testament Authors

The Cases: An Introduction[1]

In determining the relation of words to each other, case plays a large role. Although there are only five distinct case forms (nominative, vocative, genitive, dative, accusative), they have scores of functions. Further, of the almost 140,000 words in the Greek NT, about three-fifths are forms that have cases (including nouns, adjectives, participles, pronouns, and the article). Such a massive quantity, coupled with the rich variety of uses that each case can have, warrants a careful investigation of the Greek cases. The breakdown can be visualized in chart 2.

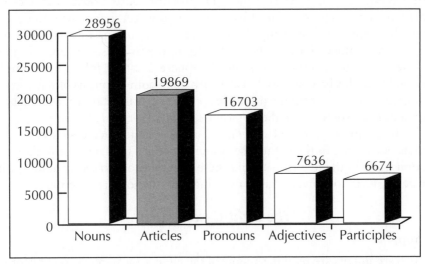

Chart 2
Frequency of Case-Forms in the New Testament (According to Word Class)

Case Systems: The Five- Vs. Eight-Case Debate

The question of how many cases there are in Greek may seem as relevant as how many angels can dance on the head of a pin. However, the question of case does have *some* significance.

(1) Grammarians are not united on this issue (although most today hold to the five-case system). This by itself is not necessarily significant. But the fact that grammars and commentaries assume two different views of case could be confusing if this issue were not brought to a conscious level.[2] (See table 2 below for a comparison of the case names in the two systems.)

---

[1] See *ExSyn* 31–35.

[2] On the side of the eight-case system are the grammars by Robertson, Dana-Mantey, Summers, Brooks-Winbery, Vaughan-Gideon, and a few others. Almost all the rest (whether grammars of the NT or of classical Greek) embrace the five-case system.

(2) The basic difference between the two systems is a question of *definition*. The eight-case system defines case in terms of *function*, while the five-case system defines case in terms of *form*.

(3) Such a difference in definition can affect, to some degree, one's hermeneutics. In both systems, with reference to a given noun in a given passage of scripture, only one case will be noted. In the eight-case system, since case is defined as much by function as by form, seeing only *one case* for a noun usually means seeing only one function. But in the five-case system, since case is defined more by form than by function, the case of a particular word *may*, on occasion, have more than one function. (A good example of the hermeneutical difference between these two can be seen in Mark 1:8—ἐγὼ ἐβάπτισα ὑμᾶς **ὕδατι,** αὐτὸς δὲ βαπτίσει ὑμᾶς ἐν πνεύματι ἁγίῳ ["I baptized you **in water,** but he will baptize you in the Holy Spirit"]. Following the eight-case system, one must see ὕδατι as either instrumental or locative, but not both. In the five-case system, it is possible to see ὕδατι as *both* the means and the sphere in which John carried out his baptism. [Thus, his baptism would have been done both by means of water and in the sphere of water.] The same principle applies to Christ's baptism ἐν πνεύματι, which addresses some of the theological issues in 1 Cor 12:13).

(4) In summary, the real *significance*[3] in this issue over case systems is a hermeneutical one. In the eight-case system there is a tendency for precision of function while in the five-case system there is more room to see an author using a particular form to convey a fuller meaning than that of one function.

The Eight-Case System

1. Support

Two arguments are used in support of the eight-case system—one historical, the other linguistic. (1) Through comparative philology (i.e., the comparing of linguistic phenomena in one language with those of another), since Sanskrit is an older sister to Greek and since Sanskrit has eight cases, Greek must also have eight cases. (2) "This conclusion is also based upon the very obvious fact that case is a matter of function rather than form."[4]

2. Critique

(1) The historical argument is *diachronic* in nature rather than synchronic. That is to say, it is an appeal to an earlier usage (in this case, to another language!), which may have little or no relevance to the present situation. But how a people understood their own language is determined much more by current usage than

---

[3] That is not to say that the issue is solved by hermeneutics, although this certainly has a place in the decision. Current biblical research recognizes that a given author may, at times, be *intentionally* ambiguous. The instances of double entendre, *sensus plenior* (conservatively defined), puns, and word plays in the NT all contribute to this fact. A full treatment of this still needs to be done.

[4] Dana-Mantey, 65.

by history. Further, the appeal to such older languages as Sanskrit is on the basis of *forms*, while the application to Greek is in terms of function. A better parallel would be that both in Sanskrit and in Greek, case is a matter of form rather than function. We have few, if any, proto-Greek or early Greek remains that might suggest more than five forms.

(2) The "very obvious fact" that case is a matter of function rather than form is not as obvious to others as it is to eight-case proponents. And it is not carried out far enough. If case is truly a matter of function only, then there should be over *one hundred* cases in Greek. The genitive alone has *dozens* of functions.[5]

3. Pedagogical Value

The one positive thing for the eight-case system is that with eight cases one can see somewhat clearly a *root idea* for each case[6] (although there are many exceptions to this), while in the five-case system this is more difficult to detect. The eight-case system is especially helpful in remembering the distinction between genitive, dative, and accusative of time.

Definition of Case Under the Five-Case System

Case is the inflectional variation in a noun[7] that encompasses various syntactical functions or relationships to other words. Or, put more simply, case is a matter of *form* rather than *function*. Each case has one form but many functions.

Five-Case System	*Eight-Case System*
Nominative	Nominative
Genitive	Genitive Ablative
Dative	Dative Locative Instrumental
Accusative	Accusative
Vocative	Vocative

Table 2
Five-Case System Vs. Eight-Case System

---

[5] We might add that to begin with semantic categories is to put the cart before the horse. Syntax must first of all be based on an examination and interpretation of the structures. To start with semantics skews the data.

[6] Indeed, much of our organization of the case uses will be built on this root idea. Thus, e.g., the genitive will have a broad section of uses called "Adjectival " and another called "Ablatival."

[7] Technically, of course, case is not restricted to nouns. Pragmatically, however, the discussion of cases focuses on nouns and other substantives because adjectives and other modifiers "piggy back" on the case of the substantive and do not bear an independent meaning.

The Nominative Case[1]
Overview of Nominative Uses

Primary Uses of the Nominative **29**
➡ 1. Subject 29
➡ 2. Predicate Nominative 30
➡ 3. Nominative in Simple Apposition 33
Grammatically Independent Uses of the Nominative **34**
➡ 4. Nominative Absolute 34
➡ 5. *Nominativus Pendens* (Pendent Nominative) 34
➡ 6. Parenthetic Nominative (Nominative of Address) 35
➡ 7. Nominative for Vocative 35
   8. Nominative of Exclamation 36

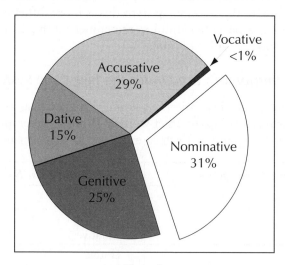

Chart 3
Frequency of Cases in the New Testament[2]

—— INTRODUCTION: UNAFFECTED[3] FEATURES ——

The nominative is the case of specific designation. The Greeks referred to it as the "naming case" for it often names the main topic of the sentence. The main

---

[1] See *ExSyn* 36–64. The nominative in proverbial expressions (54–55) and the nominative in place of oblique cases (esp. seen in the book of Revelation) (61–64) are sufficiently rare that the average intermediate Greek student can ignore them.

[2] The breakdown is as follows. Of the 24,618 nominatives in the NT, 32% are nouns (7794), 24% are articles (6009), 19% are participles (4621), 13% are pronouns (3145), and 12% are adjectives (3049).

[3] The term "unaffected" will be used throughout this book to refer to the characteristics or features of a particular morphological tag (such as nom. case, present tense, indicative mood,

topic in a sentence *semantically* is, of course, very similar to the *syntactical* subject, but the two are not always identical. Hence, the most common use of the nominative case is as subject. The nominative occurs more than any other case form in the NT, though the accusative and genitive are not far behind.

SPECIFIC USES

Primary Uses of the Nominative   ExSyn 38–49

➡ **1. Subject**   ExSyn 38–40

   a. Definition. The substantive[4] in the nominative case is frequently the subject of a finite verb.[5] The verb may be stated or implied.[6] Conversely, the subject may be implied, "embedded," as it were, in the verb (e.g., ἔρχεται means "*he* comes"). This usage is the most common for the nominative case.

   b. Amplification

   - **Relation to verb voice.** The relation of the subject to the action or state of the verb is largely determined by the voice of the verb. If the voice is *active*, the subject does the acting; if *passive*, the subject is acted upon; if *middle*, the subject acts on itself or in its own behalf, or the stress is placed on the subject. There are, of course, exceptions to this: e.g., the deponent middle and passive have active meanings, and the equative verb does not imply action, but a state.
   - **Relation to verb type.** In addition to analyzing verbs by their voice, it is profitable to analyze them as to whether they are transitive, intransitive, or equative. Briefly, *transitive* verbs take a direct object and can typically be transformed into a passive construction ("the boy hit the ball" can become "the ball was hit by the boy"). *Intransitive* verbs do not take a direct object

---

etc.) that can be seen only as an ideal composite. In other words, the unaffected features are those that, say, the present tense has when there are no intrusions on this basic meaning (such as context, lexical meaning of the verb, or other grammatical features like indicative mood, etc.). For a detailed discussion of unaffected features and specific uses, see *ExSyn* 1–11.

   [4] "Substantive" is any word functioning as a noun. Nouns will fill this role more than other words, but pronouns, adjectives, participles, and even other parts of speech can function like a noun. The following forms are capable of filling the *subject* slot: (1) noun; (2) pronoun; (3) participle (esp. articular); (4) adjective (also usually articular); (5) numeral; (6) article with various constructions; (7) an infinitive, whether anarthrous or articular; (8) preposition + numeral; (9) an entire clause that gives no morphological indication that it is the subject (such as a ἵνα or ὅτι clause).

   [5] By *finite* verb we mean any verb that, when parsed, includes *person*. Thus indicative, subjunctive, optative, and imperative verbs will take a nom. subject, while infinitives and participles technically take no subject.

   [6] The most frequent implied verb is the equative verb—usually εἰμί, and usually in the third person. Other verbs can also be implied, though almost always only if the preceding context has such a verb.

and cannot be transformed into a passive ("she came to the church" *cannot* be changed to "the church was come to by her"). *Equative* verbs are somewhat in between: they function like transitive verbs in that there are typically two substantives joined by a verb. But they also function like intransitives in that they cannot be transformed. They are unlike either in that the second substantive will be in the same case as the first substantive ("John was a man"). It is important to keep these verb types in mind as you think about syntax in general.

- **Missing elements.** The verb (especially the equative verb) may be absent from the clause, though implied (e.g., ἐγὼ φωνή ["I am a voice"] in John 1:23). Also, the subject may be absent, though implied in the verb (e.g., προσέφερον αὐτῷ παιδία ["they were bringing children to him"] in Mark 10:13).

c. Illustrations

John 3:16	ἠγάπησεν **ὁ θεός** τὸν κόσμον	**God** loved the world
Rom 6:4	ἠγέρθη **Χριστὸς** ἐκ νεκρῶν	
	Christ was raised from the dead	

➡ **2. Predicate Nominative**   *ExSyn 40–48*

a. Definition. The predicate nominative (PN) is *approximately* the same as the subject (S) and is joined to it by an equative verb, whether stated or implied. The usage is common. The equation of S and PN does not necessarily or even normally imply complete correspondence (e.g., as in the interchangeability of A=B, B=A in a mathematical formula). Rather, the PN normally describes a larger category (or *state*) to which the S belongs. It is important to keep in mind, however, that there are two distinct types of S-PN constructions; these will be discussed below.

b. Amplification

- **The kinds of verbs used.** The verbs used for this "equation" are, most frequently, εἰμί, γίνομαι, and ὑπάρχω. In addition, the passives of some transitive verbs can also be used: e.g., καλέω, εὑρίσκω.
- **Translation of subject-predicate nominative clauses.** English translation requires that the S be translated first.[7] Such is not the case in Greek. In John 1:1, for example, θεὸς ἦν ὁ λόγος should be translated "the Word was God" rather than "God was the Word." But since Greek word order is far more flexible than English, this creates a problem: How do we distinguish S from PN if word order is not a clear guide? The following section will offer a solution.
- **The semantics and exegetical significance of the subject-predicate nominative construction.**

---

[7] This is true for virtually all sentences except interrogatives where the order is reversed. Interrogatives, by their nature, indicate the unknown component and hence cannot be the subject.

(1) Two Kinds of Semantic Relationships

The significance of the S-PN construction affects more than mere translation precisely because S and PN do not normally involve total interchangeability. The usual relationship between the two is that *the predicate nominative describes the class to which the subject belongs*. This is known as a **subset proposition** (where S is a subset of PN). Thus the meaning of "the Word was flesh" is not the same as "flesh was the Word," because flesh is broader than "the Word." "The word of the cross is foolishness" (1 Cor 1:18) does not mean "foolishness is the word of the cross," for there are other kinds of foolishness. "God is love" is not the same as "love is God." It can thus be seen from these examples that *"is" does not necessarily mean "equals."*

But there is another, less frequent semantic relationship between S and PN. Sometimes called a **convertible proposition**, this construction indicates an identical exchange. That is to say, both nouns have an identical referent. The mathematical formulas of A=B, B=A are applicable in such instances. A statement such as "Michael Jordan is the greatest basketball player in NBA history" means the same thing as "the greatest player in NBA history is Michael Jordan." There is complete interchange between the two.[8] These two kinds of relationships are graphically represented in chart 4 below.

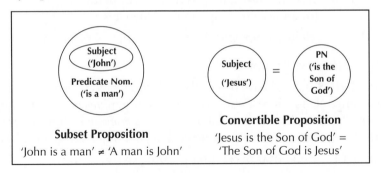

Chart 4
Semantic Relation of Subject and Predicate Nominative

Thus in examining S-PN clauses, two fundamental questions need to be answered: (1) How can we distinguish between S and PN since word order is not an infallible guide? (2) What is the semantic relationship between the two: Is the S a particular within the larger class of the PN, or is it interchangeable with the PN?

(2) How to Distinguish Subject from Predicate Nominative

The general principle for distinguishing S from PN is that the S is the *known* entity. This principle is valid for both kinds of S-PN constructions. In Greek

---

[8] However, this does not mean that it is not important to distinguish which one is the subject. The first sentence answers the question, "Who is Michael Jordan?" while the second answers "Who is the greatest player in NBA history?"

equative clauses, the known entity (S) will be distinguished from the PN in one of three ways. The significance of the following three rules is that *when only **one** nominative substantive has such a grammatical "tag," the semantic relationship will be that of particular (S) to class (PN).* That is, the construction will be a subset proposition.

(a) The subject will be a pronoun, whether stated or implied in the verb.[9]

Matt 3:17   **οὗτός** ἐστιν ὁ υἱός μου ὁ ἀγαπητός
              this is my beloved Son

Acts 2:15   ἔστιν ὥρα τρίτη τῆς ἡμέρας
              (It) is the third hour of the day

(b) The subject will be articular.[10]

John 4:24   πνεῦμα **ὁ θεός**   **God** is spirit

Mark 2:28   κύριός ἐστιν **ὁ υἱὸς** τοῦ ἀνθρώπου καὶ τοῦ σαββάτου.
              The Son of man is Lord even of the Sabbath.

(c) The subject will be a proper name.

Luke 11:30   ἐγένετο **Ἰωνᾶς** τοῖς Νινευίταις σημεῖον
              Jonah became a sign to the Ninevites

Jas 5:17   **Ἠλίας** ἄνθρωπος ἦν   **Elijah** was a man

(3) THE "PECKING" ORDER

What if *both* S and PN have one of these three tags? Which is the S, and what is the semantic relationship? First, when both substantives bear such grammatical tags, the "pecking" order is as follows: *(a) The pronoun has greatest priority;* it will be the S regardless of what grammatical tag the other substantive has

Matt 11:14   καὶ εἰ θέλετε δέξασθαι, **αὐτός** ἐστιν Ἠλίας
              and if you will receive it, **he** is Elijah

Acts 9:20   **οὗτός** ἐστιν ὁ υἱὸς τοῦ θεοῦ   **he** is the Son of God

(b) Articular nouns and proper names seem to have equal priority. In instances where one substantive is articular and the other is a proper name (or where both are articular), *word order* may be the determining factor.

John 15:1   **ὁ πατήρ** μου ὁ γεωργός ἐστιν   my **Father** is the vinedresser

Matt 13:55   οὐχ **ἡ μήτηρ** αὐτοῦ λέγεται Μαριὰμ καὶ **οἱ ἀδελφοὶ** αὐτοῦ
              Ἰάκωβος καὶ Ἰωσὴφ καὶ Σίμων καὶ Ἰούδας;
              Is not his **mother** named Mary and his **brothers** James and
              Joseph and Simon and Judas?

---

[9] This is true except for the interrogative pronoun, which is the PN.
[10] For more on this, see the chapters on the article.

(4) The Semantic Relationship: Convertible Proposition

The semantic relationship in such instances is that of a convertible proposition. That is to say, when both substantives meet one of the three qualifications for S, then they become interchangeable. (See examples in the preceding section.)

c. Substitution for Predicate Nominative (εἰς + accusative). Εἰς + the accusative is occasionally found replacing the predicate nominative in the NT. Although this construction is found in the papyri, it is usually due to a Semitic influence (Hebrew לְ). This idiom is frequent in OT quotations (as can be seen in the references below). That the construction is equivalent to the S-PN construction can be seen in Matt 19:5–6. In v. 5 the entrance into the new state is mentioned with this construction (ἔσονται οἱ δύο εἰς σάρκα μίαν ["the two shall become one flesh"]), followed in the next verse by a declaration of the resultant state with a normal PN (ὥστε οὐκέτι εἰσὶν δύο ἀλλὰ σὰρξ μία).

Mark 10:8	ἔσονται οἱ δύο **εἰς σάρκα μίαν** The two shall *become* **one flesh**
Acts 4:11	ὁ λίθος ... ὁ γενόμενος **εἰς κεφαλὴν** γωνίας The stone ... that *has become* **the chief** cornerstone

➡3. Nominative in Simple Apposition *ExSyn* 48–49

The nominative case (as well as the other cases) can be an appositive to another substantive in the *same* case. The usage is common. Four features of simple apposition should be noted (the first two are structural clues; the last two are semantic): *An appositional construction involves* (1) *two adjacent substantives* (2) *in the same case*, (3) *which refer to the same person or thing*, (4) *and have the same syntactical relation to the rest of the clause.*

The first substantive can belong to *any* category (e.g., subject, predicate nom., etc.) and the second is merely a clarification, description, or identification of who or what is mentioned. Thus, the appositive "piggy-backs" on the first nominative's use, as it were.

The appositive functions very much like a PN in a convertible proposition—that is, it refers to the same thing as the first noun. The difference, however, is that a PN makes an *assertion* about the S (an equative verb is either stated or implied); with appositives there is assumption, not assertion (no verb is in mind). In the sentence "Paul is an apostle," *apostle* is a PN; in the sentence, "Paul the apostle is in prison," *apostle* is in apposition to *Paul*.

Matt 3:1	παραγίνεται Ἰωάννης **ὁ βαπτιστὴς** κηρύσσων John **the Baptist** came preaching
Rev 1:5	ὁ μάρτυς ὁ πιστός, **ὁ πρωτότοκος** τῶν νεκρῶν the faithful witness, **the firstborn** from the dead

Grammatically Independent
Uses of the Nominative   *ExSyn 49–60*

Some grammars include nominative absolute, independent nominative, parenthetic nominative, and the *nominativus pendens* (pendent nom.) under this broad category without making any further refinement. However, not only should some distinction be made among these subgroups, but other uses of the nominative are also, technically, independent.

All independent nominatives follow this general rule: *the substantive in the nominative case is grammatically unrelated to the rest of the sentence.*

➡4. Nominative Absolute   *ExSyn 49–51*

a. Definition. The nominative absolute and the *nominativus pendens* (see next category) are two independent nominatives that are especially lumped together in most treatments. But there are distinctions in the semantic situations in which they occur. The easiest way to remember the difference between a nominative absolute and a pendent nominative is that a *nominative absolute does not occur in a sentence*, but only in titles, salutations, and other introductory phrases.

The only exception to this definition is that when a *participle* in the nominative case is grammatically unrelated to the rest of the sentence, it is traditionally *called* a nominative absolute participle (because it shares similarities with the gen. absolute participle).

b. Illustrations

Rom 1:1	Παῦλος δοῦλος Χριστοῦ Ἰησοῦ **Paul**, a bond-servant of Christ Jesus
Rev 1:1	Ἀποκάλυψις Ἰησοῦ Χριστοῦ **The revelation** of Jesus Christ

➡5. *Nominativus Pendens* (Pendent Nominative)   *ExSyn 51–53*

a. Definition. The pendent nominative is similar to the nominative absolute in that it is grammatically independent. However, while the nominative absolute is not used in a sentence, the pendent nominative is. This nominative substantive is *the logical rather than syntactical subject* at the beginning of a sentence, followed by a sentence in which this subject is now replaced by a pronoun in the case required by the syntax.

b. Clarification. The "subject" (logical, not grammatical) may be a noun or a participle,[11] which is grammatically unrelated to the rest of the sentence. The pronoun (in a different case) is used later on simply because it would be too redun-

---

[11] When the participle is the pendent nom., it is traditionally called a nom. absolute participle (see discussion under "nominative absolute").

dant to name the noun again. A helpful key to testing whether a certain nom. is pendent is the question: Can I translate the nom. at the beginning of the clause, "With reference to ... "?

c. Illustrations

Rev 3:12   ὁ νικῶν ποιήσω αὐτὸν στῦλον
the one who overcomes: I will make *him* a pillar ...

> This is a nom. absolute participle followed by a pronoun in the accusative case as required by the syntax of the sentence. This could be read, "With reference to the one who overcomes, I will make him ... "

Acts 7:40   ὁ γὰρ **Μωϋσῆς οὗτος** ... οὐκ οἴδαμεν τί ἐγένετο αὐτῷ.
for **this Moses** ... we do not know what has happened *to him*

➡6. Parenthetic Nominative   *ExSyn* 53–54

a. Definition. A parenthetic nominative is actually the subject in a clause inside a sentence that may or may not have a different subject.

b. Illustrations

John 1:6   ἐγένετο ἄνθρωπος ἀπεσταλμένος παρὰ θεοῦ, **ὄνομα** αὐτῷ Ἰωάννης.
There came a man sent from God (his **name** was John).

Matt 24:15   ὅταν οὖν ἴδητε τὸ βδέλυγμα τῆς ἐρημώσεως τὸ ῥηθὲν διὰ Δανιὴλ τοῦ προφήτου ἑστὸς ἐν τόπῳ ἁγίῳ, **ὁ ἀναγινώσκων** νοείτω, τότε
Whenever you see the abomination of desolation, spoken of by Daniel the prophet, standing in the holy place (let the **reader** understand), then ...

➡7. Nominative for Vocative (Nominative of Address)   *ExSyn* 56–59

a. Definition and Amplification. A substantive in the nominative is used in the place of the vocative case. It is used (as is the voc.) in direct address to designate the addressee.

The reason the nominative came to be used for the vocative was due to formal overlap. Note that there is no distinction in form in the plural or neuter singular, as well as in some forms of the masculine and feminine singular.

Grammarians who hold to the eight-case system typically object to the category nominative for vocative, since their definition of case is functional rather than morphological. Part of the reason for this objection, too, is that eight-case proponents tend to view language more diachronically than synchronically and more in terms of etymology than usage. But the nominative for vocative is a natural development of the nominative as the naming case, especially among peoples whose native tongue did not include a distinct vocative form.

b. Structure and Semantics. The nominative for vocative can be broken down into two structural categories: anarthrous and articular. (1) The *anarthrous* use has two further structures: with ὦ and without ὦ. Each anarthrous use parallels the similar vocative construction (viz., with the particle ὦ, the address is much more emphatic or emotional; without it, less so). (2) The *articular* use also involves two nuances: address to an inferior and simple substitute for a Semitic noun of address, regardless of whether the addressee is inferior or superior. The key for determining which use is being followed has to do with whether the text in question can be attributed to a Semitic source (such as quotation from the LXX).

c. Illustrations[12]

(1) ANARTHROUS

(a) Without ὦ

Rom 1:13   οὐ θέλω δὲ ὑμᾶς ἀγνοεῖν, **ἀδελφοί**
I do not want you to be ignorant, **brothers**

(b) With ὦ

Gal 3:1   ὦ ἀνόητοι **Γαλάται**, τίς ὑμᾶς ἐβάσκανεν;
O foolish **Galatians**! Who has bewitched you?

> The pathos of Paul is seen clearly in this text. He is deeply disturbed (or better, outraged) at the Galatians' immediate defection from the gospel.

(2) ARTICULAR

Luke 8:54   **ἡ παῖς**, ἔγειρε.   **Child**, rise.

John 20:28   Θωμᾶς εἶπεν αὐτῷ, **ὁ κύριός** μου καὶ **ὁ θεός** μου.
Thomas said to him, "My **Lord** and my **God**!"

Heb 1:8   πρὸς δὲ τὸν υἱόν, ὁ θρόνος σου, **ὁ θεός**, εἰς τὸν αἰῶνα τοῦ αἰῶνος
But to the Son [he declares], "Your throne, **O God**, is forever and ever"

> There are three syntactical possibilities for θεός here: as a subject ("God is your throne"), predicate nom. ("your throne is God"), and nom. for voc. (as in the translation above).[13]

8. Nominative of Exclamation   *ExSyn* 59–60

a. Definition and Clarification. The nominative substantive is used in an exclamation without any grammatical connection to the rest of the sentence.

---

[12] There are almost 600 instances of nom. for voc. in the NT—about twice as many as there are true vocatives. Only about 60 nominatives for vocatives are articular.

[13] For a discussion of this text and why the nom. for voc. view is the most likely interpretation, cf. *ExSyn* 59.

This use of the nominative is actually a subcategory of the nominative for vocative. However, we treat it separately and make this (somewhat) arbitrary distinction: nominative of exclamation will not be used in direct address.

b. Illustrations

Rom 7:24   ταλαίπωρος ἐγὼ **ἄνθρωπος**
           [O] wretched **man** [that] I am!

Rom 11:33   Ὦ **βάθος** πλούτου καὶ σοφίας καὶ γνώσεως θεοῦ
           O the **depth** both of the riches and wisdom and knowledge of God!

The Vocative Case[1]
Overview of Vocative Uses

Vocative as Direct Address **39**
   1. Simple Address 39
   2. Emphatic (or Emotional) Address 39
   3. The Exceptional Usage in Acts. 40
Vocative in Apposition **40**
   4. Apposition 40

—————— **DEFINITION** ——————   *ExSyn* 65–66

The vocative is the case used for addressing someone or, on occasion, for uttering exclamations. It technically has no syntactical relation to the main clause. In this respect it is much like the nominative absolute.

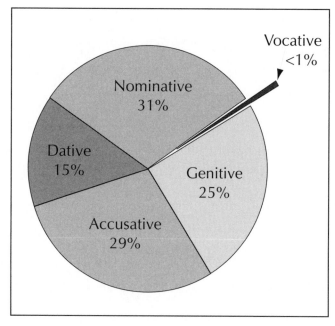

Chart 5
Frequency of Cases in the New Testament[2]

---

[1] See *ExSyn* 65–71. The vocative in exclamations (70) is a rare and disputed category; the average intermediate Greek student can ignore it.

[2] The breakdown of vocatives is as follows: 292 nouns, 0 pronouns, 0 articles, 1 participle (Acts 23:3), 24 adjectives.

As in English, the connotations of direct address vary on the circumstances, ranging from delight to astonishment to anger. Although the context plays a major role in determining the force of the vocative, the absence or presence of ὦ is also significant (see below).

─────── SPECIFIC USES ───────   *ExSyn 67–71*

There are two basic uses of the vocative: direct address and apposition. The second category, as in all simple appositions, is not really a separate syntactical category (for the case merely "piggy-backs" on the substantive to which it is in apposition). The first category, direct address, is by far the most frequent use.

There are two main keys to remembering the use and significance of the vocative. (1) *Without* ὦ preceding it (except in Acts), the vocative is simple address. (2) *With* ὦ preceding it (except in Acts), the vocative is emphatic address or vocative of exclamation.

Vocative as Direct Address   *ExSyn 67–70*

A substantive in the vocative is used in direct address to designate the addressee. Except for two texts in the NT, the addressee is always personal. This category may be divided into two main subgroups. The first category is used frequently; the second, only nine times.

1. Simple Address   *ExSyn 67–68*

a. Definition. This is the use of the vocative *without* ὦ preceding it. For the most part, no special significance is to be attached to the use of the vocative in such instances. (In many instances, however, there will obviously be great emotion in the utterance. In such cases, the context will be determinative.)

b. Illustrations

Matt 9:22   ὁ Ἰησοῦς ... εἶπεν, Θάρσει, **θύγατερ**· ἡ πίστις σου σέσωκέν σε.
Jesus said, "Take heart, **daughter**! Your faith has saved you."

Heb 1:10   Σὺ κατ᾽ ἀρχάς, **κύριε**, τὴν γῆν ἐθεμελίωσας
You, **Lord**, established the earth in the beginning

2. Emphatic (or Emotional) Address   *ExSyn 68–69*

a. Definition. This is the use of the vocative *with* ὦ preceding it. Here the presence of the particle ὦ is used in contexts where deep emotion is to be found.

b. Illustrations

Matt 15:28   ὁ Ἰησοῦς εἶπεν αὐτῇ, **Ὦ γύναι**, μεγάλη σου ἡ πίστις
Jesus said to her, '**O woman**, great is your faith!'

Jas 2:20   θέλεις δὲ γνῶναι, **ὦ ἄνθρωπε κενέ,** ὅτι ἡ πίστις χωρὶς τῶν ἔργων ἀργή ἐστιν;

Do you want to learn, **O empty man**, that faith without works is worthless?

3. The Exceptional Usage in Acts

ExSyn 69

Classical Greek was different from Hellenistic Greek in the use of the vocative in two ways: (1) the vocative with ὦ was unmarked—that is, it was the normal usage, employed in polite or simple address; (2) the vocative, whether with or without ὦ, was usually located deep in the sentence rather than at the front. Hellenistic usage has reversed especially the first trend, but also, to some degree, the second. Thus, generally speaking, ὦ with the vocative, is marked or used for emphasis, emotion, etc., and the vocative is usually near the front of the sentence. The usage in Acts is more like the classical norm than typical Koine. One cannot say, however, that this is due to Luke's more literary Koine, precisely because *the idiom occurs only in Acts, **not** in Luke.* For ὦ in the middle of a sentence without emphasis, see Acts 1:1; 18:14; 27:21; for ὦ at the beginning of a sentence, where it is emphatic, see Acts 13:10.

Vocative in Apposition

ExSyn 70–71

4. Apposition

ExSyn 70–71

a. Definition. The substantive in the vocative case can stand in apposition to another vocative. In such instances the first vocative will most likely be a direct address. The presence of an appositional vocative almost always indicates that the whole vocative construction is emphatic/emotional address rather than simple address.

b. Illustrations

Acts 1:24   Σὺ κύριε, **καρδιογνῶστα** πάντων, ἀνάδειξον ὃν ἐξελέξω ἐκ τούτων τῶν δύο ἕνα

You, Lord, **Knower of the hearts** of all men, show us which of these two you have chosen

Rev 22:20   Ναί, ἔρχομαι ταχύ. Ἀμήν, ἔρχου, κύριε **Ἰησοῦ.**

Yes, come quickly. Amen, come Lord **Jesus**!

The Genitive Case[1]
Overview of Genitive Uses

Adjectival **45**
†   1. Descriptive Genitive ("Aporetic" Genitive) 45
➡   2. Possessive Genitive 46
    3. Genitive of Relationship 47
➡   4. Partitive Genitive ("Wholative") 48
➡   5. Attributive Genitive (Hebrew Genitive, Genitive of Quality) 48
    6. Attributed Genitive 49
    7. Genitive of Material 50
    8. Genitive of Content 50
➡   9. Genitive in Simple Apposition 52
➡ 10. Genitive of Apposition (Epexegetical Genitive, Genitive of Definition) . 52
  11. Predicate Genitive 54
  12. Genitive of Subordination 54

Ablatival **55**
  13. Genitive of Separation 55
  14. Genitive of Source (or Origin) 56
➡ 15. Genitive of Comparison 56

Verbal Genitive (i.e., Genitive Related to a Verbal Noun) **57**
➡ 16. Subjective Genitive 57
➡ 17. Objective Genitive 58
  18. Plenary Genitive 59

Adverbial Genitive **60**
➡ 19. Genitive of Time 60
  20. Genitive of Means 61
  21. Genitive of Agency 61
➡ 22. Genitive Absolute 61
  23. Genitive of Reference 61
  24. Genitive of Association 62

After Certain Words **63**
➡ 25. Genitive After Certain Verbs (as a Direct Object) 63
  26. Genitive After Certain Adjectives (and Adverbs) 64
➡ 27. Genitive After Certain Prepositions 64

---

[1] See *ExSyn* 72–136. The following genitives are rare categories that the average intermediate Greek student can ignore: genitive of destination (100–101), genitive of production/producer (104–6), genitive of product (106–7), genitive of price (122), genitive of place/space (124–25), and genitive after certain nouns (135).

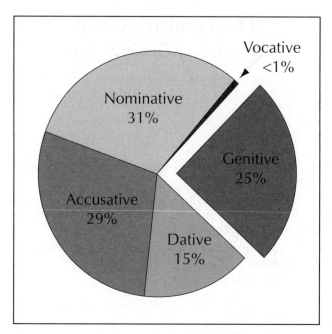

Chart 6
Frequency of Cases in the New Testament[2]

——— INTRODUCTION ———   *ExSyn 73–77*

Preliminary Remarks

1. Relation to the English Preposition "Of"

The genitive case is one of the most crucial elements of Greek syntax to master. Fortunately, for English speakers, many of the uses of the Greek genitive are similar to our preposition "of." This not only makes learning the genitive easier, but it also makes it easier to explain to a lay audience the meaning of a passage that might hinge, in part, on the use of a genitive. For example, in Rom 8:35, when Paul wrote, "What shall separate us from the love of Christ?" it is clear in both English and Greek that he meant "the love Christ has for us" rather than "the love we have for Christ."

At the same time, we should be cautioned that the Greek genitive has some different uses from the English "of" (e.g., comparison, purpose, etc.). Explaining such to a lay audience needs to be handled carefully, especially when your interpretation differs from the "of" translation the audience is using. Further, only with diligence and a desire to look at the text from the Greek viewpoint will you be able to see for yourself such interpretive possibilities.

---

[2] The genitive breakdown is as follows: 7681 nouns, 4986 pronouns, 5028 articles, 743 participles, 1195 adjectives.

2. Semantics and Exegetical Significance of the Genitive Case

Learning the genitive uses well pays big dividends. It has a great deal of exegetical significance, far more so than any of the other cases, because it is capable of a wide variety of interpretations. This, in turn, is due to three things: elasticity in its uses, embedded kernels, and antithetical possibilities.

a. Elasticity. The genitive is more elastic than any other case, able to stretch over much of the syntactical terrain. In part this is due to this one form encompassing what are frequently two case-forms in other Indo-European languages (viz., genitive and ablative—the "of" and "from" ideas).

b. Embedded kernels. Language, by its nature, is compressed, cryptic, symbolic. One of the areas of great ambiguity in language involves the genitive case. Genitives are routinely used in compressed situations that need to be unpacked. The genitive is typically related to another substantive. But what that relation involves can be quite varied. "The revelation of Jesus Christ," "the love of God," "children of wrath," "mystery of godliness" are all capable of more than one interpretation precisely because *"of" covers a multitude of semantic relationships.* In essence, the Noun-Noun$_{\text{gen}}$.[3] construction is used to compress a number of different sentence types (such as subject-predicate nominative, transitive verb-direct object, subject-transitive verb, etc.). A large part of our task in this chapter is to *unpack* the N-N$_g$ construction.

c. Antithetical possibilities. Unlike the nominative and vocative cases (whose structural clues are generally sufficient to show which usage is involved), the genitive case typically requires a nuanced examination of context, lexical meanings of the words involved (i.e., in the N-N$_g$ construction), and other grammatical features (such as articularity or number). Furthermore, in certain constructions (such as those that involve a "verbal" noun) the meaning possibilities can be somewhat antithetical. Thus, "revelation of Christ" can be unpacked to mean "the revelation *about* Christ" or "the revelation *from* Christ." Because of such widely divergent nuances, the genitive case requires careful examination.

Definition of the Genitive Case: The Unaffected Meaning[4]

1. A Note About Oblique Cases in General

The genitive is distinct from the accusative. The difference between these two is generally twofold: (a) The "genitive limits as to kind, while the accusative limits as to extent."[5] Another way to put this is that the genitive limits as to *quality*

---

[3] Traditionally called *nomen regens-nomen rectum* or head noun-gen. noun. We will use compressed and symbolic terminology: from here on called N-Ng.

[4] That is, unaffected by context, genre, lexical intrusions, etc. This is the meaning the gen. would have if it were seen in isolation.

[5] Dana-Mantey, 73.

while the accusative limits as to *quantity*. (b) The genitive is usually related to a noun while the accusative is usually related to a verb.

The genitive is distinct from the dative. While the force of the genitive is generally adjectival, the force of the dative is basically adverbial. There is some overlap between the uses of these cases, but these distinctions should help you to see more clearly the significance of each case. Also, the genitive is usually related to a noun, while the dative (as the acc.) is usually related to a verb.

2. Within the Eight-Case System

In the eight-case system, the genitive defines, describes, qualifies, restricts, limits. In this respect it is similar to an adjective, but is more emphatic. One should note that several grammars and commentaries assume the eight-case system; when they speak of the genitive, this is all they mean (i.e., the ablatival notion of separation is not included). But for those that embrace the five-case system, a more encompassing definition is needed.

3. Within the Five-Case System

Since the genitive and ablative have the same form, we shall consider them both as *one* case ("case" being defined as a matter of form rather than function). In some respects, the definition of the genitive case in the five-case system simply combines genitive and *ablative* from the eight-case system. The ablative notion is fundamentally that of *separation*. This is the *from* idea.

Another way to view the genitive case is to see all uses, both adjectival and ablatival, generating from one idea. Whether such a root idea was that of possession, or restriction, or some other notion, is of greater interest to the philologist (and the field of diachronics) than the exegete. In Hellenistic Greek, the *of* idea and the *from* idea are usually distinct—so much so that the ablatival concept is increasingly expressed with ἀπό or ἐκ rather than with the "naked" genitive form. (In the least, this suggests a growing uneasiness on the part of Koine speakers to use the gen. case to express the idea of separation.[6])

Therefore, under the five-case system, the genitive case may be defined as *the case of qualification (or limitation as to kind) and (occasionally) separation.*

———— **SPECIFIC USES** ———— *ExSyn 77–136*

Our approach to the genitive is to break its uses down into a few major categories with many subgroups under each of these. This approach (followed by many grammarians) is helpful in showing the similarities that different types of genitives have toward one another.

---

[6] Some grammars mix the naked case uses with those of preposition + case (e.g., Brooks-Winbery, 7–64).

N.B. The layout in this chapter may seem a bit industrious. The immediate reaction of looking at the following categories might be to rush through the material before the categories, like rabbits, multiply any further! What appears at first glance to be microscopic hair-splitting is governed by the principles of *semantic reality* and *exegetical significance*. That is, in light of the great diversity of established uses of the genitive, as well as of the often profound exegetical significance that this case can play in given texts, an acquaintance with these categories is justified.

Adjectival *ExSyn 78–107*

This broad category really touches the heart of the genitive. If the genitive is primarily descriptive, then it is largely similar to the adjective in functions. However, although the genitive is primarily adjectival in force, it is more emphatic than a simple adjective would be.

†1. Descriptive Genitive ("Aporetic" Genitive[7]) [characterized by, described by] *ExSyn 79–81*

a. Definition and amplification. The genitive substantive describes the head noun in a loose manner. The nature of the collocation of the two nouns in this construction is usually ambiguous.

The descriptive genitive is the "catch-all" genitive, the "drip pan" genitive, the "black hole" of genitive categories that tries to suck many a genitive into its grasp! In some respects, *all adjectival genitives are descriptive, yet no adjectival genitive is descriptive.* That is to say, although all adjectival genitives are, by their nature, descriptive, few, if any, belong only to this specific category of usage. This use truly embodies the root idea of the (adjectival) genitive. It is often the usage of the genitive when it has not been affected by other linguistic considerations—that is, when there are *no* contextual, lexemic, or other grammatical features that suggest a more specific nuance.

Frequently, however, it is close to the attributive genitive, being either *other than or broader than* the attributive use. (See chart 7 below.) Hence, this use of the genitive should be a *last resort*. If one cannot find a *narrower* category to which a genitive belongs, this is where he or she should look for solace.

b. Key to identification. For the word *of* insert the paraphrase *characterized by* or *described by*. If this fits, and if *none* of the other uses of the genitive fits, then the genitive is probably a genitive of description.[8]

---

[7] That is, the "I am at a loss" gen. (from the Greek word, ἀπορέω, "I am at a loss," a tongue-in-cheek title suggested to me by my colleague, J. Will Johnston).

[8] Commentators are often fond of merely labeling a gen. as "descriptive" without giving any more precision to the nuance involved. We suggest that an attempt at least ought to be made to see if a given gen. plugs into another category.

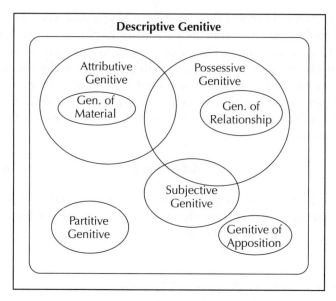

Chart 7
The Relation of Descriptive Genitive
to Various Other Genitive Uses

c. Illustrations

John 2:16   μὴ ποιεῖτε τὸν οἶκον τοῦ πατρός μου οἶκον **ἐμπορίου**
Do not make my Father's house into a house **of merchandise**

The idea is "a house in which merchandise is sold."

2 Cor 6:2   ἐν ἡμέρᾳ **σωτηρίας**
in [the] day **of salvation**

This cannot be an attributive gen., for then the idea would be "a *saved* day"! A day that is "characterized by" salvation is acceptably clear.

Rev 9:1   ἐδόθη αὐτῷ ἡ κλεὶς **τοῦ φρέατος** τῆς ἀβύσσου
the key **to the shaft** of the abyss was given to him

This is not a possessive gen., even though our idiom "belongs to" fits (for the shaft does not possess the key). The idea is "the key *that opens* the shaft of the abyss."

➡2. Possessive Genitive [belonging to, possessed by]   *ExSyn 81–83*

a. Definition. The substantive in the genitive possesses the thing to which it stands related. That is, in some sense the head noun is owned by the genitive noun. Such ownership at times can be broadly defined and need not imply the literal (and sometimes harsh) idea of possession of physical property. This usage is common.

b. Key to identification and amplification. Instead of the word *of* replace it with *belonging to* or *possessed by*. If this paraphrase fits, then the genitive is probably a genitive of possession.

Although this category can be broadly defined, it really ought to be used only when a genitive cannot fit more neatly under some other category (it will still be of common occurrence). A genitive should not be labeled possessive unless this is the *narrowest* sense it can have. If it is related to a verbal noun, then it is probably objective or subjective.[9] Further, possessive *pronouns* will be the primary words used for the genitive of possession. In fact, when you see a possessive pronoun you can *usually* assume that its primary nuance is that of possession.

c. Illustrations[10]

Matt 26:51   αὐτοῦ τὸ ὠτίον   **his** ear

John 20:28   Θωμᾶς εἶπεν αὐτῷ, ὁ κύριός **μου** καὶ ὁ θεός **μου**
              Thomas said to him, "**My** Lord and **my** God"

> The idea of possession in such expressions is not to be pressed in the sense that the Lord is owned fully by Thomas. But in a broad sense, the Lord belongs to Thomas—now, on this occasion, in a way not true before.

3. Genitive of Relationship   *ExSyn 83–84*

a. Definition and key to identification. The substantive in the genitive indicates a *familial* relationship, typically the progenitor of the person named by the head noun. This category is not very common.

This is a subset of the possessive genitive (see chart 7 above for a visual representation). The key to determining whether or not a possessive genitive is a genitive of relationship is (1) whether the noun to which the genitive is related is a *family* relation noun (e.g., son, mother, etc.) or (2) whether the noun to which the genitive is related is *understood* (i.e., must be supplied from the context) and what one supplies is a family relation noun, then the possessive genitive is a genitive of relationship. As well, the genitive noun is routinely a proper name.

Often, especially in the Gospels, the noun related to the genitive is to be supplied. If so, the genitive alone *usually* suggests the idea of "who comes from" or

---

[9] My colleague, Dr. John Grassmick, has suggested the following scheme: The subjective gen., possessive gen., and the gen. of source are closely related. Other things being equal, and if the context allows, *possession* takes precedent over source, and the *subjective* gen. takes precedent over possession *when* a verbal noun is involved.

[10] Several grammars suggest that references such as "children of God" (John 1:12), "apostle of Christ Jesus" (2 Cor 1:1); "their brothers" (Heb 7:5), and "prisoner of Christ Jesus" (Eph 3:1) embody possessive genitives. All of these are indeed genitives of possession, but their nuances also go *beyond* mere possession. E.g., "children of God" is a gen. of relationship; "apostle of Christ Jesus" is also subjective gen. (indicating that Christ Jesus sent out Paul). Hence, although in a broad sense the gen. of possession is common, in a narrow sense the instances are more restricted.

"who is a descendant of." Thus, when the noun to which the genitive is related is *not* named, it can usually be assumed that the genitive alone speaks of the ancestor.

b. Illustrations

John 21:15	Σίμων Ἰωάννου	Simon, [son] **of John**
Luke 24:10	Μαρία ἡ Ἰακώβου	Mary, the [mother] **of James**[11]

➡ **4. Partitive Genitive ("Wholative") [which is a part of]**[12]   *ExSyn* 84–86

a. Definition and explanation. The substantive in the genitive denotes *the whole of which* the head noun is a part. This usage is relatively common in the NT. Instead of the word *of* substitute *which is a part of.*

The semantics of this usage require a twofold explanation. First, this is a phenomenological use of the genitive that requires the head noun to have a lexical nuance indicating *portion.* For example, "some of the Pharisees," "one of you," "a tenth of the city," "the branch of the tree." Second, the partitive genitive is *semantically the opposite of the genitive of apposition.* While the partitive designates the whole of which the head noun is a part, the genitive of apposition designates a particular within the class described by the head noun. The important thing to keep in mind here is that, though semantically opposite, they can be structurally identical.

b. Illustrations

Luke 19:8	τὰ ἡμίσιά μου **τῶν ὑπαρχόντων**	half **of my possessions**
Rom 15:26	τοὺς πτωχοὺς **τῶν ἁγίων**	the poor **of the saints**

➡ **5. Attributive Genitive**
(Hebrew Genitive, Genitive of Quality)   *ExSyn* 86–88

a. Definition. The genitive substantive specifies an *attribute* or innate quality of the head substantive. It is similar to a simple adjective in its semantic force, though more emphatic. The category is common in the NT, largely because of the Semitic mind-set of most of its authors.

b. Key to identification. If the noun in the genitive can be converted into an attributive adjective modifying the noun to which the genitive stands related, then the genitive is likely an attributive genitive.

Semantically, there are three important points to know about attributive genitives: (1) This genitive is more emphatic than an adjective would have been.

---

[11] Occasionally, the genitive speaks of descendant rather than ancestor, as here. Cf. also Mark 16:1.

[12] The term "partitive" is confusing, for it suggests that the gen. itself will designate the part of which the head noun is the whole. Hence, it has been suggested that "wholative" is a better designation.

Chart 8
The Semantics of the Attributive Genitive

Thus, although the denotation is the same, the connotation is not. "Body of sin" has a stronger force than "sinful body." (2) The genitive of *material* is technically a subset of the attributive genitive, but it involves other nuances as well. If a genitive could be classified as either attributive or material, it should classified as the latter. (3) Certain words are frequently found in this construction, such as σῶμα as a head noun or δόξης as the genitive term.

c. Illustrations

Rom 6:6
τὸ σῶμα **τῆς ἁμαρτίας**
body **of sin** (= "**sinful** body")

Rom 8:21
τὴν ἐλευθερίαν **τῆς δόξης** τῶν τέκνων τοῦ θεοῦ
the freedom **of the glory** of the children of God (= "the **glorious** freedom of the children of God")

> Normally in gen. chains (a.k.a. concatenative genitives) each successive gen. modifies the one that precedes it, but there are many exceptions, especially with δόξης.

Jas 2:4
ἐγένεσθε κριταὶ **διαλογισμῶν** πονηρῶν
you have become judges **with** evil **motives**

> The idea here is not "you have become judges **of** evil motives" (which would be an objective gen.). But the translation "evil-motived judges" is cumbersome. This illustrates the fact that one should think about the *sense* of the passage more than merely do a translational gloss.

6. The Attributed Genitive   ExSyn 89–91

a. Definition. This is just the opposite, semantically, of the attributive genitive. The head noun, rather than the genitive, is functioning (in sense) as an attributive adjective. Although rarer than the attributive genitive, this is not altogether uncommon.

b. Key to identification. If it is possible to convert the noun to which the genitive stands related into a mere adjective, then the genitive is a good candidate for this category. One simple way to do this conversion is to omit the *of* in translation between the head noun and genitive and change the head noun into its corresponding adjective. Thus "newness *of* life" becomes "new life."

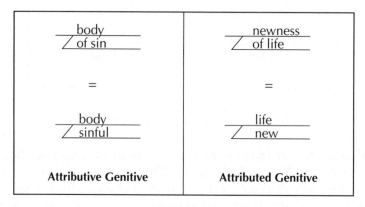

Chart 9
A Semantic Diagram of the Attributive Genitive and Attributed Genitive

c. Illustrations

Phil 1:22   τοῦτό μοι καρπὸς **ἔργου**
this [will mean] [the] fruit **of labor** to me

> Here "the fruit of labor" = "fruitful labor." An attributive gen. would mean "laboring fruit"!

1 Pet 1:7   τὸ δοκίμιον ὑμῶν **τῆς πίστεως** πολυτιμότερον χρυσίου
the genuineness **of** your **faith** that is much more precious than gold

> The idea is that their genuine faith is more precious than gold.

7. Genitive of Material [made out of, consisting of]   ExSyn 91–92

a. Definition and key to identification. The genitive substantive specifies the material out of which the head noun is made. This usage is rare in the NT (the notion of material is somewhat more frequently stated with ἐκ + gen.).

Replace the word *of* with the paraphrase *made out of* or *consisting of*. If this paraphrase fits, the genitive is probably a genitive of material.

b. Illustrations

Mark 2:21   ἐπίβλημα **ῥάκους** ἀγνάφου
a patch [made out] of unshrunk **cloth**

Rev 18:12   γόμον **χρυσοῦ** καὶ **ἀργύρου** καὶ **λίθου** τιμίου
cargo **of gold** and **silver** and precious **stone** (= cargo *consisting of* gold and silver and precious stone)

8. Genitive of Content [full of, containing]   ExSyn 92–94

a. Definition and key to identification. The genitive substantive specifies the contents of the word to which it is related. This word may be either a noun, adjective or verb. This is fairly common in the NT.

If the word to which this genitive is related is a noun, replace the word *of* with the paraphrase *full of* or *containing*. If the word is a verb, the typical translational force of the genitive is *with*. (This key is not as helpful as the others, for there are many exceptions. For this category, the real key is to notice the lexical nuance of the word to which the gen. is related.)

Two other points to note: (1) There are *two* kinds of genitive of content: one related to a noun or adjective (*nominal* gen. of content), the other to a verb (*verbal* gen. of content).[13] A genitive of content is a lexico-syntactic category in that the verb or head noun will be a term indicating *quantity*[14] (e.g., for verbs: γέμω, πίμπλημι, πληρόω; for nouns/adjectives: βαθός, μέστος, πλήρης, πλήρωμα, πλοῦτος, etc.). (2) The nominal genitive of content is distinct from the genitive of material in that content indicates the item contained while material indicates the material made out of. The figure below illustrates this difference.

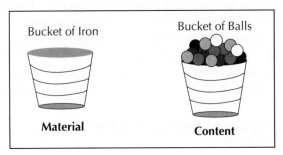

Figure 10
Genitive of Content Vs. Genitive of Material

The important thing to remember for the *verbal* use is that *in Greek the genitive, rather than the dative, is the case used to indicate the content of a verb.* Thus although the dative can frequently be translated "with," when a verb of filling is used, it is vital to examine the Greek text to see whether a genitive or dative substantive follows. If it is genitive, the translation "with" is appropriate; if a dative, some other translation (such as "by, in, because of") better reflects the Greek idiom—because *the dative case does not indicate the content of the verb.*

b. Illustrations

(1) NOMINAL GENITIVE OF CONTENT

John 21:8	τὸ δίκτυον **τῶν ἰχθύων**	the net [**full**] **of fish**
Col 2:3	πάντες οἱ θησαυροὶ **τῆς σοφίας** καὶ **γνώσεως**	
	all the treasures **of wisdom** and **knowledge**	

---

[13] Most grammars treat the verbal type under gen. direct object (with verbs of filling). Though that is an equally valid location, to list it only there would not be as helpful (since it is an important category in its own right, exegetically as well as syntactically).

[14] For the nominal usage, "the word to which the genitive is related implies a quantity or amount of the thing in the genitive, rather than being a container which is actually containing something" (Williams, *Grammar Notes*, 6).

(2) VERBAL GENITIVE OF CONTENT

John 6:13   ἐγέμισαν δώδεκα κοφίνους **κλασμάτων**
              they filled twelve baskets **with fragments**

Acts 2:4   ἐπλήσθησαν πάντες **πνεύματος** ἁγίου, καὶ ἤρξαντο λαλεῖν
              ἑτέραις γλώσσαις
              all were filled **with the** Holy **Spirit** and they began to speak in
              other tongues

➡9. Genitive in Simple Apposition   *ExSyn 94*

See the following section for a discussion of this genitive use and the genitive of apposition. These two need to be distinguished carefully. (It should be noted that the gen. in simple apposition is a legitimate category, but because of confusion over its semantics we are treating it in the next section.) Simple apposition requires that both nouns be in the same case (whether nom., gen., dat., acc., voc.), while the genitive of apposition requires only the second noun to be in the genitive case. If the syntax of the sentence requires the head noun to be in the genitive, a possibility of confusion between these two appositional uses results.

➡10. Genitive of Apposition (Epexegetical Genitive, Genitive of Definition)   *ExSyn 95–100*

This use of the genitive is common, though largely misunderstood. It is sometimes lumped in together with the genitive of content or the genitive of material, though there are legitimate semantic differences among all three categories. It is also often confused with the genitive in simple apposition.

a. Definition. The substantive in the genitive case refers to the same thing as the substantive to which it is related. The equation, however, is not exact. The genitive of apposition typically states a specific example that is a part of the larger category named by the head noun. It is frequently used when the head noun is ambiguous or metaphorical.

b. Key to identification. Every genitive of apposition, like most genitive uses, can be translated with *of* + the genitive noun. To test whether the genitive in question is a genitive of apposition, replace the word *of* with the paraphrase "which is" or "that is," "namely," or, if a personal noun, "who is." If it does not make the same sense, a genitive of apposition is unlikely; if it does make the same sense, a genitive of apposition is likely.[15]

c. Semantics: genitive of apposition distinct from simple apposition. With appositional genitives (both kinds), usually two kinds of *subject-predicate nomina-*

---

[15] The next step, of course, is to analyze this and other possibilities by way of sound exegesis.

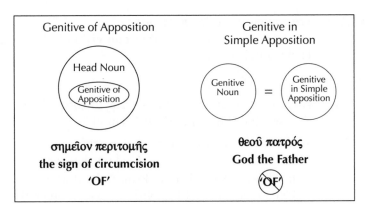

Chart 11
Genitive of Apposition Vs. Genitive in Simple Apposition

tive constructions are represented. In a *genitive of apposition* construction, the genitive is semantically equivalent to a subject that designates a particular belonging to a larger group (predicate nominative). Thus, "the sign of circumcision" can be unpacked as "circumcision is a sign" (but not "a sign is circumcision"). In this example, the lexical field of "sign" is much larger than that for "circumcision." For a *genitive in simple apposition* the two nouns are equivalent to a convertible proposition. Thus, "Paul the apostle" could be unpacked as "Paul is the apostle" or "the apostle is Paul."

d. Simplification. Two things should be noted for the appositional genitives: first, how to distinguish them from other genitive uses, and second, how to distinguish the genitive of apposition from the genitive in simple apposition. (1) *Appositional genitive vs. another genitive use*: By "appositional genitive" we mean *both* kinds of apposition (simple and gen. of apposition). The first thing to determine, of course, is whether one of the appositional uses is applicable. To do this, insert "which is," "namely," or "who is" between the head noun and the genitive noun. If this makes sense, an appositional genitive is likely. (2) *Genitive of apposition vs. simple apposition*: Both will fit the "which is" formula, so another test needs to be used to distinguish the two. If the word "of" can be used before the genitive in question, then it is a genitive of apposition. If it cannot, then it is simple apposition related to another genitive. (Keep in mind that the only time there could be any confusion is when both head noun and genitive noun are in the same case, but this does occur frequently.)

e. Illustrations

(1) OF A GENITIVE OF APPOSITION

John 2:21   ἔλεγεν περὶ τοῦ ναοῦ τοῦ **σώματος** αὐτοῦ
he was speaking concerning the temple **of** his **body** (= "the temple, **which is** his **body**")

Rom 4:11   καὶ σημεῖον ἔλαβεν **περιτομῆς**
and he received [the] sign **of circumcision** (= "the sign, **which is circumcision**")

(2) OF SIMPLE APPOSITION

Matt 2:11   εἶδον τὸ παιδίον μετὰ Μαρίας **τῆς μητρὸς** αὐτοῦ
they saw the child with Mary, his mother

Eph 1:2   χάρις ὑμῖν καὶ εἰρήνη ἀπὸ θεοῦ **πατρὸς** ἡμῶν
Grace to you and peace from God our **Father**

> If "of" were placed before "Father" the idea would be "from the God **of** our Father"! It is obviously simple apposition here.

11. Predicate Genitive   *ExSyn 102*

a. Definition. The genitive substantive makes an assertion about another genitive substantive, much like a predicate nominative does. The difference, however, is that with the predicate genitive the equative verb is a participle (in the genitive case) rather than a finite verb. This category is relatively uncommon. This kind of genitive is in reality an *emphatic kind of simple apposition* in the genitive (emphatic because of the presence of the participial form of the equative verb). Both adjectival participles and the genitive absolute participle (which is always circumstantial) can be used in this way.

b. Illustrations

Acts 7:58   νεανίου καλουμένου **Σαύλου**   a young man called **Saul**

Rom 5:8   ἔτι **ἁμαρτωλῶν** ὄντων ἡμῶν Χριστὸς ὑπὲρ ἡμῶν ἀπέθανεν
while we were yet **sinners** Christ died for us

12. Genitive of Subordination [over]   *ExSyn 103–104*

a. Definition and key to identification. The genitive substantive specifies that which is subordinated to or under the dominion of the head noun.

Instead of *of* supply the gloss *over* or something like it that suggests dominion or priority. This kind of genitive is a lexico-semantic category. That is, it is related only to certain kinds of head substantives—nouns (or participles) that lexically imply some kind of rule or authority. Words such as βασιλεύς and ἄρχων routinely belong here. For the most part, this genitive is a subset of the subjective genitive, but not always.

b. Illustrations

(1) CLEAR EXAMPLES

Matt 9:34   τῷ ἄρχοντι **τῶν δαιμονίων**   the ruler **over the demons**

Mark 15:32   ὁ βασιλεὺς **Ἰσραήλ**   the king **over Israel**

(2) Disputed Examples[16]

Eph 2:2   ποτε περιεπατήσατε ... κατὰ τὸν ἄρχοντα **τῆς ἐξουσίας** τοῦ
ἀέρος, **τοῦ πνεύματος** τοῦ νῦν ἐνεργοῦντος ἐν τοῖς υἱοῖς τῆς
ἀπειθείας
you formerly walked according to the ruler **of the domain** of
the air, [the ruler] **of the spirit** that now works in the sons of
disobedience

Col 1:15   ὅς ἐστιν εἰκὼν τοῦ θεοῦ τοῦ ἀοράτου, πρωτότοκος πάσης
κτίσεως
who is the image of the invisible God, the firstborn **over** all
creation

Ablatival *ExSyn 107–112*

The ablatival genitive basically involves the notion of *separation*. (Though frequently translated *from*, such a gloss will not work for the genitive of comparison, which requires *than* as its gloss). This idea can be static (i.e., in a separated state) or progressive (movement away from, so as to become separated). The emphasis may be on either the state resulting from the separation or the cause of separation (in the latter, origin or source is emphasized).

13. Genitive of Separation [out of, away from, from] *ExSyn 107–109*

a. Definition and key to identification. The genitive substantive is that from which the *verb* or sometimes head noun is separated. Thus the genitive is used to indicate the point of departure. This usage is rare in the NT.

For the word *of* supply the words *out of*, *away from*, or *from*. Another key is to note that *usually* this genitive will be dependent on a verb (or verbal form) rather than a noun. Two further points should be noted: (1) In Koine Greek the idea of separation is increasingly made explicit by the presence of the preposition ἀπό or sometimes ἐκ. Hence, a genitive of separation will be rare in the NT, while the preposition ἀπό (or ἐκ) + genitive will be commonly used for separation. (2) This is a lexico-syntactic category: it is determined by the lexical meaning of the word to which the genitive is related. Only if that word, usually a verb, connotes motion away from, distance, or separation can the genitive be one of separation.

b. Illustrations

Eph 2:12   ἀπηλλοτριωμένοι **τῆς πολιτείας** τοῦ Ἰσραήλ
having been alienated **from the commonwealth** of Israel

1 Pet 4:1   πέπαυται **ἁμαρτίας**
he has ceased **from** [doing] **sin**

---

[16] For discussion of these texts, cf. *ExSyn* 104.

14. Genitive of Source (or Origin)
[out of, derived from, dependent on]   *ExSyn 109–110*

a. Definition and key to identification. The genitive substantive is the source from which the head noun derives or depends. This is a rare category in Koine Greek.

For the word *of* supply the paraphrase *out of, derived from, dependent on,* or "*sourced in.*" As with the genitive of separation, the simple genitive is being replaced in Koine Greek by a prepositional phrase (in this instance, ἐκ + gen.) to indicate source. This corresponds to the fact that *source* is an emphatic idea; emphasis and explicitness often go hand in hand.

Since this usage is not common, it is not advisable to seek it as the most likely one for a particular genitive that may fit under another label. In some ways, the possessive, subjective, and source genitives are similar. In any given instance, if they all make good sense, subjective should be given priority. In cases where there is no verbal head noun, possessive takes priority over source as an apt label. The distinction between source and separation, however, is more difficult to call. Frequently, it is a matter merely of emphasis: separation stresses result while source stresses cause.

b. Illustrations

Rom 10:3   ἀγνοοῦντες τὴν **τοῦ θεοῦ** δικαιοσύνην,
            being ignorant of the righteousness **that comes from God**

2 Cor 3:3   ἐστὲ ἐπιστολὴ **Χριστοῦ**
            you are a letter **from Christ**

➡15. Genitive of Comparison [than]   *ExSyn 110–112*

a. Definition and key to identification. The genitive substantive, almost always after a comparative *adjective*, is used to indicate comparison. The genitive, then, is the standard against which the comparison is made (i.e., in "X is greater than Y," the gen. is the Y). This usage is relatively common.

The definition gives the key: a genitive after a *comparative* adjective, which requires the word *than* before the genitive (instead of the usual *of*).

b. Illustrations

Matt 6:25   οὐχὶ ἡ ψυχὴ **πλεῖόν** ἐστιν **τῆς τροφῆς**;
            Is not your life worth *more* **than food**?

Heb 1:4   **κρείττων** γενόμενος **τῶν ἀγγέλων**
            [the Son] having become *better* **than the angels**

Verbal Genitive
(i.e., Genitive Related to a Verbal Noun)   *ExSyn* 112–21

The subjective, objective, and plenary genitives are used with head nouns that involve a verbal idea. That is, the head noun has a verb as a cognate (e.g., βασιλεύς has βασιλεύω as cognate). The verbal genitive construction, then, is a sentence embed involving, typically, a transitive verbal idea in the head noun. The order below (subjective, objective, plenary) displays the descending order of frequency.

➡16. Subjective Genitive   *ExSyn* 113–16

a. Definition and key to identification. The genitive substantive functions semantically as the subject of the verbal idea implicit in the head noun. This is common in the NT.

If a subjective genitive is suspected, attempt to convert the verbal noun to which the genitive is related into a verbal form and turn the genitive into its subject. Thus, for example, "the revelation of Jesus Christ" in Gal 1:12 becomes "[What/the fact that] Jesus Christ reveals."

b. Amplification. Two points should be noted regarding the semantics of this genitive: (1) This category is lexico-syntactic—i.e., it is related to a *specific lexical meaning* for one of the words involved (in this case, the head noun). The head noun, which is here called a "verbal noun,"[17] must have an implicit verbal idea. Words such as "love," "hope," "revelation," "witness," and "word" can imply, in a given situation, a verbal idea. The perspective must, of course, be from Greek rather than English: e.g., "king" has no verbal cognate in English (there is no verb "to king"), but it does in Greek (βασιλεύς has βασιλεύω).

(2) Where objective and subjective genitives occur in the same constructions—therefore allowing for semantically opposite interpretations—the head noun implies a *transitive* verb. This is by far the more frequent type of verbal noun, however. In a given context, "love of God" could mean "[my/your/their] love for God" (objective) or "God's love for [me/you/them]." Since the lexico-syntactic features in such instances are identical, appeal must be made to context, authorial usage, and broader exegetical issues.

See Chart 12 below for a diagram of both subjective and objective genitives.

c. Illustrations

(1) CLEAR EXAMPLES

Matt 24:27   οὕτως ἔσται ἡ παρουσία **τοῦ υἱοῦ** τοῦ ἀνθρώπου
So shall the coming **of the Son** of Man be (="so shall it be when the Son of Man comes").

---

[17] Not to be confused with an infinitive, which is *syntactically* a verbal noun. The expression as used here is a *lexical* title.

Mark 14:59   οὐδὲ οὕτως ἴση ἦν ἡ μαρτυρία **αὐτῶν**
Nor was **their** testimony thus the same (="nor did they testify the same thing")

(2) POSSIBLE (AND EXEGETICALLY SIGNIFICANT) EXAMPLES

Arguably the most debated group of texts involves the expression πίστις Χριστοῦ: Should it be translated "faith *in* Christ" (objective gen.) or "the faith/faithfulness *of* Christ" (subjective gen.)?

Rom 3:22   δικαιοσύνη δὲ θεοῦ διὰ πίστεως Ἰησοῦ Χριστοῦ
even the righteousness of God, through faith **in**/the faithfulness **of Jesus Christ**[18]

➡17. Objective Genitive   *ExSyn* 116–19

a. Definition and key to identification. The genitive substantive functions semantically as the *direct object* of the verbal idea implicit in the head noun. This is common in the NT.

When an objective genitive is suspected, attempt to convert the verbal noun to which the genitive is related into a verbal form and turn the genitive into its direct object. Thus, for example, "a demonstration of his righteousness" in Rom 3:25 becomes "demonstrating his righteousness." A simpler and less fool-proof method is to supply for the word *of* the words *for, about, concerning, toward,* or sometimes *against.*

b. Amplification. Two things should be noted concerning the semantics. (1) This category is lexico-syntactic—i.e., it is related to a *specific lexical meaning* for one of the words involved (in this case, the head noun). The head noun, which is here called a "verbal noun," must have an implicit verbal idea. Words such as "love," "hope," "revelation," "witness," and "word" can imply, in a given situa-

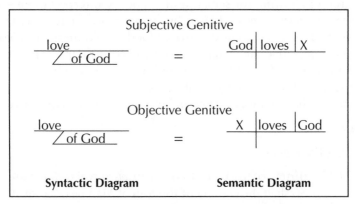

Chart 12
Diagrams of Subjective and Objective Genitive

---

[18] For discussion, cf. *ExSyn* 114–16.

tion, a verbal idea. The perspective must, of course, be from Greek rather than English: e.g., "king" has no verbal cognate in English (there is no verb "to king") but it does in Greek (βασιλεύς has βασιλεύω).

(2) Where objective and subjective genitives occur in the same constructions—therefore allowing for semantically opposite interpretations—the head noun implies a *transitive* verb. This is by far the more frequent type of verbal noun, however. In a given context, "love of God" could mean "[my/your/their] love for God" (objective) or "God's love for [me/you/them]." Since the lexico-syntactic features in such instances are identical, appeal must be made to context, authorial usage, and broader exegetical issues.

c. Illustrations

(1) CLEAR EXAMPLES

Matt 12:31   ἡ δὲ **τοῦ πνεύματος** βλασφημία οὐκ ἀφεθήσεται
            But the blasphemy **of the Spirit** shall not be forgiven (= "blasphemy **against the Spirit**" or "blaspheming the Spirit")

Luke 11:42   οὐαὶ ὑμῖν τοῖς Φαρισαίοις, ὅτι … παρέρχεσθε τὴν κρίσιν καὶ τὴν ἀγάπην **τοῦ θεοῦ**
            Woe to you Pharisees! For you have neglected justice and love **of God!**

(2) DISPUTED EXAMPLES

Rom 8:17; John 5:42; 1 Pet 3:21 ("the resurrection of Christ").[19] In addition, see the discussion under "Subjective Genitive" of the πίστις Χριστοῦ formula.

18. Plenary Genitive   *ExSyn* 119–21

a. Definition. The noun in the genitive is *both* subjective and objective. In most cases, the subjective produces the objective notion. To identify this, simply apply the keys used for the subjective and objective genitives. If *both* ideas seem to fit in a given passage *and do not contradict but rather complement one another*, then there is a good possibility that the genitive in question is a plenary (or full) genitive.

b. (Possible) Illustration

2 Cor 5:14   ἡ γὰρ ἀγάπη **τοῦ Χριστοῦ** συνέχει ἡμᾶς
            For the love **of Christ** constrains us
            It is possible that both subjective and objective genitive ideas were intended by Paul. Thus, "The love that comes from Christ produces our love for Christ—and this [the whole package] constrains us." In this example, then, the subjective *produces* the objective.

---

[19] The issue here and in similar expressions is whether we should see this as "Christ rising [from the dead]" or as "[God] raising Christ [from the dead]." Both are taught in the NT—even to the extent that Christ is considered an active participant in his own resurrection (cf. John 2:19, 21; 10:18).

Adverbial Genitive *ExSyn* 121–30

This use of the genitive is similar in force to an adverb. As well, this use of the genitive often has the force of a prepositional phrase (which, of course, is similar in force to an adverb). Thus the genitive will normally be related to a *verb* or *adjective* rather than to a noun. (Even in instances where it is dependent on a noun, there is usually an implicit verbal idea in the noun.)

➡19. Genitive of Time (within which or during which) *ExSyn* 122–24

a. Definition. The genitive substantive indicates the *kind* of time, or time *within which* the word to which is stands related takes place. The easiest way to remember the genitive of time (as opposed to the dat. and acc. of time) is to relate the genitive back to its basal significance. The genitive is the case of quality, attribute, description, or *kind*.[20] Thus, the genitive of time indicates the *kind* of time. This usage is not common, but can frequently be expected with words that lexically involve a temporal element.

b. Key to identification and amplification. The noun in the genitive expresses an indication of time. The *of* typically becomes *during* or *at* or *within*.

The semantics of this genitive should be noted: When the simple genitive (i.e., without a preposition) is used for time, it expresses the *kind* of time. However, with ἐκ or ἀπό the meaning is quite different—with emphasis placed on the beginning (cf., e.g., Mark 9:21—ἐκ παιδιόθεν ["from childhood"]).[21] This is *not* a confusion of case uses—one indicating time within which and the other indicating extent of time. The classification of a genitive indicating a time element that follows ἐκ or ἀπό is properly "object of the preposition." The preposition then needs to be classified.

An author has the choice of three cases to indicate time: genitive, dative, accusative. Generally speaking, their semantic forces are, respectively: kind of time (or time during which), point in time (answering the question, "When?"), and extent of time (answering the question, "How long?"). Such cases ought to be carefully observed to see what point an author is trying to make—a point not always easily translated into English.

c. Illustrations

Luke 18:12	νηστεύω δὶς **τοῦ σαββάτου**	I fast twice **a week**

The idea is that the Pharisee fasted twice *during* the week.

John 3:2	ἦλθεν πρὸς αὐτὸν **νυκτός**	

he came to him **during the night**

---

[20] That is, as the eight-case system defines it.

[21] This shows the fallacy of lumping preposition + case uses with simple case uses. The preposition does not simply make explicit what the simple case means; in this instance, ἐκ + gen. indicates *source* or separation, while the simple gen. indicates *kind*. But there is no simple gen. use for *time* that indicates source. This notion requires a preposition. Cf. Phil 1:5, for example, ἀπὸ τῆς πρώτης ἡμέρας ἄχρι τοῦ νῦν ("from the first day until now"): this is *not* kind of time, but span of time.

20. Genitive of Means [by]
ExSyn 125

a. Definition and key to identification. The genitive substantive indicates the means or instrumentality by which the verbal action (implicit in the head noun [or adjective] or explicit in the verb) is accomplished. It answers the question, "How?" This usage is rare. (With the preposition ἐκ this nuance is more frequent, though that technically is not a gen. of means because of the preposition.)

For *of* supply *by.* This will be followed by a noun in the genitive case that is impersonal or at least conceived of as such.

b. Illustrations

Rom 4:11   τῆς δικαιοσύνης **τῆς πίστεως**
the righteousness **by** [means of] **faith**

Jas 1:13   ὁ γὰρ θεὸς ἀπείραστός ἐστιν **κακῶν**
for God is not tempted **by evil**

21. Genitive of Agency
ExSyn 126–27

a. Definition and key to identification. The genitive substantive indicates the *personal* agent by whom the action in view is accomplished. It is almost always related to verbal adjective that is typically used as a substantive and has the characteristically passive ending -τος (e.g., ἀγαπητός, διδακτός, ἐκλεκτός); this is followed by a personal noun in the genitive. For *of* supply *by.* Thus, e.g., διδακτὸς θεοῦ, "taught of God," becomes "taught by God." This usage is fairly rare.

b. Illustrations

John 18:16   ὁ μαθητὴς ὁ ἄλλος ὁ γνωστὸς **τοῦ ἀρχιερέως**
the other disciple, who was known **by the high priest**

Rom 8:33   τίς ἐγκαλέσει κατὰ ἐκλεκτῶν **θεοῦ**;
Who will bring a charge against those chosen **by God?**

➡22. Genitive Absolute

See under "Circumstantial Participles" in chapter on participles.

23. Genitive of Reference [with reference to]
ExSyn 127–28

a. Definition and key to identification. The genitive substantive indicates that in reference to which the noun or adjective to which it stands related is true. This usage is not common.

For the word *of* supply *with reference to, with respect to.*

b. Amplification. This genitive usually modifies an adjective (although rarely it will be connected to a noun), and as such its adverbial force is self-evident. The genitive limits the frame of reference of the adjective.

All oblique cases, as well as the nominative (known as pendent nominative), can be used to indicate reference. The most common is the dative of reference. The first illustration below is with an adjective, while the second is with a noun.

c. Illustrations

Heb 3:12   καρδία πονηρὰ **ἀπιστίας**
a heart evil **with reference to unbelief**

Matt 21:21   οὐ μόνον τὸ **τῆς συκῆς** ποιήσετε
you shall do not only what [was done] **with reference to the fig tree**

24. Genitive of Association [in association with]   *ExSyn* 128–30

a. Definition and key to identification. The genitive substantive indicates the one with whom the noun to which it stands related is associated.

For *of* supply *with*, or *in association with*.

b. Amplification. The head noun to which this kind of genitival use is connected is normally prefixed with συν-. Such compound nouns naturally lend themselves to the associative idea. As well, some nouns and adjectives already embrace lexically the idea of "in association with" and hence can take a genitive of association without συν- prefixed to them.

This usage has particular exegetical weight in the Pauline letters, for it typically makes explicit some ramification of the ἐν Χριστῷ formula (since believers are said to be in Christ, because of their organic connection to him, they now associate with him in many and profound ways).

c. Illustrations

(1) Clear Examples

Eph 2:19   ἐστὲ συμπολῖται **τῶν ἁγίων**
you are fellow-citizens **with the saints**

Col 4:10   Ἀρίσταρχος ὁ συναιχμάλωτός **μου**
Aristarchus, **my** fellow-prisoner (="fellow-prisoner **with me**")

> In English usage "my" is more natural than "with me," though the force is obviously not that Paul *possesses* Aristarchus.

(2) Disputed Example

1 Cor. 3:9   **θεοῦ** γὰρ ἐσμεν συνεργοί
For we are **God's** fellow-workers

> Here, Paul *may* be saying that he and Apollos *and* God are in association with one another in the work of the ministry. However, it is better to see an ellipsis of "with one another" and to see θεοῦ as a possessive gen. (thus, "we are fellow-workers [with each other], belonging to God").[22]

---

[22] See *ExSyn* 130 for a discussion of this verse.

After Certain Words

There are some uses of the genitive that do not *neatly* fit into any of the above categories. Or, if they do fit into one of the above categories, they are related to a word *other than* a noun. These constitute the large and amorphous group known as *the use of the genitive after certain words*.

➡25. Genitive After Certain Verbs (as a Direct Object)   *ExSyn* 131–34

a. Definition and amplification. Certain verbs take a genitive substantive as direct object. These verbs commonly correspond in meaning to some other function of the genitive, e.g., separation, partitive, source, etc. The predominant uses can be grouped into four types of verbs: *sensation, emotion/volition, sharing, ruling.*[23]

For the most part, the semantic significance of genitive as direct object relates to one of the genitive functions as discussed above. But note that several of the verbs that take genitive direct objects also take accusative direct objects. Thus, when an author has a choice for the case of his direct object, the case he chooses in which to express his idea may be significant.

b. Illustrations[24]

(1) SENSATION

Mark 5:41   κρατήσας **τῆς χειρὸς** τοῦ παιδίου λέγει αὐτῇ, Ταλιθα κουμ
touching **the hand** of the little girl, he said to her, "Talitha cum"

> There is a note of tenderness seen in the gen., contrasted with the acc.

(2) EMOTION/VOLITION

Luke 10:35   ἐπιμελήθητι **αὐτοῦ**   *take care* **of him**

(3) SHARING

Heb 12:10   ὁ δὲ ἐπὶ τὸ συμφέρον εἰς τὸ *μεταλαβεῖν* **τῆς ἁγιότητος** αὐτοῦ
but he [disciplines us] for our benefit, that we might *share* **in** his **holiness**

> This is an instance of the *partitive* direct object. (Generally speaking, if a verb can take either a gen. or acc. direct object, the *accusative* will be used when the object is apprehended *as a whole*; the *genitive* will be used when the object is apprehended *in part*.) The participation that believers can have in God's holiness is not complete, but derived and partial. The gen. seems to be used to reflect this.

---

[23] Cf. BDF, 93–96 (§§169–78) for a list of such verbs (broken down into ten categories). Rather than duplicate the list here, since such genitives can easily be noted via the lexicon, the student is advised to consult BAGD under the verb in question if in doubt.

[24] Because this is such a broad category, and because the liberal use of a good lexicon reveals this usage, only a few examples will be given.

(4) RULING

Luke 22:25 οἱ βασιλεῖς τῶν ἐθνῶν *κυριεύουσιν* **αὐτῶν**
the kings of the Gentiles *lord it* **over them**

26. Genitive After Certain Adjectives (and Adverbs) *ExSyn* 134–35

a. Definition. Certain adjectives (such as ἄξιος, "worthy [of]") and adverbs normally take a genitive "object." In many instances the adjective/adverb is an embedded transitive verb, thus taking an objective genitive (e.g., "he is deserving of X" means "he deserves X") or involving a partitive idea.

b. Amplification. As with the genitive direct object, you should check BAGD under various adjectives and adverbs or BDF (98 [§182]) for a list. In reality, most of these examples also fit under some other genitive use equally well—such as partitive, objective, content, reference, etc. However, the fact that certain adjectives, by their very nature, take genitives after them renders this a predictable and stable category.

c. Illustrations

Matt 26:66 ἔνοχος **θανάτου** ἐστίν   he is *deserving* **of death**
This is the equivalent of "he deserves **death**," an objective gen.

Phil 1:27 ἀξίως **τοῦ εὐαγγελίου** τοῦ Χριστοῦ πολιτεύεσθε
conduct yourselves *worthily* **of the gospel** of Christ

➡27. Genitive After Certain Prepositions *ExSyn* 136

a. Definition. Certain prepositions take the genitive after them. See the chapter on prepositions for discussion. For review of which prepositions take which cases, cf., e.g., Mounce, *Basics of Biblical Greek*, 55–62.[25]

b. Significance. When a genitive follows a preposition, you should *not* attempt to identify the genitive's function by case usage *alone*. Rather, consult either BAGD or the chapter on prepositions for the specific usage of that case with that preposition. Many of the simple genitive uses overlap those of the preposition + the genitive (especially with ἐκ + the gen.). But the parallels are not exact; there are some simple genitive uses that cannot be duplicated with prepositions and some preposition + genitive uses that find no parallel with the simple genitive. Furthermore, where there is overlap of usage, there is usually *not* overlap of frequency of occurrence.

---

[25] In addition, forty of the forty-two "improper prepositions" take the gen. case (e.g., ἄχρι(ς), ἔμπροσθεν, ἕνεκα, ἕως, ὀψέ, πλησίον, ὑπεράνω, ὑποκάτω, χωρίς). One should consult the lexicon if in doubt.

The Dative Case[1]
Overview of Dative Uses

Pure Dative Uses. **67**
➡ 1. Dative Indirect Object 67
➡ 2. Dative of Interest (including Advantage [*commodi*]
    and Disadvantage [*incommodi*]) 68
➡ 3. Dative of Reference/Respect. 69
   4. Dative of Destination 70
   5. Dative of Possession 70
➡ 6. Dative in Simple Apposition. 71
Local Dative Uses **71**
➡ 7. Dative of Sphere 72
➡ 8. Dative of Time (when) 72
Instrumental Dative Uses. **73**
➡ 9. Dative of Association (Accompaniment, Comitative) 73
 10. Dative of Manner (or Adverbial Dative). 74
➡11. Dative of Means/Instrument. 75
† 12. Dative of Agency. 75
 13. Dative of Measure/Degree of Difference. 76
➡14. Dative of Cause 77
 15. Cognate Dative 77
The Uses of the Dative After Certain Words **78**
➡16. Dative Direct Object. 78
 17. Dative After Certain Nouns 79
 18. Dative After Certain Adjectives 79
➡19. Dative After Certain Prepositions 80

INTRODUCTION *ExSyn* 138

Preliminary Remarks

The dative case is not as exegetically significant as the genitive. This is not to say that the dative does not play a vital role in exegetical decisions. Rather, a particular instance of the dative is usually easier to classify than a given genitive. This is due to two things: (1) the broad classes of dative uses are generally more easily distinguishable; and (2) the embedded clause needs less "unpacking" since the dative is already related to a verb, while the genitive is more cryptic and elliptical since it is usually related to a noun.

---

[1] See *ExSyn* 137–75. The following datives are rare or debatable categories that the average intermediate Greek student can ignore: ethical dative (146–47), dative of recipient (148–49), dative of thing possessed (151), predicate dative (152), dative of rule (157–58), dative of material (169–70), and dative of content (170–71).

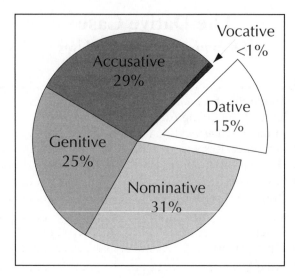

Chart 13
Frequency of Cases in the New Testament[2]

At the same time, there are some instances in which a given dative may function in more than one capacity (e.g., both instrumental and local), and not a few in which a decision is still hard to come by. In such places, the dative takes on greater significance.

Finally, the simple dative is phasing out in Koine Greek, being replaced largely by prepositions, especially ἐν + the dative. This is not to say that the simple dative and ἐν + dative mirror each other completely, as will become clear in our examination of various uses of the dative case.

Definition of the Dative Case

1. Within the Eight-Case System

"The dative, locative, and instrumental cases are all represented by the same inflectional form, but the distinction in function is very clear—much more so than the distinction between the ablative and genitive."[3] However, this does *not* mean that, within the eight-case system, it is always easy to tell to which case this particular inflectional form belongs. Furthermore, there will be a few occasions in which the same case form will have a double-duty function. The eight-case system cannot handle such a double function because such would involve two different cases. Thus, the definition of case as a matter of function rather than form can sometimes be so rigid that it excludes part of the meaning intended by the author.

---

[2] The dative breakdown is 4375 nouns, 3565 pronouns, 2944 articles, 936 adjectives, 353 participles.

[3] Dana-Mantey, 83.

The true dative is used to designate the person more remotely concerned. It is the case of *personal interest*, pointing out the person *to* or *for* whom something is done. This is not to say that the dative cannot relate to things, for there are numerous examples of this. When it does so, it has a referring force. In general, when the dative is used of persons, it speaks about the one(s) concerned about (or affected by) the action; when it is used of things, it addresses the *framework* in which an act occurs.

2. Within the Five-Case System

However, since the dative, instrumental, and locative share the same form, we will consider them as *one* case ("case" being defined as a matter of form rather than function within the five-case system).[4] The *instrumental* idea involves means and generally answers the question, "How?" The *locative* notion involves place and answers the question, "Where?" Thus, a broad view of the dative case (including pure dative, locative, and instrumental uses) suggests that it answers one of three questions: To/for whom? How? or Where?

Thus, within the five-case system the dative case may be defined as the case of *personal interest, reference/respect* (pure dative), *position* (locative), and *means* (instrumental).

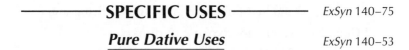

──────── **SPECIFIC USES** ────────   *ExSyn 140–75*

Pure Dative Uses   *ExSyn 140–53*

The subgroups here are specific uses built on the root idea of *personal interest* and *reference/respect*.

➡1. Dative Indirect Object   *ExSyn 140–42*

a. Definition. The dative substantive is that to or for which the action of a verb is performed. The indirect object will *only occur with a transitive verb*. When the transitive verb is in the *active* voice,[5] the indirect object receives the direct object ("the boy hit the ball *to me*"); when the verb is in the *passive* voice, the indirect object receives the subject of the verb ("the ball was hit *to me*").

Stated more succinctly: "The noun or pronoun in the dative is the person or thing to which is given (or which receives) the direct object (of a transitive verb) (or [receives the] subject of a passive verb)."[6] This category is by far the most common of the dative uses.

---

[4] It is not insignificant that even Dana-Mantey vacillate slightly here in saying "we cannot ignore form entirely while we are in the realm of syntax, for it often happens that we would be utterly unable to determine what the intended function is except for the form" (Dana-Mantey, 86).

[5] That is, active from the standpoint of English. In Greek it can sometimes be in the middle (deponent middles are treated as though they are actives).

[6] Williams, *Grammar Notes*, 15.

b. Key to identification and semantics. The key to identification is that the verb must be transitive; and if the dative can be translated with *to* or *for* it is most likely indirect object.

(1) To translate a dative as *to* or *for* with a transitive verb is easily the most common translation (like *of* for the genitive). There are many uses of the dative that actually fall under the larger umbrella of the indirect object (e.g., interest, ethical). The indirect object, therefore, is normally recognized as the most common dative.

(2) In the sentence "He gave the book to the boy," "to the boy" is the indirect object. It receives the direct object, "the book," of the transitive (and active) verb, "gave." Such a sentence can be put into a *passive transform*: "The book was given to the boy by him." Here, "the book" has become the subject (formerly the direct object), but "to the boy" is still the indirect object. The subject of the active voice verb "gave" has become the agent of the passive voice verb "was given." In both sentences the indirect object remains the same and receives the same thing semantically, though not grammatically (i.e., it receives the *book* each time, but does not receive the same part of the sentence each time).

c. Illustrations

John 4:10   καὶ ἔδωκεν ἄν **σοι** ὕδωρ ζῶν
             and he would have given **to you** living water

2 Cor 12:7   ἐδόθη **μοι** σκόλοψ τῇ σαρκί
             a thorn in the flesh was given **to me**.

             This is a passive transform of the clause, ἔδωκεν **μοι** σκόλοπα τῇ σαρκί, "He gave **me** a thorn in the flesh."

➡2. Dative of Interest (including Advantage [*commodi*] and Disadvantage [*incommodi*])   *ExSyn 142–44*

a. Definition. The dative substantive indicates the person (or, rarely, thing) interested in the verbal action. The dative of advantage has a *to* or *for* idea, while the dative of disadvantage has an *against* idea. The dative of advantage occurs more frequently than disadvantage, though both are common enough. It is important to distinguish between dative of advantage and disadvantage (since the resultant meanings are opposite).

b. Key to identification. Instead of the words *to* or *for*, supply *for the benefit of* or *in the interest of* for the dative of advantage, and *for/unto the detriment of* or *to the disadvantage of* or *against* for the dative of disadvantage. The translation *for the benefit of* and the like is helpful for getting the sense of the dative, though not as a final translation, since it is too awkward.

c. Semantics/significance. Dative of interest typically (but not always) belongs to the larger category of indirect object. The difference in the two is that in the former, interest is stressed, while in the latter it is not.

Since the root idea of the pure dative is personal interest (i.e., with reference to person), one should not think in such clear-cut categories as to divorce this idea from other uses of the pure dative. That is, *every pure dative use is a dative of interest in a general sense*. However, the category *dative of interest* really involves a more specific use of the dative, which emphasizes either advantage or disadvantage. Thus, for example, "This is food to me" would be a dative of interest in a general sense. However, a lousy meal would mean a dative of disadvantage, while *my* wife's culinary fare would mean a dative of advantage! A dative of advantage/disadvantage will usually belong to some other category as well; but when the idea of advantage/disadvantage is prominent, it is to be classified as such.

d. Illustrations

(1) ADVANTAGE (*COMMODĪ*)

1 Cor 6:13   τὰ βρώματα **τῇ κοιλίᾳ**
food is **for** [the benefit of] **the stomach**

2 Cor 5:13   εἴτε γὰρ ἐξέστημεν, **θεῷ**· εἴτε σωφρονοῦμεν, **ὑμῖν**.
for if we are beside ourselves, it is **for God**; if we are in our right minds, it is **for you**.

(2) DISADVANTAGE (*INCOMMODĪ*)

Matt 23:31   μαρτυρεῖτε **ἑαυτοῖς**   You testify **against yourselves**

1 Cor 11:29   ὁ γὰρ ἐσθίων καὶ πίνων κρίμα **ἑαυτῷ** ἐσθίει καὶ πίνει
For the one who eats and drinks eats and drinks judgment **on himself**

➡3. Dative of Reference/Respect [with reference to]   *ExSyn* 144–46

a. Definition. The dative substantive is that in reference to which something is presented as true. An author will use this dative to qualify a statement that would otherwise typically not be true. This dative can thus be called a frame of reference dative, limiting dative, qualifying dative, or contextualizing dative. This is a common use of the dative case; further, the dative is the most common case used for reference/respect.[7]

b. Key to identification and amplification. Instead of the word *to*, supply the phrase *with reference to* before the dative. (Other glosses are *concerning, about, in regard to*, etc.) When the noun in the dative is a *thing*, the sentence typically makes no sense if the dative is removed, as, e.g., in Rom 6:2—"How shall we who died [to sin] still live in it?"

---

[7] The acc. is the next most common, but it is a distant second (acc. stands first in classical Greek). There is also a gen. of reference, and, in fact, a nom. of reference (i.e., *nominativus pendens*).

The pure dative, when referring especially to things, reduces the element of interest and relation to that of reference or framework. It is frequently found with adjectives. But the dative of reference can also occasionally be used of persons.

c. Illustrations

Rom 6:11   λογίζεσθε ἑαυτοὺς εἶναι νεκροὺς μὲν **τῇ ἁμαρτίᾳ**, ζῶντας δὲ **τῷ θεῷ**
Consider yourselves to be dead **to sin**, but alive **to God**

Luke 18:31   πάντα τὰ γεγραμμένα διὰ τῶν προφητῶν **τῷ υἱῷ** τοῦ ἀνθρώ-που
all the things written by the prophets **concerning the Son** of Man

4. Dative of Destination
ExSyn 147–48

a. Definition. This dative is similar to an indirect object, except that it appears with *intransitive* verbs (esp. ἔρχομαι). It is the "to" idea when an intransitive verb is used. There is typically a transfer of something from one place to another. It indicates the final point of the verb, where the verb is going. This usage is relatively infrequent, being replaced in Koine Greek with explicit prepositions (such as ἐν, ἐπί, εἰς).

b. Key to identification. Remember that this broad "to" idea is in relation to *intransitive* verbs (i.e., verbs that do *not* take a direct object). The dative with ἔρχομαι accounts for most examples.

c. Illustrations

Matt 21:5   ὁ βασιλεύς σου ἔρχεταί **σοι**
your king is coming **to you**

Luke 15:25   ὡς ἐρχόμενος ἤγγισεν **τῇ οἰκίᾳ**
when he came, he approached **the house**

5. Dative of Possession [belonging to]
ExSyn 149–51

a. Definition. The dative of possession functions like a genitive of possession under certain conditions, occurring with equative verbs such as εἰμί, γίνομαι, and ὑπάρχω. The dative substantive possesses the noun to which it is related. In other words, it is that person or thing to which the subject of an equative verb belongs. The usage is not especially common.

b. Key to identification. Instead of the word *to*, supply *possessed by* or *belonging to*. On occasion (especially if the dative is in predicate position after an equative verb), it may be more helpful to regard the dative as the semantic equivalent of a nominative subject and put the actual subject in the predicate (i.e., treat it as direct object). For example:

Acts 8:21   οὐκ ἔστιν **σοι** μερὶς οὐδὲ κλῆρος ἐν τῷ λόγῳ τούτῳ
neither a share nor a lot in this matter **belong to you**

> This could be converted to "you have neither a share nor a lot in this matter." (The dat. becomes the subject and the subject is placed in the predicate—here, as direct object.)

c. Semantics. In general, the difference between an indirect object and a possessive dative has to do with *act* (as seen in the transitive verb) and resultant *state* (as seen in the equative verb). For example, ἔδωκεν τὸ βιβλίον μοι ("he gave me the book") becomes τὸ βιβλίον ἐστί μοι ("the book is mine").

d. Illustrations

Matt 18:12   Τί ὑμῖν δοκεῖ; ἐὰν γένηταί **τινι ἀνθρώπῳ** ἑκατὸν πρόβατα
What do you think? If a hundred sheep **[belong]** to a certain man

Rom 7:3   ἐὰν γένηται **ἀνδρὶ ἑτέρῳ**
if she becomes **to another man** (= "if she becomes another man's" or, "if she becomes possessed by another man")

➡ **6.   Dative in Simple Apposition**   *ExSyn* 152–53

a. Definition. Though not technically a syntactical category,[8] the dative case (as well as the other cases) can be an appositive to another substantive in the *same* case. An appositional construction involves two adjacent substantives that refer to the same person or thing and have the same syntactical relation to the rest of the clause. The first dative substantive can belong to *any* dative category and the second is merely a clarification of who or what is mentioned. Thus, the appositive "piggy-backs" on the first dative's use, as it were.[9] This usage is common.

b. Illustrations

Luke 1:47   ἠγαλλίασεν τὸ πνεῦμά μου ἐπὶ τῷ θεῷ **τῷ σωτῆρί** μου
my spirit rejoices in God my **Savior**

Acts 24:24   Δρουσίλλῃ **τῇ ἰδίᾳ γυναικὶ**
to Drusilla, **his wife**

Local Dative Uses   *ExSyn* 153–58

The subgroups here are specific uses built on the root idea of *position*, whether spatial, nonphysical, or temporal.

---

[8] Hence, this category could belong in the dat., locative, or instrumental groups. It is listed here for convenience' sake.

[9] For more information on simple apposition, cf. the sections on the nominative and genitive.

➡**7. Dative of Sphere [in the sphere of]**   *ExSyn*153–55

a. Definition. The dative substantive indicates the sphere or realm[10] in which the word to which it is related takes place or exists. Normally this word is a verb, but not always. This is a common use of the dative.

b. Key to identification and clarification. Before the noun in the dative supply the words *in the sphere of* or *in the realm of.* In general, it is safe to say that the dative of *reference* views the word to which the dative stands related as detached or *separated* somehow from the dative, while the dative of *sphere* views the word to which the dative stands related as *incorporated* within the realm of the dative. For example, in Rom 6:2 Paul uses the dative of reference: "How shall we who died [with reference] to sin still live in it?" Here, "we who died" is detached or separated from "sin." In Eph 2:1 we see the dative of sphere: "Though you were dead in [the sphere of] your sins." Here, "you were dead" is incorporated within the realm of sin.

c. Illustrations

Matt 5:3   οἱ πτωχοὶ **τῷ πνεύματι**   the poor **in spirit**
    Here the dat. is practically equivalent to an adverb, thus, "the spiritually poor."

1 Pet 3:18   Χριστὸς ἅπαξ περὶ ἁμαρτιῶν ἔπαθεν, δίκαιος ὑπὲρ ἀδίκων … θανατωθεὶς μὲν **σαρκί**
    Christ died once for all for sins, the just for the unjust … having been put to death **in the flesh**

➡**8. Dative of Time (when)**   *ExSyn* 155–57

a. Definition. The noun in the dative indicates the *time when* the action of the main verb is accomplished. The dative routinely denotes *point of time*, answering the question, "When?" In the eight-case system, this would be the locative of time. Though common enough, this usage is being increasingly replaced in Koine Greek with ἐν + the dative.

b. Key to identification and semantics. Remember that the noun in the dative expresses an indication of time.

The dative of time is distinct from the genitive of time as well the accusative of time (occasionally it overlaps with this category). The easiest way to remember the distinction between these cases for time is to remember the root idea of each case. The root idea of the (pure) genitive is quality, attribute, or kind; thus, the genitive of time expresses *kind* of time (or time during which). The root idea of

---

[10] Some people talk about the dative of place as a separate category, distinct from sphere. I disagree with this view. My sense is that sphere and place are simply different applications of the same category—one figurative, the other literal. The only difference is lexical, not semantic. Exegesis is not materially affected by such a distinction.

the accusative is limitation as to extent; thus, the accusative of time expresses *extent* of time. The root idea of the *local* dative is position; thus, the dative of time expresses a *point* in time.

c. Illustrations

Matt 17:23   **τῇ τρίτῃ ἡμέρᾳ** ἐγερθήσεται
[at a point in time] **on the third day** he will be raised

Matt 24:20   προσεύχεσθε δὲ ἵνα μὴ γένηται ἡ φυγὴ ὑμῶν χειμῶνος μηδὲ **σαββάτῳ**
But pray that your flight will not be during the winter nor **on the sabbath**

Instrumental Dative Uses   *ExSyn 158–171*

The subgroups here are specific uses built on the root idea of *means*, although some loosely fit under this umbrella.

➡9. Dative of Association (Accompaniment, Comitative) [in association with]   *ExSyn 159–61*

a. Definition. The dative substantive indicates the person or thing one associates with or accompanies. This usage is relatively common.

b. Key to identification and clarification. Before the noun in the dative supply the phrase *in association with*. This usage of the dative only loosely belongs under the broad category of instrumental datives. Nevertheless, it belongs here more naturally than elsewhere.

Frequently, though not always, the dative word will be related to a compound verb involving συν. This is especially so in Acts, less frequently in the Pauline letters. But not every dative following a συν- prefixed verb is a dative of association (see discussion of the debatable example below).

The difference between genitive of association and dative of association is simply this: the genitive is used with *nouns* (which begin with σύν-) while the dative is used with *verbs* (which are frequently prefixed with σύν-).

c. Caution. Although there is a close relation between means and association, one should be careful to distinguish them. In the sentence, "He walked with his friend with a cane," "with his friend" expresses association and "with a cane" expresses means. The difference is that for the purposes of walking the cane is necessary, while the friend is expendable!

d. Illustrations

(1) CLEAR EXAMPLES

Acts 9:7   οἱ δὲ ἄνδρες οἱ συνοδεύοντες **αὐτῷ**
the men who were traveling **with him**

2 Cor 6:14   μὴ γίνεσθε ἑτεροζυγοῦντες **ἀπίστοις**
do not become unequally yoked [in association] **with unbelievers**

> The first example is typical, in that there is a verb prefixed with συν. The second example has a verb root that carries an associative idea.

(2) A DEBATABLE EXAMPLE

Rom 8:16   αὐτὸ τὸ πνεῦμα συμμαρτυρεῖ **τῷ πνεύματι** ἡμῶν ὅτι ἐσμὲν τέκνα θεοῦ
the Spirit himself bears witness **along with** our **spirit** that we are God's children

> At issue, grammatically, is whether the Spirit testifies *alongside of* our spirit (dat. of association), or whether he testifies *to our spirit* (indirect object) that we are God's children. If the former, the one receiving this testimony is unstated (is it God? or believers?). If the latter, the believer receives the testimony and hence is assured of salvation via the inner witness of the Spirit. Most likely, πνεύματι should *not* be taken as association.[11]

10. Dative of Manner (or Adverbial Dative)[12]
[with, in (answering "How?")]   ExSyn 161–62

a. Definition. The dative substantive denotes the manner in which the action of the verb is accomplished. Like many adverbs, this use of the dative answers the question "How?" (and typically with a "with" or "in" phrase). The manner can be an accompanying action, attitude, emotion, or circumstance. Hence, such a dative noun routinely has an abstract quality. This usage is relatively common, though it is being supplanted by ἐν + dative (or μετά + gen.) in Koine Greek.

b. Key to identification and clarification. Supply "with" or "in" before the dative noun. Also, if the dative can be converted into an adverb (e.g., "with thanksgiving" becomes "thankfully"), it is likely a dative of manner. Note, however, that not always can one easily convert this dative into an adverb.

The real key is to ask first whether the dative noun answers the question "How?" and then ask if the dative *defines* the action of the verb (dative of means) or adds color to the verb (manner). In the sentence, "She walked with a cane, with a flare," "with a cane" expresses means, while "with a flare" expresses manner. Thus, *one* of the ways in which you can distinguish between means and manner is that a dative of manner typically employs an abstract noun while a dative of means typically employs a more concrete noun.

---

[11] See *ExSyn* 160–61 for discussion.
[12] A subcategory of dat. of manner is the cognate dat. (discussed below).

c. Illustrations

John 7:26   παρρησίᾳ λαλεῖ
he speaks **with boldness** (= **boldly**)

1 Cor 10:30   εἰ ἐγὼ **χάριτι** μετέχω
if I partake [of the food] **with thanksgiving** (= **thankfully**)

➡11. Dative of Means/Instrument [by, by means of, with]   *ExSyn 162–63*

a. Definition. The dative substantive is used to indicate the means or instrument by which the verbal action is accomplished. This is a common use of the dative, embracing as it does one of the root ideas of the dative case (viz., instrumentality).

b. Key to identification and amplification. Before the noun in the dative, supply the words *by means of* or simply *with*. The dative noun is typically concrete, as opposed to manner, where the noun is typically abstract. But the dative noun is also usually, though not always, *conceived of as impersonal*. It is distinguished from personal agency in two ways: (1) personality is not in view, and (2) means involves an agent who uses it (whether that agent is stated or implied).

c. Illustrations

John 11:2   ἐκμάξασα τοὺς πόδας αὐτοῦ **ταῖς θριξὶν** αὐτῆς
she wiped his feet **with her hair**

Rom 3:28   λογιζόμεθα δικαιοῦσθαι **πίστει** ἄνθρωπον
we maintain that a person is justified **by faith**

†12. Dative of Agency [by, through]   *ExSyn 163–66*

a. Definition. The dative substantive is used to indicate the *personal* agent by whom the action of the verb is accomplished. This is an *extremely rare* category in the NT as well as in ancient Greek in general.

b. Keys to identification, structure, and semantics. (1) According to the above definition, if the dative is used to express agency, the noun in the dative must not only be personal, but must also be the agent who performs the action. Much confusion exists among students of the NT over this category. In general, it is invoked far more often than is legitimate.[13] There are *four keys* to identification for the dative of agency: (a) *Lexical*: the dative must be personal. (b) *Contextual*: the person specified by the dative noun is portrayed as exercising volition. (c) *Grammatical*: the only clear texts involve a perfect passive verb, as in the classical idiom. (d) *Linguistic*: a good *rule of thumb* for distinguishing between agent and means is sim-

---

[13] Even by grammarians on occasion. Cf., e.g., Young, *Intermediate Greek*, 50 (his examples from Rom 8:14 and 1 Tim 3:16 are doubtful; see discussion of these texts in *ExSyn* 165–66); Brooks-Winbery, 45.

ply this: the agent of a passive verb can become the subject of an active verb, while the means normally cannot.

(2) When the dative expresses the idea of *means*, the instrument is used *by an agent*. When agent is indicated, the agent so named is *not used* by another, but is the one who either performs an act directly or uses an instrument.

c. How agency is expressed in the NT. Apart from naming the agent as the subject, there are two common ways to express agency in the NT: ὑπό + the genitive is used for *ultimate* agent; διά + the genitive is used for *intermediate* agent. For example, in Matt 1:22 we read that "all this happened in order that what was spoken **by the Lord** (ὑπὸ κυρίου) **through the prophet** (διὰ τοῦ προφήτου) might be fulfilled." The Lord is the ultimate agent, though he communicates his message through the prophet.

In summary, this clarification is important because when one sees a dative used with a person and some sort of instrumentality is implied, he/she should seek to discover the *agent* who uses the (personal) instrument.

d. Illustrations

(1) CLEAR EXAMPLES

Luke 23:15   οὐδὲν ἄξιον θανάτου ἐστὶν πεπραγμένον **αὐτῷ**
nothing worthy of death had been done **by him**

> As is apparently always the case in the NT, the only clear examples involve a perfect passive verb form.

Jas 3:7   πᾶσα γὰρ φύσις θηρίων ... δεδάμασται **τῇ φύσει τῇ ἀνθρω-πίνῃ**
For every kind of beast ... has been tamed **by humankind**

(2) DEBATABLE EXAMPLE[14]

Gal 5:16   **πνεύματι** περιπατεῖτε καὶ ἐπιθυμίαν σαρκὸς οὐ μὴ τελέσητε
walk **by the Spirit** and you will not fulfill the lust of the flesh

> Taking πνεύματι as a dat. of agency is a popular view among commentators, but there are two basic problems with this interpretation: (1) This usage is rare in the NT (unless, of course, we assume that πνεύματι on many occasions belongs here!); (2) πνεύματι does not occur with a passive verb, let alone a perfect passive; yet every clear example of dat. of agency in the NT occurs with a perfect passive verb.

13. Dative of Measure/Degree of Difference [by]   ExSyn 166–67

a. Definition and key to identification. The dative substantive, when following or preceding a comparative adjective or adverb, may be used to indicate

---

[14] Cf. *ExSyn* 165–66 for more discussion of this text as well as discussion of other passages.

the extent to which the comparison is true or the degree of difference that exists in the comparison. This usage is fairly rare.

Rather than supply "than" as with the genitive of comparison (the two ideas are similar, but not identical), supply "by" before a quantitative word in the dative. Typically the formula in Greek will be πολλῷ (the dative word) + μᾶλλον.

b. Illustrations

Phil 2:12   ὑπηκούσατε ... **πολλῷ** μᾶλλον ἐν τῇ ἀπουσίᾳ μου
you obeyed ... **much** more in my absence

Heb 1:4   **τοσούτῳ** κρείττων γενόμενος τῶν ἀγγέλων
having become **by so much** better than the angels

> A key theme in Hebrews is the superiority of the Son. In 1:4–14 the Son is contrasted to angels, with the clear implication (made explicit in v. 8) that he is God incarnate.

➡14. Dative of Cause [because of]   ExSyn 167–68

a. Definition and key to identification. The dative substantive indicates the cause or basis of the action of the verb. This usage is fairly common.

Before the dative insert the phrase *because of* or *on the basis of*. This use of the dative is similar to but not the same as the dative of means. (At times, however, it is impossible to distinguish the two.)[15] The dative of *means* indicates the *how*; the dative of *cause* indicates the *why*; the dative of *means* indicates the *method*; the dative of *cause* indicates the *basis*.

b. Illustrations

Rom 4:20   οὐ διεκρίθη **τῇ ἀπιστίᾳ**
he did not waver **because of unbelief**

Gal 6:12   μόνον ἵνα **τῷ σταυρῷ** τοῦ Χριστοῦ μὴ διώκωνται
only that they might not be persecuted **because of the cross** of Christ

15. Cognate Dative[16]   ExSyn 168–69

a. Definition and key to identification. The dative noun[17] is cognate to the verb either formally (where both noun and verb have the same root) or conceptually (where the roots are different). This is not common.

---

[15] This is because the ultimate cause may also, at times, be the accomplishing means of an action.

[16] See dat. of manner for the larger category to which this dat. belongs.

[17] This use of the dat., by definition, cannot be found with pronouns, since the *lexical* meaning of the dat. word is related to that of the verb.

The key to this use of the dative is its cognate *force*. Another clue is that the dative can usually be translated as an adverb modifying the verb.[18] The force of the cognate dative will be primarily to *emphasize the action of the verb*.

b. Illustrations

(1) COGNATE IN FORM

Luke 22:15 ἐπιθυμίᾳ ἐπεθύμησα
I desired **with desire** (= " I earnestly desired")

Jas 5:17 Ἡλίας ... **προσευχῇ** προσηύξατο
Elijah ... prayed **earnestly**

(2) COGNATE IN MEANING

1 Pet 1:8 ἀγαλλιᾶσθε **χαρᾷ**   you rejoice **with joy**

Rev 5:11–12 ἤκουσα φωνὴν ... λέγοντες **φωνῇ μεγάλῃ**
I heard a voice ... saying **with a loud voice**

The Uses of the Dative After Certain Words   ExSyn 171–75

Some uses of the dative do not *neatly* fit into any of the above categories. These constitute the large and amorphous group known as *the use of the dative after certain words*.

➡16. Dative Direct Object   ExSyn 171–73

a. Definition. A number of verbs take the dative as their direct object. Such datives are usually related to verbs implying personal relation. Thus the meanings of the verbs correspond in meaning to the basic idea of the pure dative. This category yields many illustrations.

b. Key to identification and clarification. See BAGD, a good concordance, or BDF for a list of such verbs.[19] Usually it will be obvious when the dative is the direct object. But since the dative is normally related to a *verb* rather than to a noun, there may be times of confusion.

A good rule of thumb is that verbs taking a dative direct object can usually be translated with "to" or "in." Thus ὑπακούω can be translated, "I am obedient to"; διακονῶ, "I minister to"; εὐχαριστῶ, "I am thankful to"; πιστεύω, "I trust in." (One has to use a little imagination with these verbs because they are normally rendered "I obey," "I serve," "I thank," and "I believe.")

---

[18] Some of the examples below do not fit this adverbial notion, but are cognate datives in a broader sense.

[19] Although many intermediate grammars list all such verbs, it is our conviction that grammars do much unnecessary duplication with lexica. Our approach is to try to refrain from trespassing into the domain of the lexicon as much as possible.

c. Significance. It has already been pointed out that such dative direct objects are usually related to verbs implying personal relation. This, in part, is the significance of dative direct objects. As well, some of the verbs that take dative direct objects also take accusative direct objects. Thus, when an author has a choice for the case of a direct object, the case chosen may be significant.

d. Illustrations

Gal 3:6   Καθὼς Ἀβραὰμ ἐπίστευσεν **τῷ θεῷ**, καὶ ἐλογίσθη αὐτῷ εἰς δικαιοσύνην·
Just as Abraham believed **God**, and it was reckoned to him as righteousness

Heb 1:6   ὅταν δὲ πάλιν εἰσαγάγῃ τὸν πρωτότοκον εἰς τὴν οἰκουμένην, λέγει καὶ προσκυνησάτωσαν **αὐτῷ** πάντες ἄγγελοι θεοῦ.
And when he again brings the firstborn into the [inhabited] world, he says, "And let all the angels of God worship **him**."

17. Dative After Certain Nouns   *ExSyn 173–74*

a. Definition. A few nouns take datives after them. Again, the notion of personal interest is almost always seen. This category is not particularly common. The nouns in question are *verbal* nouns (i.e., they are cognate to a verb, such as ὀφειλέτης [ὀφείλω], ὑπάντησις [ὑπαντάω]).

b. Illustrations

Matt 8:34   πᾶσα ἡ πόλις ἐξῆλθεν εἰς ὑπάντησιν **τῷ Ἰησοῦ**
all the city came out for a meeting **with Jesus**
The verbal cognate, ὑπαντάω, takes what could be called a dat. of association or dat. direct object (cf. Mark 5:2; John 4:51).

1 Cor 16:15   διακονίαν **τοῖς ἁγίοις**   service **to the saints**

18. Dative After Certain Adjectives   *ExSyn 174–75*

a. Definition and key to identification. A few adjectives are followed by the dative case. Once again, when the idea of personal interest appears, the dative is naturally used. This broad category is common.

There is no one key to identification since this is a rather amorphous group; the most common group is adjectives of "likeness" (i.e., correspondence) such as ὅμοιος, ἴσος. As well, many of the adjectives belong to the larger category of dative of *reference*.

b. Illustrations

Matt 13:31   ὁμοία ἐστὶν ἡ βασιλεία τῶν οὐρανῶν **κόκκῳ** σινάπεως
the kingdom of heaven is like a mustard **seed**

Rom 1:30   **γονεῦσιν** ἀπειθεῖς   disobedient **to parents**

➡19. Dative After Certain Prepositions *ExSyn* 175

a. Definition and key to identification. Certain prepositions take the dative after them. See the chapter on prepositions for complete discussion of this category. For review of which prepositions take which cases, cf., e.g., Mounce, *Basics of Biblical Greek*, 55–62.

b. Significance. When a dative follows a preposition, you should *not* attempt to identify the dative's function by case usage *alone*. Rather, consult BAGD for the specific usage of that case with that preposition. Although many of the case uses overlap with the uses of the preposition + the dative (especially with ἐν + the dative), the parallels are not exact. Furthermore, where there is overlap of usage, there is usually not overlap of frequency of occurrence (e.g., although the naked dative as well as ἐν + the dative can express sphere, the frequency of such usage is much higher with ἐν + the dative).

The Accusative Case[1]
Overview of Accusative Uses

Substantival Uses of the Accusative 83
➡ 1. Accusative Direct Object. 83
➡ 2. Double Accusative of Person-Thing 83
➡ 3. Double Accusative of Object-Complement 84
  4. Predicate Accusative 86
➡ 5. Accusative Subject of the Infinitive. 87
  6. Accusative of Retained Object 88
➡ 7. Accusative in Simple Apposition. 89
Adverbial Uses of the Accusative 89
  8. Adverbial Accusative (Accusative of Manner). 89
➡ 9. Accusative of Measure (or Extent of Space or Time). 90
  10. Accusative of Respect or (General) Reference 91
Special Uses of the Accusative 92
➡11. Accusative After Certain Prepositions 92

───────── **INTRODUCTION** ───────── *ExSyn 176–79*

In classical Greek, the accusative case was the "unmarked" or default case among the oblique cases (gen., dat., acc.). It was the routine case used unless there was some reason for using the genitive or dative. Unlike classical Greek, however, the NT has more nominatives than accusatives. Furthermore, typically in classical Greek the accusative outnumbers genitives and datives together, but in the NT the combination of these two cases has a significantly higher yield than accusatives.

What is to account for these differences? (1) Many of the subtleties of the language naturally began to drop out as Greek passed from classical to Koine. (2) Prepositions take a decidedly more prominent role in the NT in places where a simple case (especially the acc.) would have been used in earlier times. Many such prepositions take other than the accusative case. (3) The high proportion of genitive uses is apparently due, in part, to the Semitic influence (e.g., the "Hebrew" or attributive gen.).

General Definition

Although the accusative can justifiably be considered the default case in classical Greek, more nuancing is required to understand its role in the NT. Yes, the accusative was certainly the unmarked case as far as direct objects were concerned.

---

[1] See *ExSyn* 176–205. The following accusatives are rare categories that the average intermediate Greek student can ignore: cognate accusative (189–90), pendent accusative (198), and accusative in oaths (204–5).

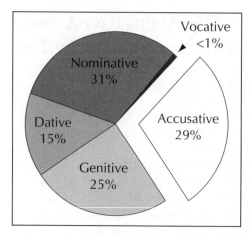

Chart 14
Frequency of Cases in the New Testament[2]

But for most other categories, it carried some semantic force. It is for this reason that we cannot simply call it the undefined case in the NT.

Instead, the least objectionable umbrella for the accusative uses is to describe it as the case of *extent*, or *limitation*. "The accusative measures an idea as to its content, scope, direction."[3] It is primarily used to *limit* the action of a verb as to *extent*, *direction*, or *goal*. Thus it most frequently answers the question, "How far?" In many respects, this will be a fluid, undefined idea. The precise force of the accusative is determined by its lexeme and that of the verb.

Relation to the Other Oblique Cases

The accusative is similar to the genitive in that both cases have as part of their root idea limitation. But the *genitive* limits as to *quality* while the *accusative* limits as to *quantity*.

Also, the accusative and the dative are similar in that both cases are primarily related to the verb. However, the dative is concerned about that to which the action of the verb is related/located/or by which it is accomplished, while the accusative is concerned about the extent and the scope of the verb's action.

———— SPECIFIC USES ———— *ExSyn 179–205*

The accusative categories can be generally grouped under one of three rubrics: substantival, adverbial, and after certain prepositions. These groupings are not entirely discrete, but may be viewed as helpful guides.

---

[2] The breakdown of acc. forms is as follows: 8815 nouns, 5009 pronouns, 5889 articles, 957 participles, 2435 adjectives (for a total of 23,105).

[3] Robertson, *Grammar*, 468. Even this does not cover every usage.

Substantival Uses of the Accusative   *ExSyn* 179–99

➡1. Accusative Direct Object   *ExSyn* 179–81

a. Definition. The accusative substantive indicates the immediate object of the action of a transitive verb, receiving the action of the verb. In this way it limits the verbal action. This usage is so common as to be routine: when one sees an accusative substantive, one normally should think of it as the direct object; conversely, when one anticipates the direct object, the case expected is usually the accusative.

b. Clarification and significance. In this use, the accusative will be related to a transitive verb. The verb is typically in the active voice, but some verbs in the middle or even the passive (deponents) take a direct object. Note that the accusative case is not the only case for the direct object; the genitive and dative also can, with certain kinds of verbs, function as the direct object. The exegetical significance of the direct object will normally be when a case *other than* the accusative is used (thus the acc. is the unmarked case as far as direct object is concerned).

c. Illustrations

Matt 5:46   ἐὰν ἀγαπήσητε τοὺς ἀγαπῶντας **ὑμᾶς**
             if you love *those who love* **you**

             Just as ὑμᾶς is the direct object of the participle ἀγαπῶντας, so ἀγαπῶντας is the direct object of the finite verb, ἀγαπήσητε.

Mark 2:17   οὐκ ἦλθον καλέσαι **δικαίους** ἀλλὰ **ἁμαρτωλούς**
             I did not come to call **the righteous** but **sinners**

Rom 8:28   τοῖς ἀγαπῶσιν τὸν θεὸν **πάντα** συνεργεῖ [ὁ θεὸς] εἰς ἀγαθόν
             God causes **all things** to work together for good to those who love God

             Sometimes it is difficult to tell whether a particular sentence even has a direct object. In this instance, such doubt is due to textual uncertainty and the syntactical range of the verb. If ὁ θεός is not authentic, then the verse could be translated "All things work together for good."[4]

➡2. Double Accusative of Person-Thing   *ExSyn* 181–82

a. Definition. Certain verbs take two direct objects, one a person and the other a thing. The thing is the nearer object; the person is the more remote object. Another way to put this is that the person is the object *affected*, while the thing is the object *effected*. This is a fairly common category.

b. Amplification. Typically we would expect the accusative of person to be in the dative rather than the accusative case. Thus "I teach you Greek," means the

---

[4] For a more detailed discussion of this text, see *ExSyn* 180–81.

same thing as "I teach Greek to you." But in Greek certain verbs take two accusatives rather than a dative of person and accusative of thing. In most instances the person *receives* the thing, just as a dative indirect object receives a direct object (hence, the person is considered the more remote object). The verbs used with person-thing double accusatives involve: (1) teaching, reminding; (2) clothing, anointing; (3) inquiring, asking; and (4) other causative ideas.

c. Illustrations

Mark 6:22   αἴτησόν **με** ὅ ἐὰν θέλῃς
             ask **me**[p] [for] **whatever**[th] you wish

John 14:26   ἐκεῖνος **ὑμᾶς** διδάξει **πάντα**
             he will teach **you**[p] **all things**[th]

Heb 1:9   ἔχρισέν **σε**... **ἔλαιον**
             he anointed **you**[p] with **oil**[th]

➡3.   Double Accusative of Object-Complement   *ExSyn* 182–89

a. Definition. An object-complement double accusative is a construction in which one accusative substantive is the direct object of the verb and the other accusative (either noun, adjective, participle, or infinitive) complements the object in that it predicates something about it. The complement may be substantival or adjectival. This common usage occurs only with certain kinds of verbs.

The proper label for the direct object in such a construction is "object in object-complement construction"; for the complement, "complement in object-complement construction," or simply "the object complement."[5]

b. Structural and semantic clues. This usage of the accusative is exegetically strategic in many texts. It is therefore important to understand how to identify it as well as how to interpret it. There is no one key to identification, but several features of this construction should be noted:

- The direct object usually combines with the verb to form a new verbal idea that has another accusative (the complement) as its object.
- Like the person-thing double accusative, this usage is lexically nuanced. That is to say, it is related to a particular kind of verb.[6] But every verb that *can* take such a construction is not *required* to do so. This creates special problems in exegesis: not infrequently a crucial issue in the text is decided on the basis of whether the two accusatives are appositional or object-complement.
- Occasionally, the construction is marked by the presence of εἰς or ὡς before the complement, or εἶναι between the two accusatives. Although such ele-

---

[5] Note that the lack of hyphen indicates this acc. term; the hyphen (object-complement) refers to the whole construction.

[6] See *ExSyn* 183, n. 24 for a list of verbs used.

ments are usually lacking, one should normally translate the construction with "as," "to be," or "namely" between the two accusatives.

- Frequently, the complement is an adjective. When this is the case, it is always a *predicate* adjective. The object is, in such cases, usually articular.

c. Identification and semantics of the components

(1) IDENTIFICATION OF THE COMPONENTS

Identification of the components in the construction is also not a given. Although normally the object comes first, twenty percent of the examples reverse this order. However, it is easy to determine which is which because *the object-complement construction is semantically equivalent to the subject-predicate nominative construction*. This is because such a construction is an embedded subject-predicate nominative clause. Thus, the principles used to sort out subject from predicate nominative can equally be used here. Specifically:

- If one of the two is a *pronoun*, it will be the object;
- If one of the two is a *proper name*, it will be the object;
- If one of the two is *articular*, it will be the object.[7]

(2) SEMANTICS OF THE COMPONENTS

In general, the *semantics* (not the identification) of the components is guided by word order. On a continuum from definite to qualitative to indefinite, the object will normally fall in the definite range, while the complement will tend toward the qualitative-indefinite range. Thus, for example, in Acts 28:6 the islanders on Malta claim Paul to be "*a god*" (ἔλεγον αὐτὸν εἶναι θεόν).

But when the order of the elements is *reversed*, the complement *tends* toward the definite-qualitative range. This is no doubt due to the prominence of its location in the clause: the more it is thrust forward, the more specific it becomes.

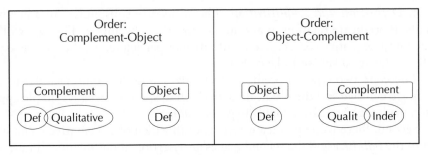

Chart 15
The Semantics of the Object-Complement Construction

---

[7] The "pecking order" between these elements seems to be the same as for the S-PN construction (see Predicate Nominative [use 2] in the chapter on the nominative): pronouns take priority, followed by (apparently) proper names, then articular nouns.

d. Illustrations. The principal verbs that can take an object-complement construction can be organized into six semantic fields: calling, designating, confessing; making, appointing; sending, expelling; considering, regarding; having, taking; and declaring, presenting.

(1) CLEAR EXAMPLES

Matt 22:43   Δαυὶδ ἐν πνεύματι καλεῖ **αὐτὸν κύριον**
            David in the Spirit calls **him**[obj] **Lord**[comp]

John 4:46   ἐποίησεν **τὸ ὕδωρ οἶνον**
          he turned **the water**[obj] [into] **wine**[comp]

Rom 3:25   ὃν προέθετο ὁ θεὸς **ἱλαστήριον**
         whom[obj] God put forth [as] **a propitiation**[comp]

Rom 6:11   λογίζεσθε **ἑαυτοὺς** εἶναι **νεκροὺς** τῇ ἁμαρτίᾳ
         consider **yourselves**[obj] to be **dead**[comp] to sin

(2) DEBATABLE PASSAGES[8]

John 4:54   **τοῦτο δεύτερον σημεῖον** ἐποίησεν ὁ Ἰησοῦς
         Jesus made **this**[obj] [to be] **the second sign**[comp]

Rom 10:9   ἐὰν ὁμολογήσῃς ἐν τῷ στόματί σου **κύριον Ἰησοῦν** ...
         σωθήσῃ
         if you confess with your mouth **Jesus** [as] **Lord** ... you shall
         be saved (or, "if you confess with your mouth [that] **Jesus** [is]
         Lord ... ")

Titus 2:10   **πᾶσαν πίστιν** ἐνδεικνυμένους **ἀγαθήν**
         showing **all faith** [to be] **good**

4. Predicate Accusative

                                                   ExSyn 190–92

a. Definition and amplification. The accusative substantive (or adjective) stands in predicate relation to another accusative substantive. The two will be joined by an equative verb, either an infinitive or participle. Neither type is especially frequent outside of Luke or Paul.

There are two types of predicate accusatives. The first one is similar to the predicate genitive and the predicate dative. That is, it is (normally) simple apposition made emphatic by a copula in *participial* form.

Second, there is the predicate accusative in which one accusative is the subject of the *infinitive* and the second makes an assertion about the first. Thus, it is similar to the nominative subject and predicate nominative construction. Frequently the infinitive will be in indirect discourse.[9]

---

[8] For a discussion of these texts, see *ExSyn* 187–89.

[9] The examples in this second category also usually belong to the object-complement category, though several are in result or purpose clauses introduced by εἰς.

b. Illustrations

Luke 4:41   ᾔδεισαν **τὸν Χριστὸν** αὐτὸν εἶναι
they knew that he was **the Christ**

Eph 2:1   ὑμᾶς ὄντας **νεκροὺς** τοῖς παραπτώμασιν
although you were **dead** in [your] trespasses

➡5. Accusative Subject of the Infinitive   *ExSyn* 192–97

a. Definition and amplification. The accusative substantive frequently functions semantically as the subject of the infinitive. Though older grammars insist that technically this is an accusative of respect, from a descriptive and functional perspective it is better to treat it as subject. This is a common use of the accusative, especially with personal pronouns.

Normally the subject of the infinitive is the same as the subject of the main verb and thus is in the nominative case. But when the infinitive requires a different agent, it is almost always put in the accusative case.

(1) ENGLISH ANALOGIES

Though this usage of the accusative is difficult to grasp, it is not without some parallels in English. In the sentence "She wanted me to learn something," "me" is both the direct object of "wanted" and the subject of "to learn." Greek usage is similar, though more varied.

(2) AN INFINITIVE WITH TWO ACCUSATIVES

Often in the NT a construction will have an accusative subject as well as an accusative predicate or an accusative direct object. In such cases, how can one tell which is which? For example, in Phil 1:7 does διὰ τὸ ἔχειν **με** ἐν τῇ καρδίᾳ **ὑμᾶς** mean "because **I** have you in my heart" or "because **you** have me in your heart"? Early analyses suggested that word order or proximity to the infinitive were the determining factors. But word order has since been shown to be at best a *secondary* consideration, and only with certain kinds of constructions. More recently, two types of constructions have been detected, each with its own set of "rules":

- **Subject accusative-predicate accusative (S-PA)** constructions need to be *treated just like their **nominative** counterparts*. Neither word order nor proximity to the infinitive are helpful guides for determining the subject. What matters is whether one of the accusatives is a pronoun or articular or a proper name (in which case, it is the subject term).[10]
- **Subject accusative-direct object (S-DO)** constructions need to be analyzed differently since there is no semantic correlation between this construction and the S-PA construction. There are only a few potentially ambiguous passages and the rest, regardless of word order, can be deciphered

---

[10] See our section on the predicate nom. (use 2 in the chapter on the nominative) for more information.

by applying *common sense* (e.g., noticing the context). Perhaps further analysis outside the NT may shed further light on this S-DO construction.

b. Illustrations

(1) Unambiguous Construction (with one Accusative Substantive)

Matt 22:3   ἀπέστειλεν **τοὺς δούλους** αὐτοῦ καλέσαι τοὺς κεκλημένους
he sent his **servants** to call those who had been invited

(2) Potentially Ambiguous Construction (with two Accusatives)[11]

The first example below is an S-PA construction involving an equative verb as the infinitive; the second is an S-DO construction with a transitive verb infinitive.

Acts 28:6   ἔλεγον **αὐτὸν** εἶναι θεόν
they were saying that **he** was a god

> In the S-PA construction, just as with subject-predicate nom. constructions (S-PN), if one of the two is a pronoun, it is the subject.

Luke 2:27   ἐν τῷ εἰσαγαγεῖν **τοὺς γονεῖς** τὸ παιδίον Ἰησοῦν
when **the parents** brought in the child Jesus

> Obviously, common sense is helpful in determining which acc. is the subject and which is the object!

6. Accusative of Retained Object   *ExSyn* 197

a. Definition. The *accusative of thing* in a double accusative person-thing construction with an active verb *retains its case* when the verb is put in the *passive*. The accusative of person, in such instances, becomes the subject. For example, "I taught you *the lesson*" becomes, with the verb converted to a passive, "You were taught *the lesson* by me." In this case, the accusative of person ("you") becomes the subject (nom.), the accusative of thing ("the lesson") is retained. This use of the accusative occurs most frequently with causative verbs, though it is rare in the NT.

b. Illustrations

1 Cor 12:13   πάντες **ἓν πνεῦμα** ἐποτίσθημεν
all were made to drink [of] **one Spirit**

> "All" is the person, put in the nom. with passive verbs. The acc. of thing, "one Spirit," is retained. If the verb had been in the active voice, the text would be read: "he made all to drink of one Spirit" (ἐπότισε πάντα ἓν πνεῦμα).

2 Thess 2:15   κρατεῖτε τὰς παραδόσεις **ἃς** ἐδιδάχθητε
hold fast to the traditions **that** you were taught

---

[11] Cf. *ExSyn* 195–97 for a discussion of several passages, including Phil 1:7 and 2 Cor 2:13.

➡7. Accusative in Simple Apposition   ExSyn 198–99

a. Definition. Though not technically a syntactical category, the accusative case (as well as the other cases) can be an appositive to another substantive in the *same* case. An appositional construction involves two adjacent substantives that refer to the same person or thing and have the same syntactical relation to the rest of the clause. The first accusative substantive can belong to *any* accusative category, and the second is merely a clarification of who or what is mentioned. Thus, the appositive "piggy-backs" on the first accusative's use, as it were. It is a common use of the accusative, though occasionally the function of the trailing accusative substantive may be difficult to determine.

b. Illustrations

Acts 16:31   πίστευσον ἐπὶ τὸν κύριον **Ἰησοῦν** καὶ σωθήσῃ σύ
believe in the Lord **Jesus** and you will be saved

Eph 1:7   ἐν ᾧ ἔχομεν τὴν ἀπολύτρωσιν διὰ τοῦ αἵματος αὐτοῦ, **τὴν ἄφεσιν** τῶν παραπτωμάτων
in whom we have the redemption through his blood, **the forgiveness** of [our] trespasses

Adverbial Uses of the Accusative   ExSyn 199–205

The difficulty with most adverbial accusatives is that they do not find ready analogies with English. The accusative in classical Greek was the workhorse of the oblique cases, functioning in many different capacities. But when the Koine language was born and nonnatives began to speak Greek, the adverbial accusatives took on a more restricted role. Many were replaced by datives or prepositional phrases. Hence, the modern student can take some measure of comfort in knowing that the unnatural feel of many adverbial accusatives was shared by other peoples learning this language as well.

8. Adverbial Accusative (Accusative of Manner)   ExSyn 200–201

a. Definition. The accusative substantive functions semantically like an adverb in that it *qualifies* the action of the verb rather than indicating *quantity* or extent of the verbal action. It frequently acts like an adverb of manner, though not always (hence, the alternative category title is really a *sub*category, although the most frequently used one). Apart from the occurrence with certain words, this usage is not common.[12]

---

[12] Many grammarians lump adverbial acc. and acc. of respect together. This is certainly legitimate, but our treatment of the adverbial acc. is more restrictive. Generally speaking, we consider an adverbial acc. *noun* to be one that can be translated like an adverb, while an acc. of respect should receive the gloss "with respect to.... "

b. Amplification and caution. This usage has structural similarities to a cognate accusative, but there the similarity ends. It is restricted to a certain group of words that, historically, were used adverbially. That is to say, many adverbs developed from the accusative form of the noun or (especially) the adjective.

There are two distinct kinds of adverbial accusatives: nominal and adjectival (one example of each is provided below). The noun δωρεάν is frequently used for an adverbial accusative. But few other nouns are so used. There is a much larger number of adjectives that are used adverbially.

c. Illustrations

Matt 10:8   **δωρεὰν** ἐλάβετε, **δωρεὰν** δότε
you received **freely, freely** give

Matt 6:33   ζητεῖτε δὲ **πρῶτον** τὴν βασιλείαν τοῦ θεοῦ
but seek **first** the kingdom of God

➡9. Accusative of Measure (or Extent of Space or Time)   *ExSyn* 201–3

a. Definition. The accusative substantive indicates the extent of the verbal action. This can either be how far (extent of space) or for how long (extent of time). The usage is quite rare with space, though somewhat common with time.

b. Key to identification and clarification. Supply before the accusative *for the extent of* or (with reference to time) *for the duration of.*

This use of the accusative has in view the basic idea of this case: limitation as to extent. The accusative of space answers the question, "How far?" while the accusative of time answers the question "How long?" It is important to specify to which subgroup a particular accusative belongs (i.e., whether it is the acc. of time or the acc. of space).

With ὥρα the accusative functions like a *dative* of time in that it answers the question "When?" In such instances, the accusative should simply be labeled an accusative of *time* (rather than acc. of *extent* of time).

c. Illustrations

(1) ACCUSATIVE FOR EXTENT OF SPACE

John 6:19   ἐληλακότες οὖν ὡς **σταδίους** εἴκοσι πέντε ἢ τριάκοντα
therefore, when they had rowed about twenty-five or thirty **stades**

(2) ACCUSATIVE FOR EXTENT OF TIME

Matt 4:2   νηστεύσας **ἡμέρας** τεσσεράκοντα καὶ **νύκτας** τεσσεράκοντα
fasting forty **days** and forty **nights**

> Had the evangelist said that Jesus was fasting forty days and forty nights with the *genitive* of time, it would have meant that he was fasting *during* that time period, but not necessarily for the whole of it.

d. Summary of genitive, dative, and accusative of time. One way to remember the distinctions between the cases used for time is to remember the root idea of each case. However, under the five-case system this may prove a bit confusing. Therefore, for the cases used for time, it may be helpful to think in terms of the *eight*-case system. The root idea of the *genitive* is *kind*. Thus the genitive of time expresses the *kind* of time or time within which. The root idea of the *locative* (not dat.) is *position*, expressing *point* in time. The root idea for the *accusative* is *extent*. Thus the accusative of time expresses the *extent* of time.

One illustration may help. If I were to say, "I worked last night" it could mean (1) during the night, (2) all night, or (3) at a point of time in the night. But in Greek, the case of *night* would indicate what I meant. If I had said νυκτός (gen.), I would mean "during the night." If I had said νυκτί (dat.) I would mean "at a point of time in the night (e.g., 1 a.m.)." If I had said νυκτά (acc.) I would mean "for the length of the night." This can be illustrated graphically as well (see chart 16 below).

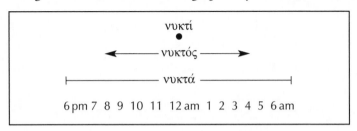

Chart 16
The Cases for Time

10. Accusative of Respect or (General) Reference   *ExSyn* 203–4

a. Definition and key to identification. The accusative substantive restricts the reference of the verbal action. It indicates *with reference to what* the verbal action is represented as true. An author will use this accusative to qualify a statement that would otherwise typically not be true. This accusative could thus be called a frame of reference accusative or limiting accusative. This is not common in Koine Greek.

Before the accusative substantive you can usually supply the words *with reference to* or *concerning*. Because this usage is rare in the NT, it should be employed as a last resort—that is, only after other categories are exhausted.

b. Illustrations

Rom 10:5   Μωϋσῆς γὰρ γράφει **τὴν δικαιοσύνην** τὴν ἐκ τοῦ νόμου
for Moses writes that, **with reference to the righteousness** that comes from the law

Rev 1:20   **τὸ μυστήριον** τῶν ἑπτὰ ἀστέρων οὓς εἶδες ἐπὶ τῆς δεξιᾶς μου
... οἱ ἑπτὰ ἀστέρες ἄγγελοι εἰσιν ...
as for the mystery of the seven stars which you saw in my right hand ... the seven stars are angels ...

Special Uses of the Accusative

➡**11. Accusative After Certain Prepositions**   *ExSyn* 205

   Definition and clarification. Certain prepositions take the accusative after them. See the chapter on prepositions for discussion. For review of which prepositions take which cases, cf. Mounce, *Basics of Biblical Greek*, 55–62.

   When an accusative follows a preposition, you should *not* attempt to identify the accusative's function by case usage *alone*. Rather, consult BAGD for the specific usage of that case with that preposition.

The Article
Part I: Origin, Function, Regular Uses, and Absence of the Article[1]
Overview

Regular Uses of the Article. **95**
  1. As a Pronoun ([partially] Independent Use). 95
➡   a. Personal Pronoun 95
➡   b. Relative Pronoun. 96
     c. Possessive Pronoun 96
  2. With Substantives (Dependent or Modifying Use) 97
     a. Individualizing Article. 97
➡   (1) Simple Identification 97
➡   (2) Anaphoric (Previous Reference). 98
       (3) Deictic ("Pointing" Article) 99
➡   (4) *Par Excellence* 99
➡   (5) Monadic ("One of a Kind" or "Unique" Article). 100
➡   (6) Well-Known ("Celebrity" Article). 100
➡   (7) Abstract (i.e., the Article with Abstract Nouns). 100
➡   b. Generic Article (Categorical Article) 101
➡   3. As a Substantiver (With Certain Parts of Speech) 103
➡   4. As a Function Marker 106
Absence of the Article. **108**
➡   1. Indefinite 108
➡   2. Qualitative. 109
  3. Definite 110
➡   a. Proper Names 110
➡   b. Object of a Preposition 110
➡   c. With Ordinal Numbers. 111
➡   d. Predicate Nominative 111
➡   e. Complement in Object-Complement Construction 111
➡   f. Monadic Nouns. 111
➡   g. Abstract Nouns 112
➡   h. A Genitive Construction (Apollonius' Corollary) 112
➡   i. With a Pronominal Adjective 113
➡   j. Generic Nouns 113

---

[1] See *ExSyn* 206–54. The following uses of the article are rare, which the average intermediate Greek student may ignore: article as alternative personal pronoun (212–13) and the kataphoric use of the article (220–21).

──────── **INTRODUCTION** ──────── *ExSyn 207–9*

The article was originally derived from the demonstrative pronoun. That is, its original force was to *point out* something. It has largely kept the force of drawing attention to something. The article is one of the most fascinating areas of study in NT Greek grammar. It is used far more frequently than any other word in the Greek NT (almost 20,000 times, or one out of seven words). As Robertson pointed out, "The article is never meaningless in Greek, though it often fails to correspond with the English idiom.... Its free use leads to exactness and finesse."[2]

Function   *ExSyn 209–10*

1. What it IS NOT

The function of the article is *not* primarily to make something definite that would otherwise be indefinite. It does *not* primarily "definitize."[3] There are at least ten ways in which a noun in Greek can be definite without the article. Further, its use with words other than nouns is not to make something definite that would otherwise be indefinite, but to *nominalize* something that would otherwise not be considered as a concept.

One further note: There is no need to speak of the article in Greek as the *definite* article because there is no corresponding indefinite article.

2. What it IS

a. At bottom, the article intrinsically has the ability to *conceptualize*. In other words, the article is able to turn just about any part of speech into a noun and, therefore, a concept. For example, "poor" expresses a quality, but the addition of an article turns it into an entity, "the poor." It is this ability to conceptualize that seems to be the basic force of the article.

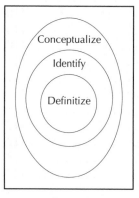

Chart 17
The Basic Forces
of the Article

b. Does it ever do more than conceptualize? Of course. A distinction needs to be made between the *essential* force of the article and what it is most *frequently* used for. In terms of basic force, the article conceptualizes. In terms of predominant *function*, it is normally used to *identify* an object. That is to say, it is used predominantly to stress the identity of an individual or class or quality.

c. The Greek article also serves a determining function at times—i.e., it definitizes. On the one hand, although it would be incorrect to say that the article's

---

[2] Robertson, *Grammar*, 756.
[3] *Contra* Brooks-Winbery, 67; Young, *Intermediate Greek*, 55.

basic function is to make something definite, on the other hand, whenever it is used, the term it modifies must of necessity be definite.

These three relationships (conceptualize, identify, definitize) can be envisioned as concentric circles: all articles that make definite also identify; all articles that identify also conceptualize.

─────────── **SPECIFIC USES** ───────────

Regular Uses of the Article   *ExSyn 210–54*

The major categories of this section (e.g., as a pronoun, with substantives, etc.) look at the article in certain constructions. But one caveat is in order: to label the use of the article in one *structural* category is not necessarily to bar it from membership in one of the *semantic* categories.

The major semantic categories normally occur with nouns, but such semantics are not infrequently found in other constructions. A good rule of thumb to follow is this: Plug the article into its appropriate structural category, then examine it to see whether it also follows one of the semantic categories as well.

1. As a Pronoun ([partially] Independent Use)   *ExSyn 211–16*

The article is not a true pronoun in Koine Greek, even though it derived from the demonstrative. But in many instances it can function semantically in the place of a pronoun.

➡ ### *a. Personal Pronoun [he, she, it]*   *ExSyn 211–12*

(1) DEFINITION. The article is often used in the place of a *third* person personal pronoun in the *nominative* case. It is only used this way with the μὲν... δέ construction or with δέ alone. (Thus, ὁ μὲν... ὁ δέ or simply ὁ δέ.) Typically, the ὁ δέ (or ὁ μέν) construction is immediately followed by a finite verb or circumstantial participle.[4]

(2) ILLUSTRATIONS

Matt 15:26–27 ὁ δὲ ἀποκριθεὶς εἶπεν· Οὐκ ἔστιν καλὸν λαβεῖν τὸν ἄρτον τῶν τέκνων ... ἡ δὲ εἶπεν ...
But **he,** answering, said, "It is not good to take the bread from the children...." But **she** said ...

Luke 5:33 οἱ δὲ εἶπαν πρὸς αὐτόν· οἱ μαθηταὶ Ἰωάννου νηστεύουσιν..., οἱ δὲ σοὶ ἐσθίουσιν καὶ πίνουσιν
But **they** said to him, "John's disciples fast..., but your [**disciples**] eat and drink."

---

[4] By definition, a circumstantial participle is *never* articular, but in such constructions the beginning student might see the article and assume that the following participle is substantival. However, if you remember that the article as a pronoun is independent and therefore *not* modifying the participle, you can see that the force of the participle is circumstantial.

➡ *b. Relative Pronoun [who, which]* ExSyn 213–15

(1) DEFINITION. Sometimes the article is equivalent to a relative pronoun in *force*. This is especially true when it is repeated after a noun before a phrase (e.g., a gen. phrase). For example, in 1 Cor 1:18 ὁ λόγος **ὁ** τοῦ σταυροῦ means "the word **which is** of the cross."

(2) AMPLIFICATION AND SEMANTICS. Specifically, this is the use of the article with second and third attributive positions in which the modifier is *not* an adjective. (The second attributive position is article-noun-article-modifier; the third attributive position is noun-article-modifier.) Thus when the modifier is (a) a *genitive*, (b) a *prepositional phrase*, or (c) a *participle*, the article is translated as a relative.

To say that the article is functioning like a relative pronoun is only an *English* way of looking at the matter. Thus it is not truly the semantic force of the article. The article is still dependent on a noun or other substantive.

When a genitive or prepositional phrase follows the substantive, the article could be omitted without altering the basic sense. Why then is the article sometimes added before genitives and prepositional phrases? It is used primarily for emphasis and secondarily for clarification.

(3) ILLUSTRATIONS. The following illustrations include as modifiers a prepositional phrase, a genitive, and a participle.

Matt 6:9	Πάτερ ἡμῶν **ὁ** ἐν τοῖς οὐρανοῖς our Father **who is** in heaven
Luke 7:32	ὅμοιοί εἰσιν παιδίοις **τοῖς** ἐν ἀγορᾷ καθημένοις they are like children **who** [are] sitting in the marketplace
Acts 15:1	ἐὰν μὴ περιτμηθῆτε τῷ ἔθει **τῷ** Μωϋσέως unless you are circumcised according to the custom **which** [is] of Moses

c. Possessive Pronoun [his, her] ExSyn 215–16

(1) DEFINITION AND AMPLIFICATION. The article is sometimes used in contexts in which possession is implied. The article itself does not involve possession, but this notion can be inferred from the presence of the article alone in certain contexts.

The article is used this way in contexts in which the idea of possession is obvious, especially when human anatomy is involved. Conversely, it is important to note that unless a noun is modified by a possessive pronoun or at least an article, possession is almost surely not implied. Thus, in Eph 5:18, πληροῦσθε ἐν πνεύματι most probably does not mean "be filled in *your own* spirit" but "be filled in/with/by the Spirit."[5]

---

[5] Some appeal to the parallel in 1 Cor 14:15, but there the article is used.

(2) ILLUSTRATIONS

Rom 7:25   ἐγὼ **τῷ** μὲν νοῒ δουλεύω νόμῳ θεοῦ, **τῇ** δὲ σαρκὶ νόμῳ
            ἁμαρτίας.
            I serve the law of God with **my** mind, but with **my** flesh, the
            law of sin.

Eph 5:25   οἱ ἄνδρες, ἀγαπᾶτε **τὰς** γυναῖκας   husbands, love **your** wives
               The article is also generic in a distributive sense: each husband
               is to love his own wife.

2. With Substantives (Dependent or Modifying Use)   *ExSyn* 216–31

The article with substantives is the most fruitful area, exegetically speaking,
to study within the realm of the article. The two broadest categories are *individualizing* and *generic*. The individualizing article particularizes, distinguishing otherwise similar objects; the generic (or categorical) article is used to distinguish
one category of individuals from another.

a. Individualizing Article   *ExSyn* 216–27

"Nearest to the real genius of [the article's] function is the use of the article
to *point out* a particular object" (italics mine).[6] But this category is not specific
enough and can be broken down into at least eight subgroups.

➡ (1) SIMPLE IDENTIFICATION   *ExSyn* 216–17

(a) Definition. The article is frequently used to distinguish one individual from
another. This is our "drip-pan" category and should be used only as a last resort.
Pragmatically, unless the article fits under one of the other six categories of the
individualizing article or under the generic use (or one of the special uses), it is
acceptable to list it as "the article of simple identification."

(b) Illustrations

Luke 4:20   πτύξας τὸ βιβλίον ἀποδοὺς **τῷ** ὑπηρέτῃ ἐκάθισεν
            he closed the book and gave it back to **the** attendant and sat down
               The book was the book of Isaiah, referred to previously in v. 17
               (thus, anaphoric). But the attendant has not been mentioned. He
               is not apparently a well-known attendant, but simply a typical
               attendant at the synagogue. The article identifies him as such.

Acts 10:9   ἀνέβη Πέτρος ἐπὶ **τὸ** δῶμα προσεύξασθαι
            Peter went up to **the** housetop to pray
               There is no previous reference to any house, but in the back-
               ground is the custom of praying on a housetop. Luke is simply
               specifying this location as opposed to some other.

---

[6] Dana-Mantey, 141.

➡   (2) Anaphoric (Previous Reference)   *ExSyn 217–20*

(a) Definition. The anaphoric article is the article denoting previous reference. (It derives its name from the Greek verb ἀναφέρειν, "to bring back, to bring up.") The first mention of the substantive is usually anarthrous because it is merely being introduced. But subsequent mentions of it use the article, for the article is now pointing back to *the* substantive previously mentioned. It is the most common use of the article and the easiest usage to identify.

(b) Amplification. Most individualizing articles will be anaphoric *in a broad sense.* That is, they will be used to point out something that had been introduced earlier—perhaps even much earlier. For example, in John 1:21 the Jews ask John the Baptist, "Are you **the** prophet?" (ὁ προφήτης εἶ σύ;). They are thinking of the prophet mentioned in Deut 18:15 ("a prophet like me"). Technically, this instance belongs under the *par excellence* article (best/extreme of a class), but again, broadly, it is anaphoric. Practically speaking, labeling an article as anaphoric requires that it have been introduced at most in the same book, preferably in a context not too far removed.

The anaphoric article may also be used with a noun whose *synonym* was mentioned previously. That is to say, although the terms used to describe may differ, the article is anaphoric if the reference is the same.

(c) Illustrations[7]

John 4:40, 43   ἔμεινεν ἐκεῖ δύο ἡμέρας ... μετὰ δὲ **τὰς** δύο ἡμέρας
                he stayed there two days ... after **the** two days ...

John 4:50   λέγει αὐτῷ ὁ Ἰησοῦς· πορεύου, ὁ υἱός σου ζῇ. ἐπίστευσεν **ὁ** ἄνθρωπος τῷ λόγῳ ὃν εἶπεν αὐτῷ ὁ Ἰησοῦς καὶ ἐπορεύετο
            Jesus said to him, "Go, your son lives." **The** man believed the word that Jesus spoke to him and went on his way.

> In v. 46 this man is introduced as τις βασιλικός ("a certain royal official"). This subsequent mention uses a rather plain synonym, ὁ ἄνθρωπος, with the article reminding us which man is in view.

Jas 2:14   Τί τὸ ὄφελος, ἀδελφοί μου, ἐὰν πίστιν λέγῃ τις ἔχειν, ἔργα δὲ μὴ ἔχῃ; μὴ δύναται **ἡ** πίστις σῶσαι αὐτόν;
            What is the benefit, my brothers, if someone says he has faith, but does not have works? **This** [kind of] faith is not able to save him, is it?

> The author introduces his topic: faith without works. He then follows it with a question, asking whether this kind of faith is able to save. The use of the article both points back to a certain kind of faith as defined by the author and is used to particularize an abstract noun.[8]

---

[7] See *ExSyn* 220 for a discussion of Phil 2:6.
[8] See *ExSyn* 219 for more discussion.

(3) Deictic ("Pointing" Article)   *ExSyn* 221

(a) Definition. The article is occasionally used to point out an object or person which/who is *present* at the moment of speaking. It typically has a demonstrative force.

(b) Illustrations

Matt 14:15	προσῆλθον αὐτῷ οἱ μαθηταὶ λέγοντες· ἔρημός ἐστιν ὁ τόπος
	the disciples came to him, saying, "**This** place is deserted"

John 19:5	ἰδοὺ ὁ ἄνθρωπος	Behold, **the** man!

Here we can envision Pilate putting Jesus on display and gesturing toward him to show the crowd precisely *which* man is on trial.

➡ (4) *Par Excellence*   *ExSyn* 222

(a) Definition. The article is frequently used to point out a substantive that is, in a sense, "in a class by itself." It is used by the speaker to point out an object as the only one worthy of the name, even though there are many other such objects by the same name.

(b) Amplification. The *par excellence* article is not necessarily used just for the *best* of a class. It could be used for the *worst* of a class—if the lexical nuance (or contextual connotation) of that particular class suggests it. In essence, *par excellence* indicates the *extreme* of a particular class. "I am **the** chief of sinners" does not mean the best of sinners, but the worst of sinners.[9]

Often "**the** gospel" (τὸ εὐαγγέλιον) and "**the** Lord" (ὁ κύριος) employ articles *par excellence*. In other words, there was only *one* gospel and *one* Lord worth mentioning as far as the early Christians were concerned.

(c) Illustrations

John 1:21	ὁ προφήτης εἶ σύ;	Are you **the** prophet?

Here the interrogators are asking John if he is *the* prophet mentioned in Deut 18:15. Of course, there were many prophets, but only one who deserved to be singled out in this way.

1 Cor 3:13	ἡ ἡμέρα δηλώσει	**the** day will reveal it

That is, the day of judgment—the *great* day.

Luke 18:13	ὁ θεός, ἱλάσθητί μοι τῷ ἁμαρτωλῷ[10]
	O God, be merciful to me, **the** sinner

---

[9] The article *par excellence* and the well-known article are often difficult to distinguish. Technically, this is due to the fact that the article *par excellence* is a subset of the well-known article. A rule of thumb here is that if the article points out an object that is not conceived as the *best* (or worst) of its category, but is nevertheless well known, it is a well-known article. The question one must always ask is, *Why* is it well known?

[10] For discussion of this text, see *ExSyn* 223.

➡ (5) MONADIC ("ONE OF A KIND" OR "UNIQUE" ARTICLE)   *ExSyn* 223–24

(a) Definition and amplification. The article is frequently used to identify monadic or one-of-a-kind nouns, such as "*the* devil," "*the* sun," "*the* Christ."

The difference between the monadic article and the article *par excellence* is that the monadic article points out a *unique* object, while the article *par excellence* points out the *extreme* of a certain category, thus, the one deserving the name more than any other. The article *par excellence*, therefore, has a superlative idea.

When the articular substantive has an adjunct (such as an adjective or gen. phrase), the entire expression often suggests a monadic notion. If no modifier is used, the article is typically *par excellence*. Thus, "**the** kingdom of God" is monadic, while "**the** kingdom" is *par excellence*.

(b) Illustrations[11]

Mark 13:24   ὁ ἥλιος σκοτισθήσεται, καὶ ἡ σελήνη οὐ δώσει τὸ φέγγος αὐτῆς
the sun will be darkened and **the** moon will not shed its light

John 1:29   ἴδε ὁ ἀμνὸς τοῦ θεοῦ ὁ αἴρων τὴν ἁμαρτίαν τοῦ κόσμου.
Behold **the** lamb of God who takes away the sin of the world!

> John's description of Jesus may be regarded as monadic as long as the gen. "of God" is considered part of the formula, for it is used alone of Jesus in the Bible.

➡ (6) WELL-KNOWN ("CELEBRITY" ARTICLE)   *ExSyn* 225

(a) Definition. The article points out an object that is well known, but for reasons *other* than the above categories (i.e., not anaphoric, deictic, *par excellence*, or monadic). Thus, it refers to a well-known object that has not been mentioned in the preceding context (anaphoric), nor is considered to be the best of its class (*par excellence*), nor is one of a kind (monadic).

(b) Illustrations

Gal 4:22   τῆς παιδίσκης . . . τῆς ἐλευθέρας
the bond-woman . . . **the** free woman

> These women were not the best of their respective categories, but were well known because of the biblical account.

Jas 1:1   ταῖς δώδεκα φυλαῖς ταῖς ἐν τῇ διασπορᾷ
to the twelve tribes that are in **the** dispersion

➡ (7) ABSTRACT (I.E., THE ARTICLE WITH ABSTRACT NOUNS)   *ExSyn* 226–27

(a) Definition. Abstract nouns by their very nature focus on a quality. However, when such a noun is articular, that quality is "tightened up," as it were, defined more closely and distinguished from other notions. This usage is frequent.

---

[11] For discussion of Matt 4:1, see *ExSyn* 224–25.

(b) Amplification. In translating such nouns into English, the article should rarely be used (typically, only when the article also fits under some other individualizing category, such as anaphoric). But in exposition, the force of the article should be brought out. Usually, the article with an abstract noun fits under the *par excellence* and well-known categories but in even a more technical way. As well, frequently it particularizes a general quality.[12]

(c) Illustrations

John 4:22   ἡ σωτηρία ἐκ τῶν Ἰουδαίων ἐστίν
             salvation is from the Jews

Rom 12:9   ἡ ἀγάπη ἀνυπόκριτος. ἀποστυγοῦντες **τὸ** πονηρόν, κολλώ-
             μενοι **τῷ** ἀγαθῷ
             Let love be without hypocrisy. Hate **the** evil; hold fast to **the** good.

> English more naturally translates the article with the last two terms because they are adjectives and, with the article, they are somewhat "concretized." Thus, τὸ πονηρόν means "that which is evil."

➡ b. Generic Article (Categorical Article) [as a class]   ExSyn 227–31

(1) DEFINITION AND KEY TO IDENTIFICATION. While the *individualizing* article distinguishes or identifies a particular object belonging to a larger class, the *generic* article distinguishes one class from another. This is somewhat less frequent than the individualizing article (though it still occurs hundreds of times in the NT). The key to determining whether or not the article might be generic is the insertion of the phrase "as a class" after the noun that the article is modifying.

(2) AMPLIFICATION. If ὁ ἄνθρωπος is understood as a generic article, the sense would be: "humankind" (i.e., human beings as a class). The use of the article here distinguishes this *class* from among other classes (such as "the animal kingdom" or "the realm of angels").

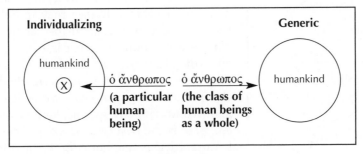

Chart 18
Individualizing Vs. Generic Article

---

[12] The article with abstract nouns often has a certain affinity with articular *generic* nouns in that both focus on traits and qualities. But there are differences: one focuses on a quality via its lexeme (abstract), while the other focuses on a category grammatically (generic).

At times, the most natural translation is to replace the article with an indefinite article. This is because both indefinite nouns and generic nouns share certain properties: while one categorizes or stresses the characteristics of a given class (generic), the other points to an individual within a class, without addressing any traits that would distinguish it from other members (indefinite).

(3) ILLUSTRATIONS[13]

Matt 18:17   ἔστω σοι ὥσπερ **ὁ** ἐθνικὸς καὶ **ὁ** τελώνης
he shall be [with reference] to you as **the** Gentile [as a class] and **the** tax-collector [as a class]

> In translation we would probably say, "**a** Gentile and **a** tax-collector." However, this is due to the fact that the *force* of the generic article is qualitative, since it indicates the class to which one belongs (thus, *kind*), rather than identifying him as a particular individual. Sometimes the English indefinite article brings out this force better.

Luke 10:7   ἄξιος **ὁ** ἐργάτης τοῦ μισθοῦ αὐτοῦ
the laborer is worthy of his wages

Eph 5:25   **οἱ** ἄνδρες, ἀγαπᾶτε τὰς γυναῖκες
Husbands [as a class], love your wives

> The command is not meant to distinguish some of the Ephesian/Asia Minor husbands as opposed to others, but to distinguish the husbands in the church as opposed to the wives or children. They are viewed collectively, as a whole.

Chart 19
The Semantic Relations of
the Individualizing Article

Chart 19 depicts the semantic relationships of the individualizing article. The chart is designed to show the student in pictorial form that the seven categories of the individualizing article are not entirely distinct. Rather, they are related, for the most part, in a general-to-specific manner. That is, every monadic article is, in a sense, a specific kind of *par excellence* article (in the sense that the only one of a class is, *ipso facto*, the best of a class). And every *par excellence* article is well known (but it is more specific, for it is well known *because* it is the best of a class). And every well-known article is anaphoric (in the broadest sense possible). But it is more specific than a simple anaphoric article would be.

---

[13] For discussion of 1 Tim 3:2, see *ExSyn* 229.

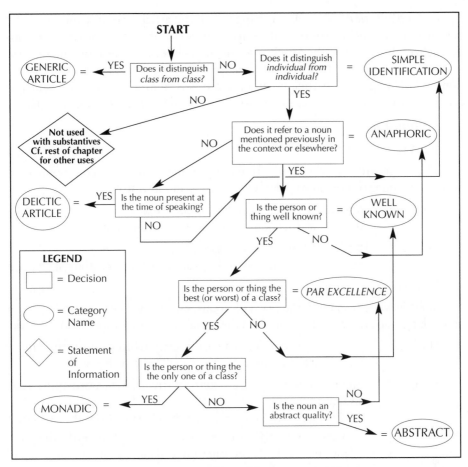

Chart 20
Flow Chart on the Article with Substantives

Chart 20 presupposes that the student understands Chart 19. In order to use the flow chart, you should attempt to find the *narrowest* category to which a particular article can belong. As long as you can say "yes" to a particular semantic force, you should continue on until you get to the narrowest category for a particular article.

➡**3. As a Substantiver (With Certain Parts of Speech)**   *ExSyn* 231–38

a. Definition. The article can turn almost any part of speech into a noun: adverbs, adjectives, prepositional phrases, particles, infinitives, participles, and even finite verbs. As well, the article can turn a phrase into a nominal entity. This incredible flexibility is part of the genius of the Greek article. Such usage is very common overall, more so with the adjective and participle than with other parts of speech.

b. Amplification. The substantiving use of the article can only minimally be considered a *semantic* category, in the sense that its essential semantic role is to conceptualize. Beyond this, the article also functions in one of the above-mentioned semantic roles; that is, it either individualizes or categorizes, just as it does with nouns. The usage with participles and adjectives is routine and unremarkable, so much so that many of these examples were discussed in the preceding sections.

c. Illustrations

(1) WITH ADVERBS   *ExSyn 232–33*

The usage with adverbs occurs frequently. Some of the more commonly used adverbs include αὔριον, ἐπαύριον, νῦν, πέραν, and πλησίον.

Acts 18:6   ἀπὸ **τοῦ** νῦν εἰς τὰ ἔθνη πορεύσομαι
from now [this point] on, I will go to the Gentiles

Col 3:2   **τὰ** ἄνω φρονεῖτε, μὴ **τὰ** ἐπὶ τῆς γῆς
Set [your] mind on **the** [things] above, not on the [things] on earth

(2) WITH ADJECTIVES   *ExSyn 233*

Adjectives often stand in the place of nouns, especially when the qualities of a particular group are stressed. Instances in the plural are especially frequently generic.

Matt 5:5   μακάριοι **οἱ** πραεῖς, ὅτι αὐτοὶ κληρονομήσουσιν τὴν γῆν
blessed are **the** meek, for they shall inherit the earth

Matt 6:13   μὴ εἰσενέγκῃς ἡμᾶς εἰς πειρασμόν, ἀλλὰ ῥῦσαι ἡμᾶς ἀπὸ **τοῦ** πονηροῦ
do not lead us into temptation, but deliver us from **the** evil [one]

> Although the KJV renders this "deliver us from evil," the presence of the article indicates not evil in general, but the evil one himself.

(3) WITH PARTICIPLES   *ExSyn 233–34*

The usage with participles is commonplace. As with adjectives, the article with participles can be individualizing or generic.

Matt 2:23   ὅπως πληρωθῇ **τὸ** ῥηθὲν διὰ τῶν προφητῶν
in order that **that** which was spoken by the prophets might be fulfilled

1 John 3:6   πᾶς **ὁ** ἁμαρτάνων οὐχ ἑώρακεν αὐτόν
everyone who sins has not seen him

(4) WITH INFINITIVES[14]   *ExSyn 234–35*

Although infinitives frequently take an article, the article is usually not used to nominalize the infinitive. This usage is relatively rare, though more common

---

[14] Cf. *ExSyn* 234–35 for a nearly exhaustive list of references in which an articular substantival infinitive is found.

in the NT letters than in narrative literature. (The infinitive can also function substantivally without the article.) The article is always neuter singular.

Acts 27:20   περιηρεῖτο ἐλπὶς πᾶσα **τοῦ** σῴζεσθαι ἡμᾶς
all hope **of** our being saved was abandoned

> The gen. articular infinitive is an objective gen. with an acc. subject of the infinitive. A woodenly literal rendering would be "all hope of the being saved with reference to us."

Rom 7:18   **τὸ** θέλειν παράκειταί μοι, **τὸ** δὲ κατεργάζεσθαι τὸ καλὸν οὔ.
the willing is present with me, but **the** doing [of] the good is not.

(5) WITH A GENITIVE WORD OR PHRASE   *ExSyn 235–36*

A non-genitive article is often followed by a genitive word or phrase. Although there is no concord, the article may be viewed as "bracketing" the word or phrase that follows. Two of the more frequent idioms are (1) the masculine singular article followed by a proper name in the genitive, where the article implies "son" (and the gen. that follows is a gen. of relationship), and (2) the neuter plural article with a genitive, where the neuter article implies "things."

Matt 10:3   Ἰάκωβος **ὁ** τοῦ Ἀλφαίου   James, **the** [son] of Alphaeus

Matt 16:23   οὐ φρονεῖς **τὰ** τοῦ θεοῦ ἀλλὰ **τὰ** τῶν ἀνθρώπων
you are not thinking **the** [things] of God, but **the** [things] of men

(6) WITH A PREPOSITIONAL PHRASE[15]   *ExSyn 236*

Similar to the use with genitive words and phrases is the use of the article to nominalize a prepositional phrase. This is a fairly common use of the article.[16]

Acts 11:2   **οἱ** ἐκ περιτομῆς
those of the circumcision [party]

1 Cor 13:9–10   ἐκ μέρους γινώσκομεν καὶ ἐκ μέρους προφητεύομεν· ὅταν δὲ ἔλθῃ τὸ τέλειον, **τὸ** ἐκ μέρους καταργηθήσεται
[now] we know in part and we prophesy in part; but when the perfect comes, **the** partial will be done away

> The article in v. 10 is anaphoric, referring back to the twofold ἐκ μέρους of v. 9. It is as if Paul said, "when the perfect comes, the 'in part' will be done away."

Phil 1:27   **τὰ** περὶ ὑμῶν
the things concerning you [= your circumstances]

---

[15] There are two more usages of the article as substantiver: with particles and with finite verbs (see *ExSyn* 237); these are sufficiently rare that the average intermediate Greek student may ignore them. For a discussion of Rev 1:4, see *ExSyn* 237.

[16] For a discussion of Phil 1:29, see *ExSyn* 236.

(7) WITH CLAUSES, STATEMENTS, AND QUOTATIONS   *ExSyn* 237–38

The neuter singular article is sometimes used before a statement, quotation, or clause. For some clauses, the article needs to be translated in various ways; only the context will help. For direct statements and quotations, it is usually best to supply the phrase "statement" after the article followed by quotation marks.

Rom 13:9   τὸ οὐ μοιχεύσεις, οὐ φονεύσεις, οὐ κλέψεις, οὐκ ἐπιθυμή-
σεις, καὶ εἴ τις ἑτέρα ἐντολή, ἐν τῷ λόγῳ τούτῳ ἀνακε-
φαλαιοῦται ἐν τῷ· ἀγαπήσεις τὸν πλησίον σου ὡς σεαυτόν.
The [list of commandments], "You shall not commit adultery,
you shall not murder, you shall not steal, you shall not covet"—
and if there is any other commandment—is summed up in this
word, namely, "You shall love your neighbor as yourself."

> The neuter article at the beginning of the verse introduces the
> second table of the Ten Commandments; ἐν τῷ toward the end
> of the verse is most likely resumptive, referring back to the mas-
> culine λόγῳ.

Eph 4:9   τὸ δὲ ἀνέβη τί ἐστιν . . . ;
Now **the** [statement], "he ascended . . . ," what does it mean . . . ?

> Although only one word from the preceding quotation of Ps
> 68:18 is repeated, the idiom suggests that the whole verse is
> under examination. In other words, the author is not asking
> "What does 'he ascended' mean?" but "What does the quota-
> tion from Ps 68:18 mean?"

➡ **4. As a Function Marker**   *ExSyn* 238–43

When the article is used as a grammatical function marker, it may or may not also bear a semantic force. But even when it does bear such a force, the grammatical (structural) use is usually prominent.

a. To Denote Adjectival Positions   *ExSyn* 239

Especially when the article is used to denote the second attributive position would we say that it has almost no semantic meaning.[17]

b. With Possessive Pronouns   *ExSyn* 239

Almost invariably the article is used when a possessive pronoun is attached to the noun. (On the other hand, the article alone can be used, in certain contexts, to imply possession [see "The Article as a Possessive Pronoun," above].)

Mark 1:41   ἐκτείνας **τὴν** χεῖρα αὐτοῦ   stretching out his hand

c. In Genitive Phrases   *ExSyn* 239–40

In genitive phrases both the head noun and the genitive noun normally have or lack the article.

---

[17] See the chapter on adjectives for examples.

This construction, known as *Apollonius' Canon*, means that both the head noun and genitive noun mimic each other with regard to articularity. Thus, we would expect either ὁ λόγος τοῦ θεοῦ or λόγος θεοῦ, but not λόγος τοῦ θεοῦ or ὁ λόγος θεοῦ. The canon, however, has many exceptions in classical Greek as well as the NT. Nevertheless, for the most part, when the article is present in the construction, it is expected with both head noun and genitive noun. In such cases, the article often carries little semantic weight,[18] because even when both nouns lack the article, they are normally definite.

Matt 3:16   εἶδεν **τὸ** πνεῦμα **τοῦ** θεοῦ καταβαῖνον ὡσεὶ περιστερὰν
he saw **the** Spirit of God coming down like a dove

> The MSS vacillate over the presence of the articles before πνεῦμα and θεοῦ. What is important to note is that the MSS *uniformly* either have both articles or lack both articles. With or without the articles, the translation and sense are the same.

Acts 26:13   **τὴν** λαμπρότητα **τοῦ** ἡλίου
the brightness of **the** sun

d. With Indeclinable Nouns   *ExSyn* 240–41

The article is used with indeclinable nouns to show the case of the noun.

Luke 1:68   εὐλογητὸς κύριος ὁ θεὸς **τοῦ** Ἰσραήλ
blessed is the Lord God of Israel

e. With Participles   *ExSyn* 241

The article before participles functions both as a substantiver and as a function marker. The presence of the article indicates a substantival (or adjectival) function for the participle. Of course, the participle can also often be substantival or adjectival without the article, though there is the greater possibility of ambiguity in such instances.

Luke 6:21   μακάριοι **οἱ** κλαίοντες νῦν
blessed are **those** who weep now

John 4:11   πόθεν οὖν ἔχεις τὸ ὕδωρ **τὸ** ζῶν;
Where then do you keep **this** living water?

f. With Demonstratives   *ExSyn* 241–42

The article is used with the demonstratives in predicate position to indicate attributive function. Demonstratives cannot stand in attributive position (e.g., between the article and noun). If they are related to an anarthrous noun, they function independently, as pronouns. Only when they are in predicate position to an *articular* noun can demonstratives be considered dependent and attributive.[19]

---

[18] One exception to this is ὁ υἱὸς τοῦ ἀνθρώπου. See *ExSyn* 240, n. 61, for discussion.

[19] Occasionally translations miss this basic rule of Greek grammar. For a discussion of John 2:11 and 4:54, see *ExSyn* 242, n. 66.

Matt 16:18   ἐπὶ ταύτῃ **τῇ** πέτρᾳ οἰκοδομήσω μου τὴν ἐκκλησίαν
on this rock I will build my church

Luke 7:44   βλέπεις ταύτην **τὴν** γυναῖκα;
Do you see this woman?

g. With Nominative Nouns (to denote subject)   ExSyn 242

Normally a subject will have the article (unless it is a pronoun or proper name).

Luke 11:7   **ἡ** θύρα κέκλεισται   **the** door is shut

h. To Distinguish Subject from Predicate Nominative and Object from Complement   ExSyn 242–43

Generally speaking, the subject will be distinguished from the predicate nominative by having the article. This rule of thumb also applies to objects in the object-complement double accusative construction.[20]

Matt 12:8   κύριος ἐστιν τοῦ σαββάτου **ὁ** υἱὸς τοῦ ἀνθρώπου
the Son of Man is lord of the Sabbath

John 5:18   πατέρα ἴδιον ἔλεγεν **τὸν** θεὸν
he was claiming God [to be] his own Father

Absence of the Article   ExSyn 243–54

It is not necessary for a noun to have the article in order for it to be definite. But conversely, a noun *cannot* be *in*definite when it has the article. Thus it *may* be definite without the article, and it *must* be definite with the article.

When a substantive is anarthrous, it may have one of three forces: indefinite, qualitative, or definite. There are not clear-cut distinctions between these three forces, however. If we were to place them on a continuum graph, we would see that the *qualitative* aspect is sometimes close to being definite, sometimes close to being indefinite:

Figure 21
The Semantics of Anarthrous Nouns

➡1. Indefinite   ExSyn 244

An indefinite noun refers to one member of a class, without specifying which member. For example, in John 4:7 we have "**A** woman from Samaria . . . " The

---

[20] Cf. discussions in the chapters on "The Nominative Case" (under predicate nominative) and "The Accusative Case" (under both object-complement and subject of infinitive).

anarthrous γυνή is indefinite, telling us nothing about this particular woman. Thus an indefinite noun is unmarked in that (next to) nothing is revealed about it apart from its membership in a class of others that share the same designation.

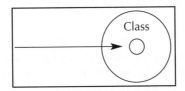

Figure 22
The Semantics of Indefinite Nouns

➡2. Qualitative   *ExSyn 244–45*

a. Definition. A qualitative noun places the stress on quality, nature, or essence. It does not merely indicate membership in a class of which there are other members (such as an indefinite noun), nor does it stress individual identity (such as a definite noun).

It is akin to a generic noun in that it focuses on the *kind*. Further, like a generic, *it emphasizes class traits.* Yet, unlike generic nouns, a qualitative noun often has in view one individual rather than the class as a whole.[21]

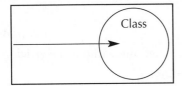

Figure 23
The Semantics of Qualitative Nouns

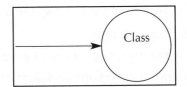

Figure 24
The Semantics of Generic Nouns

b. Illustrations

1 John 4:8   ὁ θεὸς **ἀγάπη** ἐστίν   God is **love**

Heb 1:2   ἐπ᾽ ἐσχάτου τῶν ἡμερῶν τούτων ἐλάλησεν ἡμῖν ἐν **υἱῷ**
In these last days, [God] has spoken to us in **Son**
Although this should probably be translated "a Son" (there is no decent way to express this compactly in English), the force is clearly qualitative (though, of course, on the continuum it would be closer to the indefinite than the definite category).

---

[21] Abstract nouns deserve special treatment. For the most part, they are not normally conceived of in terms of membership in a class. For example, ὁ θεὸς ἀγάπη ἐστιν cannot naturally be translated, "God is **a** love" or "God is **the** love." The lexical nature of the word ἀγάπη is abstract rather than particular. Hence, on the one hand, most abstract nouns will be qualitative; on the other hand, abstract nouns will *not* normally be generic because no *class* is in view, just a certain quality.

The point is that God, in his final revelation, has spoken to us in one who has the characteristics of a son. His credentials are vastly different from the credentials of the prophets (or from the angels, as the following context indicates).

3. Definite   *ExSyn 245–54*

A definite noun lays the stress on individual identity. It has in view membership in a class, but this particular member is already marked out by the author. Definite nouns have unique referential identity.

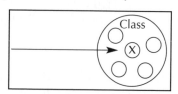

Figure 25
The Semantics of Definite Nouns

Though by definition an articular noun is definite, an anarthrous noun may also be definite under certain conditions. As was noted earlier, there are at least ten constructions in which a noun may be definite though anarthrous. The following is a brief look at these constructions.

➡   ### a. Proper Names   *ExSyn 245–47*

By the nature of the case, a proper name is definite without the article.

John 1:45   εὑρίσκει **Φίλιππος** τὸν Ναθαναήλ
Philip found Nathanael
> The article is used with Ναθαναήλ, an indeclinable name, to identify him as the direct object.

Acts 19:13   ὁρκίζω ὑμᾶς τὸν Ἰησοῦν ὃν **Παῦλος** κηρύσσει
I adjure you by the Jesus whom **Paul** preaches
> In this instance the article with Ἰησοῦν is kataphoric.

➡   ### b. Object of a Preposition   *ExSyn 247*

There is no need for the article to be used to make the object of a preposition definite. However, this is not to say that all prepositional objects are definite. An anarthrous noun as object of a preposition is not *necessarily* definite. It is often qualitative (e.g., υἱῷ in Heb 1:2, mentioned above),[22] or even occasionally indefinite (cf. μετὰ γυναικὸς ἐλάλει—"he was speaking with **a** woman" [John 4:27]). Thus, when a noun is the object of a preposition, it does not *require* the article to be definite: if it has the article, it *must* be definite; if it *lacks* the article, it *may* be definite.

---

[22] It is our impression that most anarthrous nouns after prepositions seem to be qualitative unless they are monadic, proper names, in a gen. construction, or have a qualifying adjective.

John 1:1   Ἐν ἀρχῇ ἦν ὁ λόγος
            In **the beginning** was the Word

> Here the noun is also monadic, giving it additional reason to be definite.

Rom 1:4   τοῦ ὁρισθέντος υἱοῦ θεοῦ ἐν δυνάμει κατὰ **πνεῦμα** ἁγιωσύ-
           νης ἐξ **ἀναστάσεως** νεκρῶν
           who was designated the Son of God in power according to **the Spirit** of holiness by **the resurrection** from the dead

> Two of the three prepositional phrases include definite objects; ἐν δυνάμει is qualitative.

➡ **c. With Ordinal Numbers**   *ExSyn 248*

The number identifies the "amount" of the substantive, making it definite.

Mark 15:25   ἦν **ὥρα** τρίτη καὶ ἐσταύρωσαν αὐτόν
              it was [about] **the** third **hour** when they crucified him

➡ **d. Predicate Nominative**   *ExSyn 248*

If the predicate nominative *precedes* the copula, it *may* be definite though anarthrous. For more information, see "Colwell's rule" in the chapter "Article Part II: Special Uses (and Non-Uses) of the Article."

➡ **e. Complement in Object-Complement Construction**   *ExSyn 248*

If the complement precedes the object, it may be definite though anarthrous. For more information, see "Object Complement" in the chapter on the "Accusative Case."

John 5:18   **πατέρα** ἴδιον ἔλεγεν τὸν θεόν
             he was calling God his own **father**

➡ **f. Monadic Nouns**   *ExSyn 248–49*

A one-of-a-kind noun does not, of course, require the article to be definite (e.g., "sun," "earth," "devil,"[23] etc.). One might consider πνεῦμα as monadic when it is modified by the adjective ἅγιον. If so, then the expression πνεῦμα ἅγιον is monadic and refers only to *the* Holy Spirit. In the least this illustrates the fact that we need to think of the entire *noun phrase*, not just a single word, when identifying it as monadic. The expression "Son of God," for example, is monadic, while "son" is not.

Luke 1:35   κληθήσεται **υἱὸς** θεοῦ
             he shall be called **the Son** of God

Luke 21:25   ἔσονται σημεῖα ἐν **ἡλίῳ** καὶ **σελήνῃ**
             there will be signs in **the sun** and **moon**

---

[23] For a discussion of John 6:70, see *ExSyn 249*.

➡ **g. *Abstract Nouns***   *ExSyn* 249–50

Words such as love, joy, peace, faith, etc. are commonly anarthrous though they are not *in*definite. They could be classified as qualitative-definite, however, and consequently occur with and without the article.

Luke 19:9   σήμερον **σωτηρία** τῷ οἴκῳ τούτῳ ἐγένετο
today **salvation** has come to this house

Eph 2:5, 8   **χάριτί** ἐστε σεσῳσμένοι ... τῇ **χάριτί** ἐστε σεσῳσμένοι
by **grace** you are saved ... by grace you are saved

> The first reference to χάρις is anarthrous (v. 5), followed by a resumption of the point in v. 8 with the anaphoric article. Although the force of the article is not naturally brought out in translation, its presence should not go unobserved in exegesis.

➡ ***h. A Genitive Construction (Apollonius' Corollary)***   *ExSyn* 250–52

(1) DEFINITION OF RULE AND COROLLARY. A general rule (discussed earlier in this chapter) is that *both* the head noun and the genitive noun either have the article or lack the article (known as Apollonius' Canon). It makes little semantic difference whether the construction is articular or anarthrous. Thus ὁ λόγος τοῦ θεοῦ is identical to λόγος θεοῦ.

The corollary to this rule (Apollonius' Corollary) is that *when both nouns are anarthrous, both will usually have the same semantic force.* That is, both will be, for example, definite (D-D), the most commonly shared semantic force. Somewhat less common is qualitative-qualitative (Q-Q). The least likely semantic force is indefinite-indefinite (I-I). Further, although not infrequently is there a one-step difference between the two substantives (e.g., D-Q), only rarely do the two nouns differ by two steps (either I-D or D-I).

In addition, it should be noted that (1) just as rare as I-D is I-I; (2) only rarely is the genitive noun less definite than the head noun; hence, (3) the genitive noun seems to be the "driving force" behind the construction: it tends to be definite and to make the head noun definite as well.

(2) ILLUSTRATIONS[24]

Matt 3:16   πνεῦμα θεοῦ[25]   the Spirit of God

> A nonsensical translation would be "a spirit of a god." The point of Apollonius' Corollary is that when both nouns are anarthrous and it can be determined that one is definite, then the other is also definite. Thus in the above example, if θεοῦ is definite, so is πνεῦμα.

Rom 1:18   ἀποκαλύπτεται **ὀργὴ θεοῦ**   **the wrath of God** is revealed

---

[24] For a discussion of exegetically significant texts and especially the construction ἄγγελος κυρίου, see *ExSyn* 252.

[25] This is the reading of ℵ B; most other MSS have τὸ πνεῦμα τοῦ θεοῦ.

➡ *i. With a Pronominal Adjective*   *ExSyn 253*

Nouns with πᾶς, ὅλος, etc. do not need the article to be definite, for either the class as a whole ("all") or distributively ("every") is being specified. Either way, a generic force is given to such constructions.

Matt 3:15   πρέπον ἐστὶν ἡμῖν πληρῶσαι πᾶσαν **δικαιοσύνην**
             it is fitting for us to fulfill all **righteousness**

Luke 3:5   πᾶν **ὄρος** καὶ **βουνὸς** ταπεινωθήσεται
             every **mountain** and **hill** will be brought low

Luke 5:5   ἐπιστάτα, δι᾽ ὅλης **νυκτὸς** κοπιάσαντες
             Master, we labored all **night**

➡ *j. Generic Nouns*   *ExSyn 253*

The generic article is not always necessary in order for a noun to have a generic idea. There is little semantic difference between articular generics and anarthrous generics, though it is true that some nouns usually take the article and others do not. Just as with articular generics, sometimes it is more appropriate to translate the anarthrous generic noun with an indefinite article (with the understanding that the whole class is still in view).

(1) CLEAR ILLUSTRATIONS

Luke 18:2   κριτής τις ἦν ... **ἄνθρωπον** μὴ ἐντρεπόμενος
             there was a certain judge ... who did not respect **people**

1 Cor 11:7   ἡ γυνὴ δόξα **ἀνδρός** ἐστιν
             the wife is the glory of **the husband**

             Here the article is used with γυνή, but it is not used with ἀν-
             δρός. Yet both terms are generic.

1 Tim 2:11   **γυνὴ** ἐν ἡσυχίᾳ μανθανέτω
             let **a woman** learn in silence

(2) POSSIBLE EXAMPLE

Rev 13:18   ἀριθμὸς **ἀνθρώπου** ἐστιν
             it is the number of **humankind**

             If ἀνθρώπου is generic, then the sense is, "It is [the] number of
             humankind." It is significant that this construction fits Apollo-
             nius' Canon (i.e., both the head noun and the genitive are
             anarthrous), suggesting that if one of these nouns is definite,
             then the other is too.[26]

---

[26] For a discussion of this text, see *ExSyn* 254.

The Article
Part II: Special Uses and Non-Uses of the Article[1]
Overview

Anarthrous Preverbal Predicate Nominatives
(Involving Colwell's Rule). **114**
   1. Introduction 114
➡ 2. Statement of the Rule 115
   3. Misunderstanding of the Rule 115
➡ 4. Clarification of Colwell's Rule 115
➡ 5. Significance of Colwell's Construction for Exegesis 116
➡ 6. Application of Colwell's Construction to John 1:1. 119

The Article with Multiple Substantives Connected by Καί
(Granville Sharp Rule and Related Constructions). **120**
   1. Introduction 120
➡ 2. Statement of the Rule 120
➡ 3. Validity of the Rule Within the New Testament 121
➡   a. In General 121
➡   b. For Christologically Significant Texts 122
   4. Constructions Involving Impersonal, Plural, and Proper Nouns 123
      a. Proper Names 123
➡   b. Plural Personal Constructions 123
➡   c. Impersonal Constructions. 127

In this chapter we will consider two constructions. One of these involves the nonuse of the article and the other involves the use of the article: anarthrous preverbal predicate nominatives and the article-noun-καί-noun construction. They deserve their own extended treatment both because of rich theological implications (especially related to explicit NT affirmations of the deity of Christ) and because of common abuse in NT circles. The arrows point to the most important sections.

Anarthrous Preverbal Predicate Nominatives
(Involving Colwell's Rule)   *ExSyn 256–70*

1. **Introduction**   *ExSyn 256*

a. Definition of terms. First, it would be helpful to review some basic terminology.

---

[1] See *ExSyn* 255–90.

- anarthrous = without the article
- preverbal = *before* the equative verb
- predicate nominative (PN) = the noun in the nominative case that is the same as the subject (more or less)

Therefore, an anarthrous preverbal predicate nominative is a predicate nominative that does not have the article and occurs before the equative verb. This is the kind of construction Ernest Cadman Colwell investigated when he wrote his now well-known article in 1933.[2] To economize on our verbiage, therefore, we will consider every anarthrous preverbal predicate nominative construction as a "Colwell's *construction*" (though not necessarily fitting Colwell's *rule*).

In general, we can say that a predicate nominative is anarthrous and it *follows* the copula. It is usually qualitative or indefinite.

➡ **2. Statement of the Rule**   *ExSyn 257*

Colwell's rule is as follows: "Definite predicate nouns which precede the verb usually lack the article..."[3]

He illustrated this principle with John 1:49: ἀπεκρίθη αὐτῷ Ναθαναήλ· ῥαββί, σὺ εἶ ὁ υἱὸς τοῦ θεοῦ, σὺ βασιλεὺς εἶ τοῦ Ἰσραήλ ("Nathanael answered him, 'Rabbi, you are the Son of God, you are the king of Israel'"). Colwell observed that the structural parallels between the two statements differed at two points: (1) in the second statement, the PN is anarthrous while in the first it is articular; (2) in the second statement, the PN is before the verb, while in the first it is after the verb. Yet the grammatical sense was the same for both statements: the PN in each should be regarded as definite. From this, Colwell assumed that the definiteness of the PN could be achieved either by the article or by a shift in word order. His essay dealt with the latter.

In other words, a PN that precedes the copula, and which is apparently definite *from the context*, usually lacks the article.

3. Misunderstanding of the Rule   *ExSyn 257–59*

Almost immediately many scholars (especially of a more conservative stripe) misunderstood Colwell's rule. They saw the benefit of the rule for affirming the deity of Christ in John 1:1. But what they thought Colwell was articulating was actually the *converse* of the rule, not the rule itself. That is, they thought that the rule was: An anarthrous predicate nominative that precedes the verb is usually definite. This is not the rule, nor can it be implied from the rule.

➡ **4. Clarification of Colwell's Rule**   *ExSyn 259–62*

Colwell stated that a definite PN that precedes the verb is usually anarthrous. He did *not* say the *converse*, namely, an anarthrous PN that precedes the verb is

---

[2] "A Definite Rule for the Use of the Article in the Greek New Testament," *JBL* 52 (1933): 12–21.

[3] Colwell, "A Definite Rule," 20.

usually definite. However, this is how the rule has been misunderstood by most scholars (including Colwell) since the article in *JBL* was written.

We can illustrate the fallacy of the converse of Colwell's rule this way. Suppose a little boy were to examine as best he could the relationship of rain to clouds. Every time it rains, he runs outside and notices that there are clouds in the sky. He will conclude the following principle: *if it is raining, there must be clouds in the sky.* In such a statement the *only* time the sky is examined is when it is raining. The study is not exhaustive to include all occasions in which the sky is cloudy. If this boy were to formulate the *converse* of his rule, we see its logical fallacy: *if there are clouds in the sky, it must be raining.*

With reference to Colwell's rule, only anarthrous preverbal predicate nominatives were studied that were previously determined by their contexts to be most probably definite. Not *all* anarthrous preverbal predicate nominatives were studied. But the *converse* of the rule, commonly embraced in NT scholarship, assumes that all such constructions have been examined. Other, more comprehensive studies have suggested that 80 percent of anarthrous preverbal PNs are qualitative. Therefore, when one sees an anarthrous preverbal PN, he should consider its force to be *most likely* qualitative, and only to be definite if the context or other factors strongly suggest otherwise.

The following chart displays the different databases that were examined by Colwell ("Colwell's rule") and later researchers ("Colwell's construction").

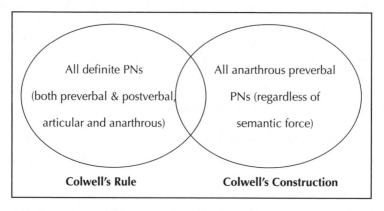

All definite PNs

(both preverbal & postverbal, articular and anarthrous)

Colwell's Rule

All anarthrous preverbal

PNs (regardless of semantic force)

Colwell's Construction

Chart 26
The Different Databases for Colwell's Rule Vs. Colwell's Construction

As can be seen from the chart, the databases were not the same. The fact of some overlap is what has given rise to the confusion over the rule.

➡5. **Significance of Colwell's Construction for Exegesis**   *ExSyn* 262–66

Later studies on this construction demonstrate that the anarthrous preverbal PN is still *closer* to definiteness than is the anarthrous *post*-copulative predicate nominative, and that an anarthrous predicate nominative that *follows* the verb will usually be either qualitative or *in*definite.[4]

A general rule about the construction can now be stated: *An anarthrous pre-verbal PN is normally qualitative, sometimes definite, and only rarely indefinite.* Two subsequent studies[5] on Colwell's construction concluded that they could not find any *indefinite* anarthrous preverbal PNs in the NT. It is entirely possible that there are some in the NT, but this is obviously the most poorly attested semantic force for such a construction.

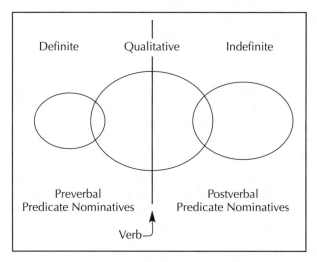

Chart 27
The Semantic Range of Anarthrous Predicate Nominatives

The chart illustrates the fact that anarthrous *preverbal* predicate nominatives usually fall within the qualitative-*definite* range, while anarthrous *postverbal* predicate nominatives usually fall within the qualitative-*indefinite* range. The presumption, therefore, when one faces an anarthrous preverbal PN is that it will be qualitative unless there are contextual or other considerations suggesting that it is definite or, less likely, indefinite.

a. Definite Predicate Nominatives

Matt 27:42   ἄλλους ἔσωσεν, ἑαυτὸν οὐ δύναται σῶσαι· **βασιλεὺς** Ἰσραήλ ἐστιν, καταβάτω νῦν ἀπὸ τοῦ σταυροῦ
He saved others, [but] he cannot save himself. He is **the king** of Israel; let him come down now from the cross . . .

> It is plain that the PN cannot be anything but definite here, for there is only one king of Israel at a time.

---

[4] That is, of course, unless there is some other ground for considering it to be definite (such as a monadic noun).

[5] See *ExSyn* 259–66 for the data on the studies.

John 1:49   σὺ εἶ ὁ υἱὸς τοῦ θεοῦ, σὺ **βασιλεὺς** εἶ τοῦ Ἰσραήλ[6]
you are the Son of God, you are **the king** of Israel

> Nathanael's response to Jesus is a twofold identification. In the first construction the PN follows the verb and has the article. In the second construction the PN precedes the verb and lacks the article. This text was Colwell's main illustration of his principle.[7]

b. Qualitative Predicate Nominatives[8]

John 1:14   ὁ λόγος **σὰρξ** ἐγένετο
the Word became **flesh**

> The idea is not that the Word became "the flesh," nor "a flesh," but simply "flesh." That is, the Word partook of humanity. Many pre–1933 exegetes (i.e., before Colwell's rule was published) saw a parallel between this verse and John 1:1, noting that both PNs were qualitative.

1 John 4:8   ὁ θεὸς **ἀγάπη** ἐστίν
God is **love**

> The meaning is certainly not convertible: "love is God." The idea of a qualitative ἀγάπη is that God's essence or nature is love, or that he has the quality of love. Thus love is an attribute, not an identification, of God.

c. Indefinite Predicate Nominatives[9]

The following examples are potential indefinite predicate nominatives in Colwell's construction.

1 Tim 6:10   **ῥίζα** πάντων τῶν κακῶν ἐστιν ἡ φιλαργυρία

> This is a difficult text to translate, having the following possibilities: (1) "the love of money is **a** root of all evils," (2) "the love of money is **the** root of all evils," (3) "the love of money motivates all evils," (4) "the love of money is **a** root of all kinds of evils," (5) "the love of money is **the** root of all kinds of evils," (6) "the love of money motivates all kinds of evils."[10]

---

[6] Several MSS place the βασιλεύς after the verb and add an article before it. Colwell noted such variants as evidence for the validity of his rule.

[7] "It was a study of these passages, especially John 1[:]49, that suggested the rule which is advocated in this study.... When the passage is scrutinized, it appears at once that the variable quantum is not definiteness but word-order" (Colwell, "A Definite Rule," 13).

[8] One of the ways to test whether a PN is qualitative or definite is to swap the S with the PN. If the sentence makes the same sense, then the PN is definite since the construction involves a convertible proposition. For a more detailed discussion, see the chapter on the Nominative Case under Predicate Nominative.

[9] For a discussion of other possible texts, see *ExSyn* 265–66.

[10] For a discussion of these possibilities, see *ExSyn* 265.

John 4:19   λέγει αὐτῷ ἡ γυνή, Κύριε, θεωρῶ ὅτι **προφήτης** εἶ σύ
> The woman said to him, "Sir/Lord, I perceive that you are
> **a/the prophet**

> Although the translation is most naturally, "Sir, I perceive that
> you are a prophet," the sense may be better characterized as
> indefinite-qualitative. It could almost be translated, "I perceive
> that you are prophetic," or "I perceive that you have the
> prophetic gift." The focus of an indefinite noun is on a *member*
> of class, while the focus of a qualitative noun is on the *attributes*
> that the class members share.

➡6. Application of Colwell's Construction to John 1:1   *ExSyn 266–69*

John 1:1 states: Ἐν ἀρχῇ ἦν ὁ λόγος, καὶ ὁ λόγος ἦν πρὸς τὸν θεόν, καὶ
θεὸς ἦν ὁ λόγος. In the last part of the verse, the clause καὶ θεὸς ἦν ὁ λόγος
(John 1:1c), θεός is the PN. It is anarthrous and comes before the verb. Therefore, it fits Colwell's *construction*, though it might not fit the rule (for the rule states
that definiteness is determined or indicated by the context, not by the grammar).
Whether it is indefinite, qualitative, or definite is the issue at hand.

a. Is Θεός in John 1:1c Indefinite?

If θεός were indefinite, we would translate it "*a god.*" If so, the theological
implication would be some form of polytheism, perhaps suggesting that the Word
was merely a secondary god in a pantheon of deities.

The grammatical argument that the PN here is indefinite is weak. Often,
those who argue for such a view do so on the sole basis that the term is
anarthrous. The indefinite notion is the most poorly attested for anarthrous preverbal predicate nominatives. Thus grammatically such a meaning is improbable.

As well, the context suggests that such is not likely, for the Word already
existed in the beginning. Further, the evangelist's own theology militates against
this view, for there is an exalted Christology in the Fourth Gospel, to the point
that Jesus Christ is identified as God (cf. 5:23; 8:58; 10:30; 20:28, etc.).

b. Is Θεός in John 1:1c Definite?

Although it is certainly possible grammatically to take θεός as a definite noun,
the evidence is not very compelling. The vast majority of *definite* anarthrous preverbal predicate nominatives are monadic, in genitive constructions, or are proper names,
none of which is true here, diminishing the likelihood of a definite θεός in John 1:1c.

Further, calling θεός in 1:1c definite is the same as saying that if it had followed
the verb, it would have had the article. Thus it would be a convertible proposition
with λόγος (i.e., "the Word" = "God" *and* "God" = "the Word"). The problem with
this argument is that the θεός in 1:1b is the Father. Thus to say that the θεός in 1:1c
is the same person is to say that "the Word was the *Father*." This, as the older grammarians and exegetes pointed out, is embryonic Sabellianism or modalism.[11]

---

[11] For references and quotations, see *ExSyn* 268.

c. Is Θεός in John 1:1c Qualitative?

The most likely candidate for θεός is qualitative. This is true both grammatically (for the largest proportion of preverbal anarthrous predicate nominatives fall into this category) and theologically (both the theology of the Fourth Gospel and of the NT as a whole). There is a balance between the Word's deity, which was already present in the beginning (ἐν ἀρχῇ ... θεὸς ἦν [1:1], and his humanity, which was added later (σὰρξ ἐγένετο [1:14]). The grammatical structure of these two statements mirror each other; both emphasize the *nature* of the Word, rather than his identity. But θεός was his nature from eternity (hence, εἰμί is used), while σάρξ was added at the incarnation (hence, γίνομαι is used).

Such an option does not at all impugn the deity of Christ. Rather, it stresses that, although the person of Christ is not the person of the Father, their *essence* is identical. The *idea* of a qualitative θεός here is that the Word had all the attributes and qualities that "the God" (of 1:1b) had. In other words, he shared the *essence* of the Father, though they differed in person. *The construction the evangelist chose to express this idea was the most **concise** way he could have stated that the Word was God and yet was distinct from the Father.*[12]

The Article with Multiple Substantives Connected by Καί (Granville Sharp Rule and Related Constructions)

ExSyn 270–91

1. Introduction

In Greek, when two nouns are connected by καί and the article precedes only the first noun, there is a close connection between the two. That connection always indicates at least some sort of *unity*. At a higher level, it may connote *equality*. At the highest level it may indicate *identity*. When the construction meets three specific demands, then the two nouns *always* refer to the same person. When the construction does not meet these requirements, the nouns may or may not refer to the same person(s)/object(s).

➡2. Statement of the Rule

ExSyn 271–72

Granville Sharp (1735–1813) was an English philanthropist and abolitionist as well as a prolific writer on various topics. As he studied the scriptures in the original Greek, he noticed a certain pattern, viz., when the construction article-substantive-καί-substantive (TSKS) involved personal nouns that were singular and not proper names, they always referred to the same person. He noticed further that such a rule applied, in several texts, to the deity of Jesus Christ. In 1798 he published a short volume entitled, *Remarks on the Definitive Article in the Greek Text of the New Testament, Containing Many New Proofs of the Divinity of Christ, from Passages Which Are Wrongly Translated in the Common English Version* [KJV].

---

[12] See *ExSyn* 269–70 for an "Appendix to Colwell's 'Construction': When the Verb is Absent."

Sharp's rule, briefly stated, is as follows: In the TSKS construction, the second substantive refers to the *same* person mentioned with the first substantive when:

- neither is *impersonal*;
- neither is *plural*;
- neither is a *proper* name.[13]

Therefore, according to Sharp, the rule applied absolutely *only* with personal, singular, and nonproper nouns. The significance of these requirements can hardly be overestimated, for those who have misunderstood Sharp's principle have done so almost without exception because they were unaware of the restrictions that Sharp set forth.[14]

➡ **3. Validity of the Rule Within the New Testament**   *ExSyn 273–77*

➡   *a. In General*

Not counting the christologically significant passages, there are 80 constructions in the NT that fit the *requirements* for Sharp's rule. But do they all fit the *semantics* of the rule—that is, do the substantives always refer to one and the same person? In a word, yes. Even Sharp's opponents could not find any exceptions; all had to admit that the rule was valid in the NT.

Below are listed several representative passages of Sharp's rule, including nouns, participles, and adjectives.

Mark 6:3   οὗτός ἐστιν ὁ τέκτων, **ὁ υἱὸς** τῆς Μαρίας **καὶ ἀδελφὸς** Ἰακώβου
             this is the carpenter, **the son** of Mary **and brother** of James

John 20:17   τὸν **πατέρα** μου **καὶ πατέρα** ὑμῶν **καὶ θεόν** μου **καὶ θεὸν** ὑμῶν
             my **Father and** your **Father and** my **God and** your **God**

> The construction here is unusual in that it involves four nouns. The possessive pronouns are used to show the differences in how Jesus and his disciples relate to God, but they do not imply that a different person is in view: the first person of the Trinity is the referent for all four nouns.
>
> It is also significant that one of the substantives is θεός. This is a good illustration of the fact that θεός is not a proper noun (from the Greek perspective), for whenever a proper name occurs in Sharp's construction two persons are in view. Yet, whenever θεός is in this construction, one person is in view.

---

[13] A *proper* noun is defined as a noun which *cannot* be "pluralized"—thus it does *not* include titles. A person's name, therefore, is proper and consequently does not fit the rule. But θεός is not proper because it can be pluralized (cf. John 10:34)—thus, when θεός is in a TSKS construction in which both nouns are singular and personal, it fits Sharp's rule.

[14] For a brief discussion of this history, see *ExSyn 272–73*.

Acts 3:14   ὑμεῖς δὲ **τὸν ἅγιον καὶ δίκαιον** ἠρνήσασθε
you have denied **the holy and righteous one**

Eph 2:14   **ὁ ποιήσας** τὰ ἀμφότερα ἓν **καὶ** τὸ μεσότοιχον τοῦ φραγμοῦ **λύσας**
the one who made both into one **and who destroyed** the middle wall of partition

> This text well illustrates that even when there are several intervening words, the construction is not thereby invalidated.

Phil 2:25   Ἐπαφρόδιτον **τὸν ἀδελφὸν καὶ συνεργὸν καὶ συστρατιώτην** μου
Epaphroditus, my **brother and fellow-worker and fellow-soldier**

> This passage illustrates the fact that a possessive pronoun added to one of the nouns does not invalidate the rule.

Heb 3:1   **τὸν ἀπόστολον καὶ ἀρχιερέα** τῆς ὁμολογίας ἡμῶν Ἰησοῦν
Jesus, **the apostle and high priest** of our confession

1 Pet 1:3   **ὁ θεὸς καὶ πατὴρ** τοῦ κυρίου ἡμῶν Ἰησοῦ Χριστοῦ
the God and Father of our Lord Jesus Christ

Rev 22:8   κἀγὼ Ἰωάννης **ὁ ἀκούων καὶ βλέπων** ταῦτα
And I, John, **the one who hears and sees** these things

➡ *b. For Christologically Significant Texts*

Titus 2:13   τοῦ μεγάλου **θεοῦ καὶ σωτῆρος** ἡμῶν Ἰησοῦ Χριστοῦ
our great **God and Savior**, Jesus Christ

> It has frequently been alleged that θεός is a proper name and, hence, that Sharp's rule cannot apply to constructions in which it is employed. We have already pointed out that θεός is not a proper name in Greek. We simply wish to note here that in the TSKS construction θεός is used over a dozen times in the NT and always (if we exclude the christologically significant texts) in reference to one person. This phenomenon is not true of any other proper name in said construction (every instance involving true proper names always points to two individuals). Since that argument carries no weight, there is no good reason to reject Titus 2:13 as an explicit affirmation of the deity of Christ.

2 Pet 1:1   τοῦ **θεοῦ** ἡμῶν **καὶ σωτῆρος**, Ἰησοῦ Χριστοῦ
our **God and Savior**, Jesus Christ

> Some grammarians have objected that since ἡμῶν is connected with θεοῦ, two persons are in view. The pronoun seems to "bracket" the noun, effectively isolating the trailing noun. However in v. 11 of this same chapter (as well as in 2:20 and 3:18), the author writes τοῦ κυρίου ἡμῶν καὶ σωτῆρος, Ἰησοῦ

Χριστοῦ, an expression that refers to one person, Jesus Christ: "Why refuse to apply the same rule to 2 Peter i. 1, that all admit … to be true of 2 Peter i. 11 [not to mention 2:20 and 3:18]?"[15]

4. Constructions Involving Impersonal, Plural, and Proper Nouns

ExSyn 277–90

a. Proper Names

ExSyn 277–78

Always in the NT, whenever proper names are in the equation, distinct individuals are in view. For example, we read of "Peter and James and John" (τὸν Πέτρον καὶ Ἰάκωβον καὶ Ἰωάννην) in Matt 17:1; "Barnabas and Saul" (τὸν Βαρναβᾶν καὶ Σαῦλον) in Acts 13:2. Yet at the same time they are united under one article for the purposes at hand. There is a reason for the lone article in every instance, viz., to conceptualize a contextually-defined coherent group. But because the nouns are proper, the article does not identify one with the other.

➡ ### b. Plural Personal Constructions

ExSyn 278–86

(1) SEMANTICS AND THE NT DATA. Since the plural construction deals with *groups*, there may be other possibilities besides absolute distinction and absolute identity. Theoretically, in fact, there are five semantic possibilities for the plural TSKS construction: (1) distinct groups, though united; (2) overlapping groups; (3) first group subset of second; (4) second group subset of first; and (5) both groups identical. In the NT all groups are represented, though they are not evenly distributed.

(2) UNAMBIGUOUS ILLUSTRATIONS

(a) Distinct Groups, Though United

At all times the lone article in the TSKS construction suggests some sort of unity. A large number of instances in the NT imply nothing more. We can readily see this in English. In the sentence "the Democrats and Republicans approved the bill unanimously," the two political parties, though distinct, are united on a particular issue.

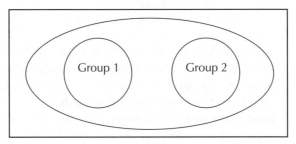

Figure 28
Distinct Groups, though United[16]

---

[15] A. T. Robertson, "The Greek Article and the Deity of Christ," *The Expositor*, 8th Series, 21 (1921): 185. For more discussion of this text, see *ExSyn* 276–77.

[16] In this and the following figures, the article before the first substantive and the καί between the substantives are omitted because the figures are intended to depict the *semantics*, not the structure, of the TSKS construction.

Matt 3:7   τῶν Φαρισαίων καὶ Σαδδουκαίων
the Pharisees and Sadducees

> Although these two parties were distinct, the article unites them for the purposes at hand. The Pharisees and the Sadducees are listed together only four other times in Matthew; in each instance the structure is TSKS and the two groups are set in opposition to Jesus.

Matt 16:21   τῶν πρεσβυτέρων καὶ ἀρχιερέων καὶ γραμματέων
the elders and chief priests and scribes

> These were the three distinct parties that comprised the Sanhedrin. (Some have erroneously insisted that this construction fits Sharp's rule because these three groups all refer to the Sanhedrin. However, to say that A + B + C = D is not the same as saying A = B = C, the latter equation being what Sharp's rule asserts.[17])

(b) Overlapping Groups

There are three kinds of overlap: simple (e.g., "the poor and sick"), first subset of second (e.g., "the angels and [other] created beings"), and second subset of first ("the created beings and [especially] angels").

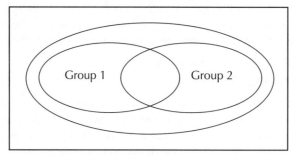

Figure 29
(Simple) Overlapping Groups

Rev 21:8   τοῖς δὲ δειλοῖς καὶ ἀπίστοις καὶ ἐβδελυγμένοις καὶ φονεῦσιν καὶ πόρνοις καὶ φαρμάκοις καὶ εἰδωλολάτραις ... τὸ μέρος αὐτῶν ἐν τῇ λίμνῃ τῇ καιομένῃ πυρὶ καὶ θείῳ
now as for the cowardly and unfaithful and abominable and murderers and fornicators and sorcerers and idolaters ...
their portion shall be in the lake that burns with fire and sulfur

> It is obvious here that the Lake of Fire is not reserved *only* for those who meet *all* of the "qualifications," nor for those meeting only one requirement. Overlapping groups is the intended meaning.

---

[17] The difference between the two formulae is the difference between equality of status and identity of referent. Only if the scribes referred to the same group as the elders could Sharp's principle be invoked.

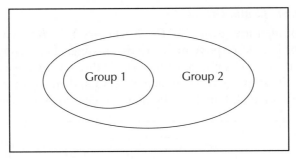

Figure 30
First Group Subset of Second

Matt 9:11   **τῶν τελωνῶν καὶ ἁμαρτωλῶν**
the tax collectors and [other] sinners

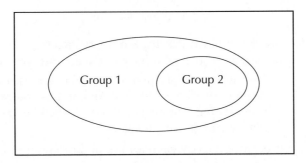

Figure 31
Second Group Subset of First

Mark 2:16   ἰδόντες ὅτι ἐσθίει μετὰ **τῶν ἁμαρτωλῶν καὶ τελωνῶν** ἔλεγον
τοῖς μαθηταῖς αὐτοῦ· ὅτι μετὰ τῶν τελωνῶν καὶ ἁμαρτωλῶν
ἐσθίει...
when they saw that he was eating with **the sinners and tax collectors**, they said to his disciples, "Why does he eat with the
tax collectors and sinners?"

There are two plural TSKS constructions in this verse, both
using the same wording but in different order. The first instance
is that of second group subset of first; the second instance is first
subset of second.

1 Cor 5:10   **τοῖς πλεονέκταις καὶ ἅρπαξιν**
the greedy and swindlers

Although one could be greedy without being branded a
swindler, it is doubtful that the reverse could be true. The idea,
then, is "the greedy and [especially] swindlers."

(c) Both Groups Identical[18]

The idea of identical groups is "the X who are Y." The second substantive functions either in a descriptive or restrictive manner. For example, "the Saint Louis Rams and world champions of football," "those eating well and exercising will get strong." This category has greater attestation than any of the others in the NT, though it is not at all found among noun+noun TSKS plural constructions.

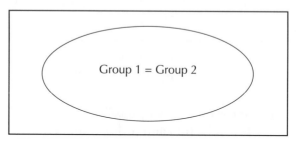

Figure 32
Both Groups Identical

John 20:29   μακάριοι **οἱ** μὴ **ἰδόντες καὶ πιστεύσαντες**
blessed are **those who have** not **seen and** [yet] **believe**

> The negative stipulation of not seeing the risen Lord is inadequate to procure a blessing. And, in this context, the Lord is pronouncing a blessing on those who believe apart from seeing him, in contrast to Thomas.

Rev 1:3   μακάριος ὁ ἀναγινώσκων καὶ **οἱ ἀκούοντες** τοὺς λόγους τῆς προφητείας **καὶ τηροῦντες** τὰ ἐν αὐτῇ γεγραμμένα
blessed is the one who reads and **those who hear** the words of this prophecy **and keep** the things written in it

> It is evident that the one who only hears the prophecy and does not obey it falls short of the blessing. The twofold response of hearing and keeping is necessary if one is to be counted among the μακάριοι.

(3) EXEGETICALLY AND THEOLOGICALLY SIGNIFICANT TEXTS. There are several ambiguous plural TSKS constructions, two of which have particular exegetical value.

Eph 4:11   αὐτὸς ἔδωκεν τοὺς μὲν ἀποστόλους, τοὺς δὲ προφήτας, τοὺς δὲ εὐαγγελιστάς, **τοὺς δὲ ποιμένας καὶ διδασκάλους**
he gave some as apostles, some as prophets, some as evangelists, **some** [as] **pastors and teachers**

> This text seems to affirm, both grammatically and exegetically, that all pastors were to be teachers, though not all teachers were to be pastors.[19]

---

[18] For a discussion of Eph 1:1, see *ExSyn* 282–83.
[19] See *ExSyn* 284 for a discussion.

Eph 2:20   ἐποικοδομηθέντες ἐπὶ τῷ θεμελίῳ **τῶν ἀποστόλων καὶ προφητῶν**

having been built upon the foundation **of the apostles and prophets**

> The strongest possibilities are either that two distinct groups are in view or the apostles are seen as a subset of the prophets. If the OT prophets are in view, then obviously two distinct groups are meant. But if NT prophets are in view, this would favor the apostles as being a subset of the prophets.[20]

➡ ### c. Impersonal Constructions   *ExSyn* 286–90

There are about 50 impersonal TSKS constructions in the NT. Theoretically, such constructions can have the same semantic range as plural personal constructions (i.e., distinct, overlapping, first subset of second, second subset of first, and identical [see figures above]). However, the "identical" category is rare, with only one clear example. Far more common is the distinct category and the overlapping groups (especially first subset of second).

(1) Unambiguous Examples

(a) Distinct Entities, Though United

Luke 21:12   διώξουσιν, παραδιδόντες εἰς **τὰς συναγωγὰς καὶ φυλακάς**

they will persecute [you], handing [you] over to **the synagogues and prisons**

> The reason for the single article is that both groups are hostile to the disciples.

Eph 3:18   **τὸ πλάτος καὶ μῆκος καὶ ὕψος καὶ βάθος**

the breadth and length and height and depth

> The author is speaking about God's love in figurative language, as if he were using a spiritual plumb-line. Although each term refers to God's love, each refers to a different aspect of it and thus the terms are *not* identical.[21]

(b) Overlapping Entities[22]

Luke 6:17   **πάσης τῆς Ἰουδαίας καὶ Ἰερουσαλήμ**
all Judea and Jerusalem

---

[20] For a discussion of this text and its theological implications, see *ExSyn* 284–86.

[21] Some have been confused over this text, assuming that it fits Sharp's rule. Generally this confusion is exacerbated because (1) all of the terms do apparently refer to God's love, yet even here it would not be appropriate to say that the length is identical with the height; (2) the figurative language compounds the problem because the imagery and its referent are both somewhat elusive; and (3) there is a widespread confusion about what Sharp's rule actually addresses: it is not mere equality, but identity that is in view.

[22] See similar section on plural personal constructions for the three different kinds of overlap possible.

2 Cor 12:21   τῶν προημαρτηκότων καὶ μὴ μετανοησάντων ἐπὶ **τῇ ἀκαθαρσίᾳ καὶ πορνείᾳ καὶ ἀσελγείᾳ**
those who have previously sinned and not repented over **the impurity and immorality and licentiousness**

Rev 9:15   ἐλύθησαν οἱ τέσσαρες ἄγγελοι οἱ ἡτοιμασμένοι εἰς **τὴν ὥραν καὶ ἡμέραν καὶ μῆνα καὶ ἐνιαυτόν**
the four angels who had been prepared for **the hour and day and month and year** were released

(c) Both Entities Identical

There is only one clear example of this in the NT: Acts 1:25.

(2) Exegetically and theologically significant texts. There are several ambiguous impersonal TSKS constructions, some of which are exegetically significant. One of them is taken up here.[23]

Acts 2:23   τοῦτον **τῇ** ὡρισμένῃ **βουλῇ καὶ προγνώσει** τοῦ θεοῦ
this [Jesus, having been delivered up] by the predetermined **plan and foreknowledge** of God

If "foreknowledge" defines "predetermination," this opens the door for the explanation that (according to one definition of πρόγνωσις) God's decree is dependent on his omniscience. But if the terms are distinguishable, the relationship may be reversed, viz., omniscience is dependent on the eternal decree. Without attempting to resolve this theological issue entirely, it can nevertheless be argued that the "identical" view is unlikely: the least attested meaning of impersonal constructions is referential identity.[24]

---

[23] For discussions of Acts 20:21 and 2 Thess 2:1, see *ExSyn* 289–90.
[24] For a more detailed discussion, see *ExSyn* 288–89.

Adjectives[1]
Overview of Adjective Uses

"Non-Adjectival" Uses of the Adjective. **129**
  1. The Adverbial Use of the Adjective 130
➡ 2. The Independent or Substantival Use of the Adjective 130
Uses of the Positive, Comparative, and Superlative Forms
of the Adjective **131**
  1. The Use of the Positive Adjective 131
➡   a. Normal Usage 131
    b. Positive for Comparative. 132
    c. Positive for Superlative 132
  2. The Use of the Comparative Adjective 132
➡   a. Normal Usage 132
    b. Comparative for Superlative 132
    c. Comparative for Elative 133
  3. The Use of the Superlative Adjective 133
➡   a. "Normal" Usage 133
➡   b. Superlative for Elative 134
➡   c. Superlative for Comparative 134
The Relation of Adjective to Noun **135**
  1. When the Article Is Present 135
➡   a. The Attributive Positions 135
➡   b. The Predicate Positions 136
    c. Summary 137
  2. When the Article Is Absent. 137
➡   a. The Anarthrous Adjective-Noun Construction 138
➡   b. The Anarthrous Noun-Adjective Construction 138
    c. Some Exegetically and Theologically Significant Passages 139

Basically, only three questions need to be asked of the adjective: (1) What is its relationship to a noun (or other substantive) and how can one tell? (2) Are the positive, comparative, and superlative forms of the adjective ever used for other than positive, comparative, and superlative ideas respectively? (3) Can the adjective function other than in dependence on a noun?

These questions will be dealt with in reverse order (or chiastically), beginning with the least significant question (exegetically) to the most significant question.

"Non-Adjectival" Uses of the Adjective   ExSyn 292–95

The basic role of the adjective is as a modifier of a noun or other substantive. As such, it can be modified by an adverb. Not infrequently, however, it deviates

---

[1] See *ExSyn* 291–314.

from this role by one step in either direction. That is, it can either stand in the place of a noun or in the place of an adverb.

Substantival	*Adjectival*	*Adverbial*
Independent	Dependent on Noun	Dependent on Adjective or Verb

Table 3
The Functions of the Adjective

1. The Adverbial Use of the Adjective

ExSyn 293

a. Definition. The adjective is sometimes used in the place of an adverb. Some of the uses are analogous to colloquial English, such as "I am doing good," or "Come here quick!" Other, more frequent instances involve idiomatic uses of the adjective, such as the accusative adjective in the neuter used adverbially. (Surprising as it may seem, this idiomatic adverbial use is frequently, if not normally, articular.) These include a large group of stereotyped words, such as βραχύ, λοιπόν, μίκρον, μόνον, πολύ, πρῶτον, ὕστερον, κτλ.

b. Illustrations

John 1:41   εὑρίσκει οὗτος **πρῶτον** τὸν ἀδελφὸν τὸν ἴδιον Σίμωνα
he **first** found his own brother, Simon

John 4:18   πέντε ἄνδρας ἔσχες καὶ νῦν ὃν ἔχεις οὐκ ἔστιν σου ἀνήρ· τοῦτο **ἀληθὲς** εἴρηκας.
You have had five husbands and the one whom you now have is not your husband; this you have spoken **truly**.

Phil 3:1   **τὸ λοιπόν**, ἀδελφοί μου, χαίρετε ἐν κυρίῳ
finally, my brothers, rejoice in the Lord

→2. The Independent or Substantival Use of the Adjective

ExSyn 294–95

a. Definition and clarification. The adjective is frequently used independently of a noun. That is, it can function as a substantive (in which case it either implies a noun or takes on the lexical nuance of a noun).

Usually, though not always, such a substantival adjective will have the article with it to point out that its use is indeed substantival. Some words, such as ἔρημος ("desert"), διάβολος ("slanderous," or, as a noun, "the devil"), and ἅγιος ("holy," or, as a noun, "saint"), often function as substantives without the article since they are either often or usually independent of nouns in the NT. Other adjectives, however, usually require the article to make clear that they are being used substantivally.

Furthermore, when the adjective is substantival, its gender is generally fixed by sense rather than by grammatical concord. That is to say, if it refers to a male, it will usually be masculine; if it refers to a female, it will usually be feminine; if it refers to an entity or concept, it will be neuter.

b. Illustrations

Matt 6:13   ῥῦσαι ἡμᾶς ἀπὸ τοῦ **πονηροῦ**
deliver us from the **evil** [one]

Acts 2:33   τῇ **δεξιᾷ** τοῦ θεοῦ ὑψωθείς
having been exalted at the **right** [hand] of God

1 Cor 13:10 ὅταν δὲ ἔλθῃ τὸ **τέλειον**, τὸ ἐκ μέρους καταργηθήσεται
whenever the **perfect** comes, the partial will be done away[2]

The Use of the Positive, Comparative, and Superlative Forms of the Adjective   *ExSyn 296–305*

The terms "positive," "comparative," and "superlative" refer to different forms of the same adjective that have to do with degree. Thus in English we have "nice" (positive form), "nicer" (comparative), and "nicest" (superlative).

The *comparative* adjective and the *superlative* adjective focus on the properties of a noun in terms of *degree*, not kind. They infer a relative rather than an absolute notion. Thus, "the taller woman" only speaks of the height of one woman in comparison with another. It may be that both are short. The issue is thus degree, since height is a quality that both share.

The *difference* between the comparative adjective and the superlative is not that of kind, or degree, but of *number*. Comparative adjectives basically compare only *two* entities (or persons, ideas, etc.). Superlative adjectives basically compare *three* or more. In the NT, however (and Koine Greek in general), there is much overlap in usage among these categories.

Finally, *elative* is a term used of either the comparative or superlative adjective to describe an *intensification* of the positive notion (with the translation *very* before the positive form). That is, like a positive adjective, an elative adjective focuses on kind rather than degree. Although the *form* of such an adjective is either comparative or superlative, in meaning it does not make an explicit comparison. For example, μείζων (comparative in form, "greater") may on occasion have an elative force, "*very* great."

1. The Use of the Positive Adjective   *ExSyn 297–98*

➡   ### a. Normal Usage

Normally, the positive adjective makes no comment about any object other than the one that it modifies (or, if a predicate adjective, the object it makes an assertion about). It simply qualifies the noun to which it stands related (e.g., "a good man" does not indicate that this particular man is *better* [the comparative idea] than other men). This usage is routine.

---

[2] For a discussion of the exegesis of this text, cf. *ExSyn 295–96*.

Rom 7:12 ἡ ἐντολὴ **ἁγία** καὶ **δικαία** καὶ **ἀγαθή**
the commandment is **holy** and **righteous** and **good**

Rev 20:2 ὁ ὄφις ὁ **ἀρχαῖος** the **old** serpent

b. Positive for Comparative

On a rare occasion, the positive adjective can be used for the comparative.

Matt 18:8 **καλόν** σοί ἐστιν εἰσελθεῖν εἰς τὴν ζωὴν κυλλόν
it is **better** to enter life crippled

c. Positive for Superlative

Occasionally, the positive adjective is used in the place of a superlative adjective. When the positive adjective is in the attributive position and is used with the *par excellence* article, it has the force of the superlative adjective. Rarely, a predicate adjective also functions as a superlative.

Matt 22:38 αὕτη ἐστὶν ἡ **μεγάλη** καὶ πρώτη ἐντολή
this is the **great** [=greatest] and first commandment

Heb 9:3 **ἅγια** ἁγίων the **Holy** of Holies
The idea is "the holiest of all holy places."

2. The Use of the Comparative Adjective ExSyn 298–301

Much less frequent than the positive form of the adjective are the comparative and superlative. There are approximately 7500 positive adjectives, 200 comparatives, and 200 superlatives in the NT.

➡ ### a. Normal Usage

The comparative adjective normally makes a comparison (as its name suggests). The largest group of instances involves an explicit comparison in which the adjective is followed by a genitive of comparison, the particle ἤ, or, less frequently, by παρά or ὑπέρ. But the comparative adjective not infrequently is used substantivally, often leaving the comparison implicit.

Matt 12:6 λέγω ὑμῖν ὅτι τοῦ ἱεροῦ **μεῖζόν** ἐστιν ὧδε
I tell you, [something] **greater** than the temple is here

Heb 4:12 ζῶν ὁ λόγος τοῦ θεοῦ καὶ ἐνεργὴς καὶ **τομώτερος** ὑπὲρ πᾶσαν μάχαιραν δίστομον
the word of God is living and active and **sharper** than any two-edged sword

b. Comparative for Superlative

Although relatively rare, the comparative adjective can be used with a superlative sense.

Luke 9:48 ὁ **μικρότερος** ἐν πᾶσιν ὑμῖν ... ἐστιν μέγας
the **least** among you all ... is greatest
Notice too that the *positive* form μέγας is used in a superlative sense.

1 Cor 13:13   νυνὶ δὲ μένει πίστις, ἐλπίς, ἀγάπη, τὰ τρία ταῦτα· **μείζων** δὲ τούτων ἡ ἀγάπη

But now remain faith, hope, love, these three. And the **greatest** of these is love

> It is sometimes disputed that μείζων is functioning in a superlative manner here.[3]

c. Comparative for Elative

Sometimes the comparative adjective is used with an elative sense. That is, the quality expressed by the adjective is intensified but is not making a comparison (e.g., ὁ ἰσχυρότερος ἀνήρ might mean "the *very* strong man" rather than "the stronger man").

(1) CLEAR EXAMPLES

Acts 13:31   ὃς ὤφθη ἐπὶ ἡμέρας **πλείους**
who appeared for **very many** days

Acts 17:22   κατὰ πάντα ὡς **δεισιδαιμονεστέρους** ὑμᾶς θεωρῶ
I perceive how **very religious** you are in every way

> The KJV has "I perceive that in all things ye are too superstitious." But such a translation is unnecessary linguistically, since the comparative has a well-established usage as an elative in Koine Greek.

(2) A POSSIBLE AND EXEGETICALLY SIGNIFICANT EXAMPLE

Matt 13:32   ὃ **μικρότερον** μέν ἐστιν πάντων τῶν σπερμάτων
[the mustard seed …] which is **smaller** than all the seeds
or perhaps which is **very small** among all the seeds

> The first translation given for this text treats the adj. in its comparative sense, while the second translation treats it in an elative sense. This text has created a theological difficulty for some American evangelicals: Jesus seems to be declaring the mustard seed to be smaller than all other seeds when, in fact, it is *not* the smallest (the wild orchid is smaller).[4]

3. The Use of the Superlative Adjective   *ExSyn* 301–5

➡   ### a. "Normal" Usage

In Hellenistic Greek, the true superlative sense for the superlative adjective is on its way out. Thus the superlative sense for the superlative adjective is "normal" more in name than in reality. Although it is more frequent than other uses, the margin is negligible.

---

[3] For discussion of this problem, see *ExSyn* 299–300.
[4] For discussion of this text, see *ExSyn* 301.

This "normal" usage is due largely to the instances of πρῶτος and ἔσχατος, which together account for most of the superlative forms in the NT. Apart from these two terms, approximately half of the superlative forms in the NT function as superlatives.

John 11:24   ἀναστήσεται ἐν τῇ ἀναστάσει ἐν τῇ **ἐσχάτῃ** ἡμέρᾳ
he will rise again in the resurrection on the **last** day

Acts 16:17   οὗτοι οἱ ἄνθρωποι δοῦλοι τοῦ θεοῦ τοῦ **ὑψίστου** εἰσίν
these men are servants of the **most high** God

Eph 3:8   ἐμοὶ τῷ **ἐλαχιστοτέρῳ** πάντων ἁγίων
to me, **less than the least** of all the saints

> This is the comparative of the superlative, perhaps coined for the occasion! A more literal translation would be something like "leaster."[5]

➡ **b. Superlative for Elative**

Apart from πρῶτος and ἔσχατος, the superlative is used about as frequently for the elative as it is for the superlative.[6] When πρῶτος and ἔσχατος are factored in, however, this category gets a smaller piece of the pie.

Mark 4:1   συνάγεται πρὸς αὐτὸν ὄχλος **πλεῖστος**
a **very great** crowd gathered before him

1 Cor 4:3   ἐμοὶ εἰς **ἐλάχιστόν** ἐστιν, ἵνα ὑφ᾽ ὑμῶν ἀνακριθῶ
to me, it is a **very small thing** that I should be judged by you

➡ **c. Superlative for Comparative**

Not infrequently, the superlative has the same sense as the comparative in that it compares only *two* things rather than three or more. This is frequent with πρῶτος (although it normally has a superlative force), rare with ἔσχατος, and nonexistent with other superlative forms.[7]

Matt 21:28   ἄνθρωπος εἶχεν τέκνα δύο. καὶ προσελθὼν τῷ **πρώτῳ** εἶπεν ...
a man had two sons. He came to the **first** and said ...

John 20:4   ὁ ἄλλος μαθητὴς ... ἦλθεν **πρῶτος** εἰς τὸ μνημεῖον
the other disciple ... came **first** to the tomb

> In classical Greek, the use of πρῶτος would usually indicate at least *three* things being compared. If this were the case here, then three disciples would be in view (*contra* οἱ δύο earlier in the verse). But the NT usage, like modern colloquial English, relaxed some of the grammatical standards of a former age.

---

[5] For discussion of this text, see *ExSyn* 302–3.

[6] Robertson inexplicably says that this usage "comprises the great majority of the superlative forms that survive in the N.T." (*Grammar*, 670). BDF make a similar comment: "In the NT the remnants of the superlative forms are used mostly with 'elative' force as in the papyri" (32–33 [§60]).

[7] For a discussion of Acts 1:1 and Luke 2:2, both of which involve debatable and exegetically significant adjectives, see *ExSyn* 304–5.

The various forces of the three forms of the adjective are conveniently summarized below.

Form	Positive	Comparative	Superlative
Function			
Positive	X	0	0
Comparative	X	X	X
Elative	0	X	X
Superlative	X	X	X

Chart 33
The Semantic Range of the Forms of the Adjective

The Relation of Adjective to Noun   ExSyn 306–14

The adjective may be either attributive or predicate in relation to the noun. That is, it may either modify the noun or assert something about it. Except for the use of pronominal adjectives with nouns (e.g., πᾶς, ὅλος, εἷς), when the article is present, it is usually easy to discern the relationship.

1. When the Article Is Present   ExSyn 306–9

➡ #### a. The Attributive Positions

(1) First Attributive Position

The first attributive position is article-adjective-noun (e.g., ὁ ἀγαθὸς βασιλεύς = the good king). In this construction "the adjective receives greater emphasis than the substantive."[8] This usage is common.

Matt 4:5   τὴν **ἁγίαν** πόλιν   the **holy** city

1 John 4:18 ἡ **τελεία** ἀγάπη ἔξω βάλλει τὸν φόβον
             perfect love casts out fear

(2) Second Attributive Position

The second attributive position is article-noun-article-adjective (e.g., ὁ βασιλεὺς ὁ ἀγαθός = the good king). This difference in the placement of the adjective is not one of relation but of position and emphasis. In the second attributive position "both substantive and adjective receive emphasis and the adjective is added as a sort of climax in apposition with a separate article."[9] A literal, though

---

[8] Robertson, *Grammar*, 776.
[9] Ibid., 777.

awkward, gloss, bringing out the force of such a construction of ὁ βασιλεὺς ὁ ἀγαθός, is "the king, the good one." This construction occurs frequently.

Acts 11:15   ἐπέπεσεν τὸ πνεῦμα τὸ **ἅγιον** ἐπ᾽ αὐτούς
the **Holy** Spirit fell on them

Heb 6:4   γευσαμένους τῆς δωρεᾶς τῆς **ἐπουρανίου**
having tasted the **heavenly** gift

(3) THIRD ATTRIBUTIVE POSITION

The third attributive position is noun-article-adjective (e.g., βασιλεὺς ὁ ἀγαθός = the good king). "Here the substantive is [often] indefinite and general, while the attribute [adjective] makes a particular application."[10] To bring out the *force* of such a construction one might translate βασιλεὺς ὁ ἀγαθός as "a king, the good one." This is the least frequent of the attributive positions, occurring only a few times with adjectives.[11]

Luke 15:22   ταχὺ ἐξενέγκατε στολὴν τὴν **πρώτην**
quickly bring out the **best** robe

> The idea is "bring out a robe—the **best** one."

John 1:18   μονογενὴς θεὸς ὁ **ὢν** εἰς τὸν κόλπον τοῦ πατρός
the unique God **who was** near the heart of the Father

> More frequent than the adj. in third attributive positions is the participle. When a participle is used, the article should normally be translated like a relative pronoun.

➡ *b. The Predicate Positions*

(1) FIRST PREDICATE POSITION

The first predicate position is adjective-article-noun (e.g., ἀγαθὸς ὁ βασιλεύς = the king is good). Here, the adjective seems to be slightly more emphatic than the noun. Thus, to bring out the *force* of such a construction, one might translate ἀγαθὸς ὁ βασιλεύς as "good is the king." This usage is relatively common.

Matt 5:9   **μακάριοι** οἱ εἰρηνοποιοί   **blessed** are the peacemakers

1 John 3:10   ἐν τούτῳ **φανερά** ἐστιν τὰ τέκνα τοῦ θεοῦ
in this the children of God are **manifest**

(2) SECOND PREDICATE POSITION

The second predicate position is article-noun-adjective (e.g., ὁ βασιλεὺς ἀγαθός = the king is good). Here, the emphasis seems to be either equally placed

---

[10] Ibid.

[11] There are only a couple dozen such examples in the NT (apart from instances with proper names). However, the third attributive position is frequent when the modifier is other than an adj. (such as a participle, prepositional phrase, or gen. adjunct). In such instances the article is translated as though it were a relative pronoun. See "Article, Part I: The Article as Relative Pronoun," for a discussion.

on both noun and adjective or is slightly heavier on the noun. This usage is relatively common.

Jas 2:26   ἡ πίστις χωρὶς ἔργων **νεκρά** ἐστιν
           faith without works is **dead**

1 Pet 2:12   τὴν ἀναστροφὴν ὑμῶν ἐν τοῖς ἔθνεσιν ἔχοντες **καλήν**
            keep your conduct among the Gentiles **good**
            The predicate adj. in this instance is also the complement of an object-complement construction.

c. Summary

When the article is present, the relation of adjective to noun is easy to determine. When the adjective is *within* the article-noun group (i.e., when it has an article immediately before it), it is attributive to the noun and hence modifies or qualifies the noun in some way. When the adjective is *outside* the article-noun group, it is predicate to the noun and hence makes an assertion about it.

The only exception to these rules when the article is present is with pronominal adjectives (i.e., words that function sometimes as adjectives and sometimes as pronouns, such as πᾶς, ὅλος). These may stand in a predicate *position* but have an attributive *relation* to the noun. Other than with pronominal adjectives, then, when the article is present, the adjective's (structural) position to the noun will determine and be the same as its (semantic) relation to the noun.

	1st	*2nd*	*3rd*
Attributive	Art-Adj-Noun (ὁ ἀγαθὸς ἄνθρωπος= the good man)	Art-Noun-Art-Adj (ὁ ἄνθρωπος ὁ ἀγαθός= the good man)	Noun-Art-Adj (ἄνθρωπος ὁ ἀγαθός= the good man)
Predicate	Adj-Art-Noun (ἀγαθὸς ὁ ἄνθρωπος= the man is good)	Art-Noun-Adj (ὁ ἄνθρωπος ἀγαθός= the man is good)	None

Table 4
Attributive and Predicate Positions of the Adjective

2. When the Article Is Absent   *ExSyn 309–14*

When no article is present, the relation of adjective to noun is more difficult to ascertain. This type of construction occurs almost 2400 times in the NT, over one fourth of all adjective-noun constructions. Conceivably, the anarthrous adjective-noun construction could express either an attributive or predicate relation. For example, βασιλεὺς ἀγαθός could mean either "a good king" or "a king is good."

➡ ### *a. The Anarthrous Adjective-Noun Construction*

Rather than treat attributive and predicate positions separately, both will be dealt with under the same structural heading. The reason for this is that only when the article is present will the structure dictate the semantics. In the anarthrous construction, since the article is absent, the position of the adjective does not determine its relation to the noun.

(1) (ANARTHROUS) FIRST ATTRIBUTIVE POSITION. Thus when it has been determined *from the context* that an adjective in an adjective-noun construction (note the order: adj., then noun) expresses an attributive relation to the noun, it is in the *first* (anarthrous) *attributive* position (e.g., ἀγαθὸς βασιλεύς = a good king). This is common enough, occurring hundreds of times in the NT.

(2) ILLUSTRATIONS

Luke 19:17   εὖγε, **ἀγαθὲ** δοῦλε   well done, **good** servant

2 Pet 1:19   ὡς λύχνῳ φαίνοντι ἐν **αὐχμηρῷ** τόπῳ
              like a lamp shining in a **dark** place

(3) (ANARTHROUS) FIRST PREDICATE POSITION. When, however, the same construction has been determined *from the context* to express a predicate relation, the adjective is in the *first* (anarthrous) *predicate* position to the noun (e.g., ἀγαθὸς βασιλεύς = a king is good). Though much less common than the attributive relation, in equative clauses (viz., a clause in which an equative verb is stated or implied), this is not uncommon.

Mark 12:31   **μείζων** τούτων ἄλλη ἐντολὴ οὐκ ἔστιν
              no other command is **greater** than these

Jas 1:12   **μακάριος** ἀνὴρ ὃς ὑπομένει πειρασμόν
              blessed is the man who endures a trial

➡ ### *b. The Anarthrous Noun-Adjective Construction*

(1) FOURTH ATTRIBUTIVE POSITION. When it has been determined *from the context* that an adjective in a noun-adjective construction expresses an attributive relation to the noun, such a construction is in the *fourth* attributive position. The reason for this is that *both* the second and third attributive positions involve an adjective following a noun. Thus, to say that an adjective is in the *fourth* attributive position is to say that the article does *not* occur in the construction at all (e.g., βασιλεὺς ἀγαθός = a good king). This usage is common.

(2) ILLUSTRATIONS

Mark 1:8   αὐτὸς βαπτίσει ὑμᾶς ἐν πνεύματι **ἁγίῳ**
              he will baptize you in the **Holy** Spirit

John 3:16   μὴ ἀπόληται ἀλλ᾽ ἔχῃ ζωὴν **αἰώνιον**
              he should not perish but have **eternal** life

(3) (ANARTHROUS) SECOND PREDICATE POSITION. When the same construction has been determined *from the context* to express a predicate relation, the adjective is

in the *second* (anarthrous) *predicate* position to the noun (e.g., βασιλεὺς ἀγαθός = a king is good). This usage is relatively common, especially in equative clauses.

Matt 13:57   οὐκ ἔστιν προφήτης **ἄτιμος** εἰ μὴ ἐν τῇ πατρίδι
a prophet is not **without honor** except in his homeland

Rom 7:8   χωρὶς νόμου ἁμαρτία **νεκρά**   apart from the law, sin is **dead**

c. Some Exegetically and Theologically Significant Passages

In anarthrous constructions there are a few passages that deserve some discussion because of their exegetical and/or theological significance. In these texts, NT scholars have seen the adjectives in question as ambiguous or definitely attributive. But a case can be made that the adjective in question is predicate.[12]

Titus 2:10   πᾶσαν πίστιν ἐνδεικνυμένους **ἀγαθήν**

There are two possibilities here: (1) "showing forth all **good** faith" and (2) "showing forth all faith [to be] **good**." The first gloss is all that is found in the literature, but the second translation is probably to be preferred.[13] If taken this way, the text seems to support the idea that saving faith does not fail, but actually results in good works.

2 Tim 3:16   πᾶσα γραφὴ **θεόπνευστος** καὶ ὠφέλιμος
every[14] scripture is **inspired** and profitable

Many scholars feel that the translation should be: "Every **inspired** scripture is also profitable." This is probably not the best translation, however. There are several contextual and grammatical arguments that could be used in defense of a predicate θεόπνευστος, but the two most important arguments are as follows:[15] (1) The fact that καί means "and" twelve times as often as it means "also," as well as the fact that it is unnatural to translate it adverbially as "also" between two adjectives in the same case, argues for a predicate θεόπνευστος. (2) In the NT, LXX, in classical and Koine Greek, the overwhelming semantic force of an adj.-noun-adj. construction in an equative clause is that the first adj. will be attributive and the second will be predicate. The evidence is so overwhelming that we may suggest a "rule": *In πᾶς + noun + adjective constructions in equative clauses the πᾶς, being by nature as definite as the article, implies the article, thus making the adjective(s) following the noun outside the implied article-noun group and, therefore, predicate.* In the least, the evidence renders translations of this verse such as the NEB's ("every inspired scripture has its use") highly suspect.

---

[12] For a discussion of Acts 19:2, see *ExSyn* 312.

[13] For a detailed discussion of this text, see *ExSyn* 312–13.

[14] It is of course possible to translate πᾶσα as "all," but normal usage would require the noun (γραφή) to be articular.

[15] For a more complete discussion of this passage, see *ExSyn* 313–14.

The Pronouns[1]
Overview of Pronouns

General Remarks 140
Semantic Categories: Major Classes 141
   1. Personal Pronouns 142
   2. Demonstrative Pronouns 144
   3. Relative Pronouns 149
   4. Interrogative Pronouns 153
   5. Indefinite Pronoun 154
   6. Possessive "Pronouns" (Adjectives) 154
   7. Intensive Pronoun 155
   8. Reflexive Pronouns 156
   9. Reciprocal Pronouns 156
Lexico-Syntactic Categories: Major Terms 156
   1. Ἀλλήλων 157
   2. Αὐτός 157
   3. Ἑαυτοῦ 157
   4. Ἐγώ 157
   5. Ἐκεῖνος 157
   6. Ἐμαυτοῦ 157
   7. Ἡμεῖς 157
   8. Ὅδε 158
   9. Ὅς 158
  10. Ὅστις 158
  11. Οὗτος 158
  12. Ποῖος 158
  13. Πόσος 158
  14. Σεαυτοῦ 158
  15. Σύ 158
  16. Τίς 158
  17. Τις 158
  18. Ὑμεῖς 159

General Remarks   *ExSyn* 316–18

1. Definition

A pronoun is a word used "to designate an object without naming it, when that which is referred to is known from context or usage, has been already mentioned or indicated, or, being unknown, is the subject or object of inquiry."[2] Since pronouns are grammatical proxies, they must indicate in some manner that to which

---

[1] See *ExSyn* 315–54.

[2] *Oxford English Dictionary*, s.v. "pronoun."

they are referring. The basic rule for the Greek pronoun is that it agrees with its antecedent in gender and number, but its case is determined by the pronoun's function in its own clause. This concord principle, however, has many exceptions.

2. Elaboration

There are over 16,000 pronouns in the NT. On the one hand, this extended use of pronouns also makes them susceptible to misinterpretation. On the other hand, pronouns are often used to *clarify*. Sometimes this penchant for clarity results in a redundant (or pleonastic) pronoun.

Pronouns are also used, at times, exclusively with *connotative* value. What they denote may be obvious from the text; but they can be used for emphasis, contrast, etc. This is especially the case with personal pronouns. But all is not cut-and-dried. Thus, even when αὐτός is used with a third person verb, it may be for emphasis *or* for clarity.

Furthermore, there is overlap in the use of the pronouns; the classical distinctions are not always maintained. The NT authors, for example, do not always maintain the near-far distinction with the demonstrative pronouns οὗτος and ἐκεῖνος.[3]

Finally, we should mention a word about terminology. When the noun (or other nominal) that the pronoun refers to *precedes* the pronoun, it is called the pronoun's *antecedent* (as in "**Bob** read the book. Then *he* gave it to Jane"). This is the most frequent usage. When the noun comes after the pronoun, it is the pronoun's *postcedent* (as in "After *he* read the book, **Bob** gave it to Jane"). In the latter case, the pronoun may be said to be "proleptic."

Semantic Categories: Major Classes   ExSyn 319–51

The number of pronoun classes in Greek is difficult to assess, though most grammars have between eight and twelve. A major part of the difficulty in determining the number of classes has to do with whether a particular term is an adjective or a pronoun.[4] Nevertheless, certain classes are not disputed as pronominal: personal, demonstrative, relative, interrogative, indefinite, intensive, reflexive, and reciprocal. These constitute the core of our discussion. In addition, the possessive pronoun will receive treatment below, but it is not a true *Greek* category.

---

[3] Dana-Mantey suggest, for example, that ἐκεῖνος is used "for that which is relatively distant in actuality or thought" (128), while οὗτος is used "for that which is relatively near in actuality or thought" (127). This is a good description of their usage in Attic Greek, but there are many exceptions in the NT.

[4] To some extent, the determination of what constitutes a pronoun is an arbitrary choice. Some words are clearly pronouns (e.g., ἐγώ), others are clearly adjectives (e.g., ἀγαθός), while several words may be classed somewhere in between, either as pronominal adjectives or adjectival pronouns. For the most part, we are regarding those words as pronouns that, when functioning substantivally, do not take the article. Adjectives, on the other hand, regularly take the article when substituting for a noun.

The relative frequency of the eight main categories can be seen in the following chart.[5]

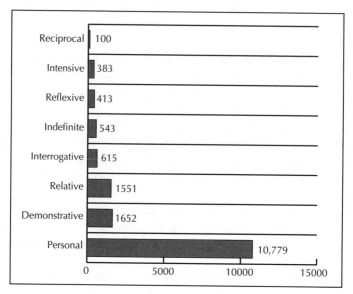

Chart 34
Frequency of Pronoun Classes in the New Testament

1. Personal Pronouns

ExSyn 320–25

a. Definition and terms used. The personal pronouns are ἐγώ (ἡμεῖς) for the first person, and σύ (ὑμεῖς) for the second person. In Hellenistic Greek, αὐτός is used for the third person pronoun (and sometimes for the first or second person).

Personal pronouns are far and away the most frequently used pronouns in the NT. Two out of three pronouns belong to this classification. About half of the instances in this class involve αὐτός. The uses of personal pronouns can be broken down by cases, viz., nominative and non-nominative (= oblique).[6]

Other pronouns that fill the slot of personal pronouns are ἐκεῖνος and οὗτος. Though technically demonstrative pronouns, not infrequently their demonstrative force is diminished (see "Demonstrative Pronouns," below, for discussion).

b. Functions

ExSyn 321–25

(1) NOMINATIVE USES

ExSyn 321–23

(a) Emphasis

The nominative personal pronoun is most commonly used for emphasis. The emphasis may involve some sort of *contrast*—either of kind (antithetical) or degree

---

[5] The statistics are those of *Accordance*, with some modification.

[6] The gen. is the most common case, accounting for about 40% of all personal pronouns. Most of these *function* semantically as possessive pronouns.

(comparison). For example, in "He washed and she dried," the contrast is comparative (both people are doing the dishes). In the sentence "He slept and she worked," the contrast is antithetical.

Emphasis may also focus on the *subject* more than the verb. The reasons for such focus may be to identify, give prominence to, clarify, etc. In such instances, contrast with other subjects is not necessarily absent, but neither is it prominent.

[1] CONTRAST

Matt 2:6   καὶ **σὺ** Βηθλέεμ, γῆ Ἰούδα, οὐδαμῶς ἐλαχίστη εἶ ἐν τοῖς ἡγεμόσιν Ἰούδα
and **you**, Bethlehem, in the land of Judah, are by no means least among the leaders of Judah

Mark 8:29   **σὺ** εἶ ὁ χριστός   **you** are the Christ
Jesus is not Elijah, one of the prophets, or John raised from the dead. He is in a league by himself. Peter's declaration as to Jesus' identity, on a discourse level, may be viewed as the pivotal point in the Gospel of Mark.

Luke 24:18   **σὺ** μόνος παροικεῖς Ἰερουσαλὴμ καὶ οὐκ ἔγνως τὰ γενόμενα ἐν αὐτῇ;
Are **you** the only one visiting Jerusalem and yet you do not know the things that have happened in it?

[2] SUBJECT FOCUS

Jas 1:13   πειράζει δὲ **αὐτὸς** οὐδένα
but **he** tempts no one

2 Pet 1:17   ὁ υἱός μου ὁ ἀγαπητός μου οὗτός ἐστιν εἰς ὃν **ἐγὼ** εὐδόκησα
this is my beloved Son, in whom **I** am well pleased

(b) Redundancy

The presence of the personal pronoun in the nominative is not always for emphasis. Occasionally, it is a mere redundancy of the pronominal notion embedded in the verb. Only the context can help determine whether a personal pronoun is emphatic or not. Many of these instances could be functioning in the narrative as a "switch-reference device, signifying a change in subject to someone or something that had been mentioned previously."[7]

Luke 5:1   Ἐγένετο δὲ ἐν τῷ τὸν ὄχλον ἐπικεῖσθαι αὐτῷ καὶ ἀκούειν τὸν λόγον τοῦ θεοῦ καὶ **αὐτὸς** ἦν ἑστὼς παρὰ τὴν λίμνην Γεννησαρέτ
When the crowd began to press on him and to hear the word of God, **he** was standing by the lake of Gennesaret.

---

[7] Young, *Intermediate Greek*, 75.

John 6:24   ὅτε οὖν εἶδεν ὁ ὄχλος ὅτι Ἰησοῦς οὐκ ἔστιν ἐκεῖ οὐδὲ οἱ μαθηταὶ αὐτοῦ, ἐνέβησαν **αὐτοὶ** εἰς τὰ πλοιάρια καὶ ἦλθον εἰς Καφαρναοὺμ ζητοῦντες τὸν Ἰησοῦν.
Then when the crowd saw that Jesus was not there, nor were his disciples, **they** got into the boats and came to Capernaum, seeking Jesus.

(2) Oblique Cases   *ExSyn* 324–25

The almost exclusive use of the personal pronouns in the oblique cases (i.e., gen., dat., acc.) is simply to stand in the place of a noun or other nominal. This use of the pronoun can be called *anaphoric* in that it refers back to its antecedent. Two other uses deserve special mention.

(a) Normal Use: Anaphoric

John 4:7   ἔρχεται γυνή . . . λέγει **αὐτῇ** ὁ Ἰησοῦς
a woman came . . . Jesus said **to her**

Acts 27:32 ἀπέκοψαν οἱ στρατιῶται τὰ σχοινία τῆς σκάφης καὶ εἴασαν **αὐτὴν** ἐκπεσεῖν
the soldiers cut the ropes of the skiff and let **it** fall

(b) Possessive

The genitive of the personal pronoun frequently, if not usually, indicates possession. As such it could be treated in one of three ways: (a) as a subclass of the normal use of the personal pronoun because it, too, refers back to the antecedent; (b) as a possessive genitive, since the notion of possession is not a part of the stem but of the case ending; (c) as a possessive pronoun (see below). It is so routine that no examples need be given here. (See the chapter on the genitive case for examples and discussion.)

(c) Reflexive

The personal pronoun is rarely used for the reflexive pronoun in the NT. In such instances it has the force of *himself, herself, itself.*

John 2:24   Ἰησοῦς οὐκ ἐπίστευεν **αὐτὸν** αὐτοῖς
Jesus was not entrusting **himself** to them

Eph 2:15   ἵνα τοὺς δύο κτίσῃ ἐν **αὐτῷ** εἰς ἕνα καινὸν ἄνθρωπον
that he might create in **himself** one new man [instead of] the two

2. Demonstrative Pronouns   *ExSyn* 325–35

a. Definition and terms used. A demonstrative pronoun is a pointer, singling out an object in a special way. The three demonstrative pronouns used in the NT are οὗτος, ἐκεῖνος, and ὅδε. (This last one is rare, occurring only ten times.) οὗτος regularly refers to the *near* object ("this"), while ἐκεῖνος regularly refers to the *far* object ("that"). There are exceptions to this rule in that both demonstratives sometimes function like personal pronouns. As well, they sometimes "violate" the general rules of concord that pronouns normally follow. Such exceptions are often freighted with exegetical significance.

b. Functions

(1) REGULAR USE (AS DEMONSTRATIVES)   *ExSyn* 325–28

The near-far distinctions of οὗτος and ἐκεῖνος can refer either to that which is near/far in (a) the context, (b) the writer's mind, or (c) the space or time of the writer or audience. Sometimes these realms are in conflict: for example, what might be the nearest antecedent contextually might not be the nearest antecedent in the author's mind. A little imagination is sometimes needed to see the reason for the pronoun.

(a) Οὗτος (Proximity)

Matt 8:27   ποταπός ἐστιν **οὗτος** ὅτι καὶ οἱ ἄνεμοι καὶ ἡ θάλασσα αὐτῷ ὑπακούουσιν;
What sort of man is **this**, that even the winds and the sea obey him?

Acts 4:11   **οὗτός** ἐστιν ὁ λίθος, ὁ ἐξουθενηθεὶς ὑφ᾽ ὑμῶν τῶν οἰκοδόμων
this is the stone, which was rejected by you builders

> The reference is to Jesus Christ, mentioned in v. 10, even though Ἰησοῦ Χριστοῦ is not the nearest antecedent in the context. But since Ἰησοῦ Χριστοῦ is the nearest psychologically, it is the antecedent.

1 Pet 1:25   τὸ ῥῆμα κυρίου μένει εἰς τὸν αἰῶνα. **τοῦτο** δέ ἐστιν τὸ ῥῆμα τὸ εὐαγγελισθὲν εἰς ὑμᾶς.
The word of the Lord abides forever. And **this** is the word that was proclaimed to you.

1 John 5:20   **οὗτός** ἐστιν ὁ ἀληθινὸς θεὸς καὶ ζωὴ αἰώνιος
this is the true God and eternal life

> This text is exegetically problematic for a variety of reasons. What concerns us here is what the antecedent is. Many scholars see ὁ θεός rather than Χριστός as the antecedent, even though Χριστός is closer.[8]

(b) Ἐκεῖνος (Remoteness)

Matt 13:11   ὑμῖν δέδοται γνῶναι τὰ μυστήρια τῆς βασιλείας τῶν οὐρανῶν, **ἐκείνοις** δὲ οὐ δέδοται
to you it has been given to know the mysteries of the kingdom of heaven, but **to those** [people] it has not been given

---

[8] Cf. *ExSyn* 326–27 for discussion of this christologically important text.

Rom 6:21   τίνα καρπὸν εἴχετε τότε ἐφ᾽ οἷς νῦν ἐπαισχύνεσθε; τὸ γὰρ
τέλος **ἐκείνων** θάνατος.
What benefit did you get then from the things of which you are
now ashamed? For the end **of those things** is death.

> Although another pronoun would in this context fit just as
> nicely, evidently ἐκεῖνος is used because of the *temporal* distance
> between the readers and their former lifestyle (notice the "then"
> and "now").

Jas 4:15   ἐὰν ὁ κύριος θελήσῃ καὶ ζήσομεν καὶ ποιήσομεν τοῦτο ἢ
ἐκεῖνο
if the Lord wills, then we will live and do this or **that**

> The activity options, though unspecified, are listed in order of
> priority. The idea is, "If we can't do this, then we will do that."

(c) Ὅδε

This pronoun is used only ten times in the NT, eight of which are in the
expression τάδε λέγει. The force of this expression is always proleptic or antici-
patory: "He says the following [things]." The pronoun is used to add solemnity to
the prophetic utterance that follows.

Rev 2:18   **τάδε** λέγει ὁ υἱὸς τοῦ θεοῦ . . .
the Son of God says **these things** . . .

(2) FOR PERSONAL PRONOUNS   *ExSyn* 328–29

Although technically οὗτος and ἐκεῖνος are demonstrative pronouns, sometimes their demonstrative force is diminished. In such cases, they act as third person personal pronouns with a simple anaphoric force. This usage is especially
frequent in John, occurring more with ἐκεῖνος than with οὗτος.

John 5:6   **τοῦτον** ἰδὼν ὁ Ἰησοῦς   when Jesus saw **him**

John 11:29   **ἐκείνη** ὡς ἤκουσεν ἠγέρθη ταχὺ καὶ ἤρχετο πρὸς αὐτόν
when **she** heard [that Jesus had arrived], she rose quickly and
came to him

2 Tim 2:26   ἀνανήψωσιν ἐκ τῆς τοῦ διαβόλου παγίδος, ἐζωγρημένοι ὑπ᾽
αὐτοῦ εἰς τὸ **ἐκείνου** θέλημα
they might return to their senses [and escape] from the snare of
the devil, after having been captured by him to [do] **his** will

> The antecedents of αὐτοῦ and ἐκείνου are not certain.[9]

(3) UNUSUAL USES (FROM AN ENGLISH PERSPECTIVE)   *ExSyn* 329–35

The following categories of usage are unusual in that the pronoun seems to
be unnecessary (redundant), is lacking in concord with its antecedent, or is used
for some other reason. Most of the uses, however, are normal in terms of the pronoun having its full demonstrative force.

---

[9] Cf. *ExSyn* 329 for discussion.

(a) Pleonastic (Redundant)   ExSyn 329–30

Occasionally a demonstrative is used when no ambiguity would result if it had been deleted. This especially occurs in the nominative case: The demonstrative repeats a subject just mentioned (usually a substantival participle), even though the verb is not introduced until *after* the pronoun. In effect, the pronoun resumes the subject that is now separated from the verb by the participial construction.

John 5:11   ὁ ποιήσας με ὑγιῆ **ἐκεῖνός** μοι εἶπεν· ἆρον τὸν κράβαττόν σου καὶ περιπάτει

The one who made me well said to me, "Take up your mattress and walk!"

Rom 8:30   οὓς δὲ προώρισεν, **τούτους** καὶ ἐκάλεσεν· καὶ οὓς ἐκάλεσεν, **τούτους** καὶ ἐδικαίωσεν· οὓς δὲ ἐδικαίωσεν, **τούτους** καὶ ἐδόξασεν

and the ones whom he predestined, **these** he also called; and the ones whom he called, **these** he also justified; and the ones whom he justified, **these** he also glorified

> The usage here seems to be emphatic and not merely resumptive. The idea is that the very ones whom God predestined, called, and justified are also glorified. The compounding of pronouns thus has a dramatic effect: No one is lost between the eternal decree and the eternal state.

2 John 9   ὁ μένων ἐν τῇ διδαχῇ, **οὗτος** καὶ τὸν πατέρα καὶ τὸν υἱὸν ἔχει

the one who abides in this teaching has both the Father and the Son

(b) Constructio ad sensum   ExSyn 330–35

A small group of demonstrative pronouns involve a *natural* agreement with their antecedents that overrides strict grammatical concord. As such, they are illustrations of constructions according to sense (*constructio ad sensum*). This natural agreement may involve gender or, much more rarely, number. Frequently, the agreement is conceptual only, since the pronoun refers to a phrase or clause rather than a noun or other substantive. As might be expected, not a few of these instances are debatable and exegetically significant.

[1] GENDER   ExSyn 331–32

[a] Clear Illustrations

Acts 8:10   **οὗτός** ἐστιν ἡ δύναμις τοῦ θεοῦ
this [man] is the power of God

Rom 2:14   ὅταν ἔθνη τὰ μὴ νόμον ἔχοντα φύσει τὰ τοῦ νόμου ποιῶσιν, **οὗτοι** νόμον μὴ ἔχοντες ἑαυτοῖς εἰσιν νόμος
whenever Gentiles who do not have the law naturally practice the things of the law, **these**, not having law, are a law unto themselves

> The pronoun's antecedent is ἔθνη which, though neuter, refers to human beings.

[b] Debatable Example

John 15:26   ὅταν ἔλθῃ ὁ παράκλητος ὃν ἐγὼ πέμψω ὑμῖν παρὰ
τοῦ πατρός, τὸ πνεῦμα τῆς ἀληθείας ὃ παρὰ τοῦ
πατρὸς ἐκπορεύεται, **ἐκεῖνος** μαρτυρήσει περὶ ἐμοῦ
whenever the Comforter comes, whom I am sending
to you from the Father—the Spirit of truth
which/who proceeds from the Father—**that one** will
testify concerning me

> The use of ἐκεῖνος here is frequently regarded by
> students of the NT to be an affirmation of the per-
> sonality of the Spirit. Such an approach is based on
> the assumption that the antecedent of ἐκεῖνος is
> πνεῦμα. But this is erroneous because πνεῦμα is
> *appositional* to a masculine noun. The gender of
> ἐκεῖνος thus has nothing to do with the natural gen-
> der of πνεῦμα. The antecedent of ἐκεῖνος is πα-
> ράκλητος, not πνεῦμα. Cf. also John 14:26 and
> 16:13–14. Although one might argue that the Spirit's
> personality is in view in these passages, the view must
> be based on the nature of a παράκλητος and the
> things said about the Comforter, not on any sup-
> posed grammatical subtleties. Indeed, it is difficult to
> find *any* text in which πνεῦμα is grammatically
> referred to with the masculine gender.[10]

[2] NUMBER   *ExSyn 332–33*

2 John 7   πολλοὶ πλάνοι ἐξῆλθον εἰς τὸν κόσμον, οἱ μὴ ὁμολογοῦντες Ἰησοῦν Χριστὸν ἐρχόμενον ἐν σαρκί· **οὗτός**
ἐστιν ὁ πλάνος καὶ ὁ ἀντίχριστος.
Many deceivers have gone out into the world, the ones
who do not confess that Jesus Christ has come in the
flesh. **This** is the deceiver and the antichrist.

> The demonstrative has virtually a generic force here:
> "Such a person is the deceiver and the antichrist."

3 John 4   μειζοτέραν **τούτων** οὐκ ἔχω χαράν, ἵνα ἀκούω τὰ ἐμὰ
τέκνα ἐν τῇ ἀληθείᾳ περιπατοῦντα
I have no greater joy than **this**, to hear that my children
are walking in the truth.

> Although the postcedent to which τούτων refers is the
> content of the ἵνα clause, the pronoun would normally
> be expected to be in the singular.

---

[10] For a discussion both of John 15:26 and the other texts (John 14:26; 16:13–14; Eph
1:13–14; 2 Thess 2:6–7; and 1 John 5:7) that are used to prove the Spirit's personality from
Greek grammar, see *ExSyn* 331–33, 338–39.

[3] CONCEPTUAL ANTECEDENT/POSTCEDENT   *ExSyn* 333–35

The neuter of οὗτος is routinely used to refer to a phrase or clause. In such cases, the thing referred to is not a specific noun or substantive. The singular is used to refer both to an antecedent and a postcedent on a regular basis, while the plural is almost exclusively limited to retrospective uses. Certain formulaic phrases are often employed, such as διὰ τοῦτο, referring back to the previous argument, or μετὰ ταῦτα, referring to the previous events.

[a] Clear Illustrations

Luke 14:20   γυναῖκα ἔγημα καὶ διὰ **τοῦτο** οὐ δύναμαι ἐλθεῖν
I have [just] married a woman and for **this reason** I cannot come

Rom 6:6   **τοῦτο** γινώσκοντες ὅτι ὁ παλαιὸς ἡμῶν ἄνθρωπος συνεσταυρώθη
since we know **this**, that our old man has been cocrucified [with him]

[b] Debatable Example

Eph 2:8   τῇ γὰρ χάριτί ἐστε σεσῳσμένοι διὰ πίστεως· καὶ **τοῦτο** οὐκ ἐξ ὑμῶν, θεοῦ τὸ δῶρον
for by grace you are saved through faith; and **this** is not of yourselves, it is the gift of God

This is the most debated text in terms of the antecedent of the demonstrative pronoun, τοῦτο. The standard interpretations include: (1) "grace" as antecedent, (2) "faith" as antecedent, (3) the concept of a grace-by-faith salvation as antecedent, and (4) καὶ τοῦτο having an adverbial force with no antecedent ("and especially"). The issues here are complex and cannot be solved by grammar alone. Nevertheless, syntactical considerations do tend toward one of the latter two views.[11]

3. Relative Pronouns   *ExSyn* 335–45

a. Definition and terms used. Relative pronouns (ὅς and ὅστις) are so called because they *relate* to more than one clause. Typically, they are "hinge" words in that they both refer back to an antecedent in the previous clause and also function in some capacity in their own clause. In other words, *the relative pronoun (RP) agrees with its antecedent in gender and number, but its case is determined by the function it has in its own clause.*

b. Functions. The definite RP is ὅς; the indefinite RP is ὅστις. These two need to be treated separately as the major exegetical issues are different for each.

---

[11] For discussion of the options, see *ExSyn* 334–36.

(1) Ὅς   *ExSyn 336–43*

(a) Regular Use   *ExSyn 336–37*

ὅς is routinely used to link a noun or other substantive to the relative clause, which describes, clarifies, or restricts the meaning of the noun.

Matt 1:16   Ἰακὼβ ἐγέννησεν τὸν Ἰωσὴφ τὸν ἄνδρα Μαρίας, ἐξ **ἧς** ἐγεννήθη Ἰησοῦς
Jacob became the father of Joseph, the husband of Mary, by **whom** was born Jesus

John 1:26   μέσος ὑμῶν ἔστηκεν **ὃν** ὑμεῖς οὐκ οἴδατε
in your midst stands [one] **whom** you do not know

Acts 4:10   Ἰησοῦ Χριστοῦ ... **ὃν** ὑμεῖς ἐσταυρώσατε, **ὃν** ὁ θεὸς ἤγειρεν ἐκ νεκρῶν
Jesus Christ ... **whom** you have crucified, **whom** God has raised from the dead

(b) "Unusual" Uses   *ExSyn 337–43*

Not infrequently relative pronouns do not follow the basic rules of agreement. Sometimes the gender of the RP does not match that of the antecedent, usually because of sense agreement superseding syntactical agreement (*constructio ad sensum*). As you recall, the rules of agreement do not normally involve *case* for the RP. Yet sometimes the case of the relative is attracted to that of the antecedent (known as attraction or direct attraction); at other times, though much less often, the antecedent is drawn to the case of the RP (known as inverse or indirect attraction).

[1] GENDER   *ExSyn 337–38*

Phlm 10   παρακαλῶ σε περὶ τοῦ ἐμοῦ τέκνου, **ὃν** ἐγέννησα ἐν τοῖς δεσμοῖς
I urge you concerning my child, **of whom** I have become a father in my bonds

> Although τέκνον is neuter, the RP is masculine because of natural gender.

1 Cor 15:10 χάριτι θεοῦ εἰμι **ὅ** εἰμι
by the grace of God I am **what** I am

> The antecedent is implicit, but it is naturally masculine. By using the neuter, Paul is not affirming his person as much as his office of apostleship.

[2] CASE   *ExSyn 338–39*

[a] Attraction (Direct Attraction)

The case of the RP, unlike its gender and number, usually has no relation to that of the antecedent, since it is normally determined by the function it has in its own clause. Sometimes, however, it is attracted to the case of the antecedent.

Matt 24:50   ἐν ὥρᾳ ᾗ οὐ γινώσκει
in an hour **which** he does not know

[b] Inverse Attraction (Indirect Attraction)

Inverse attraction takes place when the antecedent is attracted to
the case of the RP.

Mark 12:10   λίθον ὃν ἀπεδοκίμασαν οἱ οἰκοδομοῦντες, οὗτος
ἐγενήθη . . .
the stone **which** the builders rejected, this has
become . . .

[3] ANTECEDENT COMPLEXITIES   *ExSyn* 339–43

[a] Omission of Antecedent   *ExSyn* 339–42

The antecedent may be omitted for a variety of reasons in Greek.
For example, the RP may incorporate a *demonstrative* pronoun, in
which case the object is clear enough from the context. Less frequent,
but no less significant exegetically, are instances of *poetic* material woven
into the fabric of a discourse (see discussion of 1 Tim 3:16 below).

{1} EMBEDDED DEMONSTRATIVE[12]   *ExSyn* 340

John 4:18   πέντε ἄνδρας ἔσχες καὶ νῦν ὃν ἔχεις οὐκ ἔστιν σου
ἀνήρ
you have had five husbands and **[the one] whom** you
now have is not your husband

Heb 5:8   καίπερ ὢν υἱός, ἔμαθεν ἀφ᾽ ὧν ἔπαθεν τὴν ὑπακοήν
although he was a son, he learned obedience from
[those things] which he suffered

{2} POETRY   *ExSyn* 340–42

Most scholars now see hymn fragments here and there in the NT,
such as Phil 2:6–11; Col 1:15–20; 1 Tim 3:16; Heb 1:3–4. Frequently,
such texts begin with a relative clause woven into the syntax of the sur-
rounding prose discourse. Indeed, one of the standard features of
Greek poetry is the introductory use of the relative pronoun. Sometimes, however, the RP has no antecedent because the hymnic frag-
ment is introduced without syntactic connection.

1 Tim 3:16   καὶ ὁμολογουμένως μέγα ἐστὶν τὸ τῆς εὐσεβείας
μυστήριον·
ὃς ἐφανερώθη ἐν σαρκί,
ἐδικαιώθη ἐν πνεύματι,
ὤφθη ἀγγέλοις,
ἐκηρύχθη ἐν ἔθνεσιν,
ἐπιστεύθη ἐν κόσμῳ,
ἀνελήμφθη ἐν δόξῃ.

---

[12] For discussion of the exegetical difficulties in 1 Pet 1:6, see *ExSyn* 340–41.

and confessedly great is the mystery of godliness:
> **who** was manifested in the flesh,
> vindicated in the spirit,
> appeared to angels,
> proclaimed among Gentiles,
> believed on in the world,
> taken up to glory.

The rhythmic patterns of this text are obvious: six lines of parallel passive verbs, followed by parallel (ἐν +) dat. constructions. These features, coupled with an introductory ὅς, are signatures of poetry. To seek outside the hymn for an antecedent to ὅς, as some have done, is an unnecessary expedient, which, in fact, misreads the genre and misunderstands the force of τὸ τῆς εὐσεβείας μυστήριον.[13]

[b] Adverbial/Conjunctive Uses   ExSyn 342–43

The RP is often used after a preposition. Frequently, such prepositional phrases have an adverbial or conjunctive force. In such instances, the RP either has no antecedent or else its antecedent is conceptual, not grammatical.[14]

Luke 12:3   **ἀνθ᾽ ὧν** ὅσα ἐν τῇ σκοτίᾳ εἴπατε ἐν τῷ φωτὶ ἀκουσθήσεται
therefore, whatever you said in the dark will be heard in the light

Acts 26:12   **ἐν οἷς** πορευόμενος εἰς τὴν Δαμασκὸν
meanwhile/therefore, when I traveled to Damascus
> The prepositional expression could either point back to the preceding clause in a general way (="therefore," "because of these things"), or it could be temporal ("meanwhile," "in the meantime"). Cf. also Luke 12:1 (where ἐν οἷς is clearly temporal).

Rom 5:12   εἰς πάντας ἀνθρώπους ὁ θάνατος διῆλθεν, **ἐφ᾽ ᾧ** πάντες ἥμαρτον
death passed to all people, **because** all sinned
> The prepositional phrase here is often debated. It is possible that ᾧ refers back to "one man" (ἑνὸς ἀνθρώπου) mentioned earlier in the verse. If so, the idea is either "all sinned in one man," or "all sinned because of one man." But if ἐφ᾽ ᾧ functions as a conjunction, it does not look back at any antecedent, but explains how death passed to all.[15]

---

[13] For more discussion of this text, see *ExSyn* 341–42.
[14] For a discussion of the antecedent of ἐν ᾧ in 1 Pet 3:19, see *ExSyn* 343–44.
[15] For more discussion of this passage, see *ExSyn* 342–43.

(2) Ὅστις   ExSyn 343

(a) General Use

In general, ὅστις is indefinite while ὅς is definite (though ὅς used with ἄν also has an indefinite force). All but a few instances are in the nominative case. Although traditionally used, "indefinite" is not the best choice of terms for this pronoun. The notion needs to be defined broadly: It is typically either *generic* in that the RP focuses on the whole class (thus, "whoever" = "everyone who") or *qualitative* in that the RP focuses on the nature or essence of the person or thing in view. The first example below is generic and the second is qualitative.

Luke 14:27   **ὅστις** οὐ βαστάζει τὸν σταυρὸν ἑαυτοῦ καὶ ἔρχεται ὀπίσω μου, οὐ δύναται εἶναί μου μαθητής
whoever does not bear his own cross and come after me cannot be my disciple

Matt 7:15   προσέχετε ἀπὸ τῶν ψευδοπροφητῶν, **οἵτινες** ἔρχονται πρὸς ὑμᾶς ἐν ἐνδύμασιν προβάτων, ἔσωθεν δέ εἰσιν λύκοι ἅρπαγες
beware of false prophets, **the very ones who** come to you in sheep's clothing, but inside are ravenous wolves

(b) Confusion with ὅς

Not infrequently, ὅστις seems to function just like ὅς in the NT in that it has a definite referent in view. In such places there is little or no discernible difference in the force of the two pronouns. This is especially common in Luke-Acts.

Luke 9:30   ἄνδρες δύο συνελάλουν αὐτῷ, **οἵτινες** ἦσαν Μωϋσῆς καὶ Ἠλίας
two men were conversing with him, **who** were Moses and Elijah

Acts 16:12   κἀκεῖθεν εἰς Φιλίππους, **ἥτις** ἐστὶν πρώτης μερίδος τῆς Μακεδονίας πόλις
and from there to Philippi, **which** is the leading city of the district of Macedonia

4. Interrogative Pronouns   ExSyn 345–46

a. Definition and terms used. An interrogative pronoun asks a question. The most common interrogative pronoun is τίς, τί, typically asking an *identifying* question ("Who?" or "What?"). ποῖος, used far more sparingly in the NT, normally asks a *qualitative* question ("What sort?"), while πόσος asks a *quantitative* question ("How much?").

b. Functions of τίς. Τίς is used to introduce both direct and indirect questions. As such, it is used both substantivally (as a true pronoun) and adjectivally.

The neuter is also used adverbially ("Why?"). For the most part, τίς asks an identifying question, especially when a person is in view. But it is also occasionally used to ask a categorical or qualitative question ("What sort?").

Mark 8:27   τίνα με λέγουσιν οἱ ἄνθρωποι εἶναι;
Who do people say that I am?

Matt 5:46   τίνα μισθὸν ἔχετε;
What reward do you have?

Acts 1:11   τί ἑστήκατε ἐμβλέποντες εἰς τὸν οὐρανόν;
Why do you stand, gazing into heaven?

c. Functions of ποῖος and πόσος. Ποῖος and πόσος are normally qualitative and quantitative interrogative pronouns respectively: ποῖος asks "What sort?" and πόσος asks "How much?"

Mark 11:28   ἐν **ποίᾳ** ἐξουσίᾳ ταῦτα ποιεῖς;
By **what kind of** authority do you do these things?

Luke 16:7   σὺ **πόσον** ὀφείλεις;
How much do you owe?

5. Indefinite Pronoun

ExSyn 347

a. Definition and terms used. The indefinite pronoun (τις, τι) is used to introduce a member of a class without further identification. It is used both substantivally (as a true pronoun) and adjectivally. It can be translated *anyone, someone, a certain*, or simply *a(n)*. The first two examples below are substantival and the third is adjectival.

b. Illustrations

Matt 16:24   εἴ **τις** θέλει ὀπίσω μου ἐλθεῖν, ἀπαρνησάσθω ἑαυτὸν
if **anyone** wants to come after me, let him deny himself

Heb 3:4   πᾶς οἶκος κατασκευάζεται ὑπό **τινος**
every house is built by **someone**

Phil 2:1   εἴ **τις** παράκλησις ἐν Χριστῷ
if there is **any** encouragement in Christ

6. Possessive "Pronouns" (Adjectives)

ExSyn 348

a. Definition and terms used. Greek does not have a distinct possessive pronoun. Instead, it usually employs either the possessive adjective (ἐμός, σός, ἡμέτερος, ὑμέτερος) or the genitive of the personal pronoun.[16] The one *lexicalizes* possession (i.e., the notion of possession is part of the lexical root); the other *grammaticalizes* possession (i.e., the notion of possession is part of the inflection).

---

[16] The inclusion, then, of the possessive adjective in the semantic category of possession is really an English way of looking at things.

No detailed treatment needs to be given since (a) "possessive pronoun" is not a bona fide Greek category, and (b) the notion of possession can be examined either via the lexicon or other sections of this grammar.

b. How possession is expressed. Possession can be expressed in four ways in the New Testament:

- by the possessive adjectives
- by the genitive of the personal pronoun
- by the article
- by ἴδιος.

7. Intensive Pronoun   *ExSyn* 348–50

a. Definition and term used. The intensive pronoun, αὐτός, is by far the most common pronoun used in the NT. Technically, however, as an intensive (with the sense of *–self*) it is relatively infrequent. The predominant function of αὐτός is as a stand-in for the third person personal pronoun in oblique cases (see above). What will be illustrated below are the two main categories of usage *other* than as a personal pronoun.

b. Functions

(1) As an Intensive Pronoun

When αὐτός is in *predicate* position to an articular noun (or to an anarthrous proper name), it has the force of *himself, herself, itself*, etc. αὐτός can also bear this force when it stands alone, either as the subject of the verb or in any of the oblique cases. In general, the intensive use of αὐτός is intended "to emphasize identity. It is the demonstrative force intensified."[17]

Mark 12:36   **αὐτὸς** Δαυὶδ εἶπεν ἐν τῷ πνεύματι
David **himself** spoke in the Spirit

John 2:24   **αὐτὸς** Ἰησοῦς οὐκ ἐπίστευεν **αὐτὸν** αὐτοῖς διὰ τὸ **αὐτὸν** γινώσκειν πάντας
Jesus **himself** was not entrusting **himself** to them, because **he himself** knew all men

> This text affords an interesting and insightful example. It is first used as an intensifier to the subject, then as direct object (with an intensive-reflexive force). On the surface, the pronoun looks redundant, but its very repetition contrasts Jesus with the rest of humanity, setting him apart in his sinlessness.

(2) As an Identifying Adjective

When modifying an articular substantive in the *attributive* position, αὐτός is used as an identifying adjective. As such, it is translated *same*.

---

[17] Dana-Mantey, 129.

Luke 23:40   τῷ **αὐτῷ** κρίματι   in the **same** judgment

Jas 3:10   ἐκ τοῦ **αὐτοῦ** στόματος ἐξέρχεται εὐλογία καὶ κατάρα
from the **same** mouth come forth blessing and cursing

8. Reflexive Pronouns   *ExSyn 350–51*

a. Definition and terms used. The reflexive pronouns are ἐμαυτοῦ (*of myself*), σεαυτοῦ (*of yourself*), ἑαυτοῦ (*of himself*), ἑαυτῶν (*of themselves*). The force of the reflexive is *frequently* to indicate that the subject is also the object of the action of the verb. On a broader scale, the reflexive pronoun is used to *highlight the participation of the subject* in the verbal action, as direct object, indirect object, intensifier, etc.

b. Illustrations

Matt 4:6   εἰ υἱὸς εἶ τοῦ θεοῦ, βάλε **σεαυτὸν** κάτω
if you are the Son of God, throw **yourself** down

Mark 5:30   ὁ Ἰησοῦς ἐπιγνοὺς ἐν **ἑαυτῷ**
Jesus knowing within **himself**

Rom 5:8   συνίστησιν τὴν **ἑαυτοῦ** ἀγάπην εἰς ἡμᾶς ὁ θεός
God demonstrated **his own** love for us

9. Reciprocal Pronouns   *ExSyn 351*

a. Definition and terms used. The reciprocal pronoun, ἀλλήλων (*of one another*), is used to indicate an interchange between two or more groups. It is thus always *plural* and, like the reflexive pronoun, occurs only in the oblique cases. One frequently finds this pronoun in paraenetic contexts, basing the exhortation on the organic connection that believers have with the risen Christ.

b. Illustrations

Mark 9:50   εἰρηνεύετε ἐν **ἀλλήλοις**
be at peace with **one another**

John 13:34   ἀγαπᾶτε **ἀλλήλους**
love **one another**

Eph 4:25   ἐσμὲν **ἀλλήλων** μέλη
we are members **of one another**

Lexico-Syntactic Categories: Major Terms   *ExSyn 352–54*

The previous section approached the pronouns from a *semantic priority* grid. This section begins with a *formal priority*. The rationale for this is that it is more user-friendly to the student who can recognize certain words in the text as being pronouns, but may not be able to articulate to which semantic category they belong. This section, however, is little more than an outline of uses. When the student notices the various semantic options for a particular form, he or she should turn to the relevant discussions in the previous section. The semantic uses are listed in order of frequency for each word.

1. Ἀλλήλων

   Instances: 100
   Use: Reciprocal pronoun

2. Αὐτός

   Instances: 5596
   Uses

   • Personal pronoun (usually third person)
   • Possessive pronoun (gen. case)
   • Intensive pronoun (including identifying adjective)

3. Ἑαυτοῦ

   Instances: 319
   Use: Reflexive pronoun

4. Ἐγώ

   Instances: 1804
   Uses

   • Personal pronoun
   • Possessive pronoun (gen. case)

5. Ἐκεῖνος

   Instances: 265
   Uses

   • Demonstrative pronoun
   • Personal pronoun

6. Ἐμαυτοῦ

   Instances: 37
   Use: Reflexive pronoun

7. Ἡμεῖς

   Instances: 864
   Uses

   • Personal pronoun
   • Possessive pronoun (gen. case)

8. Ὅδε

Instances: 10
Use: Demonstrative pronoun

9. Ὅς

Instances: 1406
Use: Relative pronoun (definite)

10. Ὅστις

Instances: 145
Use: Relative pronoun (indefinite)

11. Οὗτος

Instances: 1387
Uses

- Demonstrative pronoun
- Personal pronoun

12. Ποῖος

Instances: 33
Use: Interrogative pronoun (qualitative)

13. Πόσος

Instances: 27
Use: Interrogative pronoun (quantitative)

14. Σεαυτοῦ

Instances: 43
Use: Reflexive pronoun

15. Σύ

Instances: 1067
Use

- Personal pronoun
- Possessive pronoun (gen. case)

16. Τίς

Instances: 546
Use: Interrogative pronoun

17. Τις

Instances: 543
Use: Indefinite pronoun

18. Ὑμεῖς

Instances: 1840
Use

- Personal pronoun
- Possessive pronoun (gen. case)

The relative frequencies of these pronouns are visually displayed in the chart below.

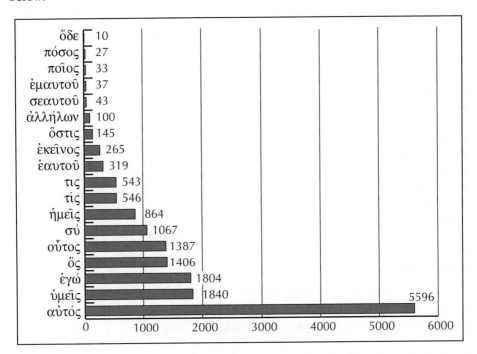

Chart 35
Frequency of Pronoun Terms in the New Testament

The Prepositions[1]
Overview of Prepositions

General Considerations **160**
  1. The Nature of Prepositions 160
  2. Spatial Functions of Prepositions 161
  3. Prepositions and Simple Case Constructions. 162
  4. Influence of Koine Greek 164

Specific Prepositions. **165**
  1. Ἀνά. 165
  2. Ἀντί. 165
➡ 3. Ἀπό 165
➡ 4. Διά 166
➡ 5. Εἰς 166
➡ 6. Ἐκ 166
➡ 7. Ἐν 167
➡ 8. Ἐπί. 168
➡ 9. Κατά 169
➡10. Μετά 169
➡11. Παρά 169
➡12. Περί 170
  13. Πρό 170
➡14. Πρός 170
➡15. Σύν. 171
➡16. Ὑπέρ 171
➡17. Ὑπό 173

General Considerations[2]

ExSyn 356–63

1. The Nature of Prepositions

ExSyn 356–57

Prepositions are, in some respects, extended adverbs. That is, they frequently modify verbs and tell how, when, where, etc. But, unlike adverbs, they govern a noun and hence can give more information than a mere adverb can.

There are exceptions to the adverbial force of prepositions. Some function adjectivally at times. In general, the prepositions that take accusative and dative case objects function adverbially, while those that take a genitive case object *often*

---

[1] See *ExSyn* 355–89.

[2] Although several intermediate grammars have a detailed chapter on the prepositions, our conviction is that grammars do much unnecessary duplication with lexica. Since anyone using this text should no doubt own a copy of BAGD, we felt that the best approach in this work is to provide things not normally accessible in a lexicon: general principles, the *basic* uses with labels consistent with our case categories, and exegetical discussions. We have given a selective treatment of lexico-syntactic categories to urge students to use BAGD and other tools.

function adjectivally. All of this is in keeping with the simple case uses: The accusative and dative are usually connected to a verb and the genitive is usually connected to a noun.

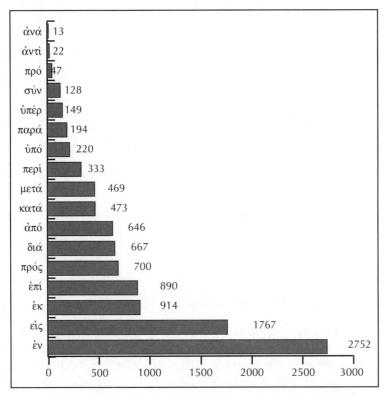

Chart 36
Frequencies of Prepositions in the New Testament[3]

2. Spatial Functions of Prepositions   *ExSyn 358–60*

a. In General

The diagram on the following page may prove helpful in understanding the local or spatial functions that prepositions have at times; it is something of a "rough and ready" guide. The circle represents the object of the preposition.

b. Motion, State, Prepositions, and Verbs[4]

One observation to be made about prepositions is whether they are stative or transitive. That is, does a given preposition suggest merely a *state* or does it imply *motion*? The chart on the next page indicates *transitive* prepositions by the use of arrows, while *stative* prepositions are displayed with simple lines having no arrows.

---

[3] This list does not include improper prepositions, so-called because they cannot be prefixed to a verb.

[4] Cf. *ExSyn* 360 for discussion of John 1:18.

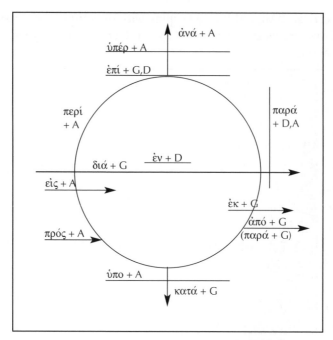

Chart 37
The Spatial Functions of Prepositions

All is not as it seems, however. A stative preposition can occur with a verb of motion, just as a transitive preposition can occur with a stative verb. In such instances, how are we to interpret the data? Note, for example, the uses of εἰς with a stative verb. εἰς generally has the meaning of movement *into from without*. However, when it is used with a stative verb, such as τηρέω, κάθημαι, εἰμί, etc., the idea of *motion* is negated by the stative nature of the verb. On the other hand, πιστεύω + ἐν is the equivalent of πιστεύω + εἰς (cf. Mark 1:15; John 3:15).[5] The idea is "put one's faith *into*" even though ἐν is used.

The general principle to follow is that *the verb takes priority: Stative verbs override transitive prepositions*, and *transitive verbs override stative prepositions*. In other words, just as the preposition virtually governs the noun, so also verbs govern the force of prepositions. There are few exceptions to this general rule.[6]

3. Prepositions and Simple Case Constructions   ExSyn 360–62

a. Do Prepositions Govern or Merely Clarify?

Older NT grammars generally denied that prepositions govern their cases. For example, Dana and Mantey argue,

---

[5] However, in some texts ἐν with πιστεύω indicates the location where belief takes place rather than the object of belief (e.g., Rom 10:9; 1 Thess 1:7; 1 Tim 3:16).

[6] The most common exception to this rule is the use of εἰμί with ἐκ. In this instance, the preposition still retains its transitive force. E.g., **ἐκ** Ναζαρὲτ δύναταί τι ἀγαθὸν εἶναι; ("Can

> It is incorrect ... to say that prepositions *govern* cases [italics mine]. But it is true that as cases limit and define the relations of verbs to substantives, so also prepositions help to express more exactly and effectively the very distinctions for which cases were created.... [7]

This statement is generally accurate for *classical* Greek, but not Koine. Some of the case uses in the classical period were quite subtle. As the language progressed in the Koine period, such subtleties were replaced with more explicit statements. For example, the genitive of separation, a common idiom in the Attic dialect, is rare in Koine. It has been replaced, by and large, by ἀπό + genitive. Likewise, ἐκ + genitive has replaced for the most part the genitive of source. Hence, the prepositional phrase does not always communicate more *explicitly* what a naked case could communicate; sometimes it communicates something *other* than what a simple case would normally communicate. In this respect it is legitimate to speak of prepositions as *governing* nouns.[8]

b. Prepositions Vs. Simple Case Constructions

Whenever any of the oblique cases follows a preposition, you should examine the use of the *preposition*, rather than the case usage, to determine the possible nuances involved.

The beginning exegete often has a tendency to treat the use of a case after a preposition as though there were no preposition present. That is, he or she attempts to determine the nuance of the case according to the categories for that case rather than according to the categories for the preposition. This is imprecise exegesis for it assumes that the preposition does not alter how the case can be used. But in Hellenistic Greek, because of the tendency toward explicitness, the preposition increasingly gained independent value. Thus, the preposition does not just clarify the case's usage; often, it *alters* it.

To restate and summarize: Prepositions are used with cases either to *clarify*, *strengthen*, or *alter* the basic case usage. For example, ἐν + the dative is very frequently, if not most frequently, used to strengthen the idea of sphere. ἐκ + the

---

any good thing *be* **from** Nazareth?") in John 1:46. In this expression the combination of preposition and verb is virtually equivalent to "Can any good thing *come* **from** Nazareth?"

[7] Dana-Mantey, 97–98 (§101). Robertson says, "The notion, therefore, that prepositions 'govern' cases must be discarded definitely" (*Grammar*, 554). Cf. also Moule, *Idiom Book*, 48. More recently, Porter, *Idioms*, argues this same point (140).

[8] Young offers the helpful insight that there are two schools of thought about prepositions: One school views them as simply clarifying the meaning of the cases, often with the result that the prepositions are not treated separately from case uses; the other school sees the preposition as the dominant element, with the result that prepositions deserve their own special treatment (Young, *Intermediate Greek*, 85). Young correctly takes the latter approach, recognizing that "in koine Greek the preposition gained more independent force, while the case lost some of its significance" (ibid.). An example of the former view is to be found in Brooks-Winbery, 2–59, where they entirely subsume the discussion of prepositions under case uses (although an appendix isolating prepositional uses is added [60–64]).

genitive often clarifies that source is the idea meant (but in Koine Greek a gen. of source is scarce). When ἀπό is used to indicate a temporal nuance, the idea is radically altered from the use of the naked genitive for time (the former speaking of the *extent* of time, stressing the beginning; the latter, speaking of the *kind* of time). Therefore, *the use of a particular preposition with a particular case **never** exactly parallels—either in category possibilities or in relative frequency of nuances—the use of a case without a preposition.*

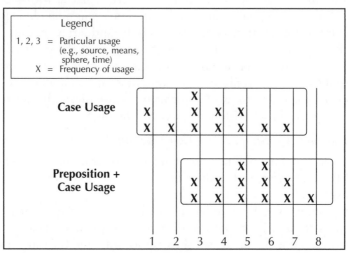

Chart 38
Semantic Overlap Between Simple Case and Preposition + Case

4. Influence of Koine Greek   *ExSyn* 362–63

In addition to the points mentioned above about preposition + case uses vs. simple case uses, Hellenistic Greek impacts prepositional uses in two other ways.

a. Overlapping Usage

Besides the tendency toward explicitness (in which prepositions are used increasingly in Koine rather than naked cases), there is also a tendency toward *laxity* in meaning. That is, many prepositions in Hellenistic Greek have overlapping semantic domains. This finds an analogy with modern English. "This morning, I jumped **in** a pool," for most English-speakers, indicates entrance into the pool, rather than an activity already within it ("I jumped **into** a pool" rather than "I jumped **within** a pool").

The overlap, however, does not flow equally in both directions. In some instances, one preposition encroaches on the meaning of another without a reciprocal laxity (such as with ὑπέρ in the place of ἀντί). In other instances, the overlap goes in both directions (e.g., εἰς and ἐν), but even here there is no equilibrium. (The significance of this point will be developed under ὑπέρ.) The most frequent examples involve ἐκ and ἀπό, εἰς and ἐν, and ὑπέρ and περί.

b. Root Fallacy

As lexicographers have long noted, the root meaning of a word is not necessarily an accurate guide to the meaning of the word in later literature. The same is true of morpho-syntactic categories: one ought not look for some kind of invariant meaning that is always present with the preposition. The meaning of words changes in time. Further, a word has a *field* of meaning rather than a *point*. Such is no less true for prepositions than for other words.[9]

Specific Prepositions   *ExSyn 364–89*

This section *outlines* the prepositions according to their basic uses and discusses a few exegetically significant texts.[10] For a more detailed treatment of the various uses of the prepositions, consult especially BAGD. The prepositions to be discussed will only be those that occur independently (i.e., not prefixed to a verb) and are considered by BAGD as "proper" prepositions.

1. Ἀνά   *ExSyn 364*

Basic uses (with accusative only)

- Distributive: *in the midst of* (ἀνὰ μέσον + gen.); *each, apiece* (with numbers)
- Spatial (in composition with verbs): *up, motion upwards.*

2. Ἀντί   *ExSyn 364–68*

Basic uses (with genitive only)

- Substitution: *instead of, in place of*[11]
- Exchange/Equivalence: *for, as, in the place of.* The notions of exchange and substitution are similar, often blending into each other.
- Cause (debatable): *because of*

➡3. Ἀπό   *ExSyn 368*

Basic uses (with genitive only). The basic force of ἀπό in classical Greek was *separation from.* "In the NT it has encroached on the domain of Att. ἐκ, ὑπό, παρά, and the gen. of separation.... "[12]

---

[9] Some grammars still seem to embrace a root meaning for each preposition. E.g., Porter, *Idioms*, 142, argues that "most prepositions have a fundamental sense related to being situated in, moving toward or moving away from a location." This leads him to the conclusion that μονογενὴς θεὸς ὁ ὢν εἰς τὸν κόλπον τοῦ πατρός in John 1:18 means "[the] only begotten [*sic*] God who is directed toward the bosom of the father") (ibid., 153).

[10] For more discussions of exegetically significant passages as well as more detailed discussions of those discussed here, see *ExSyn 364–89, passim.*

[11] For discussion of the debates about the substitutionary sense of ἀντί, especially in relation to the death of Christ, see *ExSyn 364–68.*

[12] BAGD, s.v. ἀπό, 86.

- Separation (from place or person): *away from*
- Source: *from, out of*
- Cause: *because of*
- Partitive (i.e., substituting for a partitive gen.): *of*
- Agency (rare): *by, from*

➡4. Διά   *ExSyn 368–69*

Basic uses (with genitive and accusative)

a. With genitive

- Agency: *by, through*
- Means: *through*
- Spatial: *through*
- Temporal: *through(out), during*

b. With accusative

- Cause: *because of, on account of, for the sake of*
- Spatial (rare): *through*

➡5. Εἰς   *ExSyn 369–71*

Basic uses (with accusative only)[13]

- Spatial: *into, toward, in*
- Temporal: *for, throughout*
- Purpose: *for, in order to, to*
- Result: *so that, with the result that*
- Reference/Respect: *with respect to, with reference to*
- Advantage: *for*
- Disadvantage: *against*
- In the place of ἐν (with its various nuances)

➡6. Ἐκ   *ExSyn 371–72*

Basic uses (with genitive only). In general, ἐκ has the force of *from, out of, away from, of.*

- Source: *out of, from*
- Separation: *away from, from*
- Temporal: *from, from [this point] . . . on*
- Cause: *because of*
- Partitive (i.e., substituting for a partitive gen.): *of*
- Means: *by, from*

---

[13] For a discussion of the use of εἰς in Acts 2:38, cf. *ExSyn* 369–71.

➡ **7.** ᾽Εν

a. Basic uses (with dative only). ᾽Εν is the workhorse of prepositions in the NT, occurring more frequently and in more varied situations than any other. It overlaps with the simple dative uses to a great extent, but not entirely. The following categories are for the most part painted with broad strokes.[14]

- Spatial/Sphere: *in* (and various other translations)
- Temporal: *in, within, when, while, during*
- Association (often close personal relationship): *with*
- Cause: *because of*
- Instrumental: *by, with*
- Reference/Respect: *with respect to / with reference to*
- Manner: *with*
- Thing Possessed: *with* (in the sense of *which possesses*)
- Standard (=Dative of Rule): *according to the standard of*
- As an equivalent for εἰς (with verbs of motion)

b. Significant passages involving ἐν. As varied as the uses of ἐν are, sometimes it is considered even more elastic than it really is. The following discussion focuses on a few passages in which the preposition has been viewed as expressing *agency* or *content*.[15]

(1) ᾽Εν + Dative for Personal Agency?

Some have suggested that either the naked dative or ἐν + the dative can express personal agency in the NT.[16] However, once a clear definition is given for personal agency, this will be seen to be a rare or nonexistent category. When ἐν + the dative expresses the idea of means (a *different* category), the instrument is used *by an agent.* When agency is indicated, the agent so named is not used by another, but is the one who uses an instrument.[17] Thus, ἐν + dative to express *means* can be (and often is) used of *persons*, though they are conceived of as impersonal (i.e., used as an instrument by someone else).

There are very few *clear* examples of the dative of agency in the NT, and all examples involve a perfect passive verb. The slightly different phenomenon of ἐν + the dative is considered by many to express agency on a rare occasion. Yet no

---

[14] Even BAGD (s.v. ἐν, 258) recognizes the difficulty of cataloging every usage: "The uses of this prep. are so many-sided, and oft. so easily confused, that a strictly systematic treatment is impossible. It must suffice to list the main categories, which will help in establishing the usage in individual cases." BAGD's treatment is nevertheless extensive (258–61).

[15] For a more detailed discussion of these texts, see *ExSyn* 373–76.

[16] See "Dative of Agency" in the chapter on the dative case for a discussion of other passages, especially those involving πνεύματι.

[17] It may be noted here that an intermediate agent, usually expressed by διά + the genitive, is an agent who acts *on behalf of* another or in the place of another. This agent is not, strictly speaking, *used* by another as an instrument would be.

unambiguous examples are forthcoming. Thus what can be said about the dative of agency can also be said of ἐν + the dative to express agent: it is *rare*, at best.

Mark 1:8   αὐτὸς δὲ βαπτίσει ὑμᾶς **ἐν** πνεύματι ἁγίῳ
but he shall baptize you **with** the Holy Spirit

> Here it is obvious that Christ is the agent [since αὐτός is the subject], and the Holy Spirit is the means [and perhaps sphere] that the Lord uses to baptize.

1 Cor 12:13   γὰρ **ἐν** ἑνὶ πνεύματι ἡμεῖς πάντες εἰς ἓν σῶμα ἐβαπτίσθημεν
for **by** one Spirit we all were baptized into one body

> Our contention is that this is an illustration of ἐν used for *means*. By calling "Spirit" means here does *not* deny the personality of the Holy Spirit. Rather, the Holy Spirit is the instrument that Christ uses to baptize, even though he is a person. Since πνεύματι ἁγίῳ clearly indicated means in Mark 1:8 (as in several other passages dealing with Spirit-baptism), it is surely not unreasonable to see "Spirit" as the means here.

> Furthermore, if the Holy Spirit is the agent in this text, there is a theological problem: When is the prophecy of Mark 1:8 fulfilled? When would *Christ* baptize with the Holy Spirit? Because of the grammatical improbability of πνεύματι expressing agent in 1 Cor 12:13, it is better to see it as means *and* as the fulfillment of Mark 1:8. Thus, Christ is the unnamed agent. This also renders highly improbable one popular interpretation, viz., that there are *two* Spirit baptisms in the NT, one at salvation and one later.

(2) Ἐν + Dative for Content?

Rare is the usage of the simple dative to denote the content that is used by a verb of *filling*.[18] For ἐν + the dative, this usage is debatable. Normally, a verb of filling takes a *genitive* of content. We know of no clear examples in biblical Greek in which ἐν + the dative indicates content. We should, therefore, seek some other nuance in such instances, as in Eph 5:18 (πληροῦσθε **ἐν** πνεύματι [be filled {with/by/in} the Spirit]).

➡8.   Ἐπί   *ExSyn* 376

Basic uses (with genitive, dative, and accusative)

a. With Genitive

- Spatial: *on, upon, at, near*
- Temporal: *in the time of, during*
- Cause: *on the basis of*

---

[18] See "Dative of Content" in the chapter on the dative case for discussion.

b. With Dative

- Spatial: *on, upon, against, at, near*
- Temporal: *at, at the time of, during*
- Cause: *on the basis of*

c. With Accusative

- Spatial: *on, upon, to, up to, against*
- Temporal: *for, over a period of*

➡**9.** Κατά   *ExSyn 376–77*

Basic uses (with genitive and accusative)

a.With Genitive

- Spatial: *down from, throughout*
- Opposition: *against*
- Source: *from*

b. With Accusative

- Standard: *in accordance with, corresponding to*
- Spatial: *along, through* (extension); *toward, up to* (direction)
- Temporal: *at, during*
- Distributive: *"indicating the division of a greater whole into individual parts"*[19]
- Purpose: *for the purpose of*
- Reference/Respect: *with respect to, with reference to*

➡**10.** Μετά   *ExSyn 377–78*

Basic uses (with genitive and accusative)

a. With Genitive

- Association/Accompaniment: *with, in company with*
- Spatial: *with, among*
- Manner (Attendant Circumstance): *with*

b. With Accusative

- Temporal: *after, behind*
- Spatial (rare): *after, behind*

➡**11.** Παρά   *ExSyn 378*

Basic uses (with genitive, dative, and accusative)

a. With Genitive
Generally, the idea is *from (the side of)* (almost always with a personal object).

- Source/Spatial: *from*
- Agency: *from, by*

---

[19] BAGD, s.v. κατά II.3 (406).

b. With Dative

In general, the dative uses suggest *proximity* or nearness.

- Spatial: *near, beside*
- Sphere: *in the sight of, before* (someone)
- Association: *with* (someone/something)
- Virtually equivalent to simple dative

c. With Accusative

- Spatial: *by, alongside of, near, on*
- Comparison: *in comparison to, more than*
- Opposition: *against, contrary to*

➡12. Περί   *ExSyn 379*

Basic uses (with genitive and accusative)

a. With Genitive

- Reference: *concerning*
- Advantage/Representation: *on behalf of, for* (= ὑπέρ)

b. With Accusative

- Spatial: *around, near*
- Temporal: *about, near*
- Reference/Respect: *with regard/reference to*

13. Πρό   *ExSyn 379*

Basic uses (with genitive only)

- Spatial: *before, in front of, at*
- Temporal: *before*
- Rank/Priority: *before*

➡14. Πρός   *ExSyn 380–82*

a. Basic uses (with accusative almost exclusively). This preposition occurs only once with the genitive and only six times with the dative case, but almost 700 times with the accusative. Our treatment will be restricted thus to the accusative case (for the other cases used, see BAGD's treatment).

- Purpose: *for, for the purpose of*
- Spatial: *toward*
- Temporal: *toward, for* (duration)
- Result: *so that, with the result that*
- Opposition: *against*
- Association: *with, in company with* (with stative verbs)

b. A significant passage involving πρός.[20] One of the more significant and, at the same time, most misunderstood passages (at least in popular circles) involving πρός is Rev 3:20. The text reads: Ἰδοὺ ἕστηκα ἐπὶ τὴν θύραν καὶ κρούω· ἐάν τις ἀκούσῃ τῆς φωνῆς μου καὶ ἀνοίξῃ τὴν θύραν, καὶ εἰσελεύσομαι **πρὸς** αὐτὸν καὶ δειπνήσω μετ᾽ αὐτοῦ καὶ αὐτὸς μετ᾽ ἐμοῦ ("Behold, I stand at the door and knock. If anyone hears my voice and opens the door, I will come in **to** him and will dine with him and he [will dine] with me"). The crucial phrase for our purposes is "I will come *in to* him." This text has often been taken as a text offering salvation to a lost sinner. Such a view is based on two assumptions: (1) that the Laodiceans, or at least some of them, were indeed lost, and (2) that εἰσελεύσομαι πρός means "come *into.*"

Both of these assumptions, however, are based on little evidence. With reference to the first assumption, that those in the Laodicean church were not believers, it is important to note that in the preceding verse, the resurrected Lord declares, "Those whom I love, I reprove and discipline." Here φιλέω is used for "love"—a term that is never used of God/Jesus loving unbelievers in the NT. This φιλέω must be applied to the Laodiceans here, for the verse concludes, "Be zealous, *therefore,* and repent." The inferential οὖν connects the two parts of the verse, indicating that the *Laodiceans* are to repent because Christ *loves* (φιλέω) *them!*

The second assumption is that εἰσελεύσομαι πρός means "come into." Such an assumption is based on a less than careful reading of the *English* text! The ASV, NASB, RSV, NRSV, for example, all correctly renders it "come in to" (note the space between the prepositions). The idea of "come into" would be expressed with εἰς as the independent preposition and would suggest a penetration into the person (thus, spawning the idea of entering into one's heart). However, spatially πρός means *toward,* not *into.* In all eight instances of εἰσέρχομαι πρός in the NT, the meaning is "come in toward/before a person" (i.e., enter a building, house, etc., so as to be in the presence of someone), *never penetration* into the person himself/herself.

➡**15.** Σύν   *ExSyn 382*

Basic use (with dative only). The predominant usage of this preposition is to indicate accompaniment/association: *with, in association (company) with.*

➡**16.** Ὑπέρ   *ExSyn 383–89*

a. Basic uses (with genitive and accusative)

(1) WITH GENITIVE

- Representation/Advantage: *on behalf of, for the sake of*
- Reference/Respect: *concerning, with reference to* (= περί)
- Substitution: *in place of, instead of* (= ἀντί) (such instances also involve representation)

---

[20] For a more detailed discussion, see *ExSyn* 380–81.

(2) With Accusative

- Spatial: *over, above*
- Comparison: *more than, beyond*

b. Significant passages involving ὑπέρ: concerning the substitutionary atonement (ὑπέρ + gen.).[21] The normal preposition used in texts that purportedly deal with Christ's substitutionary atonement is ὑπέρ (though ἀντί is used in Matt 20:28 / Mark 10:45). However, the case for a substitutionary sense for ὑπέρ is faced with the difficulty that the preposition can bear several other nuances that, on a lexical level, at least, are equally plausible in the theologically significant passages. It is to be noted, however, that BAGD does consider ὑπέρ to have a substitutionary sense on occasion (though they list only one text that bears on the atonement—2 Cor 5:14).

Ὑπέρ is, in fact, naturally suited to the meaning of substitution and is used in several passages dealing with the nature of Christ's atonement. On behalf of the view that ὑπέρ has at least a substitutionary sense to it in passages dealing with the atonement are the following arguments.

- The substitutionary sense is found in extra-NT Greek literature. It rarely bears this force in classical Greek, a bit more in the LXX, and extensively in the nonliterary papyri.[22] As time progressed, increasingly ὑπέρ encroached on ἀντί's domain. Indeed, one reason for previous resistance to the idea of a substitutionary ὑπέρ is that such instances were hard to find in the *classical* era. *But throughout the Koine period ὑπέρ began to encroach more and more on the meanings of ἀντί, though never fully phasing it out.* It was a relatively common phenomenon for one grammatical or lexical form to swallow up the uses of another in the Hellenistic period.

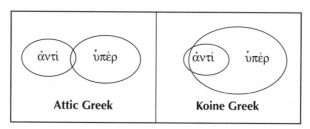

Chart 39
Overlap in Uses of Ἀντί and Ὑπέρ

- Ὑπέρ is used in a substitutionary sense in soteriologically insignificant passages in the NT, thus establishing such a nuance in the NT. Cf. Rom 9:3; Philemon 13.

---

[21] For a more detailed discussion, along with supporting evidence, see *ExSyn* 383–89.

[22] *ExSyn* 384–86 lists 78 papyrological references in which ὑπέρ is used with a substitutionary sense.

- Ὑπέρ is used with a substitutionary force in at least one soteriologically significant passage, admitted even by BAGD: 2 Cor 5:14. As well, there are other soteriologically significant texts in which it is difficult to deny a substitutionary sense to ὑπέρ: Gal 3:13; John 11:50.
- Once ὑπέρ is even used with a form of λύτρον that has been strengthened by prefixing ἀντί to it: 1 Tim 2:6.
- Ὑπέρ is a richer term than ἀντί. The question may be asked: If the Pauline doctrine of the atonement is at least a substitutionary one, why does he *never* choose the less ambiguous preposition ἀντί to express such an idea? The answer involves three points. (1) ἀντί is on its way out in the NT; ὑπέρ is encroaching on its domain. (2) As the papyri amply illustrate, the *set idiom* for substitution employs ὑπέρ instead of ἀντί. (3) The reason that this preposition was chosen was most likely that it was *more elastic* than ἀντί— i.e., ὑπέρ could involve both ideas of substitution *and* representation.

In sum, although it is possible that substitution is not the sense of ὑπέρ in some of the soteriologically significant texts, because this must be the sense in many such texts, the burden of proof falls on those who would deny such a sense in the others. In the least, in light of the well-established usage of ὑπέρ for substitution in Hellenistic Greek, there seems to be no reason not to adopt this nuance as part of the Pauline doctrine of the atonement.

➡17. Ὑπό   *ExSyn 389*

Basic uses (with genitive and accusative)

a. With Genitive

- (Ultimate) Agency: *by*[23]
- Intermediate Agency (with active verbs): *through*
- Means: *by* (rare)

b. With Accusative

- Spatial: *under, below*
- Subordination: *under* (the rule of)

---

[23] For details, see the discussion on the passive voice with agency expressed in the chapter on voice.

Person and Number[1]
Overview

Person **174**
† 1. Second Person for Third Person (*You = Someone*)?. 174
➡ 2. First Person Plural Constructions: The Scope of *We* 175
    a. Editorial *We* (Epistolary Plural) 175
    b. Inclusive *We* (Literary Plural) Vs. Exclusive *We*. 176
Number **177**
➡ 1. Neuter Plural Subject with Singular Verb 177
➡ 2. Compound Subject with Singular Verb 178
3. The Indefinite Plural (*They = Someone*). 178

In general, it can be said that a verb usually agrees with the subject in both person and number (known as *concord*). Such routine usage is already part of the intermediate student's preunderstanding and need not be discussed here.[2] There are also exceptional uses. Specifically, with regard to *person*, the lack of agreement is not between subject and verb, but between the linguistic person and the real person. With regard to *number*, there are several instances of discord between the verb number and the subject number. A few of the more interesting phenomena with regard to person and number will be noted in this chapter.[3]

Person *ExSyn 391–99*

†1. Second Person for Third Person (*You = Someone*)? *ExSyn 392–93*

In the Greek NT there is, most likely, *no indefinite second person* as there is in modern colloquial English. (By "indefinite" I mean the use of the second person for either the first or the third person.) Webster's defines the indefinite second person of modern English as referring to "a person or people generally: equivalent in sense to indefinite *one*, as, *you* can never tell!" (*New World Dictionary*). The basic exegetical point here is that the NT authors' distinctions between second and third person are not to be overlooked (because they will not be blurred in Greek as they are in English).[4]

---

[1] See *ExSyn* 390–406. The following categories are sufficiently rare, which the average intermediate Greek student may ignore: first person for the third person (391–92), the collective singular subject with a plural verb (400–401), and the categorical plural (403–6). The most important text that may fit a first person for a third person is Rom 7:7–25 (see 392).

[2] For a discussion, see Mounce, *Basics of Biblical Greek*, 116–18 (§15.3–15.5).

[3] Some grammars address one or more of these uses in other sections, such as the epistolary plural in the chapter on pronouns. Since almost all such examples occur in the nom. case as subject of the verb, thereby making an explicit pronoun dispensable (because it is embedded in the verbal inflection), it seemed more logical to discuss such in the unit on "Verbs and Verbals."

[4] For a discussion of some texts, see *ExSyn* 393.

➡**2. First Person Plural Constructions: The Scope of *We***   *ExSyn* 393–99

In many situations in the NT, especially in the letters, the use of *we* is not always clear. Does the author mean to include his associates (or coauthors), or his audience, or is this simply an *editorial* way of referring to himself? The use of the first person plural to refer only to the author is known as the *editorial we* (or *epistolary plural*); the use of the first person plural to refer to the author and his associates as distinct from the audience is called *exclusive we*; and the use of the first person plural to refer to both author(s) and his reader(s) is called the *inclusive we*. The potential referents can be diagrammed as follows.

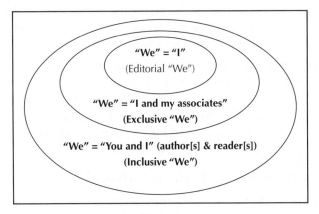

Chart 40
The Scope of "We" in the New Testament

a. Editorial **We** *(Epistolary Plural)*   *ExSyn* 394–96

(1) DEFINITION. The *editorial we* (also known as the *epistolary plural*) is the use of the first person plural by an author when he is in reality referring only to himself. The use of the epistolary plural is not common in the NT letters. Many texts are debatable; the ambiguity in such instances usually has to do with whether the author includes his associates in the first person plural or is referring only to himself; not infrequently, such passages are triply ambiguous: Does the author refer to himself alone, does he refer to himself and his associates, or does he include the *audience* in the *we*?

(2) KEYS TO IDENTIFICATION. The normal presupposition is that a given first person plural is not editorial. But when an author shifts unexpectedly from the singular to the plural, there are grounds for suspecting an epistolary plural. The *context* is thus the primary factor involved in determining whether or not *we* is editorial.[5]

---

[5] There is, however, a morphological clue as well: *the epistolary plural normally occurs in the nominative case*. Even in contexts where the oblique cases are used, the nominative usually leads off the discourse.

(3) ILLUSTRATIONS[6]

Rom 1:5   **ἐλάβομεν** χάριν καὶ ἀποστολήν
           we have received grace and an apostleship
> Paul mentions only himself as author (v. 1), rendering the plural here as most likely epistolary.

2 Cor 10:11   οἷοί **ἐσμεν** τῷ λόγῳ δι᾽ ἐπιστολῶν ἀπόντες, τοιοῦτοι καὶ παρόντες
               what **we** are when absent in word through [our] letters, these things also [we are] in deed when present
> The preceding context speaks of Paul alone as the author of his letters (vv. 9–10). The sudden change to the plural is thus best explained as an editorial *we*.

2 Cor 10:13   **ἡμεῖς** οὐκ εἰς τὰ ἄμετρα καυχησόμεθα
               we will not boast beyond the limit
> Again, the preceding context speaks only of Paul boasting, though he does seem to include reference to his companions in other things (vv. 1–2, 8 mention Paul's boasting/boldness; vv. 5, 7 seem to refer to Paul and his associates).[7]

b. Inclusive We (Literary Plural) Vs. Exclusive We   ExSyn 397–99

(1) DEFINITION. The *inclusive we* is the use of the first person plural to include both author(s) and audience. This contrasts with the *exclusive we* in which the first person plural restricts the group to the author and his associates (whether coauthors, those physically present, or even those who, distinct from the audience, have participated in some of the author's experiences, etc.).

Resolving the issue must be done on a case-by-case basis. The context and overall thrust of the book are the best clues. In particular, the presence of the second person plural in the same context often signals an exclusive *we* (but there are many exceptions).

(2) ILLUSTRATIONS[8]

(a) Of Inclusive We

Rom 5:1   δικαιωθέντες οὖν ἐκ πίστεως εἰρήνην **ἔχομεν** πρὸς τὸν θεόν
           therefore, since we have been justified by faith, **we** have peace with God

Jas 3:2   πολλὰ **πταίομεν** ἅπαντες
           we all stumble in many ways

---

[6] All of the examples of the editorial *we* in the NT are debatable, though some are excellent candidates for this category with few detractors among the commentators. For discussion of some of the debatable texts, see *ExSyn* 396–97.

[7] For more discussion of this text, see *ExSyn* 395.

[8] For a discussion of several debatable examples, see *ExSyn* 398–99.

(b) Of Exclusive We

1 Cor 4:10   ἡμεῖς μωροὶ διὰ Χριστόν, ὑμεῖς δὲ φρόνιμοι ἐν Χριστῷ· ἡμεῖς ἀσθενεῖς, ὑμεῖς δὲ ἰσχυροί
we are fools for Christ, but you are wise in Christ; **we** are weak, but you are strong

2 Thess 2:1   ἐρωτῶμεν δὲ ὑμᾶς, ἀδελφοί, ὑπὲρ τῆς παρουσίας τοῦ κυρίου ἡμῶν Ἰησοῦ Χριστοῦ καὶ ἡμῶν ἐπισυναγωγῆς ἐπ᾽ αὐτόν
Now **we** ask you, brothers, concerning the coming of our Lord Jesus Christ and our gathering together with him

> The first person plural passes almost imperceptibly from exclusive to inclusive in this verse: *"we* ask you" is clearly exclusive, while *"our* Lord" and *"our* gathering" are clearly inclusive.

Number   ExSyn 399–406

➡ **1. Neuter Plural Subject with Singular Verb**   ExSyn 399–400

Although there is a lack of concord in such constructions, they are not infrequent. Indeed, a neuter plural subject *normally* takes a singular verb. It is an example of *constructio ad sensum* (construction according to sense rather than according to strict grammatical concord). Since the neuter usually refers to impersonal things (including animals), the singular verb regards the plural subject as a *collective* whole. It is appropriate to translate the subject as a plural as well as the verb rather than translate both as singulars.

Mark 4:4   ἦλθεν **τὰ πετεινὰ** καὶ κατέφαγεν αὐτό
the birds came and devoured it

1 Cor 10:7   **τὰ τέλη** τῶν αἰώνων κατήντηκεν
the ends of the age have come

2 Cor 5:17   εἴ τις ἐν Χριστῷ, καινὴ κτίσις· **τὰ ἀρχαῖα** παρῆλθεν, ἰδοὺ γέγονεν **καινά**
if anyone is in Christ, he is a new creation; **the old things** have passed away—behold, **new things** have come!

However, when the author wants to *stress* the individuality of each subject involved in a neuter plural subject, the plural verb is used. The following are examples of the **neuter plural subject with a plural verb**.

Matt 13:38   **τὰ ζιζάνιά** εἰσιν οἱ υἱοὶ τοῦ πονηροῦ
the weeds are the sons of the evil one

John 10:27   **τὰ πρόβατα** τὰ ἐμὰ τῆς φωνῆς μου ἀκούουσιν, καγὼ γινώσκω αὐτὰ καὶ ἀκολουθοῦσίν μοι
my **sheep** hear my voice, and I know them and they follow me

➡**2. Compound Subject with Singular Verb**[9]   *ExSyn* 401–2

When two subjects, each in the singular, are joined by a conjunction, the verb is usually in the plural. However, when an author wants to *highlight* one of the subjects, the verb is put in the singular. (This even occurs when one of the subjects is in the plural.) The *first*-named subject is the one being stressed in such instances.

Matt 13:55   οὐχ **ἡ μήτηρ** αὐτοῦ λέγεται Μαριὰμ καὶ **οἱ ἀδελφοὶ** αὐτοῦ
              Ἰάκωβος καὶ Ἰωσὴφ καὶ Σίμων καὶ Ἰούδας;
              Is not his **mother** called Mary and his **brothers** [called] James
              and Joseph and Simon and Judas?

> The use of the singular verb, λέγεται, singles out Mary above
> Jesus' brothers.

John 2:2   ἐκλήθη **ὁ Ἰησοῦς** καὶ **οἱ μαθηταὶ** αὐτοῦ εἰς τὸν γάμον
              Jesus was invited to the wedding and [so were] his disciples

3. The Indefinite Plural (*They* = *Someone*)   *ExSyn* 402–3

a. Definition. The indefinite plural is the use of the third person plural to indicate no one in particular, but rather "someone." This has parallels with modern colloquial English. For example, "I understand that *they* have discovered a cure for cancer." In this sentence, "they" means "someone." Frequently it is better to convert an indefinite plural into a *passive* in which the object becomes the subject (e.g., in the sentence above, this would = "I understand that a cure for cancer has been discovered"). Sometimes the indefinite plural is a circumlocution for naming God as subject.

b. Illustrations[10]

Matt 7:16   μήτι **συλλέγουσιν** ἀπὸ ἀκανθῶν σταφυλὰς ἢ ἀπὸ τριβόλων
              σῦκα;
              they do not **gather** grapes from thornbushes, or figs from
              thistles, do they?

> Jesus had just declared that false prophets would be known by
> their fruits. Since the verb συλλέγουσιν is in concord with
> "false prophets" *grammatically* it is possible to see it referring
> back to them. But *semantically* this is absurd.

Luke 12:20   ταύτῃ τῇ νυκτὶ τὴν ψυχήν σου **ἀπαιτοῦσιν** ἀπὸ σοῦ
              in this night, **they** will require your soul from you

> Here, "they" seems to refer to God. It is not legitimate, how-
> ever, to infer from this that the Trinity is in view, for this same
> usage was found in classical Greek with reference to one person.

---

[9] For a discussion of Acts 16:31, see *ExSyn* 402.
[10] For a discussion of Mark 3:21, see *ExSyn* 403.

Voice[1]
Overview

Introduction: Definition of Terms **179**
Active Voice **180**
➡ 1. Simple Active 181
➡ 2. Causative Active (Ergative Active) 181
➡ 3. Stative Active 181
➡ 4. Reflexive Active 182
Middle Voice **182**
† 1. Direct Middle (Reflexive or Direct Reflexive) 183
➡ 2. Indirect Middle (Indirect Reflexive, Benefactive,
        Intensive, Dynamic Middle) 184
  3. Permissive Middle 185
➡ 4. Deponent Middle 185
Passive Voice **186**
  1. Passive Constructions 186
      a. The Passive with and without Expressed Agency 186
      b. Passive with an Accusative Object 190
  2. Passive Uses 190
➡   a. Simple Passive 190
➡   b. Deponent Passive 191

Introduction: Definition of Terms   ExSyn 408–10

1. Voice

Voice is that property of the verb that indicates how the subject is related to the action (or state) expressed by the verb. In general, the voice of the verb may indicate that the subject is *doing* the action (active), *receiving* the action (passive), or both doing and receiving (at least the results of) the action (middle). The three voices in Greek may be graphically (and simplistically) illustrated as shown in the chart on the following page.

2. Distinct From Transitiveness

Voice is easy to confuse with transitiveness. However, the two should be distinguished. *Transitiveness* relates the action of a verb to an *object*, while *voice* relates the action of a verb to its *subject*.[2]

---

[1] See *ExSyn* 407–41. The following categories are sufficiently rare that the average intermediate Greek student may ignore them: the redundant middle (418–19), causative middle (423–25; note exegetically important texts there), reciprocal middle (*ExSyn* 427), and causative/permissive passive (*ExSyn* 440–41).

[2] If a verb is transitive, it requires a direct object (whether stated or implied). If it is intransitive, it does not take a direct object. Further distinctions: A transitive verb has both an active

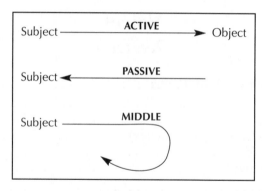

Chart 41
The Direction of the Action in Greek Voices[3]

3. Distinguishing Middle From Passive

Only in the future and aorist tenses are there distinct forms for the middle and passive voice. In the present, imperfect, perfect, and pluperfect tenses, the middle and passive forms are identical. Although for purposes of parsing, many teachers of Greek allow students to list these as simply "middle/passive," for syntactical purposes a choice needs to be made. This is not always easy and needs to be done on a case-by-case basis. A few of the exegetically significant passages discussed below are connected to this problem. As well, tagging such double-terminal voices for statistical and computer-search purposes is sometimes difficult and open to interpretation. Nevertheless, the vast majority of middle-passive forms pose no problem.

Active Voice   ExSyn 410–14

In general it can be said that in the active voice the subject *performs, produces,* or *experiences the action* or *exists* in the *state* expressed by the verb.

(or middle) and passive form, while an intransitive verb does not have a passive. The equative verb (copula) is like an intransitive verb in that it does not have a passive, but like a transitive verb in that it has a *complement* (i.e., a predicate nominative/adjective). It is different from both, however, in that its primary function is to assert a quality about the subject.

Occasionally it is difficult to tell whether a verb is transitive or intransitive (indeed, some verbs can function both ways, depending on contextual and other factors). An easy way to check for transitiveness is the "passive transform" test: Transitive verbs can be converted to the passive; when this happens, the object becomes the subject and the subject becomes the agent (after "by"). The sentence, "The boy hit the ball" can be converted to "the ball was hit by the boy." But the sentence, "the girl came home," in which the verb may look transitive, cannot be converted to "the home was come by the girl."

[3] The chart is simplistic in that it has in view only transitive verbs and depicts for the middle voice only the direct (reflexive) use. However, it may be useful for students to get a handle on the general distinctions.

➡1. Simple Active

ExSyn 411

The subject *performs* or *experiences* the action. The verb may be transitive or intransitive. This is the normal or routine use, by far the most common.

Mark 4:2   ἐδίδασκεν αὐτοὺς ἐν παραβολαῖς πολλά
he **was teaching** them many things in parables

John 1:7   οὗτος **ἦλθεν** εἰς μαρτυρίαν   he **came** for a testimony

➡2. Causative Active (Ergative Active)

ExSyn 411–12

a. Definition. The subject is not directly involved in the action, but may be said to be the ultimate source or cause of it. That cause may be volitional, but is not necessarily so. This usage is fairly common.

For the simple verb, sometimes the gloss *cause to* can be used before the verb and its object; in such cases it is usually best to convert the verb to a passive (e.g., *he causes him to be baptized*). However, this is not always appropriate.

b. Illustrations [4]

Matt 5:45   τὸν ἥλιον αὐτοῦ **ἀνατέλλει** ἐπὶ πονηροὺς καὶ ἀγαθοὺς καὶ **βρέχει** ἐπὶ δικαίους καὶ ἀδίκους
he **causes** his sun **to rise** on [both] evil and good [people], and he **causes it to rain** on [both] the righteous and unrighteous

John 19:1   **ἐμαστίγωσεν**   **he scourged** him
Pilate **caused** Jesus to be scourged, but did not perform the act himself.

➡3. Stative Active

ExSyn 412–13

a. Definition and key to identification. The subject exists in the state indicated by the verb. This kind of active includes both equative verbs (copulas) and verbs that are *translated* with an adjective in the predicate (e.g., πλουτέω—"I am rich"). This usage is common, even routine.

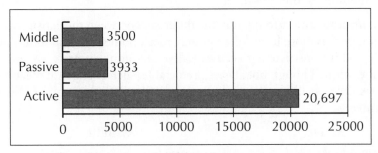

Chart 42
Voice Statistics in the New Testament

---

[4] For a discussion of Acts 21:11, see *ExSyn* 412–13.

The key to identification is simple: the stative active occurs either with the equative verb or one that in translation uses *am* + a predicate adjective ("I am X").

b. Illustrations

John 1:1   Ἐν ἀρχῇ **ἦν** ὁ λόγος   In the beginning **was** the Word

1 Cor 13:4   ἡ ἀγάπη **μακροθυμεῖ, χρηστεύεται** ἡ ἀγάπη
              love **is patient**, love **is kind**

➡**4. Reflexive Active**   *ExSyn* 413–14

a. Definition. The subject acts on himself or herself. In such cases naturally the *reflexive pronoun* is employed as the direct object (e.g., ἑαυτόν), while the corresponding reflexive middle omits the pronoun. This usage is relatively common.

b. Illustrations

Mark 15:30 **σῶσον** σεαυτόν   **save** yourself

Rev 19:7   ἡ γυνὴ αὐτοῦ **ἡτοίμασεν** ἑαυτήν
            his bride **has prepared** herself

Middle Voice   *ExSyn* 414–30

Definition. Defining the function of the middle voice is not an easy task because it encompasses a large and amorphous group of nuances. But in general, in the middle voice the subject *performs* or *experiences the action* expressed by the verb in such a way that *emphasizes the subject's participation*. It may be said that the subject acts "with a vested interest."

The difference between the active and middle is one of emphasis. The active voice emphasizes the *action* of the verb; the middle emphasizes the *actor* [subject] of the verb. "It, in some way, relates the action more intimately to the subject."[5] This difference can be expressed, to some degree, in English translation. For many middle voices (especially the indirect middle), putting the subject in *italics* would communicate this emphasis.

Clarification. Not infrequently the difference between the active and middle of the same verb is more lexical than grammatical. Sometimes the shift is between transitive and intransitive, between causative and non-causative, or some other similar alteration. Though not always predictable, such changes in meaning from active to middle usually make good sense and are true to the genius of the voices. For example:

Active	Middle
αἱρέω—*I take*	αἱρέομαι—*I choose, prefer*
ἀναμιμνῄσκω—*I remind*	ἀναμιμνῄσκομαι—*I remember*

---

[5] Dana-Mantey, 157.

ἀποδίδωμι—*I give away*   ἀποδίδομαι—*I sell*
ἐπικαλέω—*I call on, name*   ἐπικαλέομαι—*I appeal*
ἔχω—*I have, hold*   ἔχομαι—*I cling to*
κρίνω—*I judge*   κρίνομαι—*I bring a lawsuit*
παύω—*I stop* (transitive)   παύομαι—*I cease* (intransitive)
φυλάσσω—*I guard*   φυλάσσομαι—*I am on my guard*

†1. Direct Middle (Reflexive or Direct Reflexive)   *ExSyn* 416–18

a. Definition. With the direct middle, the subject acts *on* himself or herself. The genius of the middle can most clearly be seen by this use. But because of its very subtlety, nonnative speakers tended to replace this with more familiar forms. Thus although the direct middle was frequently used in classical Greek, because of the Hellenistic tendency toward explicitness, this usage has increasingly been replaced by the reflexive active. In the NT, the direct middle is quite rare, used almost exclusively with certain verbs whose lexical nuance included a reflexive notion (such as putting on clothes), or in a set idiom that had become fixed in the language.

Some grammarians dispute whether the direct middle even occurs in the NT, but such a position is overstated. Even though it is rare and not all the proposed examples are clear, there is a sufficient number to establish its usage.

b. Key to identification (verb + self [as direct object]). This is semantically equivalent to an active verb with a reflexive pronoun as object: simply add *himself, herself,* etc. as direct object to the verb.

c. Illustrations

(1) CLEAR EXAMPLES

Matt 27:5   **ἀπήγξατο**   **he hanged himself**

Acts 12:21   ὁ Ἡρῴδης **ἐνδυσάμενος** ἐσθῆτα βασιλικὴν
               Herod **clothed himself** with royal clothing

(2) A DEBATABLE AND EXEGETICALLY SIGNIFICANT PASSAGE

Rom 9:22   σκεύη ὀργῆς **κατηρτισμένα** εἰς ἀπώλειαν
              vessels of wrath, **prepared/having prepared themselves** for destruction

> The view that the perfect participle is middle, and therefore a direct middle, finds its roots in Chrysostom and is later echoed by Pelagius. The idea would be that these vessels of wrath "had prepared themselves for destruction." But to argue that κατηρτισμένα is a direct middle seems to fly in the face of grammar (the normal use of the voice and tense), lexeme, and context.[6]

---

[6] For discussion, see *ExSyn* 417–18.

➡**2. Indirect Middle (Indirect Reflexive, Benefactive,**
Intensive, Dynamic Middle)   *ExSyn* 419–23

a. Definition. The subject acts *for* (or sometimes *by*) himself or herself, or in
his or her *own interest*. The subject thus shows a special interest in the action of
the verb. This is a common use of the middle in the NT; apart from the deponent middle, it is the most common. This usage is closest to the general definition
of the middle suggested by many grammarians.

A careful examination of the usage of a particular middle voice verb in Hellenistic Greek will shed light on how much can be made of the voice. What is frequently at stake, grammatically speaking, is whether the middle is to be
considered indirect or deponent.

b. Illustrations

(1) Clear Examples

Matt 27:12   ἐν τῷ κατηγορεῖσθαι αὐτὸν ὑπὸ τῶν ἀρχιερέων καὶ πρεσβυτέρων οὐδὲν **ἀπεκρίνατο**
When he was accused by the chief priests and elders, **he**
answered nothing **[in his own defense]**.

Eph 1:4   **ἐξελέξατο** ἡμᾶς   **he chose** us **[for himself]**
Although ἐκλέγω does not occur as an active verb in the NT, it
does in Hellenistic Greek in general and hence ought not to be
taken as a deponent. God chose us *for* himself, *by* himself, or for
his own interests. This does not, of course, imply that God
needed believers. Rather, just as the chief end of human beings is
to glorify God and enjoy him forever, so too God is in the busi-
ness of glorifying himself. As is mentioned three times in Eph-
esians 1, the elect belong to God "for the praise of his glory."

Eph 5:16   **ἐξαγοραζόμενοι** τὸν καιρόν
redeeming the time **[for yourself]**

(2) A Debatable and Exegetically Significant Text

1 Cor 13:8   εἴτε προφητεῖαι, καταργηθήσονται· εἴτε γλῶσσαι, **παύσον-**
ται· εἴτε γνῶσις, καταργηθήσεται
If there are prophecies, they will be done away; if there are
tongues, **they will cease [on their own]**; if there is knowledge,
it will be done away.

If the voice of the verb here is significant, then Paul is saying
either that tongues will cut themselves off (direct middle) or,
more likely, cease of their own accord, i.e., "die out" without an
intervening agent (indirect middle). Although most NT scholars consider παύσονται to be deponent, this is unlikely.[7]

---

[7] For discussion, see *ExSyn* 422–23.

3. Permissive Middle

ExSyn 425–27

a. Definition. The subject *allows* something to be done *for* or *to* himself or herself. This usage, though rare, involves some exegetically important texts. A good "rough and ready" test is to translate the verb as a *passive*. If this makes sense—and if the notion of permission or allowance seems also to be implied—the verb is a good candidate for permissive middle. (It should be noted that most permissive middles are usually best translated as passives; the glosses provided below are intended only to illustrate the usage.)

b. Illustrations

Acts 22:16   ἀναστὰς **βάπτισαι** καὶ **ἀπόλουσαι** τὰς ἁμαρτίας σου
Rise, **have yourself baptized** and **allow** your sins **to be washed away**

1 Cor 10:2   πάντες εἰς τὸν Μωϋσῆν **ἐβαπτίσαντο**
all **were baptized** into Moses

➡4. Deponent Middle

ExSyn 428–30

a. Definition. A deponent middle is a middle voice verb that has no active *form* but is active in *meaning*. The deponent middle in the NT is very common, due to the heavy use of certain verbs. English (as well as other modern Indo-European languages) has few analogies, making analysis of this phenomenon particularly difficult.

b. Clarification. These two elements (no active form, but active force) are at the root of the definition. However, just because a verb has no active form in the *New Testament* is not reason enough to label it deponent. The following are tips for wrestling with the issue of deponency (whether for middle or passive verbs):

(1) The basic principle is this: A deponent middle verb is one that has no active form for a particular *principal part* in *Hellenistic* Greek, *and* one whose force in that principal part is evidently active. Thus, for example, ἔρχομαι has no active form for the first principal part, but it is obviously active in force. Verbs (such as ἔρχομαι) that have active forms for one or more of the principal parts are called partially deponent. Other verbs (such as δύναμαι) that have no active form in any principal part are completely deponent. Many deponent verbs never had an active form; the restriction to Hellenistic Greek is thus meant to be a bare minimum requirement.

(2) There are some verbs that never had an active form, yet the true middle force is clearly seen. For example, δέχομαι means I receive, I welcome—an idea that is inherently reflexive. It is not enough, then, to note merely that a verb lacks an active form throughout its history; it must also be demonstrated that the middle force is absent.

c. Illustrations. The following is a list of some truly deponent verbs:

- ἅλλομαι
- ἀποκρίνομαι (deponent in sixth principal part, but not in third)

- βούλομαι
- γίνομαι (but active in the fourth principal part [γέγονα])
- δύναμαι
- ἐργάζομαι
- ἔρχομαι (but active in the third and fourth principal parts [ἦλθον, ἐλήλυθα)
- λήμψομαι (the second principal part of λαμβάνω)
- πορεύομαι
- χαρίζομαι

The following is a list of verbs that look deponent but most likely are not:

- ἀρνέομαι
- ἀσπάζομαι
- βουλεύομαι
- δέχομαι
- ἐκλέγομαι
- καυχάομαι
- λογίζομαι
- μιμνήσκομαι
- παύσομαι (second principal part of παύω)[8]

Passive Voice *ExSyn* 431–41

In general it can be said that in the passive voice the subject *is acted upon* or *receives the action* expressed by the verb. No volition—nor even necessarily awareness of the action—is implied on the part of the subject. That is, the subject may or may not be aware, its volition may or may not be involved. But these things are not stressed when the passive is used.

The passive can be treated either structurally or semantically. Both ways of viewing the passive are important because they ask different questions and impact exegesis in different ways.

1. Passive Constructions *ExSyn* 431–39

a. The Passive with and without Expressed Agency

The passive voice occurs sometimes with an agent (or means) expressed, sometimes without an agent (or means) expressed. All uses of the passive (except the deponent) naturally occur both with and without an agent. Nevertheless, the issue of agency does shed much light on an author's overall meaning and ought to be included in a discussion of the passive voice.

(1) WITH AGENCY EXPRESSED *ExSyn* 431–35

Three types of agency can be expressed in Greek: ultimate agency, intermediate agency, and impersonal means. The *ultimate* agent indicates the person who

---

[8] See discussion of παύσονται in 1 Cor 13:8 in *ExSyn* 422–23.

is ultimately responsible for the action.[9] Sometimes the ultimate agent uses an *intermediate* agent who carries out the act for the ultimate agent. The *impersonal means* is that which an agent uses to perform an act. (Technically, means does not indicate agency, except in a broad sense.) Note these three further points:

- English does not formally distinguish these categories easily, but relies largely on context. "By" covers a multitude of agencies. For example, when the President of the United States wants to make a statement, sometimes he does so through his press secretary. It would be appropriate to say that "a statement was made *by the president,*" just as it would be appropriate to say that "a statement was made *by the press secretary.*" The first sentence indicates the ultimate agent; the second the intermediate agent. But in Greek, a different prepositional phrase is used to indicate each kind of agency.
- The third category is not meant to imply that the instrument used is necessarily inanimate or impersonal. Indeed, on occasion a person might be the means used by another. Impersonal means simply means that the instrument is portrayed as that which is used by another.
- Agency can be expressed with active and middle verbs, just as it can with passive verbs, although it is more common with passives.

The following table summarizes the major ways agency is expressed in the New Testament.

Agency	*Preposition (Case)*	*Translation*
Ultimate Agent	ὑπό (gen.) ἀπό (gen.) παρά (gen.)	by by, of from, by
Intermediate Agent	διά (gen.)	through, by
Impersonal Means	ἐν (dat.) dative (no prep) ἐκ (gen.)	by, with by, with by, of

Table 5
How Agency is Expressed in the New Testament

(a) Ultimate Agent ExSyn 433

The subject of a passive verb receives the action that is usually expressed by ὑπό + genitive. Sometimes ἀπό + genitive is used, rarely παρά + genitive. The ultimate agent indicates the person who is ultimately responsible for the action, who may or may not be directly involved (though he or she usually is).

---

[9] Many grammars refer to this as the *direct* agent, but this is not always an appropriate term; in fact, it could better describe the intermediate agent, because the ultimate agent's actions are often mediated through an intermediate agent.

Heb 11:23   Μωϋσῆς γεννηθεὶς **ἐκρύβη** τρίμηνον *ὑπὸ τῶν πατέρων* αὐτοῦ
After Moses was born, **he was hid** for three months *by* his parents.

> The preposition indicates that the parents were ultimately responsible for the hiding of the baby, but does not exclude the possibility that others (such as Moses' sister) also carried out the clandestine activity.

Jas 1:13   μηδεὶς πειραζόμενος λεγέτω ὅτι *ἀπὸ θεοῦ* **πειράζομαι**
let no one say when he is tempted, "**I am tempted** *by* God"

(b) Intermediate Agent   *ExSyn* 433–34

The subject of a passive verb receives the action that is expressed by διά + genitive. Here, the agent named is intermediate, not ultimate.[10] Though common, this usage is not as frequent as ὑπό + genitive for ultimate agency.

Matt 1:22   τὸ **ῥηθὲν** *ὑπὸ* κυρίου *διὰ τοῦ* προφήτου
what **was spoken** by the Lord *through* the prophet[11]

John 1:3   πάντα *δι᾽ αὐτοῦ* **ἐγένετο**
all things **came into existence** *through* him

> The Logos is represented as the Creator in a "hands-on" sort of way, with the implication that God is the ultimate agent. This is the typical (though not exclusive) pattern seen in the NT: Ultimate agency is ascribed to God the Father (with ὑπό), intermediate agency is ascribed to Christ (with διά), and "impersonal" means is ascribed to the Holy Spirit (with ἐν or the simple dative).

(c) Impersonal Means   *ExSyn* 434–35

The impersonal means by which the verbal action is carried out is expressed by ἐν + dative, the dative case alone (the most common construction), or rarely, ἐκ + genitive. The noun in the dative is not necessarily impersonal, but is conceived of as such (i.e., usually there is an implied agent who *uses* the noun in the dative as his or her instrument).

Rom 3:28   λογιζόμεθα **δικαιοῦσθαι** *πίστει* ἄνθρωπον
we maintain that a person **is justified** *by faith*

1 Cor 12:13   *ἐν ἑνὶ πνεύματι* ἡμεῖς πάντες εἰς ἓν σῶμα **ἐβαπτίσθημεν**
by one Spirit **we were** all **baptized** into one body

> By calling "Spirit" means here does not deny the personality of the Holy Spirit. Rather, the Holy Spirit is the instrument that Christ uses to baptize, even though he is a person. Just as John baptized ἐν ὕδατι, so Christ baptized ἐν πνεύματι.

---

[10] Only once is διὰ θεοῦ used in the NT (Gal 4:7 [the *v.l.* διὰ Χριστοῦ, found in numerous late MSS, indicates a scribal tension over the expression; see the discussion in J. Eadie, *Galatians* (Edinburgh: T. & T. Clark, 1869), 305–6]; Gal 1:1 comes close with διὰ Ἰησοῦ Χριστοῦ καὶ θεοῦ πατρός; cf. also 1 Cor 1:9), although διὰ θελήματος θεοῦ occurs eight times, exclusively in Paul's letters (Rom 15:32; 1 Cor 1:1; 2 Cor 1:1; 8:5; Eph 1:1; Col 1:1; 2 Tim 1:1).

[11] For discussion, see *ExSyn* 434.

(2) WITHOUT AGENCY EXPRESSED   *ExSyn 435–39*

There are a number of reasons why an agent is not always expressed with a passive verb. A few of the more common ones are as follows.

(a) The suppressed agent is often *obvious from the context* or the audience's pre-understanding. In John 3:23 there is no need for the evangelist to repeat that "John was baptizing" (from the first part of the verse) when he writes that "they were coming and **were getting baptized**" (παρεγίνοντο καὶ **ἐβαπτίζοντο**).

(b) *The focus of the passage is on the subject*; an explicit agent might detract from this focus. In Matt 2:12, for example, the magi "**were warned** in a dream" (**χρηματισθέντες** κατ᾽ ὄναρ), evidently by an angel, though this is not mentioned here.

(c) The nature of some passive verbs is such that *no agency is to be implied* (e.g., **συντελεσθεισῶν** αὐτῶν [**when** (those days) **were completed**] in Luke 4:2).

(d) The verb in question is functioning as an *equative verb* (e.g., πόλιν **λεγομένην** Ναζαρέτ ... Ναζωραῖος **κληθήσεται** [a city **called** Nazareth ... he **shall be called** a Nazarene] in Matt 2:23).

(e) Similar to this usage is an *implicit generic agent*. Greek frequently uses the simple passive without an expressed agent where colloquial English might use "they say": "They say a cure for cancer has been discovered" would often be expressed in Greek as "it is said that a cure for cancer has been found." Thus, in Matt 5:21 Jesus declares, "You have heard that **it was said**" (ἠκούσατε ὅτι **ἐρρέθη**).

(f) An *explicit agent would sometimes be obtrusive* or would render the sentence too complex, perhaps reducing the literary effect. In 1 Cor 1:13 three passives are used without an agent mentioned. **μεμέρισται** ὁ Χριστός; μὴ Παῦλος **ἐσταυρώθη** ὑπὲρ ὑμῶν, ἢ εἰς τὸ ὄνομα Παύλου **ἐβαπτίσθητε**; (**Is** Christ **divided? Was** Paul **crucified** for you, or **were you baptized** into the name of Paul?). In 1 Cor 12:13 to mention Christ as the agent who baptizes with the Spirit would be cumbersome and a mixture of metaphors, since believers are baptized into *Christ's* body (ἐν ἑνὶ πνεύματι ἡμεῖς πάντες εἰς ἓν σῶμα **ἐβαπτίσθημεν** [by one Spirit **we** all **were baptized** into one body]).

(g) Similar to the above is *the suppression of the agent for rhetorical effect*, especially for the purpose of drawing the reader into the story. Note, for example, Jesus' pronouncement to the paralytic (Mark 2:5): τέκνον, **ἀφίενταί** σου αἱ ἁμαρτίαι (child, your sins **are forgiven**). In Rom 1:13 Paul declares his desire to have visited the Romans, adding that he "was prevented" thus far (ἐκωλύθην).

(h) The passive is also used when *God is the obvious agent*. Many grammars call this a *divine passive* (or *theological passive*), assuming that its use was due to the Jewish aversion to using the divine name. For example, in the Beatitudes, the passive is used: "they shall be comforted" (παρακληθήσονται [Matt 5:4]), "they shall be filled" (χορτασθήσονται [v. 6]), "they shall receive mercy" (ἐλεηθήσονται [v. 7]). It is an overstatement, however, to claim this is always or even usually due to the author's reticence to utter the name of God.

The divine passive seems to occur frequently enough throughout the whole NT. Statements such as the following could be multiplied many times over: "a man **is justified**" (Rom 3:28); "you **were bought** with a price" (1 Cor 7:23); "you **were called** to freedom" (ὑμεῖς ἐπ᾽ ἐλευθερίᾳ **ἐκλήθητε** [Gal 5:13]); "by grace **you have been saved**" (Eph 2:5).

The divine passive is simply a specific type of one of the previous categories listed above (e.g., obvious from the passage, due to focus on the subject, otherwise obtrusive, or for rhetorical effect). That God is behind-the-scenes is self-evidently part of the worldview of the NT writers.[12]

b. Passive with an Accusative Object   *ExSyn* 438–39

(1) DEFINITION. Although it seems a bit odd to native English speakers, Greek sometimes uses an accusative with a true passive verb. The major usage for such a structure involves the accusative of retained object. In this instance, the *accusative of thing* in a double accusative person-thing construction with an active verb *retains its case* when the verb is put in the *passive*. The accusative of person, in such instances, becomes the subject. This use of the accusative occurs most frequently with causative verbs, though it is rare in the NT.

"I taught you *the lesson*" becomes, with the verb converted to a passive, "You were taught *the lesson* by me." When the verb is transformed into a passive, the accusative of person becomes the subject (nom.), the accusative of thing is retained.

(2) ILLUSTRATIONS

1 Cor 12:13   πάντες **ἓν πνεῦμα** ἐποτίσθημεν
all were made to drink [of] **one Spirit**

"All" is the person, put in the nom. with passive verbs. The acc. of thing, "one Spirit," is retained. If the verb had been in the active voice, the text would be read: "He made all to drink of one Spirit" (ἐπότισε πάντα ἓν πνεῦμα).

Luke 7:29   οἱ τελῶναι ... βαπτισθέντες **τὸ βάπτισμα** Ἰωάννου
the tax collectors, having been baptized with **the baptism** of John

2. Passive Uses   *ExSyn* 439–41

➡ ### a. Simple Passive   *ExSyn* 439–40

(1) DEFINITION. The most common use of the passive voice is to indicate that the subject receives the action. No implication is made about cognition, volition, or cause on the part of the subject. This usage occurs both with and without an expressed agent.

---

[12] For more discussion, see *ExSyn* 437–38.

(2) ILLUSTRATIONS

| Rom 5:1 | **δικαιωθέντες** οὖν ἐκ πίστεως εἰρήνην ἔχομεν πρὸς τὸν θεόν |

Therefore, **having been justified** by faith, we have peace with God

| Heb 3:4 | πᾶς οἶκος **κατασκευάζεται** ὑπό τινος |

every house **is built** by someone

➡ ***b. Deponent Passive***   *ExSyn* 441

A verb that has no active *form* may be active in meaning though passive in form. Two of the most common deponent passives are ἐγενήθην and ἀπεκρίθην. See the discussion of the deponent middle for material that is equally relevant for the deponent passive.

Moods[1]
Overview of Moods and Their Uses

The Indicative Mood **195**
➡ 1. Declarative Indicative 195
➡ 2. Interrogative Indicative. 195
➡ 3. Conditional Indicative. 195
➡ 4. Potential Indicative 196
   5. Cohortative (Command, Volitive) Indicative. 197
➡ 6. The Indicative with Ὅτι 197
     a. Substantival Ὅτι Clauses 197
     b. Epexegetical. 200
     c. Causal (Adverbial) 200

The Subjunctive Mood **201**
   1. In Independent Clauses. 202
➡   a. Hortatory Subjunctive (Volitive). 202
➡   b. Deliberative Subjunctive (Dubitative) 202
➡   c. Emphatic Negation Subjunctive. 204
➡   d. Prohibitive Subjunctive 204
   2. In Dependent (Subordinate) Clauses 205
➡   a. Subjunctive in Conditional Sentences 205
➡   b. Ἵνα + the Subjunctive 206
     c. Subjunctive with Verbs of Fearing 208
     d. Subjunctive in Indirect Questions 208
➡   e. Subjunctive in Indefinite Relative Clause. 208
➡   f. Subjunctive in Indefinite Temporal Clause 209

The Optative Mood **209**
➡ 1. Voluntative Optative (Optative of Obtainable Wish,
   Volitive Optative) 209

The Imperative Mood. **210**
➡ 1. Command 210
➡ 2. Prohibition 211
➡ 3. Request (Entreaty, Polite Command). 211
   4. Conditional Imperative. 211

──────── **INTRODUCTION** ────────   *ExSyn 443–45*

General Definition

Just as with tense and voice, mood is a morphological feature of the verb. *Voice* indicates *how* the subject *relates* to the *action* or state of the verb; *tense* is used pri-

---

[1] See *ExSyn* 443–93. The following categories are sufficiently rare that the average inter-mediate Greek student can ignore them: the oblique optative (483), the potential optative (483–

marily to portray the *kind* of action. In general, *mood* is the feature of the verb that presents the verbal action or state with reference to its *actuality* or *potentiality*. Older grammars referred to this as "mode"; others call it "attitude." There are four moods in Greek: indicative, subjunctive, optative, and imperative.[2]

There are two pitfalls to avoid in thinking about moods. (1) Mood does not have an *objective correspondence to reality*. For example, it is incorrect to say that the indicative mood signifies a "simple fact."[3] Lies are usually stated in the indicative; false perceptions are in the indicative; exaggerations and fictional accounts are in the indicative.

(2) It is imprecise to say that mood indicates a speaker's *perception* of reality. This is not the case, for otherwise misinformation, sarcasm, hyperbole, fiction, dualistic worldview, etc., could never be communicated.

Detailed Definition

A more accurate definition is as follows: Mood is the morphological feature of a verb that a speaker uses to **portray** his or her affirmation as to the certainty of the verbal action or state (whether an actuality or potentiality). The key elements in this definition are that mood (1) does not necessarily correspond to reality, (2) does not indicate even a speaker's perception of reality, but (3) does indicate a speaker's portrayal or representation.[4]

Three other points can be made. First, the general semantics of the moods can be compared as follows[5]:

Moods	Indicative	Subjunctive	Optative	Imperative
Greek example	λύεις	λύῃς	λύοις	λῦε
Portrayal	certain/asserted	probable/desirable	possible	intended
Translation	you are loosing/ you loose	you might be loosing/ you should be loosing	you may be loosing	loose!

Table 6
The Semantics of the Moods Compared

84), the permissive imperative (488–89), the pronouncement imperative (492–93) and the imperative as a stereotyped greeting (493). For the conditional optative, see the chapter on conditional clauses. The potential imperative is a disputed category (see 492) and if it occurs, it does so rarely.

[2] Most grammars do not include the infinitive or participle under the rubric of mood, and for good reason. As dependent verbals, their attitude toward certainty is dependent on some finite verb. Hence, since such an affirmation is derivative, they cannot be said to have mood per se. Nevertheless, for parsing purposes, these two verbals are usually labeled as infinitive and participle in the "mood slot."

[3] Dana-Mantey, 168 (§162). Though they add a qualification, the impression is that the indicative is somehow objectively connected to reality.

[4] In reality, *all* grammarians have to resort to shorthand definitions from time to time in order to avoid cumbersome definitions. The trade-off, then, is between pedantic accuracy and pedagogical simplicity.

[5] See *ExSyn* 445–48 for a more detailed discussion on the semantics of moods.

Second, the moods need to be seen in light of two poles. (1) The moods affirm various *degrees* of certainty; they are on a "continuum of certainty in the speaker's presentation,"[6] from *actuality* to *potentiality*. In general, the indicative mood is set apart from the others in that it is the mood normally used to address actuality, while the others—collectively known as the *oblique* moods—normally address potentiality. (2) The imperative mood is normally used to address the *volition*, while the optative, subjunctive, and especially indicative address *cognition*. In other words, the imperative appeals to the will, while the other moods appeal more frequently to the mind.

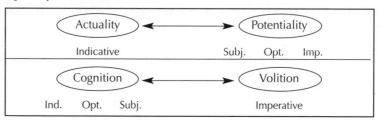

Chart 43
The Moods Viewed in Two Continua

Third, the statistics of mood frequencies in the NT are as follows:

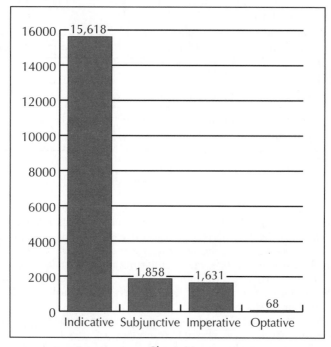

Chart 44
Mood Frequencies in the New Testament

---

[6] Credit is due Dr. Hall Harris for this nice turn of expression.

─────── **CATEGORIES** ─────── ExSyn 448–69

This chapter will deal only with the major categories of usage.

The Indicative Mood ExSyn 448–61

The indicative mood is, in general, the mood of assertion, or *presentation of certainty*. It is not correct to say that it is the mood of certainty or reality. This belongs to the presentation (i.e., the indicative may *present* something as being certain or real, though the speaker might not believe it).

➡1. Declarative Indicative ExSyn 449

a. Definition. The indicative is routinely used to *present* an assertion as a non-contingent (or unqualified) statement. This is by far its most common use.

b. Illustrations

Mark 4:3   ἐξῆλθεν ὁ σπείρων σπεῖραι   the sower **went out** to sow

Rom 3:21   χωρὶς νόμου δικαιοσύνη θεοῦ **πεφανέρωται**
Apart from the law the righteousness of God **has been manifested**.

➡2. Interrogative Indicative ExSyn 449–50

a. Definition. The indicative can be used in a question. The question *expects an assertion* to be made; it expects a declarative indicative in the answer. (This contrasts with the subjunctive, which asks a question of moral "oughtness" or obligation, or asks whether something is possible.) The interrogative indicative typically probes for information. In other words, it does not ask the *how* or the *why*, but the *what.*

Frequently an interrogative particle is used with the indicative, especially to distinguish this usage from the declarative indicative. The interrogative indicative is a common usage, though the *future* indicative is not normally used in this way (cf. deliberative subjunctive below).

b. Illustrations

Matt 27:11   σὺ **εἶ** ὁ βασιλεὺς τῶν Ἰουδαίων;
Are you the king of the Jews?

John 1:38   λέγει αὐτοῖς, Τί **ζητεῖτε**; οἱ δὲ εἶπαν αὐτῷ, Ῥαββί, ... ποῦ **μένεις**;
He said to them, "What **do you seek**?" And they said to him, "Rabbi, ... where **are you staying**?"

➡3. Conditional Indicative ExSyn 450–51

a. Definition. This is the use of the indicative in the protasis of conditional sentences. The conditional element is made explicit with the particle εἰ. This is a relatively common usage of the indicative, though much more so with the first class condition (over 300 instances) than with the second (less than 50 examples).

The first class condition indicates *the assumption of truth for the sake of argument*, while the second class condition indicates *the assumption of an untruth for the sake of argument.*[7]

b. Illustrations. The first example is a second class condition; the second is a first class condition.

1 Cor 2:8   εἰ **ἔγνωσαν**, οὐκ ἂν τὸν κύριον τῆς δόξης ἐσταύρωσαν
If **they had known**, they would not have crucified the Lord of glory

Matt 12:27   εἰ ἐγὼ ἐν Βεελζεβοὺλ **ἐκβάλλω** τὰ δαιμόνια, οἱ υἱοὶ ὑμῶν ἐν τίνι ἐκβάλλουσιν;
If I **cast out** demons by Beelzebul, by whom do your sons cast them out?

The first class condition assumes the truth of the assertion for the sake of argument; it does *not* mean that the speaker necessarily believes it to be true. The force in this verse is "If I cast out demons by Beelzebul—and let us assume that this is true for argument's sake—then by whom do your sons cast them out?"

→**4. Potential Indicative**   *ExSyn 451–52*

a. Definition. The indicative is used with verbs of obligation, wish, or desire, *followed by an infinitive*. The nature of the verb root, rather than the indicative, is what makes it look like a potential mood in its semantic force. This usage is fairly common.

Specifically, verbs indicating obligation (e.g., ὀφείλω, δεῖ), wish (e.g., βούλομαι), or desire (e.g., θέλω) are used with an infinitive.[8]

b. Illustrations

Acts 4:12   οὐδὲ ὄνομά ἐστιν ἕτερον ὑπὸ τὸν οὐρανὸν τὸ δεδομένον ἐν ἀνθρώποις ἐν ᾧ **δεῖ** σωθῆναι ἡμᾶς
There is no other name under heaven given among men by which we **must** [lit., **it is necessary** for us] be saved.

1 Tim 2:8   **βούλομαι** προσεύχεσθαι τοὺς ἄνδρας
I want the men to pray

---

[7] For a detailed treatment, see the chapter on conditional clauses.

[8] Such verbs *lexically* limit the overall assertion, turning it into a potential action. It is important to understand that the normal force of the indicative mood is not thereby denied; rather, the assertion is simply in the desire, not the doing. Thus, this usage is really a subcategory of the declarative indicative.

5. Cohortative (Command, Volitive) Indicative   *ExSyn 452–53*

a. Definition. The *future* indicative is sometimes used for a command, almost always in OT quotations (because of a literal translation of the Hebrew). However, it was used occasionally even in classical Greek. Outside of Matthew, this usage is not common. Its force is emphatic, in keeping with the combined nature of the indicative mood and future tense.

b. Illustrations

Matt 19:18   οὐ **φονεύσεις**, οὐ **μοιχεύσεις**, οὐ **κλέψεις**, οὐ **ψευδομαρ-τυρήσεις**
You shall not **murder, you shall** not **commit adultery, you shall** not **steal, you shall** not **bear false witness.**

1 Pet 1:16   ἅγιοι **ἔσεσθε**, ὅτι ἐγὼ ἅγιός εἰμι
you shall be holy, because I am holy

➡6. The Indicative with Ὅτι   *ExSyn 453–61*

The indicative mood occurs both in independent clauses and dependent clauses. One of the most frequent and complex dependent clauses in which the indicative mood occurs is the ὅτι clause.

Technically, the subcategories included here are not restricted to the syntax of the indicative mood, but involve the function of the ὅτι (+ indicative) clause. But the indicative occurs so frequently after ὅτι that a description of this construction is called for here. There are three broad groups: substantival, epexegetical, and causal.

a. Substantival Ὅτι Clauses   *ExSyn 453–59*

A ὅτι (+ indicative) frequently functions substantivally. It is known as a noun (or nominal) clause, content clause, or sometimes a declarative clause (though we prefer to use this last term for indirect discourse clauses). In such instances the translation of the ὅτι is usually "that." Like a noun, the ὅτι clause can function as subject,[9] direct object, or in apposition to another noun.

(1) DIRECT OBJECT CLAUSE   *ExSyn 454–58*

The direct object clause involves three subgroups, the latter two being common in the NT: direct object proper,[10] direct discourse, and indirect discourse. It is not always easy to distinguish these three.

(a) Direct Discourse (Recitative Ὅτι Clause [Ὅτι Recitativum])   *ExSyn 454–56*

[1] DEFINITION. This is a specialized use of the direct object clause after a verb of perception. It is a common use of the ὅτι clause. In direct discourse, the ὅτι is not to be translated; in its place you should put quotation marks.

---

[9] This usage is sufficiently rare that the average intermediate Greek student may ignore it (see *ExSyn* 453–54).

[10] This usage is sufficiently rare that the average intermediate Greek student may ignore it (see *ExSyn* 454).

[2] ILLUSTRATIONS

John 6:42   πῶς νῦν λέγει [ὅτι ἐκ τοῦ οὐρανοῦ **καταβέβηκα**];
How does he now say, ["**I have come down** from heaven"]?

John 4:17   ἀπεκρίθη ἡ γυνὴ καὶ εἶπεν αὐτῷ· οὐκ ἔχω ἄνδρα. λέγει αὐτῇ ὁ Ἰησοῦς· καλῶς εἶπας [ὅτι ἄνδρα οὐκ **ἔχω**].
The woman answered and said to him, "I do not have a husband." Jesus said to her, "Correctly you have said, ['**I do** not **have** a husband.']"

> In this text Jesus quotes the woman's words, but the word order has now been reversed. Such a change in word order does not turn this into indirect discourse; that would require, in this case, person-concord between the controlling verb (εἶπας) and the embedded verb (ἔχεις would have to be used instead of ἔχω); i.e., "Correctly you have said *that* **you do** not **have** a husband."[11]

(b) Indirect Discourse (Declarative Ὅτι Clause)   ExSyn 456–58

[1] DEFINITION. Also common is this specialized use of a ὅτι clause as the direct object clause after a verb of perception. The ὅτι clause contains *reported speech* or *thought*. This contrasts with ὅτι *recitativum*, which involves direct speech. When the ὅτι introduces indirect discourse, it should be translated *that*.

[2] CLARIFICATION/SEMANTICS. Like its recitative counterpart, the declarative ὅτι comes after a verb of perception (e.g., verbs of saying, thinking, believing, knowing, seeing, hearing). One could think of it as a recasting of an original saying or thought into a reported form. But two caveats are in order. First, in many instances there is no original statement that needs to be recast. For example, in Matt 2:16 ("when Herod saw *that* he had been tricked by the magi" [Ἡρῴδης ἰδὼν ὅτι ἐνεπαίχθη ὑπὸ τῶν μάγων]), we must not suppose that there was an original statement, "I have been tricked by the magi." Indirect discourse, then, should not be taken to mean that there is always an underlying direct discourse. Second, sometimes clauses can be taken either as declarative or recitative.

[3] TRANSLATION DIFFERENCES BETWEEN GREEK AND ENGLISH. One last point needs to be mentioned. Generally speaking, *the tense* of the Greek verb in indirect discourse is *retained* from the direct discourse. This is unlike English: In indirect discourse we usually push the *tense* back "one slot" from what it would have been in the direct discourse (espe-

---

[11] For a more detailed discussion of this text, see *ExSyn* 455–56.

cially if the introductory verb is past tense)—that is, we render a simple past as a past perfect, a present as a past tense, etc. Note the English usage in the table below.

Direct Discourse	*Indirect Discourse*
He said, "I **see** the dog"	He said that he **saw** the dog
He said, "I **saw** the dog"	He said that he **had seen** the dog
"I **am doing** my chores"	I told you that I **was doing** my chores
"I **have done** my chores"	I told you that I **had done** my chores

Table 7
English Tenses in Direct and Indirect Discourse

[4] ILLUSTRATIONS

Matt 5:17   μὴ νομίσητε [ὅτι **ἦλθον** καταλῦσαι τὸν νόμον ἢ τοὺς προφήτας]
Do not think [*that* **I have come** to destroy the law or the prophets].

> This summarizes the views of Jesus' opponents. The supposed direct discourse would have been, "He has come to destroy the law and the prophets."

Mark 2:1   ἠκούσθη [ὅτι ἐν οἴκῳ **ἐστίν**]
It was heard [*that* **he was** at home].

> Note that although the equative verb ἐστίν is here translated as a past tense, it is *not* a historical present. The semantics of historical presents are quite different from the present tense retained in indirect discourse.

John 4:1   ὡς ἔγνω ὁ Ἰησοῦς [ὅτι **ἤκουσαν** οἱ Φαρισαῖοι [ὅτι Ἰησοῦς πλείονας μαθητὰς **ποιεῖ** καὶ **βαπτίζει** ἢ Ἰωάννης]]
when Jesus knew [*that* the Pharisees **had heard** [*that* Jesus **was making** and **baptizing** more disciples than John]]

> This text involves indirect discourse embedded within *another* indirect discourse. It affords a good illustration of the differences between English and Greek. The Greek retains the tenses from the direct discourse, while English moves them back one slot. Thus, ἤκουσαν is translated *had heard* even though it is aorist (the original statement also would have been aorist: "the Pharisees have heard ... "). And both ποιεῖ and βαπτίζει, although present tenses, are translated as though they were imperfects (the original statement would have been "Jesus *is* making and baptizing more disciples than John).

(2) Apposition [*NAMELY, THAT*]   *ExSyn 458–59*

(a) Definition and key to identification. Not infrequently a ὅτι clause stands in apposition to a noun, pronoun, or other substantive. When it does so the translation of the ὅτι as *namely, that* should make good sense (although *that* will also work). Another way to test whether a ὅτι clause is appositional is to try to *substitute* the clause for its antecedent (in which case you translate the ὅτι simply as *that*). This contrasts with the epexegetical ὅτι clause, which cannot be substituted for its antecedent. This usage is normally in apposition to the demonstrative τοῦτο in such expressions as "I say *this* to you, *namely, that* . . . " and the like.

(b) Illustrations

Luke 10:20   ἐν τούτῳ μὴ χαίρετε ὅτι τὰ πνεύματα ὑμῖν **ὑποτάσσεται**
               Do not rejoice in this, [*namely, that* the spirits **are subject** to you].

> The ὅτι clause stands in apposition to ἐν τούτῳ. It could replace it entirely ("Do not rejoice *that* the spirits are subject to you"), as is done in the second half of this verse.

Rom 6:6   τοῦτο γινώσκοντες [ὅτι ὁ παλαιὸς ἡμῶν ἄνθρωπος **συνεσταυρώθη**]
               knowing this, [*namely, that* our old man **was cocrucified**]

b. Epexegetical   *ExSyn 459–60*

The ὅτι clause is sometimes used epexegetically. That is, it *explains, clarifies,* or *completes* a previous word or phrase. This is similar to the appositional ὅτι clause except that the epexegetical ὅτι clause (1) does not identify or name, but instead explains its antecedent; and (2) *cannot be substituted for its antecedent*; and (3) can explain (or complement) something other than a substantive. In some instances (especially after a substantive) the gloss *to the effect that* brings out the explanatory force of the ὅτι clause. Many examples, however, could be treated either as appositional or epexegetical.

Luke 8:25   τίς οὗτός ἐστιν [ὅτι καὶ τοῖς ἀνέμοις **ἐπιτάσσει** καὶ τῷ ὕδατι, καὶ **ὑπακούουσιν** αὐτῷ;]
               Who is this man [*that* **he commands** the winds and the sea, and **they obey** him?]

Rom 5:8   συνίστησιν τὴν ἑαυτοῦ ἀγάπην εἰς ἡμᾶς ὁ θεός, [ὅτι ἔτι ἁμαρτωλῶν ὄντων ἡμῶν Χριστὸς ὑπὲρ ἡμῶν **ἀπέθανεν**]
               God demonstrated his own love toward us [*to the effect that* while we were yet sinners, Christ **died** for us]

c. Causal (Adverbial) [because]   *ExSyn 460–61*

(1) Definition. Frequently ὅτι introduces a dependent causal clause. In such instances it should be translated *because* or *for*. It is important to distinguish this usage from the declarative ὅτι, even though in many contexts there may be some

ambiguity. There are two questions to ask of a particular ὅτι clause: (a) Does it give the *content* (declarative) or the *reason* (causal) for what precedes? (b) Are the verb tenses in the ὅτι clause translated normally (causal), or should they be moved back one "slot" (declarative)?

(2) ILLUSTRATIONS

Matt 5:3   μακάριοι οἱ πτωχοὶ τῷ πνεύματι, ὅτι αὐτῶν **ἐστιν** ἡ βασιλεία τῶν οὐρανῶν
             Blessed are the poor in spirit, *because* the kingdom of heaven **is** theirs.

Eph 4:25   λαλεῖτε ἀλήθειαν ἕκαστος μετὰ τοῦ πλησίον αὐτοῦ, ὅτι **ἐσμὲν** ἀλλήλων μέλη
             Speak the truth, each one [of you], with his neighbor, *because* **we are** members of one another.

The Subjunctive Mood   *ExSyn 461–80*

Definition. The subjunctive is the most common of the oblique moods in the NT. In general, the subjunctive can be said to *represent the verbal action (or state) as uncertain but probable.* It is *not* correct to call this the mood of uncertainty because the optative also presents the verb as uncertain. Rather, it is better to call it the mood of *probability* so as to distinguish it from the optative. Still, this is an overly simplistic definition in light of its usage in the NT.

Detailed description. The subjunctive mood encompasses a multitude of nuances. An adequate description of it requires more nuancing than the mere notion of probability, especially in the Hellenistic era. The best way to describe it is in relation to the other potential moods, the optative and the imperative.

In relation to the optative. We begin by noting that the optative in Koine Greek was dying out; it was too subtle for people acquiring Greek as a second language to grasp fully. In the NT there are 1858 subjunctives and less than 70 optatives—a ratio of 27:1! This simple statistic reflects the fact that in the Hellenistic era *the subjunctive is encroaching on the uses of the optative.* The subjunctive thus, at times, is used for mere *possibility* or even *hypothetical* possibility (as well as, at other times, probability).

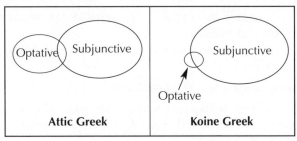

Chart 45
Semantic Overlap of Subjunctive and Optative

On the other hand, sometimes the subjunctive acts like a future indicative. In dependent clauses, for example, often it functions more like an indicative than an optative. When used in result clauses, for example, the subjunctive cannot be said to express "probability." In any event, the one-word descriptions for the moods are meant to be mere handles, not final statements.

In relation to the imperative. The imperative is the primary volitional mood. However, *the subjunctive is also frequently used for volitional notions*, in particular as a hortatory subjunctive and prohibitive subjunctive. Even in dependent clauses (such as after ἵνα), the subjunctive commonly has a volitional flavor to it. An acceptable gloss is often *should*, since this is equally ambiguous (it can be used for *probability, obligation,* or *contingency*).

In sum, the subjunctive is used to grammaticalize *potentiality*. It normally does so in the realm of *cognitive probability*, but may also be used for *cognitive possibility* (overlapping with the optative) or *volitional intentionality* (overlapping with the imperative).

It should be added here that the tenses in the subjunctive, as with the other potential moods, involve only *aspect* (kind of action), not time. Only in the indicative mood is time a part of the tense.

1. In Independent Clauses   *ExSyn 463–69*

There are four primary uses of the subjunctive in independent clauses: hortatory, deliberative, emphatic negation, and prohibition. The first two are usually found without negatives, while the latter two, by definition, are preceded by negative particles. Hortatory and prohibitive subjunctive appeal to the volition; deliberative may be volitional or cognitive; emphatic negation is cognitive.

➡   *a. Hortatory Subjunctive (Volitive) [let us]*   *ExSyn 464–65*

(1) DEFINITION. The subjunctive is commonly used to exhort or command oneself and one's associates. This function of the subjunctive is used "to urge some one to unite with the speaker in a course of action upon which he has already decided."[12] This use of the subjunctive is an exhortation in the *first person plural*. The typical translation, rather than *we should*, is *let us.* . . .

(2) ILLUSTRATIONS[13]

Mark 4:35   καὶ λέγει αὐτοῖς . . . **Διέλθωμεν** εἰς τὸ πέραν
And he said to them . . . "**Let us go** to the other side."

1 Cor 15:32 εἰ νεκροὶ οὐκ ἐγείρονται, **φάγωμεν** καὶ **πίωμεν**, αὔριον γὰρ ἀποθνῄσκομεν
If the dead are not raised, **let us eat** and **drink**, for tomorrow we die.

➡   *b. Deliberative Subjunctive (Dubitative)*   *ExSyn 465–68*

(1) DEFINITION. The deliberative subjunctive asks either a *real* or *rhetorical* question. In general, it can be said that the deliberative subjunctive is "merely the

---

[12] Chamberlain, *Exegetical Grammar*, 83.
[13] For discussion of Rom 5:1, see *ExSyn 464–65*.

hortatory turned into a question," though the semantics of the two are often quite different. Both imply some *doubt* about the response, but the *real* question is usually in the *cognitive* area (such as "How can we . . . ?" in which the inquiry is about the means), while the *rhetorical* question is *volitive* (e.g., "Should we . . . ?" in which the question has to do with moral obligation). Because of this difference in the semantics it is best to distinguish the two kinds of questions. The table below illustrates the *usual* differences.

Name	Type of Question	Expected Response	Area of Doubt
Real	Is it *possible*?	resolution of problem	cognitive
Rhetorical	Is it *right*?	volitional/behavioral	conduct

Table 8
The Semantics of Deliberative Questions

(a) Deliberative Real Subjunctive

[1] DEFINITION. As the name implies, the *real* question expects some kind of answer and is a genuine question. In the speaker's presentation, there is uncertainty about the answer. Unlike the interrogative indicative, it does not ask a question of fact, but of *possibility, means, location,* etc. In other words, it typically does not ask *What?* or *Who?*, but *How? Whether?* and *Where?* Occasionally it can ask a question of moral obligation, like the rhetorical question, but when it does, the expected answer is in doubt.

[2] ILLUSTRATIONS

Matt 6:31   μὴ μεριμνήσητε λέγοντες· τί **φάγωμεν**; ἤ· τί **πίωμεν**; ἤ· τί **περιβαλώμεθα**;
Do not be anxious, saying, "What **should we eat**?" or "What **should we drink**?" or "What **should we wear**?"

Although the question appears to be asking for a specific content, as indicated by the τί (thus, a question of fact), the subjunctive tells a different story. The subjunctive indicates some doubt as to *whether* food or drink or clothing will be available.

Mark 6:37   λέγουσιν αὐτῷ· ἀπελθόντες **ἀγοράσωμεν** δηναρίων διακοσίων ἄρτους καὶ δώσομεν αὐτοῖς φαγεῖν;
They said to him, "**Should we** go and **buy** two hundred denarii worth of bread and give it to them to eat?"

The question here is one of possibility. The disciples are essentially asking, *How* do you expect us to feed these people? To be noted is the future indicative, δώσομεν, that is joined to the aorist subjunctive. It, too, is deliberative.

(b) Deliberative Rhetorical Subjunctive

[1] DEFINITION. As the name implies, the *rhetorical* question expects no *verbal* response but is in fact a thinly disguised statement, though couched in such a way as to draw the listener into the text. In the speaker's presentation, there is uncertainty about whether the listener will heed the implicit command. Unlike the interrogative indicative, it does not ask a question of fact, but of *obligation*. It is supremely a question of "oughtness."

[2] ILLUSTRATIONS

Mark 8:37   τί **δοῖ** ἄνθρωπος ἀντάλλαγμα τῆς ψυχῆς αὐτοῦ;
What **can** a person **give** in exchange for his life?

> Although the question appears to be asking whether such an exchange is possible, it is really an indictment against gaining the world and losing one's life in the process.

Rom 10:14   πῶς **ἀκούσωσιν** χωρὶς κηρύσσοντος;
How **can they hear** without a preacher?

> The implication is that there is no way that they will hear without a preacher.

➡ c. Emphatic Negation Subjunctive   ExSyn 468–69

(1) DEFINITION. Emphatic negation is indicated by οὐ μή plus the *aorist subjunctive* or, less frequently, οὐ μή plus the future indicative. This is the strongest way to negate something in Greek.[14]

(2) ILLUSTRATIONS

John 10:28   δίδωμι αὐτοῖς ζωὴν αἰώνιον καὶ *οὐ μή* **ἀπόλωνται**
I give them eternal life, and **they will** *not at all* **perish**

Heb 13:5   *οὐ μή* σε **ἀνῶ** οὐδ᾽ *οὐ μή* σε **ἐγκαταλίπω**
I will *not at all* **fail** you nor **will I** *ever* **leave** you

➡ d. Prohibitive Subjunctive   ExSyn 469

(1) DEFINITION. This is the use of the subjunctive in a prohibition—that is, a negative command. It is used to forbid the occurrence of an action. The structure is usually μή + *aorist subjunctive*, typically in the *second* person.[15] Its force is equivalent to an imperative after μή; hence, it should be translated *Do not* rather than *You should not*. The prohibitive subjunctive is frequently used in the NT.

---

[14] One might think that the negative with the subjunctive could not be as strong as the negative with the indicative. However, while οὐ + the indicative denies a *certainty*, οὐ μή + the subjunctive denies a *potentiality*. The negative is not weaker; rather, the affirmation that is being negatived is less firm with the subjunctive. οὐ μή rules out even the idea as being a possibility.

[15] In fact, nowhere in the NT is the *second person aorist imperative* used after μή.

(2) ILLUSTRATIONS

John 3:7   μὴ **θαυμάσῃς** ὅτι εἶπόν σοι· δεῖ ὑμᾶς γεννηθῆναι ἄνωθεν.
            Do *not* **be amazed** that I said to you, "You must be born again."

Rev 22:10   μὴ **σφραγίσῃς** τοὺς λόγους τῆς προφητείας τοῦ βιβλίου τούτου
            Do *not* **seal up** the words of the prophecy of this book

2. In Dependent (Subordinate) Clauses   *ExSyn* 469–80

The following categories of the subjunctive are the primary uses when the subjunctive is in a dependent or subordinate clause. By far the most common category is the use of the subjunctive after ἵνα.

➡ ### a. Subjunctive in Conditional Sentences   *ExSyn* 469–71

(1) DEFINITION. This is the use of the subjunctive in the protasis of conditional sentences. The conditional element is made explicit by the particle ἐάν.

(2) CLARIFICATION AND SEMANTICS. The subjunctive is used in the *third class condition* as well as the *fifth class condition*. Structurally, these two are virtually identical: The *fifth* class condition requires a present indicative in the apodosis, while the *third* class can take virtually any mood-tense combination, including the present indicative.

Semantically, their meaning is a bit different. The *third* class condition encompasses a broad range of potentialities in Koine Greek. It depicts what is *likely to occur* in the *future*, what could *possibly occur*, or even what is only *hypothetical* and will not occur.

The *fifth* class offers a condition the fulfillment of which is realized in the *present time*. This condition is known as the *present general condition*. For the most part this condition is a *simple* condition; that is, the speaker gives no indication about the likelihood of its fulfillment. His presentation is neutral: "If A, then B."

Because of the broad range of the third class condition and the undefined nature of the fifth class, many conditional clauses are open to interpretation.[16]

(3) ILLUSTRATIONS

Matt 4:9   ταῦτά σοι πάντα δώσω, ἐὰν πεσὼν **προσκυνήσῃς** μοι
            I will give you all these things, *if* **you will** fall down and **worship** me

            This is a true third class since the apodosis involves a future indicative.

John 5:31   ἐὰν ἐγὼ **μαρτυρῶ** περὶ ἐμαυτοῦ, ἡ μαρτυρία μου οὐκ ἔστιν ἀληθής
            If **I bear testimony** about myself, my testimony is not true

            The present tense in the apodosis (ἔστιν) permits this to be taken as a fifth class condition. In the context, it seems to be the

---

[16] For a detailed treatment on the subjunctive in conditions, see the chapter on conditional clauses.

best option: Jesus is not saying that it is probable that he will bear testimony about himself. Rather, he is simply stating a supposition ("If A, then B").

➡ ### b. Ἵνα + the Subjunctive   *ExSyn 471–77*

The single most common category of the subjunctive in the NT is after ἵνα, comprising about *one third* of all subjunctive instances. There are seven basic uses included in this construction: purpose, result, purpose-result, substantival, epexegetical, complementary, and command.[17]

(1) PURPOSE Ἵνα CLAUSE (FINAL OR TELIC Ἵνα)   *ExSyn 472*

The most frequent use of ἵνα clauses is to express purpose. The focus is on the *intention* of the action of the main verb, whether accomplished or not. In keeping with the genius of the subjunctive, this subordinate clause answers the question *Why?* rather than *What?* An appropriate translation would be *in order that*, or, where fitting, as a simple infinitive (*to . . .*).[18]

Acts 16:30   τί με δεῖ ποιεῖν ἵνα **σωθῶ**;
             What must I do *to* **be saved**?

1 John 2:1   ταῦτα γράφω ὑμῖν ἵνα μὴ **ἁμάρτητε**
             I am writing these things to you *in order that* **you might** not **sin**

(2) PURPOSE-RESULT Ἵνα CLAUSE   *ExSyn 473–74*

A purpose-result ἵνα indicates *both the intention and its sure accomplishment*. "In many cases purpose and result cannot be clearly differentiated, and hence ἵνα is used for the result which follows according to the purpose of the subj[ect] or of God. As in Jewish and pagan thought, purpose and result are identical in declarations of the divine will."[19]

John 3:16   τὸν υἱὸν τὸν μονογενῆ ἔδωκεν, ἵνα πᾶς ὁ πιστεύων εἰς αὐτὸν μὴ **ἀπόληται** ἀλλ᾽ **ἔχῃ** ζωὴν αἰώνιον
             He gave his only Son, *in order that* everyone who believes in him **should** not **perish** but **should have** eternal life.

> The fact that the subjunctive is all but required after ἵνα does not, of course, argue for uncertainty as to the fate of the believer. This fact is obvious, not from this text, but from the use of of οὐ μή in John 10:28 and 11:26, as well as the general theological contours of the Gospel of John.

---

[17] Of these seven uses, the result (see *ExSyn* 473), the epexegetical (476), and the command (476-77) uses are sufficiently rare that the average intermediate Greek student may ignore them.

[18] This use of the subjunctive does not necessarily imply any doubt about the fulfillment of the verbal action on the part of the speaker. This may or may not be so; each case must be judged on its own merits.

[19] BAGD, s.v., ἵνα, II. 2. (p. 378).

Phil 2:9–11   ὁ θεὸς αὐτὸν ὑπερύψωσεν . . . **ἵνα** ἐν τῷ ὀνόματι Ἰησοῦ πᾶν γόνυ **κάμψῃ**. . .καὶ πᾶσα γλῶσσα **ἐξομολογήσηται** ὅτι κύριος Ἰησοῦς Χριστός

God highly exalted him . . . *in order that* at the name of Jesus every knee **should bow** . . . and every tongue **should confess** that Jesus Christ is Lord

> Paul here is not declaring *only* God's *intention* in exalting Christ. It is much more than that. The apostle is indicating that what God intends he will carry out.[20]

(3) Substantival Ἵνα Clause (Subfinal Clause)   *ExSyn 474–76*

As with ὅτι plus the indicative, ἵνα plus the subjunctive can be used substantively. There are four basic uses: subject, predicate nominative, direct object, and apposition. As with substantival ὅτι clauses, the ἵνα clause will be bracketed so as to highlight its substantival force. None is especially frequent. Below are examples of predicate nominative, direct object, and apposition.

John 4:34   ἐμὸν βρῶμά ἐστιν [**ἵνα ποιήσω** τὸ θέλημα τοῦ πέμψαντός με καὶ **τελειώσω** αὐτοῦ τὸ ἔργον]

My food is [*that* **I should do** the will of the one who sent me and **complete** his work].

Luke 4:3   εἰ υἱὸς εἶ τοῦ θεοῦ, εἰπὲ τῷ λίθῳ τούτῳ [**ἵνα γένηται** ἄρτος]

If you are God's Son, say to this stone [*that* **it should become** bread].

John 17:3   αὕτη ἐστιν ἡ αἰώνιος ζωὴ [**ἵνα γινώσκωσιν** σὲ τὸν μόνον ἀληθινὸν θεόν]

This is eternal life, [*namely, that* **they might know** you, the only true God].

(4) Complementary Ἵνα   *ExSyn 476*

The complementary ἵνα *completes* the meaning of a helping verb such as θέλω, δύναμαι, and the like. In classical Greek this would have been expressed by a complementary infinitive. Although complementary, the force of the entire construction (verb + ἵνα clause) is usually that of *purpose* (in keeping with the lexeme of the main verb).

Luke 6:31   καθὼς θέλετε **ἵνα ποιῶσιν** ὑμῖν οἱ ἄνθρωποι ποιεῖτε αὐτοῖς ὁμοίως

Just as you wish [*that* people **should do** to you], do likewise to them.

---

[20] For discussion, see *ExSyn* 474.

1 Cor 14:5   θέλω πάντας ὑμᾶς λαλεῖν γλώσσαις, μᾶλλον δὲ [ἵνα προφη-
             τεύητε]
             I want you all to speak in tongues, but even more [*to* **prophesy**]

> Note the parallel between the first half of the verse, which uses
> a complementary infinitive, and the second half, which uses a
> complementary ἵνα clause.

c. Subjunctive with Verbs of Fearing, etc.   *ExSyn* 477

(1) DEFINITION. Μή plus the subjunctive can be used after verbs of *fearing,
warning, watching out for*, etc. Not unusual in the better writers (Paul, Luke,
Hebrews), this construction serves as a warning or suggests caution or anxiety.

(2) ILLUSTRATIONS

Luke 21:8   βλέπετε μὴ πλανηθῆτε
             Watch out that **you are** *not* **deceived**

Heb 4:1   φοβηθῶμεν ... μήποτε ... δοκῇ τις ἐξ ὑμῶν ὑστερηκέναι
             Let us fear ... *lest* ... anyone of you **should appear** to have
             failed

d. Subjunctive in Indirect Questions   *ExSyn* 478

(1) DEFINITION. The subjunctive is sometimes used in indirect questions. In
such a usage, it follows the main verb, but appears awkward, even unconnected,
in the sentence structure. Because of this the subjunctive (and its accompanying
interrogative particle) needs to be smoothed out in translation.

(2) ILLUSTRATIONS

Matt 15:32   ἤδη ἡμέραι τρεῖς προσμένουσίν μοι καὶ οὐκ ἔχουσιν τί
             φάγωσιν
             They have already been with me [for] three days and they do
             not have anything **to eat.**

> Literally, "they do not have *what* **they might eat.**" The direct
> question would have been, τί φάγωμεν ("What are we to eat?").

Luke 9:58   ὁ υἱὸς τοῦ ἀνθρώπου οὐκ ἔχει ποῦ τὴν κεφαλὴν κλίνῃ
             The Son of Man has no place where **he could lay** his head.

➡ ### e. Subjunctive in Indefinite Relative Clause   *ExSyn* 478–79

(1) DEFINITION. The subjunctive is frequently used after ὅστις (ἄν/ἐάν) or
ὅς (δ᾽) ἄν. The construction normally indicates a generic (or sometimes an uncertain) subject; hence, the particle of contingency and the need for a subjunctive.
The construction is roughly the *equivalent of a third class or fifth class condition.*[21]

---

[21] The difference is that in indefinite relative clauses the element of contingency is not
that of time but of person. Hence, the subjunctive is often translated like an indicative, since the
potential element belongs to the subject rather than the verb.

(2) ILLUSTRATIONS

John 4:14 ὅς δ᾿ ἄν **πίῃ** ἐκ τοῦ ὕδατος οὗ ἐγὼ δώσω αὐτῷ, οὐ μὴ διψή-
σει εἰς τὸν αἰῶνα
Whoever **drinks** of the water that I will give him will never thirst
again.

Gal 5:10 ὁ ταράσσων ὑμᾶς βαστάσει τὸ κρίμα, ὅστις ἐὰν **ᾖ**
The one who is troubling you will bear [his] judgment, *whoever*
he is.

→ *f. Subjunctive in Indefinite Temporal Clause*   *ExSyn* 479–80

(1) DEFINITION. The subjunctive is frequently used after a *temporal adverb* (or
improper preposition) meaning *until* (e.g., ἕως, ἄχρι, μέχρι), or after the temporal
conjunction ὅταν with the meaning, *whenever*. It indicates a future contingency
from the perspective of the time of the main verb.

(2) ILLUSTRATIONS

Matt 5:11 μακάριοί ἐστε ὅταν **ὀνειδίσωσιν** ὑμᾶς
Blessed are you *whenever* **they revile** you

1 Cor 11:26 τὸν θάνατον τοῦ κυρίου καταγγέλλετε *ἄχρι* οὗ **ἔλθῃ**
you do proclaim the Lord's death *until* **he comes**

The Optative Mood   *ExSyn* 480–84

There are less than 70 optatives in the entire NT. In general, it can be said
that the optative is the mood used when a speaker wishes to portray an action as
possible. It usually addresses cognition, but may be used to appeal to the volition.

→1. **Voluntative Optative (Optative of Obtainable Wish,**
     Volitive Optative)   *ExSyn* 481–83

a. Definition. This is the use of the optative in an independent clause to
express an *obtainable wish* or a *prayer*. It is frequently an appeal to the *will*, in particular when used in prayers.

This optative fits one of three nuances: (1) *mere possibility* that something will
take place; (2) *stereotyped formula* that has lost its optative "flavor": μὴ γένοιτο
usually has the force of abhorrence, and may in some contexts be the equivalent
of οὐ μή + aorist subjunctive (a very strong negative); or (3) *polite request* without
necessarily a hint of doubting what the response will be.

The voluntative optative is the most common optative category (at least 35
of the 68–69 uses belong here). One set idiom makes up almost half of all the voluntative optatives: μὴ γένοιτο, an expression that occurs 15 times (14 of which
occur in Paul).

b. Illustrations[22]

Rom 3:3–4   εἰ ἠπίστησάν τινες, μὴ ἡ ἀπιστία αὐτῶν τὴν πίστιν τοῦ θεοῦ
καταργήσει; μὴ **γένοιτο**· γινέσθω δὲ ὁ θεὸς ἀληθής, πᾶς δὲ
ἄνθρωπος ψεύστης
If some did not believe, their unbelief will not nullify the faithfulness of God, will it? **May it** never **be**! But let God be [found]
true, and every man [be found] a liar!

2 Tim 1:16   **δῴη** ἔλεος ὁ κύριος τῷ Ὀνησιφόρου οἴκῳ
May the Lord **grant** mercy on the house of Onesiphorus!

The Imperative Mood   ExSyn 485–93

The imperative mood is the mood of *intention*. It is the mood furthest
removed from certainty. Ontologically, as one of the potential or oblique moods,
the imperative moves in the realm of *volition* (involving the imposition of one's
will upon another) and *possibility*. There are many exceptions to this twofold "flavor" of the imperative in actual usage, although in almost every instance the
rhetorical power of the imperative is still felt.

➡1. **Command**   ExSyn 485–86

a. Definition. The imperative is most commonly used for commands,[23] out-
numbering prohibitive imperatives about five to one. As a command, the imperative is usually from a superior to an inferior in rank. It occurs frequently with
the aorist and present (only rarely with the perfect tense).

The basic force of the imperative of command involves somewhat different
nuances with each tense. With the *aorist*, the force generally is to *command the
action as a whole*, without focusing on duration, repetition, etc. In keeping with its
aspectual force, the aorist puts forth a *summary command*. With the *present*, the
force generally is to *command the action as an ongoing process*. This is in keeping
with the present's aspect, which portrays an *internal* perspective.

One final note: the *third person* imperative is normally translated *Let him do*,
etc. This is easily confused in English with a permissive idea. Its force is more
akin to *he must*, however, or periphrastically, *I command him to....*

b. Illustrations

Mark 2:14   **ἀκολούθει** μοι   **Follow** me!

Jas 1:5   εἰ τις ὑμῶν λείπεται σοφίας, **αἰτείτω** παρὰ τοῦ ... θεοῦ
If anyone of you lacks wisdom, **let him ask** of God.

The force of the imperative is probably not a mere urging or
permission, but a command, in spite of the typical English ren-
dering. An expanded gloss is, "If anyone of you lacks wisdom,
he must ask of God."

---

[22] For a discussion of 1 Thess 3:11, see *ExSyn* 482–83.

[23] See the chapter on volitional clauses for a more detailed discussion.

➡2. Prohibition

ExSyn 487

a. Definition. The imperative is commonly used to forbid an action.[24] It is simply a negative command (see discussion above). μή (or a cognate) is used before the imperative to turn the command into a prohibition. Almost all instances in the NT involve the present tense. The aorist is customarily found as a prohibitive *subjunctive*.

b. Illustrations

Mark 5:36   μὴ **φοβοῦ**, μόνον πίστευε.   **Do** *not* **be afraid**; only believe.

Rom 6:12   μὴ **βασιλευέτω** ἡ ἁμαρτία ἐν τῷ θνητῷ ὑμῶν σώματι
Do *not* **let** sin **reign** in your mortal body.

➡3. Request (Entreaty, Polite Command)

ExSyn 487–88

a. Definition. The imperative is often used to express a request. This is normally seen when the speaker is addressing a superior. Imperatives (almost always in the *aorist* tense) directed toward God in prayers fit this category. The request can be a positive one or a *negative* one (*please, do not . . .*); in such cases the particle μή precedes the verb.

b. Illustrations

Matt 6:10–11 **ἐλθέτω** ἡ βασιλεία σου· **γενηθήτω** τὸ θέλημά σου . . . τὸν ἄρτον ἡμῶν τὸν ἐπιούσιον **δὸς** ἡμῖν σήμερον
Let your kingdom **come**, **let** your will **be done** . . . **give** us today our daily bread

2 Cor 5:20   δεόμεθα ὑπὲρ Χριστοῦ, **καταλλάγητε** τῷ θεῷ
We ask you for the sake of Christ, **be reconciled** to God.

4. Conditional Imperative

ExSyn 489–92

a. Definition. The imperative may at times be used to state a condition (protasis) on which the fulfillment (apodosis) of another verb depends. There are at least twenty such imperatives in the NT.

b. Structure and semantics. This use of the imperative is always or almost always found in the construction *imperative* + καί + *future indicative*. The idea is "If X, then Y will happen." As well, there are a few constructions in which the verb in the apodosis is either another imperative or οὐ μή + subjunctive, though all of these are disputed.

Even if these disputed constructions are valid, it is significant that in each one of them *the trailing verb is semantically equivalent to a future indicative*. Take John 1:46, for example: εἶπεν αὐτῷ Ναθαναήλ· ἐκ Ναζαρὲτ δύναταί τι ἀγαθὸν εἶναι· λέγει αὐτῷ ὁ Φίλιππος· **ἔρχου** καὶ **ἴδε**. (Nathanael said to him, "What good

---

[24] See the chapter on volitional clauses for a more detailed discussion, particularly of the use of tenses in prohibitions.

thing can come out of Nazareth?" Philip said to him, "**Come** and **see**!") If ἔρχου is conditional, then the trailing imperative bears the force of a future indicative: "If you come, you will see."

All of the disputed examples display these same semantics, viz., that the trailing verb functions as though it were a future indicative. Further, *none of the undisputed conditional imperatives seems to have lost its injunctive force.* That is to say, even though the imperative is translated by *if you do* and the like, the imperative was used precisely because it communicated something that another mood could not.

c. Illustrations

(1) CLEAR EXAMPLES

Matt 7:7   **αἰτεῖτε** καὶ δοθήσεται ὑμῖν
           Ask and it will be given to you
                The idea is "If you ask (and you should), it will be given to you."

Jas 4:7   **ἀντίστητε** τῷ διαβόλῳ, καὶ φεύξεται ἀφ᾽ ὑμῶν·
           Resist the devil and he will flee from you.

(2) A DEBATABLE AND EXEGETICALLY SIGNIFICANT TEXT

Eph 4:26   **ὀργίζεσθε** καὶ μὴ ἁμαρτάνετε
           Be angry and do not sin
                Although many NT scholars regard ὀργίζεσθε as a conditional imperative, this is unlikely because it does not fit the semantics of other conditional imperatives. Not only are there no undisputed examples of conditional imperatives in the construction imperative + καί + imperative in the NT, all of the possible conditional imperatives in the construction imperative + καί + imperative require the trailing imperative to function semantically like a *future indicative*. If applied to Eph 4:26, this would mean, "If you are angry, you will *not sin*"—an obviously ludicrous meaning. It is thus best to take ὀργίζεσθε as a command. As such, the force is something of a shorthand for church discipline, a theme quite appropriate in this context.[25]

---

[25] See the discussion in *ExSyn* 491–93.

Tenses: An Introduction[1]
Overview

Definition of Tense. 213
The Element of Time. 213
  1. Three Kinds of Time and the Verb Mood. 213
  2. Portrayal Vs. Reality of Time. 215
The Element of Aspect (Kind of Action). 215
  1. Definition of Aspect 215
  2. Types of Action Possible. 216
  3. Portrayal Vs. Reality of Aspect. 217

Definition of Tense   *ExSyn 496–97*

In general, *tense* in Greek involves two elements: *aspect* (kind of action, [sometimes called *Aktionsart*, though a difference does need to be made between the two]) and *time*. Aspect is the primary value of tense in Greek and time is secondary, if involved at all. In other words, *tense is that feature of the verb that indicates the speaker's presentation of the verbal action (or state) with reference to its aspect and, under certain conditions, its time.* [2]

The tenses in Greek are the present, future, perfect, imperfect, aorist, and pluperfect.[3]

The Element of Time   *ExSyn 497–98*

1. Three Kinds of Time and the Verb Mood

Three kinds of time may be portrayed by tense: past, present, future. These are natural to English, but some languages employ other ideas—e.g., past, non-past; near, far; completed, uncompleted; etc. For the most part, the *mood* of the verb dictates whether or not time is an element of the tense.

a. Indicative. Time is clearly involved. We could in a sense speak of time as *absolute* (or *independent*) in the indicative in that it is dependent directly on the speaker's time frame, not something within the utterance itself. There are occasions, of course, when time is not involved in the indicative. This is due to other phenomena such as genre, lexeme, the nature of the subject or object (e.g., whether general or specific), etc. But in their unaffected meaning (i.e., in their essence, undisturbed by other considerations), the tenses in the indicative mood include a temporal marker.

---

[1] See *ExSyn* 494–512.

[2] It is our conviction that the Greek tense does grammaticalize time; this chapter and the chapters on the tenses assume that. For a discussion of whether tenses grammaticalize time, see *ExSyn* 504–12.

[3] The future perfect also occurs, but in the NT only in periphrasis.

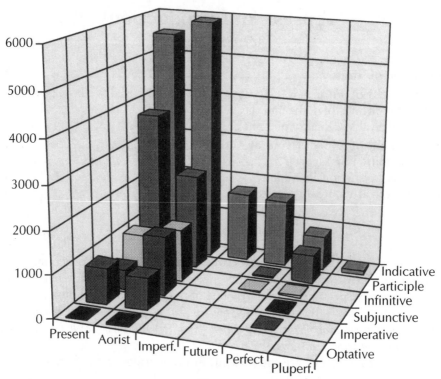

Chart 46
Relative Frequency of Tenses in the New Testament[4]

b. Participle.[5] Time is very often involved in a participle, although here it is *relative* (or *dependent*). Time with participles (especially adverbial participles) depends on the time of the main verb. The participle is not directly connected to the time frame of the speaker and hence cannot be said to be absolute. Still, the three kinds of time are the same: past, present, future. But with the participle "past" means past with reference to the verb, not the speaker (it is called *antecedent*), present is present in relation to the verb (*contemporaneous*), and future is future only with reference to the verb (*subsequent*). The times are for the most part the same; the frame of reference is all that has changed.

c. Subjunctive, Optative, Imperative, Infinitive. Except in indirect discourse, time is not seen with these moods. Thus an aorist in the subjunctive would have a futuristic (or potential) flavor, while in the indicative it would have a past idea. We can say, then, that for the most part time is irrelevant or nonexistent in the oblique (nonindicative) moods.

---

[4] The specific breakdown of each tense is as follows: present—11,583; aorist—11,606; imperfect—1682; future—1623; perfect—1571; pluperfect—86. These numbers do not take into account periphrastics.

[5] Participles and infinitives are technically not moods; but since they take the place of a mood, it is both convenient and semantically suitable to discuss them with reference to time.

To sum up: In general, time is absolute in the indicative, relative in the participle, and nonexistent in the other moods.

2. Portrayal Vs. Reality of Time

Although an author may use a tense in the indicative, the time indicated by that tense *may* be other than or broader than the *real* time of the event. All such examples belong to phenomenological categories. As such, there will normally be sufficient clues (context, genre, lexeme, other grammatical features) to signal the temporal suppression.

a. Other than. Examples of time *other than* what the tense (in the indicative) signifies include the historical present, futuristic present, proleptic aorist, and epistolary aorist.

b. Broader than. Examples of time *broader than* what the tense (in the indicative) signifies include the gnomic present, extension-from-past present, the gnomic aorist, and the gnomic future.

The Element of Aspect (Kind of Action)   *ExSyn* 499–504

1. Definition of Aspect   *ExSyn* 499–500

a. Basic definition. Verbal aspect is, in general, the portrayal of the action (or state) as to its *progress*, *results*, or *simple occurrence*.

b. Aspect versus Aktionsart. It is important to distinguish aspect from *Aktionsart*. In general, we can say that *aspect* is the unaffected meaning while *Aktionsart* is aspect in combination with lexical, grammatical, or contextual features. Thus, the present tense views the action from within, without respect to beginning or end (aspect), while some uses of the present tense can be iterative, historical, futuristic, etc. (all of these belong to *Aktionsart* and are meanings of the verb affected by other features of the language). This is the same kind of distinction we have earlier called ontological vs. phenomenological (terms that can be applied to any morpho-syntactic category, not just the verb tense).

It is not technically correct to say that aspect is subjective while *Aktionsart* is objective. Such a statement tacitly assumes that there is a one-to-one correspondence between language and reality. *Aktionsart* is not actually objective, although it may be presented as more in tune with the actual event.[6]

Pragmatically, this distinction between aspect and *Aktionsart* is helpful in three ways. (1) The basic definition of a given tense deals with aspect, while the various categories of usage deal with *Aktionsart*. Thus, although the basic definition is the "purest," least-affected meaning, it is also the most artificial. What we

---

[6] To argue that *Aktionsart* is objective is akin to saying that the indicative mood is the mood of fact. There is no necessary reality that corresponds to either the indicative or a particular *Aktionsart*.

see is a verb that has as many as seven different morphological tags to it (one of which may be present tense), one lexical tag (the stem)—and all this in a given context (both literary and historical). Although we may be, at the time, trying to analyze the meaning of the present tense, all of these other linguistic features are crowding the picture.

(2) One error in this regard is to see a particular category of usage (*Aktionsart*) as underlying the entire tense usage (aspect). This is the error of *saying too much*. Statements such as "the aorist means once-for-all action" are of this sort. It is true that the aorist may, under certain circumstances, describe an event that is, in reality, momentary. But we run into danger when we say that this is the aorist's unaffected meaning, for then we force it on the text in an artificial way. We then tend to ignore such aorists that disprove our view (and they can be found in every chapter of the NT) and proclaim loudly the "once-for-all" aorists when they suit us.

(3) Another error is to assume that nothing more than the unaffected meaning can ever be seen in a given tense usage. This is the error of *saying too little*. To argue, for example, that the aorist is always the "unmarked" tense, or "default" tense, fits this. This view fails to recognize that the tense does not exist in a vacuum. Categories of usage are legitimate because the tenses combine with other linguistic features to form various fields of meaning.

2. Types of Action Possible   *ExSyn 500–501*

Greek has essentially three aspects or types of action: internal, external, and perfective-stative. Admittedly, these terms are not very descriptive. Perhaps an illustration might help. To sit in the stands as a spectator and watch a parade as it is passing by is an *internal* perspective: One views the parade in its progression, without focusing on the beginning or end. To view the parade from a blimp as a news commentator several hundred feet in the air is an *external* perspective: One views the whole of the parade without focusing on its internal makeup. To walk down the street after the parade is over as part of the clean-up crew is a *perfective-stative* view: While recognizing that the parade is completed (external), one stands in the midst of the ongoing results (internal)!

a. Internal (or progressive). The internal portrayal *"focuses on* [the action's] *development or progress and sees the occurrence in regard to its internal make-up, without beginning or end in view."*[7] This is the detailed or open-ended portrayal of an action. It is sometimes called *progressive*; it "basically represents an activity as in process (or in progress)."[8] The tense-forms involved are the *present* and *imperfect*.

---

[7] Fanning, *Verbal Aspect*, 103. Italics in the original. "Linear" (or "durative") is the old description with which most are familiar.

[8] McKay, "Time and Aspect," 225. Although this gives one a better handle on the idea, it is often too restrictive in its application.

b. External (or summary). The external portrayal "presents an occurrence *in summary, viewed as a whole from the outside, without regard for the internal make-up of the occurrence.*"[9] The tense-form involved is the aorist. As well, the future apparently belongs here.

c. Perfective-stative (stative, resultative, completed). The unaffected meaning is a combination of the external and internal aspects: The *action* is portrayed *externally* (summary), while the *resultant state* proceeding from the action is portrayed *internally* (continuous state). The tense-forms involved are the *perfect* and *pluperfect.*

3. Portrayal Vs. Reality of Aspect   *ExSyn 502–4*

a. Lack of precise correspondence. There is a genuine difference between *portrayal* of action and the real *progress* of the action. An author may *portray* the action as summary, or he may portray the action as progressive, stative, etc. In some respects, it may be helpful to see the various aspects as analogous to photography. The aorist would be a *snapshot*, simply viewing the action as a whole without further adieu. It would be the establishment shot, or the portrayal that keeps the narrative moving at a brisk pace. The imperfect would be a *motion picture*, portraying the action as it unfolds. This is more of an "up close and personal" kind of portrayal.

The same event might be portrayed with two different tenses, even within the same gospel. This illustrates the fact that *an author often has a choice in the tense he uses* and that *portrayal is not the same as reality.* For example:

Mark 12:41   πλούσιοι **ἔβαλλον** πολλά
the rich **were casting in** much

> The imperfect is used because the scene is in progress. Thus it looks at the incident from the inside.

Mark 12:44   πάντες γὰρ ἐκ τοῦ περισσεύοντος αὐτοῖς **ἔβαλον**
For these all, out of their abundance, **cast** [their money] **in**

> The aorist is now used at the conclusion of Jesus' story as a summary of the event just witnessed.

b. The issue of choice. (1) *Selected by the speaker.* A basic issue in the tense used is *how much* a speaker wants to say about the progress or results of an action, or what he wants to *emphasize.* This is not a question of accurate description vs. inaccurate description, but of fuller description vs. simple statement of action, *or* of one emphasis vs. another of the *same* action. For example:

---

[9] Fanning, *Verbal Aspect*, 97. Cf. also McKay, "Time and Aspect," 225. Again, it is important to remember that this is a definition of the aorist's *aspect*, not its *Aktionsart*, for the latter is a combination of this ontological meaning with other features of the language. Thus, in a given context and with a given verb in the aorist tense, an author may indicate something of the internal make-up of the occurrence.

Rom 3:23   πάντες γὰρ **ἥμαρτον**   for all **have sinned**

> The *aorist* is used here, leaving the action in some sense unde-
> fined. However, it is an equally true statement that: "all sin"
> (present—customary) *and* "all have sinned" (perfect—past
> action with continuing results). Therefore, Paul's choice of the
> aorist was used to emphasize one aspect or possibly to say less
> (or to *stress* the *fact* of humanity's sinfulness) than the present or
> perfect would have done. However, any of these three tenses
> could have been used to describe the human condition. An
> author's portrayal is thus selective at times and simply brings out
> the aspect that he wants to emphasize at the time rather than
> giving the full-orbed reality of the event.

(2) *Restricted by the lexeme, context, etc.* Many actions are restricted to a particular tense. For example, if a speaker wishes to indicate an action that is intrinsically *terminal* (such as "find" or "die" or "give birth to"), the choice of tense is
dramatically reduced. We would not usually say "he was finding his book." The
imperfect, under normal circumstances, would thus be inappropriate. By contrast,
if an author wished to speak of the unchanging nature of a *state* (such as "I have"
or "I live"), the aorist would normally not be appropriate. Indeed, when the aorist
of such stative verbs is used, the emphasis is most frequently on the *entrance into
the state.*

The point is that often the choice of a tense is made for a speaker by the
action being described. At times the tense chosen by the speaker is the *only* one
that could be used to portray the idea. Three major factors determine this: lexical meaning of the verb (e.g., whether the verb stem indicates a terminal or punctual act, a state, etc.), contextual factors, and other grammatical features (e.g.,
mood, voice, transitiveness, etc). This is precisely the difference between aspect
and *Aktionsart*: Aspect is the basic meaning of the tense, unaffected by considerations in a given utterance, while *Aktionsart* is the meaning of the tense as used
by an author in a particular utterance, affected as it were by other features of the
language.

The Present Tense[1]
Overview of Uses

Narrow-Band Presents **221**
➡ 1. Instantaneous Present (Aoristic or Punctiliar Present) 221
➡ 2. Progressive Present (Descriptive Present) 222
Broad-Band Presents **222**
3. Extending-from-Past Present 222
➡ 4. Iterative Present 223
➡ 5. Customary (Habitual or General) Present 224
➡ 6. Gnomic Present 224
Special Uses of the Present **225**
➡ 7. Historical Present (Dramatic Present) 226
8. Perfective Present 227
9. Conative (Tendential, Voluntative) Present 228
a. In Progress, but not Complete (True Conative) 228
b. Not Begun, but About/Desired to be Attempted
(Voluntative/Tendential) 229
➡10. Futuristic Present 229
a. Completely Futuristic 229
b. Mostly Futuristic (Ingressive-Futuristic?) 230
➡11. Present Retained in Indirect Discourse 230

———————— INTRODUCTION ———————— *ExSyn 514–16*

Aspect

With reference to *aspect*, the present tense is *internal* (that is, it portrays the action from the inside of the event, without special regard for beginning or end), but it makes no comment as to fulfillment (or completion). The present tense's portrayal of an event *"focuses on its development or progress* and sees the occurrence *in regard to its internal make-up, without beginning or end in view."*[2] It is sometimes called *progressive*: It "basically represents an activity as in process (or in progress)."[3]

Time

With reference to *time*, the present *indicative* is usually present time, but it may be other than or broader than the present time on occasion (e.g., with the historical present and gnomic present respectively).

---

[1] See *ExSyn* 513–39.

[2] Fanning, *Verbal Aspect in New Testament Greek*, 103 (italics in original).

[3] K. L. McKay, "Time and Aspect," 225. Although this gives one a better handle on the idea, it is often too restrictive in its application.

Aspect + Time (The Unaffected Meaning)

What is fundamental to keep in mind as you examine each of the tenses is the difference between the unaffected meaning and the affected meaning and how they relate to each other. Part of this difference is between aspect and *Aktionsart*. (The other part has to do with the temporal element of tense [restricted to the indicative mood].) Together, aspect and time constitute the "ontological meaning" or unaffected meaning of a given tense in the indicative. In this case, it is the meaning the present tense would have if we could see such a tense in a vacuum—without context, without a lexical intrusion from the verb, and without other grammatical features (either in the verb itself or in some other word in the sentence that is impacting the tense). In other words, the unaffected meaning of the present tense is its *basic idea*. However, this unaffected meaning is only theoretical. No one has ever observed it for any of the tenses, simply because we cannot observe a tense that is not attached to a verb (which has lexical value): -ω is a morpheme, while πιστεύω is a present tense verb. The unaffected meaning, then, is something that has been extrapolated from actual usage.

What is the value of having such a theoretical knowledge of the tenses? It helps us in at least two ways. (1) Since the affected meanings are what we call "Specific Uses," the more we know how the tense is affected, the more certain we can be of its usage in a given passage. *The three intrusions mentioned above (lexical, contextual, grammatical) are the staple things that make up affected meanings.* The more we analyze such intrusions, the better we can predict when a given tense (or case or voice or any other morpho-syntactic element of the language) will fit into a particular category of usage.

(2) It is important to understand that the unaffected meaning can be overridden—to some degree but not entirely—by the intrusions. That is to say, it is not correct to say that the unaffected meaning will always be present in full force in any given context. The unaffected meaning is not, therefore, the lowest common denominator of the tense uses. But neither will it be completely abandoned. An author chooses his particular tense for a reason, just as he chooses his mood, lexical root, etc. All of these contribute to the meaning he wishes to express. They are all, as it were, vying for control.

In sum, it is imperative that one pay close attention to the various influences affecting the meaning of the tense. All of these influences, in combination with the present tense, contribute to the specific category of usage under question.

———— SPECIFIC USES ————   *ExSyn 516–39*

The specific uses of the present tense can be categorized into three large groups: narrow-band presents, broad-band presents, and special uses. "Narrow-band" means that the action is portrayed as occurring over a relatively short interval; "broad-band" means that the action is portrayed as occurring over a longer interval; "special uses" include instances that do not fit into the above categories, especially those involving a time frame that is *other than* the present.[4]

Narrow-Band Presents   *ExSyn 516–19*

The action is portrayed as being in progress or as occurring.[5] In the *indicative* mood, it is portrayed as occurring in the present time ("right now"), that is, at the time of speaking. This involves two particular uses of the present: instantaneous and progressive.

➡1.   Instantaneous Present (Aoristic or Punctiliar Present)[6]   *ExSyn 517–18*

a. Definition and clarification. The present tense may be used to indicate that an action is completed at the *moment* of speaking. This occurs *only* in the *indicative*. It is relatively common.

The element of *time* becomes so prominent that the progressive aspect is entirely suppressed in this usage. The instantaneous present is typically a lexically influenced present tense: It is normally a verb of *saying* or *thinking* (a *performative* present).[7] The act itself is completed at the moment of speaking.

Past	Present	Future
	.	

Diagram 47
The Force of the Instantaneous Present

Note: The diagrams used for the tenses that have time indicators relate absolutely only to the indicative mood. The time element is included because of the relatively large percentage of indicative tenses. For those uses that have examples outside the indicative, one should simply ignore the time frame.

b. Illustrations

John 3:3	ἀμὴν ἀμὴν **λέγω** σοι	verily, verily, **I say** to you
Acts 9:34	εἶπεν αὐτῷ ὁ Πέτρος· Αἰνέα, **ἰᾶταί** σε Ἰησοῦς Χριστός	Peter said to him, "Aeneas, Jesus Christ **heals** you."

[4] Pragmatically, it is helpful to think in terms of *time* when thinking through these categories. This is not because the present tense always includes a temporal marker, but rather because most present tenses (like other tenses) are found in the indicative. Further, some uses are restricted to the indicative (such as historical present); such can only be thought of in terms of time.

[5] The alternative title, "durative" present, to describe both the instantaneous and progressive present is hardly an adequate description for the instantaneous present, since the aspectual force of the present tense is entirely suppressed.

[6] Instantaneous present is a much more satisfactory term since aoristic and punctiliar continue erroneous views about the aorist—viz., that it in reality refers to a momentary act.

[7] Fanning, *Verbal Aspect*, 202. Fanning notes a second type, viz., an act that is simultaneous to the time of speaking but is not identical with it. For our purposes, we can treat them both simply as instantaneous presents.

➡**2. Progressive Present (Descriptive Present)** *ExSyn* 518–19

a. Definition and key to identification. The present tense may be used to describe a scene in progress, especially in narrative literature. It represents a somewhat broader time frame than the instantaneous present, though it is still narrow when compared to a customary or gnomic present. The difference between this and the iterative (and customary) present is that the latter involves a *repeated* action, while the progressive present normally involves *continuous* action. The progressive present is common,[8] both in the indicative and oblique moods. The key to identification is *at this present time, right now*.

Past	Present	Future
	——	

Diagram 48
The Force of the Progressive Present

b. Illustrations

Mark 1:37   πάντες **ζητοῦσίν** σε
           all **are** [right now] **searching for** you

Rom 9:1   ἀλήθειαν **λέγω** . . . οὐ **ψεύδομαι**
           I am telling the truth. . . **I am** not **lying**

            What follows is a discourse about Paul's sorrow over the nation of Israel.

Broad-Band Presents   *ExSyn* 519–25

The following four categories of the present tense include those that are used to indicate an event or occurrence taking place over a long interval or an extended sequence of events.

**3. Extending-from-Past Present
(Present of Past Action Still in Progress)** *ExSyn* 519–20

a. Definition and key to identification. The present tense may be used to describe an action that, begun in the past, continues in the present. The emphasis is on the present time. Note that this is different from the *perfect* tense in that the perfect speaks only about the *results* existing in the present time. It is different from the progressive present in that it reaches back in time and usually, if not always, has some sort of temporal indicator, such as an adverbial phrase, to show

---

[8] The descriptive present, in many grammars, is presented as different from the progressive present. The difference is that the descriptive involves a narrower sequential band than does the progressive present. We have put both together for convenience' sake.

this past-referring element. Depending on how tightly one defines this category, it is either relatively rare or fairly common.[9]

The key to this usage is normally to translate the present tense as an *English present perfect*. Some examples might not fit such a gloss, however.

Past	Present	Future
	•	

Diagram 49
The Force of the Extending-from-Past Present

b. Illustrations

Luke 15:29   τοσαῦτα ἔτη **δουλεύω** σοι
I have served you for these many years

1 John 3:8   ἀπ᾽ ἀρχῆς ὁ διάβολος **ἁμαρτάνει**
the devil **has been sinning** from the beginning

➡4. **Iterative Present**   *ExSyn* 520–21

a. Definition and key to identification. The present tense may be used to describe an event that *repeatedly* happens. (The *distributive* present belongs here, too: the use of the present tense for individual acts distributed to more than one object.) This usage is frequently found in the imperative mood, since an action is urged to be done. The iterative present is common. The key to identification is translated using the English words "repeatedly" or "continuously."

Past	Present	Future
	• • • • •	

Diagram 50
The Force of the Iterative Present

b. Illustrations

Matt 7:7   **Αἰτεῖτε** ... **ζητεῖτε** ... **κρούετε**   **Ask ... seek ... knock**
The force of the present imperatives is "Ask repeatedly, over and over again ... seek repeatedly ... knock continuously, over and over again."

Matt 17:15   πολλάκις **πίπτει** εἰς τὸ πῦρ   often **he falls** into the fire

Luke 3:16   ἐγὼ ὕδατι **βαπτίζω** ὑμᾶς   **I baptize** you in water
This is an instance of a distributive present: John baptizes each person only once, but the action is repeated.

---

[9] Fanning takes it to be a rare category, limiting it by description: "It always includes an *adverbial phrase* or other time-indication" (*Verbal Aspect*, 217). But Brooks-Winbery define it more broadly (*Syntax*, 77; see discussion in Fanning, *Verbal Aspect*, 217, n. 30).

➡5. Customary (Habitual or General) Present   *ExSyn* 521–22

a. Definition. The customary present is used to signal either an action that *regularly occurs* or an *ongoing state*. The action is usually *iterative*, or repeated, but not without interruption. This usage is quite common. The difference between the customary (proper) and the iterative present is mild. Generally, however, it can be said that the *customary* present is *broader* in its idea of the "present" time and describes an event that occurs *regularly*.

There are two types of customary present, repeated action and ongoing state. The stative present is more pronounced in its temporal restrictions than the customary present or the gnomic present.

b. Key to identification. For action verbs, one can use the gloss *customarily*, *habitually*. For stative verbs one can use the gloss *continually*.

Past	Present	Future
. . . .		
	or	

Diagram 51
The Force of the Customary Present

c. Illustrations

Luke 18:12   **νηστεύω** δὶς τοῦ σαββάτου
I [customarily] **fast** twice a week

John 3:16   πᾶς ὁ **πιστεύων** εἰς αὐτὸν μὴ ἀπόληται
everyone who [continually] **believes** in him should not perish
> This could also be taken as a gnomic present, but if so it is not a proverbial statement, nor is it simply a general maxim. In this Gospel, there seems to be a qualitative distinction between the ongoing act of believing and the simple fact of believing.

John 14:17   παρ᾽ ὑμῖν **μένει** καὶ ἐν ὑμῖν ἔσται
he **continually remains** with you and he shall be in you

➡6. Gnomic Present   *ExSyn* 523–25

a. Definition. The present tense may be used to make a statement of a general, timeless fact. "It does not say that something *is* happening, but that something *does* happen."[10] The action or state continues without time limits. The verb is used "in proverbial statements or general maxims about what occurs at *all* times."[11] This usage is common.

b. Semantics and semantic situations. The gnomic present is distinct from the customary present in that the *customary* present refers to a regularly recurring

---

[10] Williams, *Grammar Notes*, 27.
[11] Fanning, *Verbal Aspect*, 208.

action while the *gnomic* present refers to a general, timeless fact. It is distinct from the stative present (a subcategory of the customary) in that the stative present involves a temporal restriction while the gnomic present is generally *atemporal*.

There are two predominant semantic situations in which the gnomic present occurs. The *first* includes instances that depict *deity or nature as the subject of the action*. Statements such as "the wind blows" or "God loves" fit this category. Such gnomic presents are true *all* the time. There is a *second* kind of gnomic, slightly different in definition: the use of the present in *generic* statements to describe something that is true *any* time (rather than a universal statement that is true *all* the time). This usage involves a particular grammatical intrusion: *The gnomic verb typically takes a generic subject or object*. Further, the present participle, especially in such formulaic expressions as πᾶς ὁ + *present participle* and the like, routinely belongs here.

c. Key to identification. As a general rule, if one can use the phrase *as a general, timeless fact*, it is a gnomic present (though this is not always applicable).

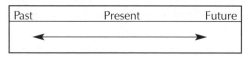

Diagram 52
The Force of the Gnomic Present

d. Illustrations[12]

Matt 5:32   πᾶς ὁ **ἀπολύων** τὴν γυναῖκα αὐτοῦ
everyone who **divorces** his wife

John 3:8   τὸ πνεῦμα ὅπου θέλει **πνεῖ**
the wind **blows** where it desires

2 Cor 9:7   ἱλαρὸν γὰρ δότην **ἀγαπᾷ** ὁ θεός
God **loves** [as a general, timeless fact] a cheerful giver

Special Uses of the Present   *ExSyn 526–39*

Five uses of the present tense do not easily fit into the above categories. These include the historical present, perfective present, conative present, futuristic present, and present retained in indirect discourse. The first four may be viewed temporally for pragmatic purposes (as most of them occur only in the indicative), moving from *simple past* (historical present), to *past + present result* (perfective present), to *presently incomplete or potential* (conative present), to *futuristic* (futuristic present). The fifth category, the present retained in indirect discourse, is technically not a syntactical category but a structural one.

---

[12] For a discussion on 1 John 3:6, 9 and 1 Tim 2:12, both of which are debatable and exegetically significant texts, see *ExSyn 524–26*.

➡7. **Historical Present (Dramatic Present)**   *ExSyn* 526–32

a. Definition and amplification. The historical present is used fairly frequently in narrative literature to describe a past event.

The *reason* for the use of the historical present is normally to portray an event *vividly*, as though the reader were in the midst of the scene as it unfolds. Such vividness might be *rhetorical* (to focus on some aspect of the narrative) or *literary* (to indicate a change in topic). The present tense may be used to describe a past event, either for the sake of *vividness* or to *highlight* some aspect of the narrative.

However, with λέγει and other verbs introducing (in)direct discourse, the historical present is for the most part a stereotyped idiom that has lost its original rhetorical powers. λέγει/λέγουσιν is by far the most common verb used as a historical present, accounting for well over half of all the instances.

The *aspectual* value of the historical present is normally, if not always, reduced to zero.[13] The verbs used, such as λέγει and ἔρχεται, normally introduce an action in the midst of aorists without the slightest hint that an internal or progressive aspect is intended.[14] The historical present has suppressed its aspect, but not its time. But the time element is rhetorical rather than real.[15] The diagram below reflects this.

Past	Present	Future
·		

Diagram 53
The Force of the Historical Present

Regarding use and genre, the historical present occurs mostly in less educated writers as a function of colloquial, vivid speech. More literary authors, as well as those who aspire to a distanced historical reporting, tend to avoid it (John [162], Mark [151], Matthew [93], Luke [11], Acts [13]). The historical present is preeminently the storyteller's tool and as such occurs exclusively (or almost exclusively) in *narrative* literature.

b. Clarification/semantic situation. Because the historical present occurs primarily in *narrative*, it is natural that it is used *only* in the third person. More-

---

[13] So BDF, 167 (§321); Robertson, *Grammar*, 867 (though he says that some instances are equal to an imperfect); Fanning, *Verbal Aspect*, 227–31.

[14] If the nontemporal view of tense were true, we would expect the aspect to be in full flower. Porter argues that this is indeed the case (*Verbal Aspect*, 195). Yet in his description he argues for *vividness* (rather than a progressive portrayal) as the force of the aspect. This seems better suited to the temporal view.

[15] Fanning has arrived at similar conclusions (*Verbal Aspect*, 228): "The point of the historical present is not how the occurrence is viewed, but that it occurs (rhetorically) 'now.'" He goes on to say that "the *temporal* meaning predominates and neutralizes the *aspectual* force." Although we fully agree, it does seem that this description goes against the grain of Fanning's "invariant meaning" for the tenses (in this case, that the present tense has an invariant meaning of an internal aspect).

over, since it is used for vividness or highlighting, it is equally natural that it occurs with verbs of *action*.

The *one* verb that is *not* used as a historical present is the *equative verb* (εἰμί).[16] Also, when γίνομαι functions as an equative verb, it is not used as a historical present. However, it may function as other than an equative verb at times.

Since time is an element of tense only absolutely in the indicative, it stands to reason that the historical present can only legitimately be used in the *indicative* mood.

c. Illustrations

(1) CLEAR EXAMPLES

Matt 26:40   **ἔρχεται** πρὸς τοὺς μαθητὰς καὶ **εὑρίσκει** αὐτοὺς καθεύδοντας, καὶ **λέγει** ...
he **came** to the disciples and **found** them sleeping, and **he said** ...

Mark 1:41   αὐτοῦ ἥψατο καὶ **λέγει** αὐτῷ ...
he touched him and **said** to him ...

(2) DEBATABLE TEXT[17]

John 5:2   **ἔστιν** δὲ ἐν τοῖς Ἱεροσολύμοις ... κολυμβήθρα
Now there **is** in Jerusalem ... a pool

> Although ἔστιν is usually assumed to be a historical present, since the equative verb is nowhere else clearly used as a historical present in the NT, the present tense should be taken as indicating present time from the viewpoint of the speaker.[18]

8. Perfective Present

ExSyn 532–33

a. Definition and clarification. The present tense may be used to *emphasize* that the results of a past action are still continuing. This usage is not very common.

There are *two types*: one lexical, the other contextual. The *lexical* type involves certain words (most notably ἥκω, which almost always has a perfective force to it).[19] The other type is *contextual*: This use of the present is especially frequent with λέγει as an introduction to an OT quotation.[20] Its usual force seems to be

---

[16] Although the copula may be used as a present tense retained in indirect discourse, which is an entirely different idiom. Much confusion has arisen over the similarities in *translation* between these two.

[17] For a discussion of John 8:58, see *ExSyn* 530–31; for a discussion of Rom 7:14–24, see *ExSyn* 531–32.

[18] See *ExSyn* 531–32 for a discussion of this text; for a more complete discussion, see D. B. Wallace, "John 5,2 and the Date of the Fourth Gospel," *Bib* 71 (1990): 177–205.

[19] According to Fanning, the following verbs also occasionally function as perfective presents: ἀπέχω, ἀκούω, πάρειμι (see *Verbal Aspect*, 239–40 for a discussion).

[20] This usage is so distinct that it could be given a different label, something like the *introductory formula present*.

that although the statement was spoken in the past, it still speaks today and is binding on the hearers.[21]

Past	Present	Future
•(————)		

Diagram 54
The Force of the Perfective Present

Note: The symbol (————) indicates the *results* of an action.

b. Illustrations

1 Tim 5:18   **λέγει** ἡ γραφή· βοῦν ἀλοῶντα οὐ φιμώσεις
the scripture **says,** "You shall not muzzle the ox while it is treading out the grain"

1 John 5:20   ὁ υἱὸς τοῦ θεοῦ **ἥκει**, καὶ δέδωκεν ἡμῖν διάνοιαν
the Son of God **has come** and has given us understanding

The perfective present is here joined by καί to a perfect tense, illustrating its force.

9. Conative (Tendential, Voluntative) Present   *ExSyn 534–35*

This use of the present tense portrays the subject as *desiring* to do something (*voluntative*), *attempting* to do something (*conative*), or at the point of *almost doing* something (*tendential*). This usage is relatively rare.

We will break this down into two categories: in progress, but not complete (true conative); and not begun, but about/desired to be attempted (voluntative, tendential).

This general category needs to be distinguished from the futuristic present, which typically connotes certainty that an action will be carried out.

a. In Progress, but not Complete (True Conative)

(1) DEFINITION AND KEY TO IDENTIFICATION. The present tense is used to indicate that an *attempt* is *being made* in the present time (indicative mood). Often it bears the connotation that the action will *not* be completed. The key to identification is to use *is attempting (unsuccessfully)*

Past	Present	Future
	————O	

Diagram 55
The Force of the (True) Conative Present

Note: The symbol O is used for all actions that are either not accomplished or not begun.

---

[21] In some respects it could be treated as a *testimonium* present, which is followed by a content clause: "This is the statement of Scripture. . . . " Cf. John 1:19 (αὕτη ἐστὶν ἡ μαρτυρία τοῦ Ἰωάννου).

(2) ILLUSTRATIONS

Gal 5:4   οἵτινες ἐν νόμῳ **δικαιοῦσθε**
[you] who **are attempting to be justified** by the Law

> If this were a durative present of some sort, the translation would be, "you who *are being justified* by the Law"! Obviously, such a meaning for this text would contradict the whole point of Galatians. Paul is not declaring that they *are* being justified by the Law, but that they *think* they are (or they are trying to be), though their attempt can only end in failure.

b. Not Begun, but About/Desired to be Attempted (Voluntative/Tendential)

(1) DEFINITION AND KEY TO IDENTIFICATION. The present tense is used to indicate that an *attempt* is *about to be made* or one that is *desired to be made* in the present time (or very near future time). The action may or may not be carried out. The key to identification is *about to*.

Past	Present	Future
		O

Diagram 56
The Force of the Tendential Present

(2) ILLUSTRATIONS

John 10:32   διὰ ποῖον αὐτῶν ἔργον ἐμὲ **λιθάζετε**;
For which of these works **are you about to stone** me?

➡10. Futuristic Present
ExSyn 535–37

The present tense may be used to describe a future event, though (unlike the conative present) it typically adds the connotations of immediacy and certainty. Most instances involve verbs whose *lexical* meaning involves anticipation (such as ἔρχομαι, -βαίνω, πορεύομαι, etc.). This usage is relatively common.

a. Completely Futuristic

(1) DEFINITION AND KEY TO IDENTIFICATION. The present tense may describe an event that is *wholly* subsequent to the time of speaking, as though it were present. It focuses on either the *immediacy* or the *certainty* of the event; the context needs to be examined to determine which notion is being emphasized. As a key to identification one can use *is soon going to, is certainly going to, will*.

Past	Present	Future
		·

Diagram 57
The Force of the Completely Futuristic Present

(2) ILLUSTRATIONS

Rom 6:9   Χριστὸς ... οὐκέτι **ἀποθνῄσκει**
Christ ... **is** not **going to die**

> Obviously, the stress here is on certainty, as evidenced by οὐκέτι.

Rev 22:20   ναί, **ἔρχομαι** ταχύ   Yes, **I am coming** quickly.

> This is a difficult text to assess. It may be that the stress is on the certainty of the coming or on the immediacy of the coming. But one's view does not hinge on the futuristic present, but on the adverb ταχύ. The force of the sentence may then mean, "Whenever I come, I will come *quickly*," in which case the stress is on the *certainty* of the coming (cf. Matt 28:8). Or it may mean, "I am on my way and I intend to be there *very soon*." If so, then the stress is on the *immediacy* of the coming.

b. Mostly Futuristic (Ingressive-Futuristic?)

(1) DEFINITION AND KEY TO IDENTIFICATION. The present tense may describe an event *begun* in the present time, but completed in the future. This is especially used with verbs of coming, going, etc., though it is rarer than the wholly futuristic present. As for the key to identification, often the verb can be translated as a present tense (e.g., *is coming*).

Past	Present	Future
	•	

Diagram 58
The Force of the Mostly Futuristic Present

(2) ILLUSTRATIONS

Mark 10:33   **ἀναβαίνομεν** εἰς Ἱεροσόλυμα
We are going up to Jerusalem

➡11. Present Retained in Indirect Discourse   *ExSyn* 537–39

a. Definition. Generally speaking, *the tense* of the Greek verb in indirect discourse is *retained* from the direct discourse. (Indirect discourse occurs after a verb of perception [e.g., verbs of saying, thinking, believing, knowing, seeing, hearing]. It may be introduced by a declarative ὅτι, λέγων, εἶπεν, etc.[22]) This is unlike English: In indirect discourse we usually push the *tense* back "one slot" from what it would have been in the direct discourse (especially if the introductory verb is past tense)— that is, we render a simple past as a past perfect, a present as a past tense, etc.

---

[22] For a general discussion of the indicative mood in declarative ὅτι clauses, see "Indicative Mood."

In Greek, however, the tenses of the original utterance are retained in the indirect discourse. The *present* tense is one of these. This usage is common, especially in the Gospels and Acts.

This use of the present tense is not, technically, a syntactical category. That is to say, the present tense also belongs to some other present tense usage. The retained present is a *translational* category, not a syntactical one.

b. Clarification. A retained present is usually progressive, but not in the present time (that is, according to *English*). Do *not* confuse this with the historical present, however. Equative verbs are frequently used in indirect discourse (and thus are to be translated as a past tense, though present in Greek); such verbs do not occur as historical presents, however (see above).

c. Illustrations

Mark 2:1   ἠκούσθη ὅτι ἐν οἴκῳ **ἐστίν**
It was heard that **he was** at home

> Note that although the equative verb ἐστίν is here translated as a past tense, it is *not* a historical present. The semantics of historical presents are quite different from the present tense retained in indirect discourse.

John 4:1   ὡς ἔγνω ὁ Ἰησοῦς ὅτι **ἤκουσαν** οἱ Φαρισαῖοι ὅτι Ἰησοῦς πλείονας μαθητὰς **ποιεῖ** καὶ **βαπτίζει** ἢ Ἰωάννης
when Jesus knew that the Pharisees **had heard** that Jesus **was making** and **baptizing** more disciples than John

> This text involves indirect discourse embedded within *another* indirect discourse. It affords a good illustration of the differences between English and Greek. The Greek retains the tenses from the direct discourse, while English moves them back one slot. Thus, ἤκουσαν is translated *had heard* even though it is aorist (the original statement would have been aorist: "the Pharisees heard . . . "). And both ποιεῖ and βαπτίζει, although present tenses, are translated as though they were imperfects (the original statement would have been, "Jesus *is making* and *baptizing* more disciples than John").

The Imperfect Tense[1]
Overview of Uses

Narrow-Band Imperfects **233**
➡ 1. Progressive (Descriptive) Imperfect 233
➡ 2. Ingressive (Inchoative, Inceptive) Imperfect 233

Broad-Band Imperfects **234**
➡ 3. Iterative Imperfect. 234
➡ 4. Customary (Habitual or General) Imperfect 235

Special Uses of the Imperfect. **236**
5. Conative (Voluntative, Tendential) Imperfect 236
   a. In Progress, but not Complete (True Conative) 236
   b. Not Begun, but About/Desired to be Attempted
      (Voluntative/Tendential) 237
➡ 6. Imperfect Retained in Indirect Discourse 237

——— INTRODUCTION ——— *ExSyn 541*

As a tense of the first principal part, the imperfect mirrors the present tense both in its general aspect and its specific uses (the only difference being, for the most part, that the imperfect is used for past time).

Like the present tense, the imperfect displays an *internal aspect*.[2] That is, it portrays the action from within the event, without regard for beginning or end. This contrasts with the aorist, which portrays the action in summary fashion. For the most part, the aorist takes a *snapshot* of the action while the imperfect (like the present) takes a *motion picture*, portraying the action as it unfolds. As such, the imperfect is often incomplete and focuses on the *process* of the action.[3]

With reference to *time*, the imperfect is almost always *past*. (Note that since the imperfect only occurs in the indicative mood, this tense always grammatical-izes time.) However, occasionally it portrays time other than the past (e.g., the conative imperfect may have this force to it sometimes; also the imperfect in second class conditions connotes present time—but such is due more to the aspect than the time element of the tense). In general, the imperfect may be diagrammed as follows:

---

[1] See *ExSyn* 540–53. The instantaneous imperfect (see 542–43) and the "pluperfective" imperfect (see 549) are sufficiently rare that the average intermediate Greek student may ignore them.

[2] For a discussion on the difference between unaffected meaning and specific uses, see the introduction to the present tense.

[3] On the different aspectual forces of the aorist and imperfect, see "Portrayal Vs. Reality of Aspect" in "The Tenses: An Introduction."

Past	Present	Future
—		

Diagram 59
The Basic Force of the Imperfect

——————— SPECIFIC USES ———————   *ExSyn 541–53*

Narrow-Band Imperfects   *ExSyn 541–45*

The action is portrayed as being in progress or as occurring in the *past time* (since all imperfects are in the indicative). This involves two specific types of imperfect: progressive and ingressive.

➡**1. Progressive (Descriptive) Imperfect**   *ExSyn 543–44*

a. Definition and key to identification. The imperfect is often used to describe an action or state that is in progress in past time from the viewpoint (or, more accurately, portrayal) of the speaker. The action (or state) is more narrowly focused than that of the customary imperfect. It speaks either of *vividness* or *simultaneity* with another action.

For its key to identification, use *was (continually) doing, was (right then) happening*.

Past	Present	Future
—		

Diagram 60
The Force of the Progressive Imperfect

b. Illustrations

Matt 8:24   σεισμὸς μέγας ἐγένετο ἐν τῇ θαλάσσῃ ... αὐτὸς δὲ **ἐκάθευδεν**
a massive storm came on the sea ... but **he was sleeping**

Acts 3:2   τις ἀνὴρ χωλὸς ἐκ κοιλίας μητρὸς αὐτοῦ ὑπάρχων **ἐβαστάζετο**
a certain man, who was lame from birth, **was being carried**

➡**2. Ingressive (Inchoative, Inceptive) Imperfect**   *ExSyn 544–45*

a. Definition and clarification. The imperfect is often used to stress the beginning of an action, with the implication that it continued for some time.

The difference between the ingressive *imperfect* and the ingressive *aorist* is that the imperfect stresses beginning but implies that the action *continues*, while the aorist stresses beginning but does not imply that the action continues. Thus the translation (and key to identification) for the inceptive imperfect ought to be "began *doing*" while the inceptive aorist ought to be translated "began *to do*."

b. Semantic situation. The ingressive imperfect is especially used in narrative literature when a change in activity is noted. It is possibly the most common imperfect in narrative because it introduces a topic shift. The following examples may be treated as progressive imperfects, but the context of each indicates a topic shift or new direction for the action.

Past	Present	Future
•———		

Diagram 61
The Force of the Ingressive Imperfect

c. Illustrations

Mark 9:20   πεσὼν ἐπὶ τῆς γῆς **ἐκυλίετο** ἀφρίζων
             He fell on the ground and **began rolling about**, foaming at the mouth.

John 4:30   ἐξῆλθον ἐκ τῆς πόλεως καὶ **ἤρχοντο** πρὸς αὐτόν
             They came out of the city and **began coming** to him.

             There is a subtle contrast between the aorist and imperfect here. The aorist gets the Samaritans out of Sychar, in a summary fashion; the imperfect gets them on the road to Jesus. But it looks at the action from the inside. The evangelist leaves the reader hanging with this tantalizing morsel: They were coming to Jesus but had not arrived yet. Dramatically, the scene shifts to the dialogue between Jesus and his disciples, leaving the reader with some unfinished business about the Samaritans. They appear on the scene again a few moments later when Jesus declares, "Lift up your eyes, for they are white for the harvest" (4:35). The Samaritans have arrived.

Broad-Band Imperfects   *ExSyn 546–48*

Like the present tense, several imperfects involve a time frame that is fairly broadly conceived. However, unlike the present tense, there is no *gnomic* imperfect.

➤3. Iterative Imperfect   *ExSyn 546–47*

a. Definition. The imperfect is frequently used for *repeated* action in past time. It is similar to the customary imperfect, but it is not something that regularly recurs. Further, the iterative imperfect occurs over a shorter span of time.

There are two types of iterative imperfect: (1) **Iterative** proper, in which the imperfect indicates *repeated action by the same agent*; and (2) **Distributive**, in which the imperfect is used for *individual acts of multiple agents*.

b. Clarification. Many grammarians make no distinction between the iterative and the customary imperfect. However, while the customary is repeated action in past time, it has two elements that the iterative imperfect does not have: (1) regularly recurring action (or action at regular intervals), and (2) action that tends to take place over a long span of time. Thus, in some sense, it might be said that the customary imperfect is a *subset* of the iterative imperfect. The difference between these two will be seen more clearly via the illustrations.

c. Key to identification. Often the gloss *kept on doing, going,* etc., helps the student to see the force of this use of the imperfect, though this is not always the case, especially with distributive imperfects. Another gloss is *repeatedly, continuously doing.*

Past	Present	Future
. . . . .		

Diagram 62
The Force of the Iterative Imperfect

d. Illustrations

Matt 3:6   ἐβαπτίζοντο ἐν τῷ Ἰορδάνῃ ποταμῷ ὑπ᾽ αὐτοῦ
They were being baptized in the Jordan River by him.

John 19:3   ἔλεγον, Χαῖρε
they kept on saying, "Hail!"

➡4. **Customary (Habitual or General) Imperfect**   *ExSyn 548*

a. Definition. The imperfect is frequently used to indicate a *regularly* recurring activity in past time (habitual) *or* a *state* that continued for some time (general).[4]

The difference between the customary (proper) and the iterative imperfect is not great. Generally, however, it can be said that the *customary* imperfect is *broader* in its idea of the past time and it describes an event that occurred *regularly.*

b. Key to identification. The two types of customary imperfect are lexically determined: One is repeated action (habitual imperfect [*customarily, habitually*]), while the other is ongoing state (stative imperfect [*continually*]). The habitual imperfect can be translated with the gloss *customarily, used to, were accustomed to.*

Past	Present	Future
. . . . ———— or ————		

Diagram 63
The Force of the Customary Imperfect

---

[4] Some grammarians distinguish between stative imperfects and habitual imperfects. In terms of type of action portrayed, this is a legitimate distinction. In terms of time frame, the two are close together. Like the customary present, we have lumped them together for convenience' sake.

c. Illustrations

Luke 2:41　ἐπορεύοντο οἱ γονεῖς αὐτοῦ κατ᾽ ἔτος εἰς Ἰερουσαλήμ
　　　　　his parents **used to go** to Jerusalem each year

Rom 6:17　ἦτε δοῦλοι τῆς ἁμαρτίας
　　　　　you were [continually] slaves of sin

Special Uses of the Imperfect　*ExSyn 549–53*

Three uses of the imperfect tense do not naturally fit into the above categories. These include the "pluperfective" imperfect (not included here), conative imperfect, and imperfect retained in indirect discourse. The first two are true syntactical categories, while the third is technically not a syntactical category but a structural one.

5. Conative (Voluntative, Tendential) Imperfect　*ExSyn 550–52*

This use of the imperfect tense occasionally portrays the action as something that was *desired* (*voluntative*), *attempted* (*conative*), or at the point of *almost happening* (*tendential*).[5] There are two types: in progress, but not complete (true conative); and not begun, but about/desired to be attempted (voluntative, tendential).

a. In Progress, but not Complete (True Conative)

(1) DEFINITION AND KEY TO IDENTIFICATION. The imperfect tense is used to indicate that an *attempt* was *being made* in the past time. The implications are that it was not brought to a successful conclusion. As a key to identification, use *was attempting (unsuccessfully)*.

Past	Present	Future
——O		

Diagram 64
The Force of the (True) Conative Imperfect

Note: The symbol O is used for all actions that are either not accomplished or not begun.

(2) ILLUSTRATIONS

Matt 3:14　ὁ δὲ Ἰωάννης **διεκώλυεν** αὐτόν
　　　　　but John **was trying to prevent** him

Mark 15:23　**ἐδίδουν** αὐτῷ ἐσμυρνισμένον οἶνον· ὃς δὲ οὐκ ἔλαβεν
　　　　　They were attempting to give him wine mixed with myrrh, but he did not accept it.

---

[5] Nevertheless, the conative imperfect is much more common than the conative present.

b. Not Begun, but About/Desired to be Attempted (Voluntative/Tendential)

(1) DEFINITION AND KEY TO IDENTIFICATION. The imperfect tense is used to indicate that an *attempt* was *about to be made* or that one was almost *desired to be made*. The action, however, was not carried out. Often the notion conveyed is that the action was contemplated more than once (hence, the imperfect is naturally used).

What is portrayed with this usage frequently is *present* time, in which the action is entirely unrealized in the present. The imperfect seems to be used to indicate the unreal present situation.

As the key to identification, use *was about to, could almost wish*.

Past	Present	Future
O O O		

Diagram 65
The Force of the Tendential Imperfect

(2) ILLUSTRATIONS

Luke 1:59   ἐκάλουν αὐτὸ ἐπὶ τῷ ὀνόματι τοῦ πατρὸς αὐτοῦ Ζαχαρίαν
They wanted to call him by the name of his father, Zachariah.

Rom 9:3   ηὐχόμην γὰρ ἀνάθεμα εἶναι αὐτὸς ἐγώ
For **I could almost wish** myself accursed

➡6. Imperfect Retained in Indirect Discourse   *ExSyn* 552–53

a. Definition. Like the present, the imperfect can be retained from the direct discourse in the indirect.[6] In English, however, we translate it as though it were a past perfect. As with the retained present, this is a *translational* category, not a *syntactical* one.[7]

Indirect discourse occurs after a verb of perception (e.g., verbs of saying, thinking, believing, knowing, seeing, hearing). It may be introduced by a declarative ὅτι, λέγων, εἶπεν, etc.[8] This is unlike English: In indirect discourse we usually push the *tense* back "one slot" from what it would have been in the direct discourse (especially if the introductory verb is past tense)—that is, we render a simple past as a past perfect, a present as a past tense, etc.

---

[6] There are exceptions to this general rule. Not infrequently, the imperfect stands in the place of the present.

[7] For a more detailed explanation, see the discussion of tenses retained in indirect discourse in the previous chapter.

[8] For a general discussion of the indicative mood in declarative ὅτι clauses, see "Indicative Mood."

b. Illustrations

John 2:22   ἐμνήσθησαν οἱ μαθηταὶ αὐτοῦ ὅτι τοῦτο **ἔλεγεν**
his disciples remembered that **he had said** this

John 9:18   οὐκ ἐπίστευσαν οἱ Ἰουδαῖοι ... ὅτι **ἦν** τυφλός
the Jews did not believe ... that **he had been** blind

The Aorist Tense[1]
Overview of Uses

➡ 1. Constative (Complexive, Punctiliar, Comprehensive, Global) Aorist . 241
➡ 2. Ingressive (Inceptive, Inchoative) Aorist 241
➡ 3. Consummative (Culminative, Ecbatic, Effective) Aorist 241
   4. Epistolary Aorist 242
   5. Proleptic (Futuristic) Aorist 242
   6. Immediate Past Aorist/Dramatic Aorist 242

INTRODUCTION

Aspect and Time

1. Aspect: "Snapshot"

The aorist tense "presents an occurrence in summary, viewed as a whole from the outside, without regard for the internal make-up of the occurrence."[2] This contrasts with the present and imperfect, which portray the action as an ongoing process. It may be helpful to think of the aorist as taking a snapshot of the action while the imperfect (like the present) takes a motion picture, portraying the action as it unfolds.

2. Time

In the *indicative*, the aorist usually indicates *past* time with reference to the time of speaking (thus, "absolute time"). Aorist *participles* usually suggest *antecedent* time to that of the main verb (i.e., *past* time in a *relative* sense). There are exceptions to this general principle, of course, but they are due to intrusions from other linguistic features vying for control (see below).

Outside the indicative and participle, time is not a feature of the aorist,[3]

Past	Present	Future
.		

Diagram 66
The Force of the Aorist Indicative

---

[1] See *ExSyn* 554–65. The gnomic aorist (see 562) is sufficiently rare that the average intermediate Greek student may ignore it.

[2] Fanning, *Verbal Aspect*, 97.

[3] Indirect discourse aorists are an exception to this rule. But this is because such aorists *represent* an indicative of the direct discourse. See chapter on "Moods" for discussion.

Thawing Out the Aorist: The Role of the Context and Lexeme

The aorist is not always used merely to summarize. In combination with other linguistic features (such as lexeme or context) the aorist often does more. Some actions, for instance, are shut up to a particular tense. If a speaker wishes to indicate an action that is intrinsically *terminal* (such as "find," "die," or "give birth to"), the choice of tense is dramatically reduced. We would not usually say "he was finding his book." The imperfect, under normal circumstances, would thus be inappropriate.

By contrast, if a speaker wants to speak of the unchanging nature of a *state* (such as "I have" or "I live"), the aorist is not normally appropriate. Indeed, when the aorist of such stative verbs is used, the emphasis is most frequently on the *entrance into the state*.

The point is that often the choice of a tense is made for a speaker by the action he or she is describing. At times the tense chosen by the speaker is the *only* one that could have been used to portray the idea. Three major factors determine this: lexical meaning of the verb (e.g., whether the verb stem indicates a terminal or punctual act, a state, etc.), contextual factors, and other grammatical features (e.g., mood, voice, transitiveness, etc). This is the difference between aspect and *Aktionsart*: Aspect is the basic meaning of the tense, unaffected by considerations in a given utterance, while *Aktionsart* is the meaning of the tense as used by an author in a particular utterance, affected, as it were, by other features of the language.

The use of the aorist in any given situation depends, then, on its combination with other linguistic features.

The Abused Aorist: Swinging the Pendulum Back

There are two errors to avoid in treating the aorist: saying too little and saying too much.

First, some have *said too little* by assuming that nothing more than the unaffected meaning can ever be seen when the aorist is used. This view fails to recognize that the aorist tense (like other tenses) does not exist in a vacuum. Categories of usage are legitimate because the tenses combine with other linguistic features to form various fields of meaning.

Second, many NT students see a particular category of usage (*Aktionsart*) as underlying the entire tense usage (aspect). This is the error of *saying too much*. Statements such as "the aorist means once-for-all action" are of this sort. It is true that the aorist may, under certain circumstances, describe an event that is, in reality, momentary. But we run into danger when we say that this is the aorist's unaffected meaning, for then we force it on the text in an artificial way. We then tend to ignore such aorists that disprove our view (and they can be found in virtually every chapter of the NT) and proclaim loudly the "once-for-all" aorists when they suit us.

──────── **SPECIFIC USES** ────────   *ExSyn 557–65*

**➡1. Constative (Complexive, Punctiliar,
      Comprehensive, Global) Aorist**   *ExSyn 557–58*

  a. Definition. The aorist normally views the action *as a whole*, taking no interest in the internal workings of the action. It describes the action in summary fashion, without focusing on the beginning or end of the action specifically. This is by far the most common use of the aorist, especially with the indicative mood.

  The constative aorist covers a multitude of actions. The event might be iterative in nature, or durative, or momentary, but the aorist says none of this. It places the stress on the fact of the occurrence, not its nature.

  b. Illustrations

  Matt 8:3   ἐκτείνας τὴν χεῖρα **ἥψατο** αὐτοῦ
                He stretched out his hand and **touched** him

  Rom 5:14   **ἐβασίλευσεν** ὁ θάνατος ἀπὸ Ἀδὰμ μέχρι Μωϋσέως
                death **reigned** from Adam until Moses

➡2. Ingressive (Inceptive, Inchoative) Aorist   *ExSyn 558–59*

  a. Definition. The aorist tense may be used to stress the beginning of an action or the entrance into a state. Unlike the ingressive imperfect, there is no implication that the action continues. This is simply left unstated. The ingressive aorist is quite common.

  b. Clarification and key to identification. This use of the aorist is usually shut up to two kinds of verbs: (1) It occurs with *stative* verbs, in which the stress is on *entrance into the state.* (2) It also occurs with verbs that denote activities, especially in contexts where the action is introduced as a new item in the discourse. As the key to identification, use *began to do, became.*

  c. Illustrations

  Matt 9:27   **ἠκολούθησαν** αὐτῷ δύο τυφλοί
                two blind men **began to follow** him

  Matt 22:7   ὁ δὲ βασιλεὺς **ὠργίσθη**
                now the king **became angry**

➡3. Consummative (Culminative, Ecbatic, Effective) Aorist   *ExSyn 559–61*

  a. Definition. The aorist is often used to stress the cessation of an act or state. Certain verbs, by their *lexical* nature, virtually require this usage. For example, "he died" is usually not going to be an ingressive idea. The context also assists in this usage at times; it may imply that an act was already in progress and the aorist then brings the action to a conclusion.

b. Illustrations[4]

Mark 5:39   τὸ παιδίον οὐκ **ἀπέθανεν** ἀλλὰ καθεύδει
the little girl **has** not **died**, but is sleeping

> The difference between the aorist and the present is clearly seen in this dominical saying: The girl's life is not at an end (aorist); there is more to come (present).

Rev 5:5   **ἐνίκησεν** ὁ λέων ὁ ἐκ τῆς φυλῆς Ἰούδα
the Lion from the tribe of Judah **has overcome**

4. Epistolary Aorist   *ExSyn 562–63*

a. Definition. This is the use of the aorist indicative in NT letters in which the author self-consciously describes his letter from the time frame of the audience. The aorist indicative of πέμπω is naturally used in this sense. This category is not common, but it does have some exegetical significance.

b. Illustrations

Gal 6:11   ἴδετε πηλίκοις ὑμῖν γράμμασιν **ἔγραψα** τῇ ἐμῇ χειρί.
See with what large letters **I have written** to you, with my own hand.

Phil 2:28   **ἔπεμψα** αὐτόν   **I have sent** him

> This, of course, is from the standpoint of the readers, for Epaphroditus, the one being sent, was the one who would be carrying the letter to the Philippians.

5. Proleptic (Futuristic) Aorist   *ExSyn 563–64*

a. Definition and clarification. The aorist *indicative* can be used to describe an event that is not yet past as though it were already completed. This usage is not common, though several exegetically significant texts involve possible proleptic aorists.

An author sometimes uses an aorist for the future to stress the certainty of an event. It involves a "rhetorical transfer" of a future event as though it were past.

b. Illustration

Rom 8:30   οὓς δὲ ἐδικαίωσεν, τούτους καὶ **ἐδόξασεν**
those whom he justified, these **he** also **glorified**

> From Paul's perspective, the glorification of those who have been declared righteous is as good as done.

6. Immediate Past Aorist/Dramatic Aorist   *ExSyn 564–65*

a. Definition. The aorist indicative can be used of an event that happened rather recently. Its force can usually be brought out with something like *just now*,

---

[4] For a detailed discussion of οἰκοδομήθη in John 2:20 (viz., whether it is a constative or consummative aorist), see *ExSyn 560–61*.

as in *just now I told you*. This may be lexically colored (occurring with verbs of *emotion* and *understanding*), but more often it is due to Semitic coloring, reflecting a Semitic stative perfect. As well, it is sometimes difficult to tell whether the aorist refers to the immediate past or to the present (dramatic).

b. Illustrations

Matt 9:18   ἄρχων εἷς ἐλθὼν προσεκύνει αὐτῷ λέγων ὅτι ἡ θυγάτηρ μου ἄρτι **ἐτελεύτησεν**
A certain ruler came and bowed down before him, saying, "My daughter **has** just now **died**."

Matt 26:65   ἴδε νῦν **ἠκούσατε** τὴν βλασφημίαν
Behold, just now you **heard** his blasphemy

The Future Tense[1]
Overview of Uses

➧ 1. Predictive Future. 244
   2. Imperatival Future. 245
   3. Deliberative Future 245

─────────── **INTRODUCTION** ─────────── *ExSyn 566–67*

With reference to *aspect*, the future seems to offer an *external* portrayal, something of a temporal counterpart to the aorist indicative.[2] The external portrayal "presents an occurrence *in summary, viewed as a whole from the outside, without regard for the internal make-up of the occurrence.*"[3] With reference to *time*, the future tense is always future from the speaker's presentation (or, when in a participial form, in relation to the time of the main verb).

The future occurs in the indicative, participle, and infinitive forms in the NT, though the bulk are indicatives.

In general, the future tense may be charted as follows (with respect to both time and aspect):

Past	Present	Future
		•

Diagram 67
The Force of the Future Tense

─────────── **SPECIFIC USES** ─────────── *ExSyn 568–71*

➧**1. Predictive Future** *ExSyn 568*

a. Definition. The future tense may indicate that something will take place or come to pass. The portrayal is external, summarizing the action: "it will happen." The predictive future is far and away the most common use of this tense.

b. Illustrations

Acts 1:11   οὗτος ὁ Ἰησοῦς ... **ἐλεύσεται**
             this Jesus ... **will come**

─────────────────

[1] See *ExSyn* 566–71. The following categories are sufficiently rare that the average intermediate Greek student may ignore them: the gnomic future (see 571) and the future as equivalent to a subjunctive (see 571).

[2] Not all grammarians agree with this (tentative) assessment. For a discussion, see *ExSyn* 566–67.

[3] Fanning, *Verbal Aspect*, 97.

Phil 1:6   ὁ ἐναρξάμενος ἐν ὑμῖν ἔργον ἀγαθὸν **ἐπιτελέσει** ἄχρι ἡμέρας
Χριστοῦ Ἰησοῦ
the one who began a good work in you **will perfect** it until the
day of Christ Jesus

> Wedged as it is between the past (ἐναρξάμενος) and an end-
> point in the future (ἄχρι), the future tense seems to suggest a
> progressive idea. But the future in itself says none of this.

2. Imperatival Future ExSyn 569–70

a. Definition. The future indicative is sometimes used for a command, almost
always in OT quotations (the result of a literal translation of the Hebrew). However, it was used in this manner even in classical Greek, though sparingly. Outside of Matthew, this usage is not common. The force of the imperatival future is
not identical with an imperative. Generally speaking, it has a universal, timeless,
and/or solemn force to it.

b. Illustrations

Matt 19:18   οὐ **φονεύσεις**, οὐ **μοιχεύσεις**, οὐ **κλέψεις**, οὐ **ψευδομαρ-
τυρήσεις**
You shall not **murder, you shall** not **commit adultery, you
shall** not **steal, you shall** not **bear false witness.**

1 Pet 1:16   ἅγιοι **ἔσεσθε**, ὅτι ἐγὼ ἅγιός εἰμι
You shall be holy, because I am holy.

3. Deliberative Future ExSyn 570

a. Definition. The deliberative future asks a question that implies some doubt
about the response. The question, asked in the *first person* singular or plural, is
generally either *cognitive* or *volitional*. Cognitive questions ask, "How will we?"
while volitional questions ask, "Should we?" Thus, the force of such questions is
one of "oughtness"—that is, possibility, desirability, or necessity. The aorist subjunctive is more common in deliberative questions than the future indicative.

b. Illustrations

Mark 6:37   ἀγοράσωμεν δηναρίων διακοσίων ἄρτους καὶ **δώσομεν** αὐτοῖς φαγεῖν;
Should we buy two hundred denarii worth of food and **give** it
to them to eat?

Heb 2:3   πῶς ἡμεῖς **ἐκφευξόμεθα** τηλικαύτης ἀμελήσαντες σωτηρίας;
How **shall we escape** if we neglect so great a salvation?

The Perfect and Pluperfect Tenses[1]
Overview of Tense Uses

The Perfect Tense **246**
➡ 1. Intensive Perfect (Resultative Perfect) 247
➡ 2. Extensive Perfect (Consummative Perfect) 248
   3. Aoristic Perfect (Dramatic or Historical Perfect) 249
➡ 4. Perfect with a Present Force. 249
The Pluperfect Tense **250**
➡ 1. Intensive Pluperfect (Resultative Pluperfect) 251
➡ 2. Extensive Pluperfect (Consummative Pluperfect) 252
➡ 3. Pluperfect with a Simple Past Force 252

For the most part, the perfect and pluperfect tenses are identical in aspect though different in time. Thus both speak of an event accomplished in the past (in the indicative mood, that is) with results existing afterwards—the perfect speaking of results existing in the present, the pluperfect speaking of results existing in the past.

The *aspect* of the perfect and pluperfect is sometimes called *stative, resultative, completed,* or *perfective-stative.* Whatever it is called, the kind of action portrayed (in its unaffected meaning) is a combination of the external and internal aspects: The *action* is presented *externally* (summary), while the *resultant state* proceeding from the action is presented *internally* (continuous state).

As to *time*, note the treatments below under each tense.

The Perfect Tense   *ExSyn 573–82*

The primary uses of the perfect are easy to comprehend, though they are not insignificant. As Moulton points out, the perfect tense is "the most important, exegetically, of all the Greek Tenses."[2] The perfect is used less frequently than the present, aorist, future, or imperfect; when it is used, there is usually a deliberate choice on the part of the writer.

The force of the perfect tense is simply that it describes an event that, completed in the past (we are speaking of the perfect indicative here), has results existing in the present time (i.e., in relation to the time of the speaker). BDF suggest that the perfect tense "combines in itself, so to speak, the present and the aorist in that it denotes the *continuance* of *completed action*."[3] It is incorrect, however, to

---

[1] See *ExSyn* 572–86. The gnomic perfect (see 580), the proleptic or futuristic perfect (see 581), and the perfect of allegory (see 581–82) are sufficiently rare that the average intermediate Greek student may ignore them.

[2] Moulton, *Prolegomena*, 140.

[3] BDF, 175 (§340).

say that the perfect signifies abiding results; such conclusions belong to the realm of theology, not grammar.

Past	Present	Future
• (————)		

Diagram 68
The Force of the Perfect

Note: The symbol (————) indicates the *results* of an action.

The chart shows that the perfect may be viewed as combining the aspects of both the aorist and present tense. It speaks of completed action (aorist) with existing results (present). The basic question to be asked is which of these aspects is emphasized in a given context.

The uses of the perfect tense may be broken down into three main groups: normative, collapsed, and specialized. The *normative* uses involve both the external and internal aspects, but with a slightly different emphasis. The *collapsed* perfects are those that collapse (or suppress) either the internal or external aspect, because of contextual or lexical interference, respectively. The *specialized* perfects are rare uses that detour from the normal usage in a more pronounced way than the collapsed perfects do.

➡1.   Intensive Perfect (Resultative Perfect)   *ExSyn 574–76*

a. Definition. The perfect may be used to *emphasize* the results or present state produced by a past action. The English present often is the best translation for such a perfect. This is a common use of the perfect tense.

b. Caution. The average student learning NT Greek typically knows Greek grammar better than English grammar after a couple of years of study. Consequently, the aspect of the Greek perfect is sometimes imported into the English perfect. That is, there is a tendency to see the English perfect as placing an emphasis on existing results—a notion foreign to English grammar. One ought to be careful when translating the perfect into English to resist the temptation of translating it as an English perfect at all times. When so translated, the Greek perfect should be extensive, not intensive.

c. Semantics/key to identification. This use of the perfect does not exclude the notion of a completed act; rather, it *focuses* on the resultant state. Consequently, *stative* verbs are especially used in this way. Often the best translation of the intensive perfect is as a *present* tense. (Nevertheless, many perfects are open to interpretation and could be treated either as intensive or extensive.) The only difference in the chart below and the previous chart (on the unaffected meaning of the perfect) is that the resultant state is here emphasized.

Past	Present	Future
· (———————)		

Diagram 69
The Force of the Intensive Perfect

d. Illustrations

Luke 5:20   ἄνθρωπε, **ἀφέωνταί** σοι αἱ ἁμαρτίαι σου
man, your sins **are forgiven**

Rom 3:10   καθὼς **γέγραπται** ὅτι οὐκ ἔστιν δίκαιος οὐδὲ εἷς
Just as **it is written**, "There is none righteous, no, not one."

This common introductory formula to OT quotations seems to be used to emphasize that the written word still exists. It implies a present and binding authority.[4]

➡2. Extensive Perfect (Consummative Perfect)   ExSyn 577

a. Definition. The perfect may be used to *emphasize* the completion of a past action or the process from which a present state emerges. It should normally be translated in English as a present perfect. This usage is common.

b. Semantics/key to identification. The emphasis is on the completed event in the past time rather than the present results. As with the intensive perfect, this does not mean that the other "half" of its aspect has disappeared, just that it does not receive the greatest emphasis. For example, **ἐγήγερται** τῇ ἡμέρᾳ τῇ τρίτῃ ("**he has been raised** on the third day") in 1 Cor 15:4, though extensive, still involves current implications for Paul's audience. (Many perfects are open to interpretation and could be treated either as intensive or extensive.) One key is that *transitive* verbs often belong here.

Past	Present	Future
● (┬————————)		

Diagram 70
The Force of the Extensive Perfect

c. Illustrations

John 1:34   **ἑώρακα** καὶ **μεμαρτύρηκα** ὅτι οὗτός ἐστιν ὁ ἐκλεκτός τοῦ θεοῦ.
I have seen and **I have testified** that this is the elect one of God.

The portrayal of John's testimony seems to place an emphasis more on the completed event in the past than on the present results. In other words, there is stress on his having seen enough of Jesus [completed action] to make a reliable report.

---

[4] As contrasted with λέγει, which seems to emphasize immediate applicability of the word.

Rom 5:5   ἡ ἀγάπη τοῦ θεοῦ **ἐκκέχυται** ἐν ταῖς καρδίαις ἡμῶν
the love of God **has been poured out** in our hearts

> This verse is wedged in the middle of the section of Romans 5 that deals with God's work in salvation, setting the groundwork for sanctification. The stress, therefore, seems to be slightly more on what Christ's finished work on the cross accomplished as a solid basis for the believers' present sanctification.

3. Aoristic Perfect (Dramatic or Historical Perfect)   *ExSyn 578–79*

a. Definition. The perfect indicative is rarely used in a rhetorical manner to describe an event in a highly vivid way. The aoristic/dramatic perfect is "used as a simple past tense without concern for present consequences. . . . "[5] In this respect, it shares a kinship with the historical present. This use is informed by *contextual* intrusions (narrative). The *key* to detecting a dramatic perfect is the absence of any notion of existing results.

It may be best to think of it as an *intensive extensive perfect* used in narrative (i.e., it is an intensive use of the extensive perfect). That is to say, it focuses so much on the act that there is no room left for the results. It occurs in contexts where one would expect the aorist.

Past	Present	Future
.		

Diagram 71
The Force of the Dramatic Perfect

b. Illustration

Acts 7:35   τοῦτον ὁ θεὸς. . . **ἀπέσταλκεν**
this [Moses] God . . . **sent**

➡4. Perfect with a Present Force   *ExSyn 579–80*

a. Definition and semantics. Certain verbs occur frequently (or exclusively) in the perfect tense without the usual aspectual significance. They have come to be used just like present tense verbs.[6] This usage is common.

Οἶδα is the most commonly used verb in this category. But other verbs also seem to be used this way, such as the perfects ἕστηκα, πέποιθα, and μέμνημαι. The reason why such perfects have the same semantics as presents is frequently that *there is very little distinction between the act and its results*. They are *stative* verbs.

---

[5] Fanning, *Verbal Aspect*, 301.

[6] It should be noted that such perfects are not restricted to the indicative since the issue is not just time but aspect as well. The charts here are restricted to indicatives to show their temporal placement.

The result of knowing is knowing. When one comes to stand, he or she still stands. The result of persuading someone is that he or she is still persuaded. Thus this usage occurs especially with verbs where the act slides over into the results.

Past	Present	Future
	———	

Diagram 72
The Perfect with Present Force

Both in semantics and semantic situation, this use of the perfect is at the opposite end of the spectrum from the aoristic perfect.

Aoristic Perfect	Regular Perfect	Perf w/Pres Force
Past	Past | Present	Present
•	• (———)	———
contextual intrusion (narrative)		lexical intrusion (usu. stative)

Diagram 73
The Aoristic Perfect and Perfect with Present Force Compared

In sum, it is important to remember that (1) this usage of the perfect is always *lexically influenced* (i.e., it occurs only with certain verbs), and (2) a large number of perfects must be treated as presents without attaching any aspectual significance to them. (Οἶδα alone constitutes over one fourth of all perfects in the NT!)

b. Illustrations

Mark 10:19   τὰς ἐντολὰς **οἶδας**   **you know** the commandments

John 1:26   μέσος ὑμῶν **ἕστηκεν** ὃν ὑμεῖς οὐκ **οἴδατε**
in your midst **stands** one whom **you do** not **know**

The Pluperfect Tense   *ExSyn* 583–86

As was stated in the general introduction to both the perfect and the pluperfect, for the most part, these two tenses are identical in aspect though different in time. That is, both speak of the state resulting from a previous event—the perfect speaking of existing results in the present (with reference to the speaker), the pluperfect speaking of existing results in the *past* (as this tense occurs only in the indicative mood). Thus, it may be said that *the pluperfect combines the aspects of the aorist (for the event) and the imperfect (for the results).*

To put this another way, the force of the pluperfect tense is that it describes an event that, completed in the past, has results that existed in the past as well (in relation to the time of speaking). *The pluperfect makes no comment about the results existing up to the time of speaking.* Such results may exist at the time of speaking or they may not; the pluperfect contributes nothing either way. (Often, however, it can be ascertained from the context whether or not the results do indeed exist up to the time of speaking.)

Past	Present
• (————————)	

Diagram 74
The Force of the Pluperfect

Note: The symbol (————————) indicates the *results* of an action.

There are only 86 simple pluperfects in the NT. In addition, there are a number of pluperfect periphrastic constructions (i.e., εἰμί in the indicative + a perfect participle).

➡ **1. Intensive Pluperfect (Resultative Pluperfect)**   *ExSyn* 584–85

a. Definition. This use of the pluperfect places the emphasis on the results that existed in past time. Its force can usually be brought out by translating it as a simple past tense. This is different from an aorist, however, in that the aorist is not used to indicate a resultant state from the event. It is different from an imperfect in that the imperfect describes the event itself as progressive, while the pluperfect only describes the state resulting from the event as continuing. This usage is relatively common.

Past	Present
• (————————)	

Diagram 75
The Force of the Intensive Pluperfect

As with its counterpart, the intensive perfect, some of the examples below might better belong to the extensive usage, since the difference between the two is only one of emphasis.

b. Illustrations

Matt 9:36   ἰδὼν δὲ τοὺς ὄχλους ἐσπλαγχνίσθη περὶ αὐτῶν, ὅτι **ἦσαν ἐσκυλμένοι** καὶ **ἐρριμμένοι** ὡσεὶ πρόβατα μὴ ἔχοντα ποιμένα.

But when he saw the crowds he felt compassion for them, because **they were weary** and **were lying down**, as sheep that do not have a shepherd.

> The periphrastic participles are used to indicate the current status of the crowd when Jesus saw them. There may be a hint in Matthew's use of the pluperfect, esp. in collocation with the shepherd motif, that this situation would soon disappear.

Luke 4:29   ἤγαγον αὐτὸν ἕως ὀφρύος τοῦ ὄρους ἐφ᾽ οὗ ἡ πόλις
ᾠκοδόμητο αὐτῶν
they led him to the brow of the hill on which their city
was built

> This is a good example of what the pluperfect does not tell us:
> It makes no comment about the present time (from the per-
> spective of the speaker). The pluperfect, being essentially a nar-
> rative tense, cannot be employed here to mean that the city no
> longer stood!

➡2. Extensive Pluperfect (Consummative Pluperfect)   *ExSyn* 585–86

a. Definition. The pluperfect may be used to emphasize the completion of
an action in past time, without focusing *as much* on the existing results. It is usually best translated as a past perfect (*had* + perfect passive participle). (Some examples might better belong to the intensive category.) This usage is relatively
common, especially in the Fourth Gospel.

Past	Present
• (————————)	

Diagram 76
The Force of the Extensive Pluperfect

b. Illustrations

Mark 15:46   ἔθηκεν αὐτὸν ἐν μνημείῳ ὃ **ἦν λελατομημένον** ἐκ πέτρας
he placed him in a tomb that **had been hewn** out of a rock

John 9:22   ἤδη γὰρ **συνετέθειντο** οἱ Ἰουδαῖοι
for the Jews **had** already **agreed**

➡3. Pluperfect with a Simple Past Force   *ExSyn* 586

a. Definition. Certain verbs occur frequently (or exclusively) in the perfect
and pluperfect tenses without the usual aspectual significance. Οἶδα (ᾔδειν) is the
most commonly used verb in this category. But other verbs also are used this way,
such as the perfects and pluperfects of ἵστημι, εἴωθα, πείθω, παρίστημι. These
are typically stative verbs; in all cases this pluperfect is due to *lexical intrusion*.
Instances are common in the NT (constituting the largest group of pluperfects).
(See the treatment under the perfect tense's counterpart, "Perfect with a Present
Force," for more discussion.)

The periphrastic constructions often resemble an imperfect more than an
aorist in translation.

b. Illustrations

Mark 1:34   οὐκ ἤφιεν λαλεῖν τὰ δαιμόνια, ὅτι **ᾔδεισαν** αὐτόν.
he would not permit the demons to speak, because **they knew**
him

Rev 7:11   πάντες οἱ ἄγγελοι **εἱστήκεισαν** κύκλῳ τοῦ θρόνου
all the angels **stood** around the throne

The Infinitive[1]
Overview of Uses

SEMANTIC CATEGORIES **255**
Adverbial Uses. **256**
➡ 1. Purpose 256
➡ 2. Result. 257
➡ 3. Time 258
➡ 4. Cause 259
➡ 5. Complementary (Supplementary) 259
Substantival Uses **260**
➡ 1. Subject. 260
2. Direct Object. 261
➡ 3. Indirect Discourse 261
➡ 4. Appositional. 262
➡ 5. Epexegetical. 263

STRUCTURAL CATEGORIES **264**
Anarthrous Infinitives. **264**
1. Simple Infinitive 264
2. Πρίν (ἤ) + Infinitive 264
3. Ὡς + Infinitive. 264
4. Ὥστε + Infinitive 264
Articular Infinitives. **264**
1. Without Governing Preposition. 264
   a. Nominative Articular Infinitive 264
   b. Accusative Articular Infinitive. 264
   c. Genitive Articular Infinitive 264
2. With Governing Preposition 264
   a. Διὰ τό + Infinitive 264
   b. Εἰς τό + Infinitive 264
   c. Ἐν τῷ + Infinitive 265
   d. Μετὰ τό + Infinitive 265
   e. Πρὸς τό + Infinitive. 265
   f. Miscellaneous Prepositional Uses. 265

---

[1] See *ExSyn* 587–611. The infinitive of means (see 597–97) and the independent use of the infinitive (see 608–9) are sufficiently rare that the average intermediate Greek student may ignore them.

Definition and Basic Characteristics

The infinitive is an *indeclinable verbal noun*. As such, it participates in some of the features of the verb and some of the noun.

Like a verb, the infinitive has tense and voice, but not person or mood. It can take an object and be modified by adverbs. Its number is always singular. Like the oblique moods (i.e., non-indicative moods), the infinitive is normally negated by μή rather than οὐ.

Like a noun, the infinitive can have many of the case functions that an ordinary noun can have (e.g., subject, object, apposition). It can function as the object of a preposition, be anarthrous and articular, and be modified by an adjective. Although technically infinitives do not have gender, often the neuter singular article is attached to them. So, from a structural perspective, it would be appropriate to speak of infinitives as neuter (though this is never a part of the parsing). The *neuter* article really has no other significance than a formal attachment (though the *case* of the article at times may be important to observe). One ought not to read into a given infinitive any impersonal idea simply because the neuter article is used!

The infinitive often occurs after *prepositions*. When it does so, the infinitive is *always articular*. However, it would be incorrect to assume that the infinitive is for this reason functioning substantivally. One needs the broader picture here: Prepositional phrases are routinely attached to verbs and hence are adverbial in nature. When the infinitive occurs after a preposition, the preposition combines with the infinitive for an adverbial force.

Structure Vs. Semantics?

Our approach is first to lay out the infinitive by its *semantic* categories (e.g., purpose, result, cause, time, etc.). A discussion of these categories will help the student see the different shades of meaning that each can have. This is important for a general understanding of how infinitives function. However, this approach is not very helpful when one begins with the *text*.

When you are looking at an infinitive in the Greek text, you need to note the structural clues and then turn to the "Structural Categories" section to see what meanings are possible. Then, read the material under "Semantic Categories" for a more detailed discussion of the meaning.

──────── SEMANTIC CATEGORIES ────────

The infinitive, as we noted above, partakes of the noun and the verb. True to its nature, we can organize it around these two parts of speech. When the infinitive has a verbal emphasis, it is normally dependent—i.e., it is adverbial in nature. On rare occasions, it can be independent verbally. When its emphasis falls on the nominal side, it can likewise be dependent (adjectival) or independent (substantival). This semantic categorization is visualized in the chart below. (However, because of the relative rarity of the independent verbal and dependent adjectival uses, we will follow a different pattern of organization.)

	Verbal	Nominal
Independent	**(Verbal)** Imperatival Absolute	**(Substantival)** Subject, object, etc.
Dependent	**(Adverbial)** Purpose, Result, Cause, Means, etc.	**(Adjectival)** Epexegetical

Chart 77
The Semantic Range of the Infinitive

Adverbial Uses

ExSyn 590–99

There are five basic adverbial uses of the infinitive: purpose, result, time, cause, and complementary.

➡ **1. Purpose [*to, in order to, for the purpose of*]**   *ExSyn 590–92*

a. Definition and structural clues. The infinitive is used to indicate the purpose or goal of the action or state of its controlling verb. It answers the question "Why?" in that it looks ahead to the anticipated and intended result. This is one of the most common uses of the infinitive.

The purpose infinitive is normally expressed by one of the following structural patterns:

- Simple or "naked" infinitive (usually following an [intransitive] verb of motion)
- τοῦ + infinitive
- εἰς τό + infinitive
- πρὸς τό + infinitive

b. Key to identification. Although a simple *to* idea will in most instances be the most appropriate translation, you should expand on this for the sake of testing to see if the infinitive in question fits another category. If you suspect a purpose infinitive, insert the gloss *in order to* or *for the purpose of* (and translate the infinitive as a gerund), *in order that*.

c. Illustrations

Matt 5:17   μὴ νομίσητε ὅτι ἦλθον **καταλῦσαι** τὸν νόμον
Do not think that I came **to destroy** the law

John 1:33   ὁ πέμψας με **βαπτίζειν**
the one who sent me **to baptize**

> This text illustrates (1) that the controlling verb of an infinitive is not necessarily the main verb of the sentence (in this case, a substantival participle); and (2) that the gloss *in order to* is for testing purposes only, as it would be too awkward if made the final translation ("the one who sent me in order to baptize").

➡ **2. Result** [*so that, so as to, with the result that*]   *ExSyn* 592–94

a. Definition and clarification.[2] The infinitive of result indicates the outcome produced by the controlling verb. In this respect it is similar to the infinitive of purpose, but the former puts an emphasis on intention (which may or may not culminate in the desired result) while the latter *places the emphasis on effect* (which may or may not have been intended). This usage is relatively common.

The result infinitive may be used to indicate either *actual* or *natural* result. *Actual* result is indicated in the context as having occurred; *natural* result is what is assumed to take place at a time subsequent to that indicated in the context.

The result infinitive is normally expressed by one of the following structural patterns:

- Simple or "naked" infinitive (usually following an [intransitive] verb of motion)
- τοῦ + infinitive
- εἰς τό + infinitive
- ὥστε + infinitive (the most frequent structure for a result infinitive)

Note that the first three parallel the first three structural patterns of the purpose infinitive, making syntactical decisions sometimes difficult.

b. Key to identification. Unlike the purpose infinitive, the simple *to* idea will often not be sufficient. In fact, it will frequently be misleading (even to the point of producing a confusing translation). The gloss *so that, so as to,* or *with the result that* brings out the force of this infinitive.[3]

---

[2] There are really two kinds of result infinitives: One is the actual, chronologically sequential result of the controlling verb; the other is the implication or significance of what the controlling verb actually accomplishes (almost an epexegetical idea, but not quite like the epexegetical inf. Its gloss would be "this is what the controlling verb means" or "here's what I mean when I say X").

[3] However, in modern colloquial English, *so that* also indicates purpose.

c. Illustrations

Luke 5:7   ἔπλησαν ἀμφότερα τὰ πλοῖα **ὥστε βυθίζεσθαι** αὐτά
they filled both the boats **so that they began to sink**

> This text illustrates the difference between result and purpose. The boats did not *intend* to sink (purpose). But the result was that they were so full of fish they began to sink.

1 Cor 13:2   ἐὰν ἔχω πᾶσαν τὴν πίστιν **ὥστε ὄρη μεθιστάναι**
if I have all faith **so as to remove** mountains

➡3. Time   *ExSyn 594–96*

This use of the infinitive indicates a temporal relationship between its action and the action of the controlling verb. It answers the question, "When?" There are three types, all carefully defined structurally: antecedent, contemporaneous, and subsequent. You should distinguish between them rather than labeling an infinitive merely as "temporal."[4]

a. Antecedent (μετὰ τό + infinitive) [after . . .]   *ExSyn 594–95*

The action of the infinitive of antecedent time occurs *before* the action of the controlling verb. Its *structure* is μετὰ τό + the infinitive and should be translated *after* plus an appropriate *finite* verb.[5]

Matt 26:32   μετὰ δὲ τὸ **ἐγερθῆναί** με προάξω ὑμᾶς εἰς τὴν Γαλιλαίαν.
And *after* I **have been raised**, I will go before you into Galilee.

b. Contemporaneous (ἐν τῷ + infinitive) [while, as, when . . .]   *ExSyn 595*

The action of the infinitive of contemporaneous time occurs *simultaneously* with the action of the controlling verb. Its *structure* is ἐν τῷ + the infinitive. It should be translated *while* (for present infinitives) or *as, when* (for aorist infinitives) plus an appropriate *finite* verb.

Matt 13:4   ἐν τῷ **σπείρειν** αὐτὸν ἃ μὲν ἔπεσεν παρὰ τὴν ὁδόν
while he **was sowing**, some fell on the road

---

[4] The contemporaneous inf. use is by far the most common. The antecedent inf. is relatively rare, but should be learned in conjunction with the other uses.

[5] There is confusion in some grammars about the proper labels of the temporal infinitives. More than one has mislabeled the antecedent infinitive as the subsequent infinitive, and vice versa. This confusion comes naturally: If we are calling this use of the infinitive *antecedent*, why then are we translating it as *after*? The reason is that this infinitive explicitly tells when the action of the *controlling verb* takes place, as in "*after* he got in the boat, it sank." In this sentence, "he got in" is the infinitive and "sank" is the main verb. The sinking comes after the getting in, or conversely, the getting in comes before the sinking. Thus the action of the infinitive occurs before that of the controlling verb.

Students are often confused about this point. Some have even queried, "Then why shouldn't we translate the sentence, 'Before the boat sank, he got in'?" The reason is that there is no word *before*, and the verb is not in the prepositional phrase (where we find the word *after*). It may be helpful to remember it this way: **After** *the infinitive comes the verb.*

Luke 3:21   *ἐν τῷ* **βαπτισθῆναι** *ἅπαντα τὸν λαὸν*
             when all the people **were baptized**

c. Subsequent (πρὸ τοῦ, πρίν, or πρὶν ἤ + infinitive)
[before . . .]
ExSyn 596

The action of the infinitive of subsequent time occurs *after* the action of the controlling verb. Its *structure* is πρὸ τοῦ, πρίν, or πρὶν ἤ + the infinitive. The construction should be *before* plus an appropriate *finite* verb.[6]

Matt 6:8   *οἶδεν ὁ πατὴρ ὑμῶν ὧν χρείαν ἔχετε πρὸ τοῦ ὑμᾶς* **αἰτῆσαι** *αὐτόν*
            your Father knows what you need *before* you **ask** him

➡4. Cause
ExSyn 596–97

a. Definition and structural clues. The causal infinitive indicates the reason for the action of the controlling verb. In this respect, it answers the question "Why?" Unlike the infinitive of purpose, however, the causal infinitive gives a *retrospective* answer (i.e., it looks back to the ground or reason), while the purpose infinitive gives a *prospective* answer (looking forward to the intended result). In Luke-Acts this category is fairly common, though rare elsewhere.

The infinitive of cause is usually expressed by διὰ τό + infinitive. As its key to identification, use *because* + a finite verb appropriate to the context.

b. Illustrations

Mark 4:6   *διὰ τὸ μὴ* **ἔχειν** *ρίζαν ἐξηράνθη*
            because it **had** no root, it withered

Heb 7:24   *ὁ δὲ διὰ τὸ* **μένειν** *αὐτὸν εἰς τὸν αἰῶνα ἀπαράβατον ἔχει τὴν ἱερωσύνην*
            but *because* he **remains** forever, he maintains his priesthood permanently

➡5. Complementary (Supplementary)
ExSyn 598–99

a. Definition and structural clues. The complementary infinitive is frequently used with "helper" verbs to complete their thought. Such verbs rarely occur without the infinitive. This finds a parallel in English.

The key to this infinitive use is the helper verb. The most common verbs that take a complementary infinitive are ἄρχομαι, βούλομαι, δύναμαι (the most commonly used helper verb), ἐπιτρέπω, ζητέω, θέλω, μέλλω, and ὀφείλω. The infinitive itself is the *simple* infinitive.[7]

---

[6] See note above on antecedent infinitives for discussion on why there is confusion over terminology between these two categories.

[7] A second clue is that the complementary infinitive is especially used with a *nominative* subject, as would be expected. For example, in Luke 19:47 we read οἱ γραμματεῖς *ἐζήτουν* αὐτὸν **ἀπολέσαι** ("the scribes *were seeking* **to kill** him"). But when the infinitive requires a

b. Illustrations

Matt 6:24   οὐ δύνασθε θεῷ **δουλεύειν** καὶ μαμωνᾷ
               *you can*not **serve** God and mammon

Phil 1:12   **γινώσκειν** δὲ ὑμᾶς βούλομαι, ἀδελφοί, ὅτι τὰ κατ᾽ ἐμὲ ...
               now *I want* you **to know**, brothers, that my circumstances ...

Substantival Uses   *ExSyn 600–7*

There are four basic uses of the substantival infinitive: subject, direct object, appositional, and epexegetical.[8] A specialized use of the direct object is indirect discourse. But because it occurs so frequently, it will be treated separately. Thus, pragmatically, there are five basic uses of the substantival infinitive: subject, direct object, indirect discourse, appositional, and epexegetical.

➡1. Subject   *ExSyn 600–1*

a. Definition and structural clues. An infinitive or an infinitive phrase frequently functions as the subject of a finite verb. This category especially includes instances in which the infinitive occurs with *impersonal verbs* such as δεῖ, ἔξεστιν, δοκεῖ, etc.[9]

This infinitive may or may not have the article. However, this usage of the infinitive does not occur in prepositional phrases.

b. Key to identification. Besides noting the definition and structural clues, one helpful key to identification is to do the following. In place of the infinitive (or infinitive phrase), substitute X. Then say the sentence with this substitution. If X can be replaced by an appropriate noun functioning as subject, then the infinitive is most likely a subject infinitive.

For example, in Phil 1:21 Paul writes, "For to me, to live is Christ and to die is gain." Substituting X for the infinitives we get, "For to me, X is Christ and X is gain." We can readily see that X can be replaced by a noun (such as "life" or "death").

c. Illustrations

Mark 9:5   ὁ Πέτρος λέγει τῷ Ἰησοῦ· ῥαββί, καλόν ἐστιν ἡμᾶς ὧδε **εἶναι**
               Peter said to Jesus, "Rabbi, for us **to be** here is good"

---

different agent, it is put in the accusative case (e.g., **γινώσκειν** ὑμᾶς βούλομαι ["I want *you* **to know**"] in Phil 1:12). The infinitive is still to be regarded as complementary. For a discussion on the subject of the inf., see the chapter on the acc. case.

[8] The epexegetical use might more properly be called adjectival or dependent substantival.

[9] Technically, there are no impersonal subjects in Greek as there are in English. Instances of the inf. with, say, δεῖ, are actually subject infinitives. Thus, δεῖ με ἔρχεσθαι means "to come is necessary for me" rather than "it is necessary for me to come." One way to see the force of the Greek more clearly is to translate the inf. as a gerund.

Phil 1:21   ἐμοὶ γὰρ **τὸ ζῆν** Χριστὸς καὶ **τὸ ἀποθανεῖν** κέρδος
For to me, **to live** is Christ and **to die** is gain

2. Direct Object

ExSyn 601–3

a. Definition and structural clues. An infinitive or an infinitive phrase occasionally functions as the direct object of a finite verb. Apart from instances of indirect discourse, this usage is rare. Nevertheless, this is an important category for exegesis.

This infinitive may or may not have the article. However, this usage of the infinitive does not occur in prepositional phrases.

b. Key to identification. Besides noting the definition and structural clues, one helpful key is to do the following: In place of the infinitive (or infinitive phrase), substitute X. Then say the sentence with this substitution. If X could be replaced by an appropriate noun functioning as direct object, then the infinitive is most likely a direct object infinitive. (This works equally well for indirect discourse infinitives.)

c. Illustrations

2 Cor 8:11   νυνὶ δὲ καὶ **τὸ ποιῆσαι** ἐπιτελέσατε
but now also complete **the doing** [of it]

Phil 2:13   θεὸς γάρ ἐστιν ὁ ἐνεργῶν ἐν ὑμῖν καὶ **τὸ θέλειν** καὶ **τὸ ἐνεργεῖν** ὑπὲρ τῆς εὐδοκίας
For the one producing in you both **the willing** and **the working** (for [his] good pleasure) is God[10]

➡3. Indirect Discourse

ExSyn 603–5

a. Definition. This is the use of the infinitive (or infinitive phrase) after a verb of *perception* or *communication*. The controlling verb introduces the indirect discourse, of which the infinitive is the main verb. "When an infinitive stands as the object of a verb of mental perception or communication and expresses the content or the substance of the thought or of the communication it is classified as being in indirect discourse."[11] This usage is quite common in the NT.

b. Clarification and semantics. We can see how indirect discourse functions by analogies with English. For example, "I told you to do the dishes" involves a verb of communication ("told") followed by an infinitive in indirect discourse ("to do"). The infinitive in indirect discourse represents a *finite* verb in the direct discourse. The interpreter has to reconstruct the supposed direct discourse. In this example, the direct discourse would be, "Do the dishes." What we can see from this illustration is that the infinitive of indirect discourse may represent an *imperative* on occasion.

---

[10] For discussion of this text, see *ExSyn* 602–3.

[11] J. L. Boyer, "The Classification of Infinitives: A Statistical Study," *GTJ* 6 (1985): 7.

But consider the example, "He claimed to know her." In this sentence the infinitive represents an *indicative*: "He claimed, 'I know her.'"

From these two illustrations we can see some of the sentence "embedding" in infinitives of indirect discourse. The general principle for these infinitives is that *the infinitive of indirect discourse retains the **tense** of the direct discourse and usually represents either an **imperative** or **indicative***.

c. Introductory verbs. The verbs of perception/communication that can introduce an indirect discourse infinitive are numerous. The list includes verbs of knowing, thinking, believing, speaking, asking, urging, and commanding. The most common verbs are δοκέω, ἐρωτάω, κελεύω, κρίνω, λέγω, νομίζω, παραγγέλλω, and παρακαλέω.

d. Illustrations

Mark 12:18   Σαδδουκαῖοι ... οἵτινες *λέγουσιν* ἀνάστασιν μὴ **εἶναι**
Sadducees ... who *say* **there is** no resurrection

Jas 2:14   τί τὸ ὄφελος, ἀδελφοί μου, ἐὰν πίστιν *λέγῃ* τις **ἔχειν** ἔργα δὲ μὴ ἔχῃ;
What is the benefit, my brothers, if someone *claims* **to have** faith but does not have works?

> The direct discourse would have been, "I have faith." If the original discourse had been "I have faith but I do not have works," the subjunctive ἔχῃ would have been an infinitive as well.

Eph 4:21–22   ἐν αὐτῷ *ἐδιδάχθητε* ... **ἀποθέσθαι** ὑμᾶς ... τὸν παλαιὸν ἄνθρωπον
you have been taught in him ... that you **have put off** ... the old man

> The other translation possibility is, "You have been taught in him that you *should* put off the old man." The reason that either translation is possible is simply that the infinitive of indirect discourse represents either an imperative or an indicative in the direct discourse, while its tense remains the same as the direct discourse. Hence, this verse embeds either "Put off the old man" (aorist imperative), or "You have put off the old man."[12]

➡**4. Appositional [namely]**   *ExSyn* 606–7

a. Definition. Like any other substantive, the substantival infinitive may stand in apposition to a noun, pronoun, or substantival adjective (or some other substantive). The appositional infinitive typically refers to a specific example that falls within the broad category named by the head noun. This usage is relatively common.

This category is easy to confuse with the epexegetical infinitive. The difference is that the epexegetical infinitive *explains* the noun or adjective to which it is

---

[12] For discussion of this text, see *ExSyn* 605–6.

related, while apposition *defines* it. That is to say, apposition differs from epexegesis in that an appositional infinitive is more substantival than adjectival. This subtle difference can be seen in another way: An epexegetical infinitive (phrase) cannot typically substitute for its antecedent, while an appositional infinitive (phrase) can.

b. Key to identification. Insert the word *namely* before the infinitive. Another way to test it is to replace the *to* with a colon (though this does not always work quite as well[13]). For example, Jas 1:27 ("Pure religion ... is this, to visit orphans and widows") could be rendered "Pure religion is this, *namely*, to visit orphans and widows," or "Pure religion is this: visit orphans and widows."

c. Illustrations

Jas 1:27   θρησκεία καθαρὰ ... αὕτη ἐστίν, **ἐπισκέπτεσθαι** ὀρφανοὺς καὶ χήρας
pure religion ... is this, **namely, to visit** orphans and widows

Phil 1:29   ὑμῖν ἐχαρίσθη τὸ ὑπὲρ Χριστοῦ, οὐ μόνον **τὸ** εἰς αὐτὸν **πιστεύειν** ἀλλὰ καὶ **τὸ** ὑπὲρ αὐτοῦ **πάσχειν**
it has been granted to you, for the sake of Christ, not only **to believe** in him, but also **to suffer** for him

> The article with ὑπὲρ Χριστοῦ turns this expression into a substantive functioning as the subject of ἐχαρίσθη. Thus, "the-[following]-on-behalf-of-Christ has been granted to you."

➡ **5. Epexegetical**   *ExSyn* 607

a. Definition. The epexegetical infinitive clarifies, explains, or qualifies a noun or adjective.[14] This use of the infinitive is usually bound by certain lexical features of the noun or adjective. That is, they normally are words indicating ability, authority, desire, freedom, hope, need, obligation, or readiness. This usage is fairly common.[15]

b. Illustrations

Luke 10:19   δέδωκα ὑμῖν τὴν ἐξουσίαν τοῦ **πατεῖν** ἐπάνω ὄφεων καὶ σκορπίων
I have given you authority **to tread** on serpents and scorpions

1 Cor 7:39   ἐλευθέρα ἐστὶν ᾧ θέλει **γαμηθῆναι**
she is free **to be married** to whom[ever] she desires

---

[13] The reason is that dropping the *to* turns the inf. into an imperative. Only if the context allows for it will this be an adequate translation.

[14] Some grammars also say that it can qualify a verb. But when the inf. qualifies a verb, it should be treated as complementary.

[15] This use of the infinitive is easy to confuse with the appositional infinitive. On the distinction between the two, see the discussion under "Appositional Infinitive."

—— STRUCTURAL CATEGORIES —— *ExSyn 609–11*

Anarthrous Infinitives   *ExSyn 609*

The great majority of infinitives in the NT are anarthrous (almost 2000 of the 2291 infinitives).

1. Simple Infinitive

The simple infinitive is the most versatile of all structural categories, displaying a wide variety of semantic uses: purpose, result, complementary, subject, direct object (rare), indirect discourse, apposition, and epexegesis.

2. Πρίν (ἤ) + Infinitive (subsequent time only)

3. ῾Ως + Infinitive

This category of the infinitive can express purpose or result.

4. ῞Ωστε + Infinitive

This category of the infinitive can express purpose (rare) or result.

Articular Infinitives   *ExSyn 610*

Of the 314 articular infinitives in the NT, about two-thirds are governed by a preposition. Conversely, all infinitives governed by a preposition are articular.

1. Without Governing Preposition

a. *Nominative Articular Infinitive*

A nominative articular infinitive can function as the subject in a sentence or be in apposition (rare).

b. *Accusative Articular Infinitive*

An accusative articular infinitive can function as the object in a sentence or be in apposition.

c. *Genitive Articular Infinitive*

A genitive articular infinitive can denote purpose, result, contemporaneous time (rare), cause (also rare), or epexegesis; it can also be in apposition.

2. With Governing Preposition

a. *Διὰ τό + Infinitive:* Cause

b. *Εἰς τό + Infinitive:* Purpose, Result, or Epexegesis

c. Ἐν τῷ + *Infinitive:* **Result (rare) or Contemporaneous Time**

d. Μετὰ τό + *Infinitive:* **Antecedent Time**

e. Πρὸς τό + *Infinitive:* **Purpose or Result**

f. Miscellaneous Prepositional Uses

For a list and discussion of other prepositions used with the infinitive as well as the "normal" prepositions used with infinitives in an "abnormal" way, see Burton's *Moods and Tenses*, 160–63 (§406–17).

The Participle[1]
Overview of Uses

Adjectival Participles. **269**
➡ 1. Adjectival Proper (Dependent) 270
➡ 2. Substantival (Independent) 270
Verbal Participles **271**
   1. Dependent Verbal Participles 271
      a. Adverbial (or Circumstantial) 272
➡   (1) Temporal 272
            (2) Manner 274
➡   (3) Means 274
➡   (4) Cause 275
➡   (5) Condition 276
➡   (6) Concession 277
➡   (7) Purpose (Telic) 277
➡   (8) Result 278
➡   b. Attendant Circumstance 279
      c. Indirect Discourse 281
➡   d. Periphrastic 281
      e. Redundant (Pleonastic) 282
† 2. Independent Verbal Participles: Imperatival 283
The Participle Absolute **283**
   1. Nominative Absolute 283
➡ 2. Genitive Absolute 284

——— INTRODUCTION ———   *ExSyn* 613–17

1. The Difficulty with Participles

It is often said that mastery of the syntax of participles is mastery of Greek syntax. Why are participles so difficult to grasp? The reason is threefold: (1) *usage*—the participle can be used as a noun, adjective, adverb, or verb (and in any mood!); (2) *word order*—the participle is often thrown to the end of the sentence or elsewhere to an equally inconvenient location; and (3) *locating the main verb*—sometimes it is verses away; sometimes it is only implied; and sometimes it is not even implied! In short, the participle is difficult to master because it is so versatile. But this very versatility makes it capable of a rich variety of nuances, as well as a rich variety of abuses.

---

[1] See *ExSyn* 612–55. The complementary participle (see 646) and the indicative independent participle (see 653) are sufficiently rare that the average intermediate Greek student may ignore them.

2. The Participle as a Verbal Adjective

The participle is a *declinable verbal adjective*. From its verbal nature it derives tense and voice; from its adjectival nature, gender, number, and case. Like the infinitive, the participle's verbal nature is normally seen in a *dependent* manner. That is, it is normally adverbial (in a broad sense) rather than functioning independently as a verb. Its adjectival side is seen in both substantival (independent) and adjectival (dependent) uses; both are frequent (though the substantival is far more so).

a. The Verbal Side of the Participle

(1) TIME. The *time* of the participle's verbal nature requires careful consideration. Generally speaking, the tenses behave as they do in the indicative. The only difference is that now the point of reference is the controlling verb, not the speaker. Thus, time in participles is relative (or dependent), while in the indicative it is absolute (or independent).

	PAST	PRESENT	FUTURE
ABSOLUTE (Indicative)	Aorist Perfect Imperfect Pluperfect	Perfect	Future
RELATIVE (Participle)	Aorist Perfect	Perfect (Aorist)	Future

Chart 78
Time in Participles

The *aorist* participle, for example, usually denotes *antecedent* time to that of the controlling verb.[2] But if the main verb is also aorist, this participle *may* indicate contemporaneous time. The *perfect* participle also indicates *antecedent* time. The *present* participle is used for *contemporaneous* time. (This contemporaneity, however, is often quite broadly conceived, depending especially on the tense of the main verb.) The *future* participle denotes subsequent time.

This general analysis should help us in determining whether a participle can even belong to a certain adverbial usage. For example, participles of *purpose* are normally future, sometimes present, (almost) never aorist or perfect.[3] Why? Because the purpose of the controlling verb is carried out *after* the time of the main verb (or sometimes contemporaneously with it). Likewise, *causal* participles

---

[2] We are speaking here principally with reference to adverbial (or circumstantial) participles.

[3] Some have noted that the aorist participle can, on a rare occasion, have a telic force in Hellenistic Greek, because the future participle was not normally a viable choice in the conversational and vulgar dialect.

will not be in the future tense (though the perfect adverbial participle is routinely causal; the aorist often is and so is the present).[4] *Result* participles are never in the perfect tense. Participles of *means*? These are normally present tense, though the aorist is also amply attested (especially when a progressive aspect is not in view).

(2) ASPECT. As for the participle's *aspect*, it still functions for the most part like its indicative counterparts. There are two basic influences that shape the participle's verbal side, however, which are almost constant factors in its *Aktionsart*.[5] First, because the participle has embodied two natures, neither one acts completely independently of the other. Hence, the verbal nature of participles has a permanent *grammatical intrusion* from the adjectival nature. This *tends* to dilute the strength of the aspect. Many nouns in Hellenistic Greek, for instance, were participles in a former life (e.g., ἄρχων, ἡγεμών, τέκτων). The constant pressure from the adjectival side finally caved in any remnants of verbal aspect. This is not to say that no participles in the NT are aspectually robust—many of them are! But one must not assume this to be the case in every instance. In particular, when a participle is *substantival*, its aspectual element is more susceptible to reduction in force.

Second, many substantival participles in the NT are used in generic utterances. The πᾶς ὁ ἀκούων (or ἀγαπῶν, ποιῶν, etc.) formula is always or almost always generic. As such it is expected to involve a *gnomic* aspect.[6] Most of these instances involve the present participle. But if they are already gnomic, we would be hard-pressed to make something more out of them—such as a progressive idea.[7] Thus, for example, in Matt 5:28, "everyone who looks at a woman" (πᾶς ὁ βλέπων γυναῖκα) with lust in his heart does not mean "continually looking" or "habitually looking," any more than four verses later "everyone who divorces his wife" (πᾶς ὁ ἀπολύων τὴν γυναῖκα αὐτοῦ) means "repeatedly divorces"! This is not to deny a habitual *Aktionsart* in such gnomic statements. But it is to say that caution must be exercised. In the least, we should be careful not to make statements such as, "The present participle βλέπων [in Matt 5:28] characterizes the man by his act of *continued* looking."[8] This may well be the meaning of the *evangelist*, but the present participle, by itself, can hardly be forced into this mold.

b. The Adjectival Nature of the Participle

As an adjective, a participle can function dependently or independently. That is, it can function like any ordinary adjective as an attributive or predicate. It also can act substantivally, as is the case with any adjective.

---

[4] That the present participle could be causal may seem to deny its contemporaneity. But its contemporaneity in such cases is either broadly conceived or the participle functions as the *logical* cause though it may be *chronologically* simultaneous.

[5] For a discussion of the difference between aspect and *Aktionsart*, see our introductory chapter on verb tenses.

[6] See the discussion under gnomic present tense.

[7] Nevertheless, the present substantival participle, even when gnomic, can have a progressive force as well.

[8] Lenski, *St. Matthew's Gospel* (Columbus, Ohio: Lutheran Book Concern, 1932), 226.

c. Summary

All participles fit one of two categories (in keeping with the fact that they are verbal adjectives): Every participle emphasizes either its verbal or its adjectival aspect. Within each of these emphases, every participle is either dependent or independent. If you can keep this simple grid in mind, you will have a broad, organizational understanding of the participle.[9]

	Verbal	Adjectival
Independent	**(Verbal)** Imperatival Indicative	**(Substantival)** Subject, object, etc.
Dependent	**(Adverbial)** Temporal, Causal, Means, Manner, etc.	**(Adjectival)** Attributive Predicate

Chart 79
The Semantic Range of the Participle

———————— SPECIFIC USES ————————   *ExSyn 617–55*

Adjectival Participles   *ExSyn 617–21*

This category involves both the dependent and independent adjectival participles (i.e., both the adjectival proper and substantival). For a structural clue, the student should note the article: If it stands before a participle and functions as a modifying article (normal use), then that participle *must* be adjectival. If the participle does *not* have the article, it *may* be adjectival. Therefore, the first question one needs to ask when attempting to determine the nuance of a particular participle is, *Does it have the article?* If the answer is yes, it is adjectival;[10] if the answer is no, it may be adjectival or any other kind of participle (such as adverbial).

---

[9] Although every participle fits under either an adjectival emphasis or verbal emphasis and is either dependent or independent, I have not listed one large category of participles (known as participles absolute). These will be treated separately from the above mentioned categories, even though they in fact fit under these categories. The reason for a separate treatment of the participle absolute is that it has particular structural clues (especially a specific case) that require further explanation.

[10] There is one seeming exception to this rule. When the construction is ὁ μέν + participle or ὁ δέ + participle, the article may be functioning like a personal pronoun. In such instances it is not modifying the participle but is the subject of the sentence. The participle will then be adverbial. See the discussion of this phenomenon in "The Article, Part I."

➡1. Adjectival Proper (Dependent)

ExSyn 617–21

a. Definition. The participle may function like an adjective and either modify a substantive (attributive) or assert something about it (predicate). The attributive participle is common; the predicate participle is rare.

b. Clarification/key to identification. The way in which one determines whether a participle is attributive or predicate is exactly the same as how one determines whether an *adjective* is attributive or predicate. The adjectival participle may occupy any of the three attributive positions and both predicate positions. You should normally translate the *attributive* participle as though it were a relative clause (e.g., ὁ πατήρ σου ὁ **βλέπων** ἐν τῷ κρυπτῷ ἀποδώσει σοι ["your Father *who* **sees** in secret will reward you"] in Matt 6:4).

As a refinement, therefore, we should add that a *predicate* participle never has the article (only the attributive and substantival participles do).

c. Illustrations

(1) ATTRIBUTIVE PARTICIPLES

Matt 2:7	τοῦ **φαινομένου** ἀστέρος	the **shining** star
John 4:11	τὸ ὕδωρ τὸ **ζῶν**	the **living** water
John 4:25	Μεσσίας … ὁ **λεγόμενος** χριστός	
	Messiah … **the one called** Christ	

(2) PREDICATE PARTICIPLES

Heb 4:12	**ζῶν** ὁ λόγος τοῦ θεοῦ	the word of God is **living**
Jas 2:15	ἐὰν ἀδελφὸς ἢ ἀδελφὴ γυμνοὶ ὑπάρχωσιν καὶ **λειπόμενοι** τῆς ἐφημέρου τροφῆς	
	if your brother or sister is naked and **lacking** [their] daily food	

➡2. Substantival (Independent)

ExSyn 619–21

a. Definition. This is the independent use of the adjectival participle (i.e., not related to a noun). It functions in the place of a substantive. As such, it can function in virtually any capacity that a noun can, such as subject, direct object, indirect object, apposition, etc. This category is found quite frequently in the NT.

b. Key to identification and clarification. First, of course, if the participle has the article it must be either adjectival (proper) or substantival. Second, if it is articular and is not related in a dependent fashion to any substantive in the sentence, then it is substantival. The translation is often *the one who/the thing which* with the participle then translated as a finite verb (e.g., ὁ ποιῶν is translated *the one who does*).

The substantival participle may or may not be articular, although most are. Its case is determined as any ordinary noun's case is determined, viz., by its function in the sentence.

c. Semantics. First, in relation to the infinitive: Although participles and infinitives are often translated the same (especially when the infinitive is translated as a gerund), there is a distinct difference. "Whereas the infinitive is abstract, speaking of the *act* or *fact* of doing, the participle is concrete, speaking of the *person who* or *thing which* does."[11]

Second, with reference to its verbal nature: Just because a participle is adjectival or substantival, this does *not* mean that its verbal aspect is entirely diminished. Most substantival participles still retain *something* of their aspect. A *general* rule of thumb is that *the more particular (as opposed to generic) the referent, the more of the verbal aspect is still seen.*

Third, the aspect of the *present* participle can be diminished if the particular context requires it. Thus, for example, ὁ βαπτίζων in Mark 1:4 does not mean "the one who continually baptizes" but simply "the baptizer." Indeed, it cannot mean this in Mark 6:14, for otherwise John would be baptizing without a head ("John the baptizer has been raised from the dead")!

d. Illustrations

Luke 1:45	μακαρία ἡ **πιστεύσασα**	blessed is **she who believed**
John 3:16	πᾶς ὁ **πιστεύων**	everyone **who believes**

John 3:16 The idea seems to be both gnomic and continual: "everyone who continually believes." This is not due to the present tense only, but to the use of the present participle of πιστεύω, especially in soteriological contexts in the NT.[12]

John 6:39   τοῦτο δέ ἐστιν τὸ θέλημα τοῦ **πέμψαντός** με
now this is the will of **the one who sent** me

Verbal Participles *ExSyn 621–53*

This category involves those participles that emphasize the verbal over the adjectival nuance. The category includes both independent and (far more commonly) dependent verbal participles. By way of clarification, it should again be stated that the verbal element of *any* participle, whether it be adjectival or verbal in emphasis, is not usually absent (note the partial exceptions above in which the aspect is diminished, even though the voice still retains its force). However, when a participle is labeled as verbal, we simply indicate that its verbal nature is in the forefront.

1. Dependent Verbal Participles *ExSyn 622–50*

This is far and away the larger of the two categories of participles and includes the following subcategories: adverbial (or circumstantial), attendant circumstance, indirect discourse, periphrastic, and redundant.[13]

---

[11] Williams, *Grammar Notes*, 50.

[12] See *ExSyn* 621 for discussion.

[13] Broadly speaking, of course, all (verbal) dependent participles are adverbial.

a. Adverbial (or Circumstantial)

ExSyn 622–40

DEFINITION. The adverbial participle is grammatically subordinated to its controlling verb (usually the main verb of the clause). Like an ordinary adverb, the participle modifies the verb, answering the question, *When?* (temporal), *How?* (means, manner), *Why?* (purpose, cause), etc.

Many grammars prefer to call this participle *circumstantial*, but that title is too vague. To call this participle *adverbial* communicates more clearly and fits the general idea better: Adverbial participles, like adverbs, are dependent on a verb.

AMPLIFICATION AND KEY TO IDENTIFICATION. First, as we have said earlier, the context plays a major role in determining the force of the Greek participle. This is especially so with the adverbial participle.

Second, since the subject of the participle is usually the subject of a finite verb, the participle will usually be in the *nominative* case (almost 70% of the time).

Third, there is often a strong translational correspondence between the English participle and the Greek (more so than for the respective infinitives). In *this* respect, the participle is not difficult to master.

Fourth, related to this, the English participle is generally more ambiguous than the Greek. Greek participles for the most part follow carefully defined patterns (e.g., word order, tense of participle, tense of controlling verb), allowing us to limit our choices in a given text more than we could if we depended on the English alone. It is for this reason that the student is encouraged to translate the force of the participle with more than an —*ing* gloss.

SPECIFIC NUANCES OF THE ADVERBIAL PARTICIPLE. Most adverbial participles belong to one of *eight* categories: temporal, manner, means, cause, condition, concession, purpose, or result.

➡ (1) TEMPORAL

ExSyn 623–27

(a) Definition. In relation to its controlling verb, the temporal participle answers the question *When?* Three kinds of time are in view: antecedent, contemporaneous, and subsequent. The *antecedent* participle should be translated *after doing, after he did*, or if very close to the time of the main verb, *when.* The *contemporaneous* participle should normally be translated *while doing.* And the *subsequent* participle should be translated *before doing, before he does*, etc.[14] This usage is common.

(b) Key to identification. If a particular adverbial participle is to be labeled as temporal, this should be the *primary* element the author wishes to stress (because almost all participles, whether adverbial or not, are temporal in at least a secondary sense).[15]

---

[14] In reality, almost all subsequent participles fit some other category, especially purpose and result. Hence, *before* is not normally a viable translation.

[15] Although the temporal participle is commonly found, students tend to appeal to this category too often. If a participle is labeled as temporal, this does not necessarily mean that such is its only force. Often a secondary notion is present, such as means or cause (see *ExSyn* 624 for further discussion).

Therefore, if you have identified a participle as having temporal force, you should go on and ask whether another, more specific semantic value is intended. You should probe the participle's usage with questions such as, "Is the author *only* describing when this happened or is he also indicating *why* or *how* it happened?"

(c) *Amplification.* The *aorist participle* is normally, though by no means always, *antecedent* in time to the action of the main verb. But when the aorist participle is related to an *aorist* main verb, the participle will often be contemporaneous (or simultaneous) to the action of the main verb. With a present tense main verb, the aorist participle is usually antecedent in time.

The *present participle* is normally *contemporaneous* in time to the action of the main verb. This is especially so when it is related to a present tense main verb. But this participle can be broadly antecedent to the time of the main verb, especially if the participle is articular. As well, the present participle is occasionally subsequent *in a sense* to the time of the main verb. This is the case when the participle has a telic (purpose) or result flavor to it.

The *future participle* is always *subsequent* in time to the action of the main verb.

The *perfect participle* is almost always *antecedent* with reference to the main verb. When it is contemporaneous, such is due to either an intensive use of the perfect or to a present force of the perfect in its lexical nuance.

The following chart notes the tenses normally used for the various temporal relations, especially as these relate to the other adverbial uses of the participle.

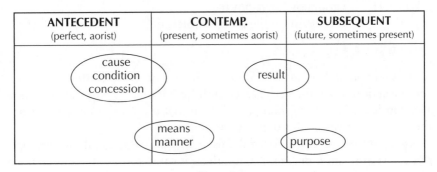

Chart 80
The Tenses of Adverbial Participles

(d) *Illustrations*

Matt 4:2	**νηστεύσας** ... ὕστερον ἐπείνασεν
	after he fasted ... he became hungry
Mark 2:14	**παράγων** εἶδεν Λευὶν τὸν τοῦ Ἀλφαίου
	while going on, he saw Levi, the son of Alphaeus
Mark 9:15	πᾶς ὁ ὄχλος **ἰδόντες** αὐτὸν ἐξεθαμβήθησαν
	when all the crowd **saw him**, they were amazed

(2) Manner [BY + PARTICIPLE OF EMOTION OR ATTITUDE]   *ExSyn 627–28*

(a) Definition and key to identification. The participle indicates the *manner* in which the action of the finite verb is carried out. First, there is much confusion between this participle and the participle of means. The reason is that both answer the question, *How?* But beyond this initial question, there is usually little similarity. The participle of manner is relatively rare in comparison with the participle of means.[16]

Second, pragmatically, the participle of manner refers to the *emotion* (or sometimes *attitude*)[17] that accompanies the main verb. In this sense, it "adds color" to the story. It could appropriately be called *the participle of style.* This contrasts with the participle of means, which *defines* the action of the main verb. The key question that must be asked is, Does this participle *explain or define* the action of the main verb (means), or does it merely add *extra color* to the action of the main verb (manner)?

(b) Illustrations

Matt 19:22   ἀπῆλθεν **λυπούμενος**   he went away **grieving**

Notice that the participle does answer the question, "How?" but it does not define the mode of transportation. If we were to ask, "How did he go away?" *grieving* would be a participle of manner, while *walking* would be a participle of means.

Acts 5:41   ἐπορεύοντο **χαίροντες**
they went on their way **rejoicing**

➡   (3) Means [BY MEANS OF]   *ExSyn 628–30*

(a) Definition and key to identification. This participle indicates the means by which the action of a finite verb is accomplished; it may be physical or mental. It can be considered an *epexegetical* participle in that it *defines* or *explains* the action of the controlling verb. This usage is common.

As we pointed out above, both the participle of manner and the participle of means answer the question, *How?* Thus, there is some confusion between the two. Thus, one should supply *by* or *by means of* before the participle in translation. If this does not fit, it is not a participle of means.

Here are some further guidelines that you should use to distinguish between means and manner:

---

[16] Most grammars and commentaries make either little distinction between these two or define manner in a way that is much closer to our definition of means. However, there are usually clear semantic differences. What is at stake is for the most part a terminological issue, not a substantive one. When commentators speak of the "modal participle" (a term that fits both means and manner), it is best to regard most such identifications as participles of *means.*

[17] The attitude, however, may be expressed by a participle of means—if it is an *essential* or defining characteristic of the main verb.

- The participle of means asks "How?" but here (as opposed to the participle of manner) it seems a more necessary and implicit question.[18]
- If the participle of means is absent (or removed), the *point* of the main verb is removed as well (this is not normally true with manner).
- In some sense, the participle of means almost always defines the action of the main verb; i.e., it makes more explicit what the author intended to convey with the main verb.[19]

(b) Illustrations

Matt 27:4   ἥμαρτον **παραδοὺς** αἷμα ἀθῷον
I have sinned **by betraying** innocent blood

Acts 9:22   Σαῦλος ... συνέχυννεν τοὺς Ἰουδαίους ... **συμβιβάζων** ὅτι οὗτός ἐστιν ὁ χριστός.
Saul ... confounded the Jews ... **by proving** that [Jesus] was the Christ.

1 Pet 5:6–7   ταπεινώθητε ὑπὸ τὴν κραταιὰν χεῖρα τοῦ θεοῦ ... πᾶσαν τὴν μέριμναν ὑμῶν **ἐπιρίψαντες** ἐπ᾽ αὐτόν, ὅτι αὐτῷ μέλει περὶ ὑμῶν.
Humble yourselves under the mighty hand of God ... **by casting** all your cares on him, because he cares for you.

> Although treated as an independent command in several modern translations (e.g., NRSV, NIV), the participle should be connected with the verb of v. 6, ταπεινώθητε (so NET). As such, it is not offering a new command, but is defining *how* believers are to humble themselves. Taking the participle as means enriches our understanding of both verbs: Humbling oneself is not a negative act of self-denial per se, but a positive one of active dependence on God for help.

Phil 2:7   ἑαυτὸν ἐκένωσεν μορφὴν δούλου **λαβών**
he emptied himself **by taking on** the form of a servant[20]

→ (4) CAUSE [*BECAUSE*]   *ExSyn* 631–32

(a) Definition and key to identification. The causal participle indicates the *cause, reason,* or *ground* of the action of the finite verb. This is a common usage.

---

[18] The participle of means gives the *anticipated* answer to the question *How?* while manner normally does not. Thus, to the question, "How did he go to the ballgame?" one could answer "by driving his car" (means) or "hoping for a victory" (manner).

[19] Note that this participle is frequently used with vague, general, abstract, or metaphorical finite verbs. Further, it usually *follows* its verb. The reason for these two features (one lexical, the other structural) is that the participle explains the verb. If the verb needs explaining, then it is the vaguer term. The verb comes first and is general in its lexical range. The participle of means then follows, defining more exactly what the verbal action is.

[20] For a discussion of this text, see *ExSyn* 630.

It answers the question, *Why?* The thought of this participle can be brought out by *since* or *because*. (*Because* is normally preferable, however, in that *since* is often used of a temporal rather than a causal nuance.)

Two further clues (one on the *tenses* used, the other on *word order*) should be noted. (1) Aorist and perfect participles are amply represented, but the present participle is also frequently found here.[21] (2) The causal participle normally *precedes* the verb it modifies (though there are many exceptions).

(b) Illustrations

Matt 1:19	Ἰωσὴφ . . . δίκαιος **ὢν**
	Joseph . . . **because he was** a righteous man
John 4:6	ὁ Ἰησοῦς **κεκοπιακὼς** . . . ἐκαθέζετο
	because Jesus **was wearied** . . . he sat
John 11:38	Ἰησοῦς οὖν πάλιν **ἐμβριμώμενος** . . . ἔρχεται εἰς τὸ μνημεῖον
	Then Jesus, **because he was deeply moved** . . . came to the tomb

➥ (5) CONDITION [*IF*]   *ExSyn* 632–33

(a) *Definition.* This participle implies a condition on which the fulfillment of the idea indicated by the main verb depends. Its force can be introduced by *if* in translation. This usage is fairly common.

(b) *Clear illustrations*

Matt 21:22	πάντα ὅσα ἂν αἰτήσητε ἐν τῇ προσευχῇ **πιστεύοντες** λήμψεσθε.
	Whatever you ask for in prayer, **if you believe**, you will receive it.
Gal 6:9	θερίσομεν μὴ **ἐκλυόμενοι**
	we shall reap **if we do** not **lose heart**

(c) *Debatable text*

Heb 6:4–6	ἀδύνατον τοὺς ἅπαξ φωτισθέντας . . . καὶ **παραπεσόντας**, πάλιν ἀνακαινίζειν εἰς μετάνοιαν
	it is impossible to restore again to repentance those who have once been enlightened. . . **if they have fallen away**
	παραπεσόντας is often construed as conditional (a tradition found in the KJV and repeated in most modern translations and by many commentators [but cf. NET]); this is unwarranted.[22]

---

[21] The aorist fits many other categories of usage, but the perfect adverbial participle (including perfects used as presents, such as οἶδα) almost always belongs here. The present causal participle may be conceived as broadly contemporaneous with the controlling verb, just as the customary present is broadly contemporaneous with present time. The NT knows of no future causal participles.

[22] For further discussion, see *ExSyn* 633.

➡   (6) CONCESSION

(a) Definition and amplification. The concessive participle implies that the state or action of the *main verb* is true *in spite of* the state or action of the participle. Its force is usually best translated with *although*. This category is relatively common.

This is semantically the opposite of the causal participle but structurally identical (i.e., it typically precedes the verb and fits the contours of a causal participle—i.e., antecedent time and thus aorist, perfect, or sometimes present). There are, however, often particles that help to make the concessive idea more obvious (such as καίπερ, καίτοιγε, κτλ.).

(b) Illustrations

Eph 2:1   ὑμᾶς **ὄντας** νεκρούς
           although you were dead

1 Pet 1:8 ὃν οὐκ **ἰδόντες** ἀγαπᾶτε
           although you have not **seen** him, you love him

Phil 2:6   ὃς ἐν μορφῇ θεοῦ **ὑπάρχων**
           who, **although he existed** in the form of God

           The translation of this participle as concessive is not entirely clear upon a casual reading of the text. The two options are either causal or concessive.[23]

➡   (7) PURPOSE (TELIC)   *ExSyn* 635–37

(a) Definition. The telic participle indicates the purpose of the action of the finite verb. Unlike other participles, a simple -*ing* flavor will miss the point. Almost always this can (and usually should) be translated like an English *infinitive*. This usage is somewhat common.

(b) Key to identification/semantics. First, to *clarify* that a particular participle is telic, one can either translate it as though it were an infinitive or simply add the phrase *with the purpose of* before the participle in translation.

Second, since purpose is accomplished *as a result* of the action of the main verb, perfect participles are excluded from this category (since they are typically antecedent in time). The future adverbial participle *always* belongs here; the present participle frequently does. The aorist participle only rarely does.[24]

Third, many present participles that fit this usage are lexically influenced. Verbs such as *seek* (ζητέω) or *signify* (σημαίνω), for example, involve the idea of purpose lexically.

Fourth, the telic participle almost always *follows* the controlling verb. Thus, the word order emulates what it depicts. Some participles, when following their controlling verbs, virtually demand to be taken as telic (e.g., πειράζω).

---

[23] For further discussion of this text, see *ExSyn* 634–35.

[24] The aorist participle can, on a rare occasion, have a telic force in Hellenistic Greek, because the future participle was not normally a viable choice in the conversational and vulgar dialect.

(c) *Significance.* This participle, like the participle of cause, answers the question, *Why?* But the participle of purpose looks forward, while the participle of cause looks back. As well, the difference between the participle of purpose and the infinitive of purpose is that the participle emphasizes the *actor* while the infinitive emphasizes the *action*.

(d) *Illustrations*

Matt 27:49   εἰ ἔρχεται Ἠλίας **σώσων** αὐτόν
              if Elijah is going to come **with the purpose of saving** him

John 12:33   τοῦτο δὲ ἔλεγεν **σημαίνων** ποίῳ θανάτῳ ἤμελλεν
              ἀποθνῄσκειν.
              Now he said this **to signify** by what sort of death he would die.

Acts 3:26   ἀπέστειλεν αὐτὸν **εὐλογοῦντα** ὑμᾶς
              he sent him [for the purpose of] **blessing** you

➡ (8) RESULT   *ExSyn* 637–40

(a) *Definition.* The participle of result is used to indicate the actual outcome or result of the action of the main verb. It is similar to the participle of purpose in that it views the *end* of the action of the main verb, but it is dissimilar in that the participle of purpose also indicates or emphasizes intention or design, while result emphasizes what the action of the main verb actually accomplishes. This usage is somewhat common.[25]

(b) *Amplification and semantics.* The participle of result is not necessarily opposed to the participle of purpose. Indeed, many result participles describe the result of an action *that was also intended.* The difference between the two, therefore, is primarily one of emphasis. The relation between purpose and result can be visually represented as in Chart 81.

There are *two types* of result participle:

- *Internal* or *logical result:* This indicates an *implication* of the action of the controlling verb. It is thus actually *simultaneous*, giving the *logical* outcome of the verb. Thus, John 5:18: "He was calling God his own Father, [**with the result of**] **making** (ποιῶν) himself equal to God."
- *External* or *temporal result:* This indicates the true result of the action of the controlling verb. It is *subsequent*, stating the *chronological* outcome of the verb. Thus, Mark 9:7: "a cloud came [**with the result that it**] **covered** (ἐπισκιάζουσα) them."

(c) *Key to identification.* The result participle will be a *present* tense participle and will *follow* (in word order) the main verb. The student should insert the phrase

---

[25] Although most grammars do not include this as a separate category, this is due to it being mixed in with the attendant circumstance participle. But that is looking at the matter purely from an English viewpoint. The two should be distinguished because of structural and semantic differences. See the discussion below under "Attendant Circumstance."

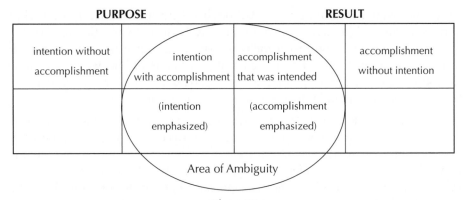

Chart 81
The Semantic Overlap of Purpose and Result Participles

with the result of/that before the participle in translation in order to see if the participle under examination is indeed a result participle.

(d) Illustrations

Luke 4:15   αὐτὸς ἐδίδασκεν ἐν ταῖς συναγωγαῖς αὐτῶν **δοξαζόμενος** ὑπὸ πάντων.
He taught in their synagogues, [**with the result that he was**] **being glorified** by all.

Eph 2:15   ἵνα τοὺς δύο κτίσῃ ἐν αὐτῷ εἰς ἕνα καινὸν ἄνθρωπον **ποιῶν** εἰρήνην
in order that he might create in himself the two into one new man, [**with the result of**] **making** peace

Eph 5:18–21 πληροῦσθε ἐν πνεύματι ... **λαλοῦντες** ... **ᾄδοντες** καὶ **ψάλλοντες** ... **εὐχαριστοῦντες** ... **ὑποτασσόμενοι**
Be filled with the Spirit ... [**with the result of**] **speaking** ... **singing** and **making melody** ... **being thankful** ... **being submissive.**[26]

➡ **b. Attendant Circumstance**   *ExSyn* 640–45

(1) DEFINITION. The attendant circumstance participle is used to communicate an action that, in some sense, is coordinate with the finite verb. In this respect it is not dependent, for it is translated like a verb. Yet it is still dependent *semantically*, because it cannot exist without the main verb. It is translated as a finite verb connected to the main verb by *and*. The participle then, in effect, "piggybacks" on the mood of the main verb. This usage is relatively common, but widely misunderstood.

(2) CLARIFICATION. First, we are treating this participle as a *dependent* verbal participle because it never stands alone. That is, an attendant circumstance will

---

[26] For a discussion of this text, see *ExSyn* 639–40.

always be related to a finite verb. Although it is translated as a finite verb, it derives its "mood" (semantically, not syntactically) from that of the main verb.

Second, it is important to argue from *sense* rather than from translation. In order to see more clearly what the sense of a participle will be, we need to apply the following criterion: If a participle makes good sense when treated as an adverbial participle, we should not seek to treat it as attendant circumstance.[27]

(3) STRUCTURE AND SEMANTICS. As to *structure*, in the NT (as well as other ancient Greek literature) certain structural patterns emerge regarding the attendant circumstance participle. These are not absolute. We may, however, say that they follow a "90% rule." That is to say, ***all** five of the following features occur in at least 90% of the instances of attendant circumstance.* The conclusion from this is that if these five features are not present (or if one or two of them are not present), to label a participle as attendant circumstance needs strong corroborative evidence. It is not impossible, of course, but one should double-check other possibilities before tagging the participle. The five features are:

- The tense of the participle is usually *aorist.*
- The tense of the main verb is usually *aorist.*
- The mood of the main verb is usually *imperative* or *indicative.*
- The participle will *precede the main verb*—both in word order and time of event (though usually there is a close proximity).
- Attendant circumstance participles occur frequently in narrative literature, infrequently elsewhere.

As to *semantics*, the relative semantic weight in such constructions is that *a greater emphasis is placed on the action of the main verb than on the participle.* That is, the participle is something of a prerequisite before the action of the main verb can occur.

(4) ILLUSTRATIONS

Luke 16:6	**καθίσας** ταχέως γράψον πεντήκοντα **Sit down** quickly **and** write fifty
Acts 5:5	ἀκούων δὲ ὁ Ἀνανίας τοὺς λόγους τούτους **πεσὼν** ἐξέψυξεν but when Ananias heard these words, **he fell down and** died
Acts 10:13	**ἀναστάς**, Πέτρε, θῦσον καὶ φάγε. **Rise**, Peter, **and** kill and eat.
Matt 28:19–20	**πορευθέντες** οὖν μαθητεύσατε πάντα τὰ ἔθνη, βαπτίζοντες αὐτοὺς εἰς τὸ ὄνομα τοῦ πατρὸς καὶ τοῦ υἱοῦ καὶ τοῦ ἁγίου πνεύματος, διδάσκοντες ... **Go**, therefore, **and** make disciples of all the nations, baptizing them in the name of the Father and of the Son and of the Holy Spirit, teaching ...

---

[27] The confusion has arisen over a couple of things: loose translation and mixing the participle of result in with the attendant circumstance participle.

Although many argue against πορευθέντες being an attendant circumstance participle, it clearly has that force. The trailing participles, βαπτίζοντες, and διδάσκοντες, should be taken as indicating *means*.[28]

c. Indirect Discourse

ExSyn 645–46

(1) DEFINITION. An anarthrous participle in the *accusative* case, in conjunction with an accusative noun or pronoun, sometimes indicates indirect discourse after a verb of perception or communication. This usage is fairly common (especially in Luke and Paul). As with the infinitive of indirect discourse, the participle of indirect discourse retains the tense of the direct discourse.

(2) ILLUSTRATIONS

Acts 7:12   ἀκούσας δὲ Ἰακὼβ **ὄντα** σιτία εἰς Αἴγυπτον
when Jacob heard that **there was** grain in Egypt

Phil 2:3   ἀλλήλους ἡγούμενοι **ὑπερέχοντας** ἑαυτῶν
by regarding one another **as more important** than yourselves

2 John 7   ὁμολογοῦντες Ἰησοῦν Χριστὸν **ἐρχόμενον** ἐν σαρκί
confessing Jesus Christ **coming** in the flesh (*or* confessing Jesus Christ **to have come** in the flesh; *or* confessing **that** Jesus Christ **has come** in the flesh)

➡ ### d. Periphrastic

ExSyn 647–49

(1) DEFINITION. An anarthrous participle can be used with a verb of being (such as εἰμί or ὑπάρχω) to form a finite verbal idea. This participle is called periphrastic because it is a *roundabout* way of saying what could be expressed by a single verb. As such, it more naturally corresponds to English: ἦν ἐσθίων means *he was eating*, just as ἤσθιεν does. This usage is common with the present participle and perfect participle, but not with other tenses.

(2) STRUCTURE AND SEMANTICS. First, regarding semantics, in classical Greek this construction was used to highlight aspectual force. By the Hellenistic era and particularly in the NT, such emphasis is often, if not usually, lost.

Second, as to structure, the participle is almost always nominative case and usually follows the verb. And, as Dana-Mantey succinctly stated long ago,

This mode of expression, common to all languages, is extensively employed in Greek. It occurs in all the voices and tenses, though rare in the aorist.... Certain tense forms in Greek were expressed exclusively by the periphrastic construction; namely, the perfect middle-passive subjunctive and optative. As the finite verb, εἰμί is generally used, though also γίνομαι and ὑπάρχω, and possibly ἔχω in the perfect (cf. Lk. 14:18; 19:20) and pluperfect (Lk. 13:6). The periphrastic imperfect is the form most common in the New Testament.[29]

---

[28] For futher discussion, see *ExSyn* 645–46.

[29] Dana-Mantey, 231.

Finally, various verb-participle combinations are used to constitute a single finite verb tense, as noted in the following table.

Finite Verb (of εἰμί)	+	Participle	=	Finite Tense Equivalent
Present	+	Present	=	Present
Imperfect	+	Present	=	Imperfect
Future	+	Present	=	Future
Present	+	Perfect	=	Perfect
Imperfect	+	Perfect	=	Pluperfect

Table 9
The Forms of the Periphrastic Participle

(3) ILLUSTRATIONS

(a) Present Periphrastic

Col 1:6   καθὼς καὶ ἐν παντὶ τῷ κόσμῳ *ἐστὶν* **καρποφορούμενον**
just as in all the world it *is* **bearing fruit**

(b) Imperfect Periphrastic

Matt 7:29   *ἦν* **διδάσκων** αὐτούς   *he was* **teaching** them

(c) Future Periphrastic[30]

Mark 13:25   καὶ οἱ *ἀστέρες ἔσονται* ... **πίπτοντες**
and the stars *will be* **falling**

(d) Perfect Periphrastic

Eph 2:8   τῇ γὰρ χάριτί *ἐστε* **σεσωσμένοι**
For by grace *you have been* **saved** [or *you are* **saved**]

(e) Pluperfect Periphrastic

Acts 21:29   *ἦσαν* γὰρ **προεωρακότες** Τρόφιμον
for they *had* **previously seen** Trophimus

e. Redundant (Pleonastic)   *ExSyn* 649–50

(1) DEFINITION. A verb of saying (or sometimes thinking) can be used with a participle with basically the same meaning (as in ἀποκριθεὶς εἶπεν). Because such an idiom is foreign to English, many modern translations simply render the controlling verb.[31]

---

[30] Because of the combination of the future finite verb and the present participle, the aspect of this use of the future is progressive (unlike its simple tense-form counterpart). This category is rare but is included here for sake of completeness.

[31] Some call this a pleonastic (=redundant) or appositional participle. In a sense, it is a subset of the participle of *means*, for it defines the action of the main verb. For the most part, it is probably due to a Semitic idiom.

(2) ILLUSTRATIONS

Luke 12:17 διελογίζετο ἐν ἑαυτῷ **λέγων**
            he was thinking within himself, **saying**

Matt 11:25 **ἀποκριθεὶς** ὁ Ἰησοῦς εἶπεν   Jesus, **answering**, said
            The construction ἀποκριθεὶς εἶπεν "became to such an extent
            an empty formula that it is even sometimes used when there is
            nothing preceding to which an 'answer' can be referred. . ."[32]

†2. Independent Verbal Participles: Imperatival   *ExSyn* 650–52

Included in this category are those participles that function as though they
were finite verbs and are not dependent on any verb in the context for their mood
(thus, distinct from attendant circumstance). The independent verbal participles
may function as either indicatives or imperatives, though both of these are
extremely rare. The imperatival participle is discussed below.

a. Definition. The participle may function just like an imperative. This use of
the participle is not to be attached to any verb in the context, but is grammatically independent. The imperatival participle is quite rare. "In general it may be
said that no participle should be explained in this way that can properly be connected with a finite verb."[33]

b. Illustrations[34]

Rom 12:9   **ἀποστυγοῦντες** τὸ πονηρόν, **κολλώμενοι** τῷ ἀγαθῷ
            hate the evil, **cleave** to the good

1 Pet 2:18 οἱ οἰκέται, **ὑποτασσόμενοι** . . . τοῖς δεσπόταις
            Servants, **submit yourselves** . . . to your masters

The Participle Absolute   *ExSyn* 653–55

In this final section on participles, we will be dealing with participles that occur
in particular case constructions (known as nominative absolute and genitive
absolute). These participles do, however, fit under the above two broad categories
(adjectival and verbal). They are treated here separately because they involve structural clues related to their cases and, to some degree, they express an *additional*
nuance beyond what has been described in the above two major categories.

1. Nominative Absolute   *ExSyn* 654

a. Definition. The nominative absolute participle is in reality simply a substantival participle that fits the case description of *nominativus pendens*. Although

---

[32] Zerwick, *Biblical Greek*, 127.

[33] Robertson, *Grammar*, 1134.

[34] For a discussion (and rejection) of unlikely imperatival participles in Eph 4:1–3; 5:19–
21, see *ExSyn* 651–52.

it is called "nominative absolute," it is not to be confused with the *case* category of nominative absolute. To refresh your memory, the *nominativus pendens* (pendent nominative) "consists in the enunciation of the logical (not grammatical) subject at the beginning of the sentence, followed by a sentence in which that subject is taken up by a pronoun in the case required by the syntax."[35]

b. Clarification. Although this participle has *some* affinity with the genitive absolute participle, the *nominative* absolute participle is always *substantival* while the genitive absolute participle is always *adverbial* or, at least, dependent-verbal.

c. Illustrations

John 7:38   ὁ **πιστεύων** εἰς ἐμέ ... ποταμοὶ ἐκ τῆς κοιλίας αὐτοῦ ῥεύσουσιν
the **one who believes** in me ... rivers will flow out of his belly

Rev 3:21   ὁ **νικῶν** δώσω αὐτῷ καθίσαι
the **one who conquers**, to him I will give to sit

➡2. Genitive Absolute *ExSyn* 654–55

a. Definition. We can define the genitive absolute participial construction *structurally* or *semantically*.

Structurally, the genitive absolute consists of the following:

- a noun or pronoun in the genitive case (though this is sometimes absent);
- a genitive *anarthrous* participle (always);
- the entire construction at the front of a sentence (usually).

Semantically, there are again three items to note, once the structure has been identified (note that the above stated structure is not limited to the genitive absolute construction):

- This construction is unconnected with the rest of the sentence (i.e., its subject—the genitive noun or pronoun—is different from the subject of the main clause);
- the participle is *always* adverbial (circumstantial) or, at least, dependent-verbal (i.e., it cannot be an adjectival or substantival participle);
- the participle is normally (about 90% of the time) *temporal*, though on occasion it can express any of the adverbial ideas.

b. Illustrations

Matt 9:18   ταῦτα αὐτοῦ **λαλοῦντος** ... ἄρχων εἷς ἐλθὼν προσεκύνει αὐτῷ
while he was saying these things ... a certain ruler came and bowed down before him

---

[35] Zerwick, *Biblical Greek*, 9.

Rom 7:3   **ζῶντος** τοῦ ἀνδρὸς ... γένηται ἀνδρὶ ἑτέρῳ
while her husband **is still alive** ... she becomes another man's [wife]

> This is a *somewhat* rare example in that it is found in the NT letters (cf. also Eph 2:20). Most gen. absolutes are in the Gospels and Acts.

Introduction to Greek Clauses[1]
Overview

Introduction 286
Two Types of Clauses 286
Classification of Independent Clauses 287
Classification of Dependent Clauses 288

Introduction   *ExSyn* 656–57

Approach of this Chapter

This chapter is intended to offer little more than an outline of basic clause structure in the NT. Because the specific categories are treated elsewhere in the grammar, a minimal treatment is required here.

Definition

Clauses are units of thought forming part of a compound or complex sentence. Each clause normally contains a subject and predicate or a nonfinite verbal form (i.e., either an infinitive or participle).

A *compound* sentence is one in which two or more clauses are connected in a coordinate relation, known as *paratactic* structure.

A *complex* sentence is one in which one or more clauses are subordinate to another clause, known as *hypotactic* structure.

Two Types of Clauses   *ExSyn* 657

1. Independent Clause

An independent clause is a clause that is *not* subordinate to another clause.

An independent clause normally has for its nucleus: subject—verb—(object). A coordinating conjunction makes two independent clauses coordinate (paratactic) to each other (thus forming a compound sentence).

- "She ate a hot dog *but* he drank milk."
- "He went to the library *and* (he) worked on his assignment."

2. Dependent Clause

A dependent clause is a clause that stands in a substantival or subordinate (hypotactic) relationship to another clause, either an independent clause or another dependent clause.

---

[1] See *ExSyn* 656–65.

- "He went to the library *in order to* work on his assignment." (subordinate relation)
- "The student *who* went to the library completed his assignment on time." (substantival relation)

Classification of Independent Clauses   ExSyn 657–58

1. Introduced by a Coordinating Conjunction

The function of an independent clause is usually determined by the "logical" function of the *coordinating conjunction* introducing the clause. This function may be:

- *connective*, most often involving καί or δέ
- *contrastive*, most often involving ἀλλά, δέ, or πλήν
- *correlative*, usually involving μέν … δέ or καί … καί
- *disjunctive*, involving ἤ
- *explanatory*, usually involving γάρ
- *inferential*, most often involving ἄρα, διό, οὖν, or ὥστε
- *transitional*, usually involving δέ or οὖν

2. Introduced by a Prepositional Phrase

Sometimes an independent clause will be introduced by a *prepositional phrase* whose function determines the function of the independent clause. For example:

- διὰ τί—"why?" (cf. Matt 9:11)
- διὰ τοῦτο—"for this reason" (cf. Matt 13:13)
- εἰς τί—"why?" (cf. Mark 14:4)
- ἐκ τούτου—"as a result of this" (cf. John 6:66)
- ἐπὶ τοῦτο—"for this reason" (cf. Luke 4:43)
- κατὰ τί—"how?" (cf. Luke 1:18)
- μετὰ τοῦτο—"after this" (cf. Rev 7:1)

3. Asyndeton (no Formal Introduction)

Occasionally, an independent clause is *not* introduced by a conjunctive word or phrase. This phenomenon is known as *asyndeton* (a construction "not bound together"). In such cases the function of the independent clause is implied from the literary context. Asyndeton is a vivid stylistic feature that occurs often for emphasis, solemnity, or rhetorical value (staccato effect), or when there is an abrupt change in topic. Thus, it is found, for example, with:

- commands and exhortations, put forth in rapid succession (cf. 1 Thess 5:15–22)
- sentences in a series (cf. Matt 5:3–11; 2 Tim 3:15–16)
- sentences unrelated to each other/topic shift (cf. 1 Cor 5:9)[2]

---

[2] For discussion of Eph 5:21–22, see *ExSyn* 659, n. 6.

Classification of Dependent Clauses   ExSyn 659–65

Dependent clauses can be analyzed in terms of structural form or syntactical function. There are four basic structures (infinitival, participial, conjunctive, and relative clauses) and three syntactical functions (substantival, adjectival, and adverbial clauses).

1. Structure   ExSyn 659–60

Four kinds of constructions are involved in dependent clauses.

a. *infinitival* clauses: contain an infinitive.

b. *participial* clauses: contain a participle.

c. *conjunctive* clauses: introduced by a subordinate conjunction.

d. *relative* clauses: introduced by

- a relative *pronoun* (ὅς [*who, which*])
- a relative *adjective* (οἶος [*such as, as*], ὅσος [*as much/many as*])
- a relative *adverb* (ὅπου [*where*], ὅτε [*when*]).

Note that relative clauses can also be analyzed according to *syntactical function*:

a. *Definite* relative clause. This type of clause contains a verb in the *indicative* mood and refers to a specific individual or group, or to a specific fact, event, or action (e.g., οὐδείς ἐστιν **ὃς** ἀφῆκεν οἰκίαν [*there is no one **who** has left home*] in Mark 10:29). The relative pronoun refers back to its *antecedent* in the sentence (a noun, pronoun, or noun phrase). It has concord with its antecedent in *number* and *gender*, but its *case* is determined by its function in the relative clause.

b. *Indefinite* relative clause. An indefinite relative clause contains a verb in the *subjunctive* mood plus the particle ἄν (or ἐάν) and refers to an unspecified individual or group, or to an event or action (e.g., ὃ ἐὰν ᾖ δίκαιον [*whatever is right*] in Matt 20:4; ὃς ἂν θέλῃ ἐν ὑμῖν εἶναι πρῶτος [*whoever wants to be first among you*] in Matt 20:27). Indefinite relative clauses have *no antecedent*.

2. Syntactical Function   ExSyn 660–65

There are three broad syntactical functions of dependent clauses: substantival, adjectival, and adverbial.

a. Substantival Clause   ExSyn 660–61

In this usage the dependent clause functions like a noun.

(1) STRUCTURE. This function of the dependent clause can be expressed by the following structural forms:[3]

  (a) Substantival *infinitive* clause
  (b) Substantival *participial* clause

---

[3] Each of the following structures follows a specific pattern as well. See the respective chapters for details.

(c) Substantival *conjunctive* clause

(d) Substantival *relative pronoun* clause

(2) BASIC USES

(a) Subject

[1] Substantival *infinitive* (e.g., Heb 10:31)

[2] Substantival *participle* (e.g., John 3:18)

[3] ὅτι + *indicative mood* (e.g., Gal 3:11)

[4] ἵνα + *subjunctive mood* (e.g., 1 Cor 4:2)

[5] *Relative pronoun* ὅ (e.g., Matt 13:12)

(b) Predicate Nominative

[1] Substantival *infinitive* (e.g., Rom 1:12)

[2] Substantival *participle* (e.g., John 4:26)

[3] ἵνα + *subjunctive* (e.g., John 4:34)

(c) Direct Object

[1] Substantival *infinitive* (e.g., 1 Tim 2:8)

[2] Substantival *participle* (e.g., Phil 3:17)

[3] ὅτι + *indicative* (e.g., John 3:33)

[4] ἵνα + *subjunctive* (e.g., Matt 12:16)

[5] *Relative pronoun* ὅ (e.g., Luke 11:6)

(d) Indirect Discourse

[1] Substantival *infinitive* (e.g., Luke 24:23; 1 Cor 11:18)

[2] Substantival *participle* (e.g., Acts 7:12; 2 Thess 3:11)

[3] ὅτι + *indicative* (e.g., Matt 5:17; John 4:1)

(e) Apposition

[1] Substantival *infinitive* (e.g., Jas 1:27)

[2] ὅτι + *indicative* (e.g., Luke 10:20)

[3] ἵνα + *subjunctive* (e.g., John 17:3)

b. Adjectival Clauses   *ExSyn* 661–62

The dependent clause may function like an adjective and modify a noun, noun phrase, or other substantive.

(1) STRUCTURE. This function of the dependent clause can be expressed by the following structural forms:[4]

(a) Epexegetical *infinitive* clause

(b) (Attributive) adjectival *participial* clause

(c) *Conjunctive* clause

(d) *Relative pronoun* and *relative adjective* clauses

---

[4] See the respective chapters for particular structures that each of these takes (e.g., an adjectival participle is normally articular).

(2) BASIC USES. Every adjectival clause *describes, explains,* or *restricts* a noun, pronoun, or other substantive. It has no functional subcategories. The following structural forms express this basic function:

    (a) Epexegetical *infinitive* (e.g., Rom 1:15)
    (b) Adjectival *participle* (e.g., 2 Cor 3:3)
    (c) ὅτι + *indicative mood* (e.g., Luke 8:25)
    (d) ἵνα + *subjunctive mood* (e.g., John 2:25)
    (e) *Relative pronoun* clause (e.g., Eph 6:17; 1 John 2:7)

c. Adverbial Clause   *ExSyn* 662–65

In this usage the dependent clause functions like an adverb in that it modifies a verb.

(1) STRUCTURE. This function of the dependent clause can be expressed by the following structures:

    (a) *Infinitival* clause
    (b) *Adverbial Participial* clause
    (c) *Conjunctive* clause
    (d) *Relative pronoun* and *relative adverb* clause

(2) BASIC USES

    (a) Cause (all four constructions)
        [1] *infinitive* (e.g., Jas 4:2)[5]
        [2] adverbial *participle* (e.g., Rom 5:1)
        [3] ὅτι + *indicative* (e.g., Eph 4:25)
        [4] *relative pronoun* οἵτινες (e.g., Rom 6:2)
    (b) Comparison (conjunctive and relative clauses)
        [1] καθώς + *indicative* (e.g., Eph 4:32)
        [2] *relative* adjective ὅσος (e.g., Rom 6:2)
    (c) Concession (all four constructions *except infinitive* clauses)
        [1] adverbial *participle* (e.g., Phil 2:6)
        [2] εἰ καί + *indicative* (e.g., Luke 11:8)[6]
        [3] *relative pronoun* οἵτινες (e.g., Jas 4:13–14)
    (d) Condition (all four constructions *except infinitive* clauses)
        [1] adverbial *participle* (e.g., Heb 2:3)
        [2] conjunctive clause:

           • In the *first class condition* the speaker assumes that the condition stated in the protasis (the "if" clause) is true for the sake of argument, and thus the content of the apodosis (the "then" clause) follows, naturally and logically. Frequently the protasis is in fact *not* true, but is still presented by the speaker as true for the sake of argument.

---

  [5] Virtually all causal infinitives follow διὰ τό. See the chapter on infinitives for discussion.
  [6] εἰ καί is used more frequently in concessive clauses than any other structure (except for adverbial participles, though they often involve no structural clues).

- In the *second class condition* the condition is assumed to be *not* true (contrary to fact). The speaker then states in the apodosis what would have been true had the protasis been true. The protasis can, of course, be true, but this is either not known to be the case by the speaker or is presented with some irony.
- In the *third class condition* there is a wide variety of nuances found in the protasis, from hypothetical to probable. Some examples also involve a "present general" reality.

    [3] *relative adjective* ὅσοι (e.g., Rom 2:12)

(e) Complementary (infinitive and conjunctive clauses)

    [1] *infinitive* (e.g., 1 John 3:16)

    [2] ἵνα + *subjunctive* (e.g., Luke 6:31; John 8:56)

(f) Location (conjunctive and relative adverb clauses)

    [1] οὗ + *indicative* (e.g., Rom 4:15)

    [2] *relative adverb* ὅπου (e.g., Mark 4:5)

(g) Manner/Means (*all* four constructions *except conjunctive* clauses)

    [1] articular *infinitive* (e.g., ἐν τῷ + *infinitive* in Acts 3:26)[7]

    [2] adverbial *participle* (e.g., Acts 16:16)[8]

    [3] *relative pronoun* ὅν (e.g., Acts 1:11)

(h) Purpose (*all* four constructions)

    [1] *infinitive* (e.g., 1 Tim 1:15)

    [2] adverbial *participle* (e.g., 1 Cor 4:14)

    [3] ἵνα + *subjunctive* (e.g., 1 Pet 3:18)

    [4] *relative pronoun* οἵτινες (e.g., Matt 21:41)

(i) Result (*all* four constructions)

    [1] *infinitive* (e.g., Gal 5:7)

    [2] adverbial *participle* (e.g., John 5:18)[9]

    [3] ἵνα + *subjunctive* (e.g., Rom 11:11)

    [4] *relative adverb* ὅθεν (e.g., Heb 8:3)

(j) Time (*all* four constructions)

    [1] articular *infinitive* (e.g., πρὸ τοῦ + *infinitive* in Matt 6:8)[10]

    [2] adverbial *participle* (e.g., Matt 21:18, 23)[11]

    [3] ὅτε + *indicative* (e.g., Matt 19:1)

    [4] *relative pronoun* clause (e.g., ἀφ᾽ ἧς ... in Col 1:9; ἐν ᾧ ... in Mark 2:19)

---

[7] The infinitive of means is normally expressed by ἐν τῷ + infinitive. However, this construction is more often used of contemporaneous time.

[8] Means and manner need to be distinguished for participles, in light of resultant exegetical differences. See the chapter on participles for a discussion.

[9] The participle of result is sometimes confused with the attendant circumstance participle. But the structure and semantics of each type of participle are different. See the chapter on participles for a discussion.

[10] The infinitive of time involves antecedent, contemporaneous, and subsequent time.

[11] Like the infinitive, these can indicate antecedent, contemporaneous, or subsequent time.

3. How To Classify a Dependent Clause   *ExSyn 665*

a. Identify the structural *form* of the clause: Infinitival? Participial? Conjunctive? Relative?

b. Identify the syntactical *function* of the clause by classifying the key structural marker in the clause (viz., the infinitive, participle, conjunction, or relative pronoun). This involves two steps:

(1) Identify the main functional category: substantival, adjectival, or adverbial.

(2) Identify the appropriate functional subcategory under the main category (e.g., under *Adverbial,* is it cause, condition, purpose, result, time, etc.?)

(3) Note the word or words in the context to which the dependent clause is related.

The Role of Conjunctions[1]
Overview

Introduction 293
Specific Semantic Categories 295
   1. Logical Conjunctions 296
      a. Ascensive Conjunctions. 296
      b. Connective Conjunctions (continuative, coordinated) 296
      c. Contrastive Conjunctions (adversative) 297
      d. Correlative Conjunctions (paired conjunctions) 297
      e. Disjunctive (Alternative) Conjunctions 298
      f. Emphatic Conjunctions 298
      g. Explanatory Conjunctions. 298
      h. Inferential Conjunctions 298
      i. Transitional Conjunctions. 299
   2. Adverbial Conjunctions. 299
      a. Causal Conjunctions 299
      b. Comparative Conjunctions (manner) 299
      c. Conditional Conjunctions. 300
      d. Local Conjunctions (sphere). 300
      e. Purpose Conjunctions 301
      f. Result Conjunctions 301
      g. Temporal Conjunctions. 301
   3. Substantival Conjunctions 302
      a. Content Conjunctions. 302
      b. Epexegetical Conjunctions 302

Introduction

ExSyn 666–69

1. Definition

The term *conjunction* comes from the Latin verb *conjungo*, which means "join together." A conjunction is a word that connects words, clauses, sentences, or paragraphs, and as a result links the component parts and/or the thought units of a language together. It is a linking word.

2. Characteristics of conjunctions

The primary characteristic of conjunctions is that of making connections in a language. They can make two types of structural connections: coordinate (*paratactic*) or subordinate (*hypotactic*). The *coordinate* conjunction links equal elements together, e.g., a subject (or other part of speech) to a subject (or other part of

---

[1] See *ExSyn* 666–78.

speech), sentence to sentence, or paragraph to paragraph.[2] The *subordinate* conjunction links a dependent clause to an independent clause or another dependent clause, either of which supplies the controlling idea that the subordinate conjunction and its clause modifies. Some English examples are supplied below followed by Greek examples.

*John **and** Jim are Greek scholars.*

And is a coordinate conjunction linking two nouns, both of which are subjects.

*I study Greek **in order to** improve my Bible study skills.*

In order to is a subordinate conjunction introducing a clause that modifies the controlling idea, "I study Greek." The dependent clause gives the **purpose** for my study of Greek.

John 1:1   Ἐν ἀρχῇ ἦν ὁ λόγος, **καὶ** ὁ λόγος ἦν πρὸς τὸν θεόν
In the beginning was the Word, **and** the Word was with God

καί is a coordinate conjunction linking two independent clauses.

John 3:16   Οὕτως **γὰρ** ἠγάπησεν ὁ θεὸς τὸν κόσμον, **ὥστε** . . . , **ἵνα** πᾶς ὁ πιστεύων. . . .
For God so loved the world, **with the result that** . . . , **in order that** whoever believes. . . .

γάρ is a coordinate conjunction linking this sentence to the previous idea in John 3:14, explaining why God makes eternal life available. **ὥστε** is a subordinate conjunction, introducing the result of God's love for the world, namely, he gave his Son. **ἵνα** is a subordinate conjunction, introducing the purpose God had in giving his Son, viz., that everyone who believes in him might have eternal life.

3. The use of conjunctions in exegesis

Conjunctions are important in exegesis because they relate the thoughts of a passage to one another. A key to determining their use is identifying the two sets of ideas that the conjunction links together. One must determine the controlling idea that the conjunction modifies, that is, the element in the sentence or larger literary unit to which the conjunction is to be connected. Often more than one possible connection exists. When this situation occurs, context and authorial expression are two key ways to determine the most likely connection.

---

[2] Although the two elements might be equal *syntactically*, there is often a *semantic* notion of subordination. For example, on the surface "I went to the store *and* I bought bread" involves two coordinate clauses joined by *and*. But on a "deep structure" level, it is evident that coordinate ideas are not involved: "I went to the store *in order that* I might buy bread." Semitic languages are especially paratactic, as are the lower echelons of Hellenistic Greek. Narrative literature often reflects this, even among the more literary writers.

*I walked home and studied Greek **in order to** be able to watch the baseball game tonight.*

> In this sentence it is unclear whether the subordinate clause introduced by "in order to" gives the purpose for walking home, the purpose for studying Greek, or the purpose of both.

Contrast this example with the earlier example from John 3:16. In that passage it is clear that the ἵνα clause gives the purpose for which God gave his Son and not the purpose for which God loved the world, because the latter idea does not make contextual sense. Sometimes, however, the elements that a conjunction (particularly a subordinate conjunction like ἵνα or ὅτι) connects together can be disputed. That is why it is necessary to state clearly what ideas a conjunction links together and the nature of the connection. When there are several possible connections, try to be aware of the options. Test each option with an interpretive translation in determining the best one.

4. Common Greek conjunctions

The most common *coordinating* conjunctions are (in order): καί, δέ, γάρ, ἀλλά, οὖν, ἤ, τε, οὐδέ, οὔτε, and εἴτε.

The most common *subordinating* conjunctions that usually govern the *indicative* mood are (in order): ὅτι, εἰ, καθώς, ὡς, γάρ, and ὅτε.

The most common *subordinating* conjunctions that usually govern the *subjunctive* mood are: ἵνα, ὅταν, ἐάν, ὅπως, ἕως, μή, and μήποτε.

Specific Semantic Categories   *ExSyn 669–78*

The following survey gives some of the major categories of usage for Greek conjunctions. Conjunctions can be organized three ways: semantically, structurally, and lexically.

Semantic (functional) categories. Conjunctions can be divided into three semantic/functional categories: *substantival*, *adverbial*, and *logical*. The *substantival* category refers to content uses, such as direct and indirect discourse, or to epexegetical uses. The *adverbial* category includes uses indicating time, place, purpose, result, or other ideas that are commonly regarded as adverbial. The *logical* category includes uses indicating a movement of thought in the passage in terms of addition, contrast, conclusion, transition, or other such relationships.

Structural categories. It is also possible to divide conjunctions into two broad structural categories: *coordinate* and *subordinate*. But these are not as helpful to the student exegetically as the more semantically sensitive divisions given here.

Lexical categories. Finally, conjunctions can be organized lexically, i.e., alphabetically according to their form. A lexicon takes this approach. It is important that students use a lexicon such as BAGD when working with conjunctions. The outline of conjunctions given in this chapter is intended to supplement, not supplant, the description of conjunctions in the standard lexica.[3]

Our approach is to organize the data by the broad semantic/functional categories of logical, adverbial, and substantival.[4]

1. Logical Conjunctions

ExSyn 670–75

These conjunctions relate the movement of thought from one passage to another by expressing logical relationships between the connected ideas. For the most part, coordinate conjunctions are used here.

a. Ascensive Conjunctions [even]

(1) DEFINITION. This use expresses a *final addition* or *point of focus*. It is often translated *even*. This classification is usually determined by the context. Conjunctions that function this way are καί, δέ, and μηδέ.

(2) ILLUSTRATIONS

1 Cor 2:10   τὸ πνεῦμα πάντα ἐραυνᾷ, **καὶ** τὰ βάθη τοῦ θεοῦ
the Spirit searches all things, **even** the deep things of God

Eph 5:3   πορνεία δὲ καὶ ἀκαθαρσία πᾶσα . . . **μηδὲ** ὀνομαζέσθω ἐν ὑμῖν
but do **not** let immorality and all uncleanliness . . . **even** be named among you

b. Connective Conjunctions (continuative, coordinate) [and, also]

(1) DEFINITION. This use simply *connects an additional element* to a discussion or adds an additional idea to the train of thought. It is translated *and*, though if it is emphatic, it can be translated *also*, indicating a key addition. This latter use (*also*) is sometimes called **adjunctive**. The major connective conjunctions are καί and δέ. δέ as a connective conjunction may often be left untranslated.

(2) ILLUSTRATIONS

Eph 1:3   εὐλογητὸς ὁ θεὸς **καὶ** πατὴρ τοῦ κυρίου ἡμῶν Ἰησοῦ Χριστοῦ
blessed be the God **and** Father of our Lord Jesus Christ

Luke 6:9   εἶπεν **δὲ** ὁ Ἰησοῦς πρὸς αὐτούς
and Jesus said to them

---

[3] Besides supplying a rich bibliography and a few exegetical insights, BAGD attempt, in most cases, to "cover all the bases" of usage. Such an approach contrasts with this chapter, which only addresses the basic categories of usage.

[4] For an outline of the broad structural categories, see the chapter, "Introduction to Greek Clauses."

c. Contrastive Conjunctions (adversative) [but, rather, however]

(1) DEFINITION. This use suggests a *contrast* or opposing thought to the idea to which it is connected. It is often translated *but, rather, yet, though,* or *however.* Major contrastive conjunctions include: ἀλλά, πλήν, καί (if indicated by the context), and δέ (if indicated by the context).

(2) ILLUSTRATIONS

Matt 5:17	οὐκ ἦλθον καταλῦσαι, **ἀλλὰ** πληρῶσαι
	I did not come to destroy, **but** to fulfill [the Law]

Matt 12:43   διέρχεται δι᾽ ἀνύδρων τόπων ζητοῦν ἀνάπαυσιν **καὶ** οὐχ εὑρίσκει
[An unclean spirit ...] goes through waterless places seeking rest **but** it does not find [it]

John 15:16   οὐχ ὑμεῖς με ἐξελέξασθε, **ἀλλ᾽** ἐγὼ ἐξελεξάμην ὑμᾶς
you did not choose me, **but** I chose you

> The contrast between Jesus and the disciples is categorical: Election was accomplished by him, a point strengthened by the ἀλλά. A comparative contrast would mean, "You did not choose me as much as I chose you," but that is foreign to the context.

d. Correlative Conjunctions (paired conjunctions)

(1) DEFINITION. These are *paired conjunctions* that express various relationships. Such pairs include: μέν ... δέ (*on the one hand ... on the other hand*); καί ... καί (*both ... and*); μήτε ... μήτε (*neither ... nor*); οὔτε ... οὔτε (*neither ... nor*); οὐκ ... ἀλλά or δέ (*not ... but*); οὐ ... ποτέ (*not ... ever*); ποτέ ... νῦν (*once ... now*); τέ ... τέ (*as ... so*) or (*not only ... but also*); ἤ ... ἤ (*either ... or*).

(2) ILLUSTRATIONS

Matt 9:37   ὁ **μὲν** θερισμὸς πολύς, οἱ **δὲ** ἐργάται ὀλίγοι
On the one hand, the harvest is plentiful, **but on the other hand** the laborers are few

> A smoother translation should normally be used: "The harvest is plentiful, but the laborers are few." The above was given to show the contrast in balance that the μέν ... δέ construction suggests.

Mark 14:68   **οὔτε** οἶδα **οὔτε** ἐπίσταμαι σὺ τί λέγεις
I **neither** know **nor** understand what you are saying

Luke 24:20   ὅπως **τε** παρέδωκαν αὐτὸν οἱ ἀρχιερεῖς καὶ οἱ ἄρχοντες ἡμῶν εἰς κρίμα θανάτου **καὶ** ἐσταύρωσαν αὐτόν
how our chief priests and rulers **both** betrayed him to a sentence of death **and** crucified him

e. Disjunctive (Alternative) Conjunctions [or]

(1) DEFINITION. This use gives an *alternative* possibility to the idea to which it is connected. It is translated *or*. The major disjunctive conjunction is ἤ. It can suggest opposite or related alternatives.

(2) ILLUSTRATIONS

Matt 5:17   μὴ νομίσητε ὅτι ἦλθον καταλῦσαι τὸν νόμον **ἤ** τοὺς προφήτας
Do not think that I came to destroy the Law **or** the prophets

Matt 5:36   οὐ δύνασαι μίαν τρίχα λευκὴν ποιῆσαι **ἢ** μέλαιναν
you are not able to make one hair white **or** black

f. Emphatic Conjunctions [certainly, indeed]

(1) DEFINITION. This use appears in various forms and is determined by the context. It usually involves *intensifying* the normal sense of a conjunction. Examples are as follows: ἀλλά intensified is translated *certainly*; οὐ with μή becomes *certainly not* or *by no means*; οὖν becomes *certainly*. True emphatic conjunctions include: γέ, δή, μενοῦνγε, μέντοι, ναί, and νή.

(2) ILLUSTRATIONS

Rom 8:32   ὅς **γε** τοῦ ἰδίου υἱοῦ οὐκ ἐφείσατο
who **indeed** did not spare his own Son

Phil 3:8   ἀλλὰ **μενοῦνγε** καὶ ἡγοῦμαι πάντα ζημίαν εἶναι
but **indeed** also I count all things to be loss

g. Explanatory Conjunctions

(1) DEFINITION. This use indicates that additional information is being given about what is being described. It can often be translated *for*, *you see*, or *that is*, *namely*. Key conjunctions here are: γάρ, δέ, εἰ (after verbs of emotion), and καί.

(2) ILLUSTRATIONS

John 3:16   οὕτως **γάρ** ἠγάπησεν ὁ θεὸς τὸν κόσμον
for God so loved the world

John 4:8   οἱ **γὰρ** μαθηταὶ αὐτοῦ ἀπεληλύθεισαν εἰς τὴν πόλιν
for his disciples had gone into the city

h. Inferential Conjunctions [therefore]

(1) DEFINITION. This use gives a *deduction*, *conclusion*, or *summary* to the preceding discussion. Common inferential conjunctions include: ἄρα, γάρ, διό, διότι, οὖν, πλήν, τοιγαροῦν, τοινῦν, and ὥστε.

(2) Illustrations

Rom 12:1   παρακαλῶ **οὖν** ὑμᾶς . . . παραστῆσαι τὰ σώματα ὑμῶν
I urge you **therefore** . . . to present your bodies

Rom 15:7   **διὸ** προσλαμβάνεσθε ἀλλήλους, καθὼς καὶ . . .
therefore receive one another, even as also [Christ received you]

i. Transitional Conjunctions [now, then]

(1) Definition. This use involves the change to a new topic of discussion. It can often be translated *now* (though οὖν is frequently translated *then*). Major conjunctions with this force are: οὖν and δέ. δέ is by far the most common. The use of οὖν is reserved for narrative material, especially John.

(2) Illustrations

Matt 1:18   τοῦ **δὲ** Ἰησοῦ Χριστοῦ ἡ γένεσις οὕτως ἦν
Now the birth of Jesus Christ was as follows

John 5:10   ἔλεγον **οὖν** οἱ Ἰουδαῖοι τῷ τεθεραπευμένῳ
Then the Jews were saying to the one who had been healed

2. Adverbial Conjunctions

ExSyn 675–77

These conjunctions amplify the verbal idea in a specific way. These uses usually involve *subordinate* conjunctions.

a. Causal Conjunctions [because, since]

(1) Definition. This use expresses the basis or ground of an action. Major conjunctions used this way are: γάρ, διότι, ἐπεί, ἐπειδή, ἐπειδήπερ, καθώς, ὅτι, and ὡς. They are often translated *because* or *since*.

(2) Illustrations

Luke 1:34   Πῶς ἔσται τοῦτο, **ἐπεὶ** ἄνδρα οὐ γινώσκω;
How can this be, **since** I do not know a man?

John 5:27   ἐξουσίαν ἔδωκεν αὐτῷ κρίσιν ποιεῖν, **ὅτι** υἱὸς ἀνθρώπου
ἐστίν
he gave authority to him to render judgment, **because** he is the Son of Man

b. Comparative Conjunctions (manner)

(1) Definition. This use suggests an *analogy* or *comparison* between the connected ideas or tells how something is to be done. Major conjunctions used this way are: καθάπερ, καθώς, οὕτως, ὡς, ὡσαύτως, ὡσεί, and ὥσπερ. They are often translated *as, just as, in the same way, thus,* or *in this manner.*

(2) ILLUSTRATIONS

1 Cor 2:11   **οὕτως** καὶ τὰ τοῦ θεοῦ οὐδεὶς ἔγνωκεν εἰ μὴ τὸ πνεῦμα τοῦ θεοῦ
In the same way also no one has known the things of God except the Spirit of God.

> The comparison here is to the spirit of a human being knowing a human being's thought (v. 10).

Eph 4:32   γίνεσθε εἰς ἀλλήλους χρηστοί ... χαριζόμενοι ἑαυτοῖς **καθὼς** καὶ ὁ θεὸς ἐν Χριστῷ ἐχαρίσατο ὑμῖν
Be kind to one another ... forgiving each other, **just as** God in Christ forgave you.

c. Conditional Conjunctions [if]

(1) DEFINITION. This use introduces a condition in the presentation of the speaker that must occur before a certain action or conclusion can occur. This conditional clause may not reflect reality, but rather simply the writer's presentation or perception of reality. As part of a conditional clause this conjunction introduces the **protasis** (or *if* part of the *if ... then* statement). εἰ and ἐάν are the major conditional conjunctions. They are translated *if*.[5]

(2) ILLUSTRATIONS

1 Cor 2:8   **εἰ** γὰρ ἔγνωσαν, οὐκ ἂν τὸν κύριον τῆς δόξης ἐσταύρωσαν
For **if** they had known [the wisdom of God], [then] they would not have crucified the Lord of glory.

John 5:31   **ἐὰν** ἐγὼ μαρτυρῶ περὶ ἐμαυτοῦ, ἡ μαρτυρία μου οὐκ ἔστιν ἀληθής
If I testify concerning myself, [then] my testimony is not true.

d. Local Conjunctions (sphere)

(1) DEFINITION. This use gives the location or sphere (metaphorically), that is, the context in which an action takes place. Major conjunctions used this way are: ὅθεν, ὅπου, and οὗ. Translations include *where, from where,* or *the place which.*

(2) ILLUSTRATIONS

Matt 6:19   μὴ θησαυρίζετε ὑμῖν θησαυροὺς ἐπὶ τῆς γῆς, **ὅπου** σὴς καὶ βρῶσις ἀφανίζει
Do not store for yourselves treasures on the earth, **where** moth and rust destroy

Rom 4:15   οὗ δὲ οὐκ ἔστιν νόμος, οὐδὲ παράβασις
but **where** there is no law, there is no transgression

> Note the difference between the conjunction (οὗ) and the negative adverb (οὐ).

---

[5] See the chapter on conditional sentences for a detailed discussion.

e. Purpose Conjunctions [in order that]

(1) DEFINITION. This use indicates the goal or aim of an action. Major conjunctions for this category are: ἵνα, ὅπως, μήπως (the negative purpose), μήπου (negative purpose), and μήποτε (negative purpose). By far the most common is ἵνα. Translations for this use are: *in order that, with the goal that, with a view to, that*.

(2) ILLUSTRATIONS

John 3:16   τὸν υἱὸν τὸν μονογενῆ ἔδωκεν, **ἵνα** πᾶς ὁ πιστεύων εἰς αὐτόν ...

he gave his only Son, **in order that** everyone who believes in him [should not perish but should have eternal life]

John 5:34   ἀλλὰ ταῦτα λέγω **ἵνα** ὑμεῖς σωθῆτε

but I say these things **in order that** you might be saved

Acts 9:24   παρετηροῦντο δὲ καὶ τὰς πύλας ἡμέρας τε καὶ νυκτὸς **ὅπως** αὐτὸν ἀνέλωσιν

And they were also watching the gates, both day and night, **in order that** they might kill him

f. Result Conjunctions [so that, with the result that]

(1) DEFINITION. This use gives the outcome or consequence of an action. The focus is on the outcome of the action rather than on its intention. Major conjunctions used this way are: ὥστε, ὡς, ὅτι, and less frequently, ἵνα. This use can be tranlsated *that, so that,* or *with the result that*. By far the most common is ὥστε.

(2) ILLUSTRATIONS

John 3:16   οὕτως γὰρ ἠγάπησεν ὁ θεὸς τὸν κόσμον, **ὥστε** τὸν υἱὸν τὸν μονογενῆ ἔδωκεν

for God so loved the world, **that** he gave his only Son

John 9:2   τίς ἥμαρτεν ... **ἵνα** τυφλὸς γεννηθῇ;

Who sinned ... **with the result that** [this man] was born blind?

g. Temporal Conjunctions

(1) DEFINITION. This use gives the time of the action. Major conjunctions used this way are: ἄχρι, ἕως, ὅταν, ὅτε, οὐδέποτε (negative temporal), οὐκέτι (negative temporal), οὔπω (negative temporal), ποτέ, and ὡς. Translation varies depending on the conjunction used.

(2) ILLUSTRATIONS

Luke 21:24   Ἰερουσαλὴμ ἔσται πατουμένη ὑπὸ ἐθνῶν, **ἄχρι οὗ** πληρωθῶσιν καιροὶ ἐθνῶν

Jerusalem will be trampled under foot by the Gentiles **until the time when** the times of the Gentiles be fulfilled

John 6:24   **ὅτε** οὖν εἶδεν ὁ ὄχλος ὅτι Ἰησοῦς οὐκ ἔστιν ἐκεῖ

now **when** the crowd saw that Jesus was not there

3. Substantival Conjunctions

ExSyn 677–78

These uses are limited to instances where the conjunction introduces a noun content clause and to epexegesis.

a. Content Conjunctions [that]

(1) DEFINITION. This use involves a conjunction that introduces a subject, predicate nominative, direct object, or an appositional noun clause. Direct and indirect discourse are specialized object clauses following verbs of expression or perception. Major conjunctions here include: ἵνα, ὅπως, ὅτι, and ὡς. ἵνα and ὅτι are the most common.[6] This use of the conjunction is translated *that* or, if introducing direct discourse (e.g., a *recitative* ὅτι), it is left untranslated.

(2) ILLUSTRATIONS

1 Cor 15:3   παρέδωκα γὰρ ὑμῖν . . . **ὅτι** Χριστὸς ἀπέθανεν ὑπὲρ τῶν ἁμαρτιῶν ἡμῶν
For I passed on to you . . . **that** Christ died for our sins
> This is a direct object clause.

John 4:17   Καλῶς εἶπας **ὅτι** Ἄνδρα οὐκ ἔχω
[Jesus said to her], "Correctly you have said, 'I do not have a husband.'"
> This is a direct discourse object clause.

John 4:19   κύριε, θεωρῶ **ὅτι** προφήτης εἶ σύ
Sir, I perceive **that** you are a prophet
> This is an indirect discourse object clause.

b. Epexegetical Conjunctions [that]

(1) DEFINITION. This use involves a conjunction introducing a clause that completes the idea of a noun or adjective. It often functions like an epexegetical infinitive. Major conjunctions used this way are ἵνα and ὅτι. The normal translation for this use is *that*.

(2) ILLUSTRATIONS

Luke 7:6   οὐ ἱκανός εἰμι **ἵνα** ὑπὸ τὴν στέγην μου εἰσέλθῃς
I am not worthy **that** you should enter under my roof.

Matt 8:27   ποταπός ἐστιν οὗτος **ὅτι** καὶ οἱ ἄνεμοι καὶ ἡ θαλασσα αὐτῷ ὑπακούουσιν;
What sort of man is this **that** both the winds and the sea obey him?

---

[6] See the chapter on moods, under indicative (for ὅτι) and subjunctive (for ἵνα), for a more detailed discussion.

Conditional Sentences[1]
Overview

Introduction **303**
Conditional Sentences in General **304**
   1. Definition 304
   2. General Guidelines for Interpreting Conditional Sentences. 306
      a. The Conditional Element. 306
      b. Relation to Reality. 306
      c. Converse of the Condition (Semantically) 307
      d. Reverse of the Condition (Semantically) 307
      e. Summary 308
Conditional Sentences in Greek (Especially the NT) **308**
   1. Ways to Convey the Conditional Idea in Greek 308
      a. Implicitly 308
      b. Explicitly 308
   2. Structural Categories of Conditional Sentences 309
   3. Semantic Categories of Conditional Sentences 309
➡   a. First Class Condition (Assumed True for Argument's Sake) 309
➡   b. Second Class Condition (Contrary to Fact). 312
➡   c. Third Class Condition 313
      d. Fourth Class Condition (Less Probable Future) 314

Introduction   *ExSyn* 680–81

1. Importance of Conditional Sentences in the New Testament

There are over 600 *formal* conditional sentences in the NT (i.e., with an explicit *if*). This works out to an average of about one per page in Nestle–Aland[27]. Besides these formal conditions, there are hundreds of implicit conditions. Thus, a proper understanding of conditions impacts one's exegesis at every turn of the page.

Some of the great themes of biblical theology cannot be properly understood apart from a correct understanding of conditions. Widespread misunderstanding persists about the Greek conditions. On any Sunday misinformation about conditional clauses is communicated from pulpit to pew. Whole theological systems and lifestyles are sometimes built on such misunderstandings.

2. How to Approach Conditional Sentences

There are essentially three approaches we can take in analyzing conditional sentences: structural, semantic, and pragmatic. The *structural* (or formal)

---

[1] See *ExSyn* 679–712. Pp. 701–12 are an appendix on advanced information about conditional sentences, including the history of the discussion among classical Greek grammarians, a proposed solution to the debate, and a brief discussion of speech act theory.

approach looks at the conditional particle (whether εἰ or ἐάν) and the moods and tenses used in the protasis (*if* clause) and apodosis (*then* clause). From these structural groups emerge the basic meanings that conditions display.

The *semantic* (or universal grammar) approach asks essentially what the two halves of conditions mean. That is, how do they relate to each other? This approach begins with the basic structure (*if . . . then*), but addresses more general issues that are true of all conditions, such as whether the relationship of protasis to apodosis is cause to effect or something else.

The *pragmatic* (or speech act theory) approach examines what people are trying to communicate when they use conditional sentences in a broad way. This approach is not concerned with how the two halves relate to each other, but whether a conditional sentence is uttered as a veiled threat, request, command, or the like.

All of these are valid approaches. We will focus on the first two since the pragmatic approach is too far removed from form for us to get an easy handle on it; that is, it more properly belongs to discourse analysis than to syntax.

Conditional Sentences in General   ExSyn 682–87

Certain features of conditional sentences are true of all languages. In a given instance, such features are intuitively recognized. But these need to be brought out in the open initially to overcome several misconceptions about how conditions behave in cherished texts.

1. Definition   ExSyn 682–84

Conditional sentences can be defined structurally or semantically.

a. Structurally. A conditional sentence has two parts: an "if" part (the protasis) and a "then" part (the apodosis).

b. Semantically. Conditions can be defined semantically in terms of the overall construction as well as the individual components. There are two aspects to examine here.

(1) THE MEANING OF THE CONSTRUCTION (I.E., THE RELATION OF THE PROTASIS TO THE APODOSIS)

There is often a tacit assumption that the protasis of a condition indicates the *cause* and the apodosis tells the *effect*. But this is not the only relation the two can have. In essence, there are three basic relations that a protasis can have to an apodosis: cause–effect, evidence–inference, and equivalence. It is a profitable exercise to examine the biblical text in light of these basic nuances.

(a) *Cause–Effect*

The first relation the two parts can have is that of cause and effect. "If" = cause; "then" = effect. For example:

- "If you put your hand in the fire, you will get burned."
- "If you eat three pounds of chocolate every day for a month, you will look like a blimp!"

The NT has its share of illustrations as well:[2]

Matt 4:9   ταῦτά σοι πάντα δώσω, ἐὰν πεσὼν προσκυνήσῃς μοι.
             I will give you all these things, if you fall down and worship me.

(b) Evidence–Inference

The second relation the protasis can have to the apodosis is that of ground (or evidence) to inference. Here the speaker infers something (the apodosis) from some evidence. That is, he makes an induction about the *implications* that a piece of evidence suggests. For example:

- "If it's Tuesday, this must be Belgium" (title of an old movie).
- "If she has a ring on her left hand, then she's married."

Notice that the protasis is not the *cause* of the apodosis. In fact, it is often just the opposite: "If she gets married, she will wear a ring on her left hand." Thus, often, though not always, the ground–inference condition will semantically be the *converse* of the cause–effect condition.

Rom 8:17   εἰ δὲ τέκνα, καὶ κληρονόμοι
             Now if [we are] children, then [we are] heirs.

1 Cor 15:44 εἰ ἔστιν σῶμα ψυχικόν, ἔστιν καὶ πνευματικόν.
             If there is a physical body, there is also a spiritual [body].

             Obviously, the physical body does not *cause* the spiritual one; rather, Paul simply infers that there must be a spiritual body from the evidence of a physical one.

(c) Equivalence

The third relation the two parts can have to one another is one of equivalence. That is, we could put this formula this way; "If A, then B" means the same thing as "A = B." (This often looks similar to evidence–inference.) For example:

- "If you are Henry's son, then Henry is your father."
- "If you are obedient to God, you are living righteously."
  (more loosely equivalent)

Jas 2:11   εἰ ... φονεύεις δέ, γέγονας παραβάτης νόμου.
             But if you commit murder, you have become a law-breaker.

(d) Principles

A few principles emerge from this brief analysis.

- The three types of conditions are not entirely distinct. There is much overlap between them.[3]

---

[2] This cause-effect relationship occurs in the first, second, and third class conditions.

[3] The equivalence type especially can often be treated as a specific kind of evidence–inference construction. Not all evidence–inference constructions, however, involve equivalence.

- Nevertheless, it is important exegetically for the student to *try* to distinguish, if possible, these three nuances. We will see this more clearly when we examine the "General Guidelines" section.
- *A compound protasis does not necessarily mean that both conditions have the same relation to the apodosis.* Note, for example, the following illustration: Suppose a quarterback tells his tailback, "If you veer right and go ten yards, you'll make a first down." But both protases do not have the same relation to the apodosis. The tailback could also veer left or plow straight ahead. The essential thing, though, is that he make ten yards!

(2) The Meaning of the Components

Basically, the meaning of the components is that of supposition–consequence.

(a) Apodosis. The apodosis is *grammatically independent, but semantically dependent.* That is, it can stand on its own as a full-blown sentence (e.g., "If I die, *I die*"), but it depends for its "factuality" on the fulfillment of the protasis ("If he wins this race, he'll be the new champion").

(b) Protasis. The protasis, on the other hand, is *grammatically dependent, but semantically independent.* That is, it does not form a complete thought ("*If I go swimming tomorrow*, I'll catch a cold"), but its fulfillment is independent of whether the apodosis is true.

2. General Guidelines for Interpreting Conditional Sentences ExSyn 685–87

a. The Conditional Element

Only the *protasis* is the conditional element. That is, the contingency lies with the *if*, not the *then*. If the protasis is fulfilled, the apodosis is also fulfilled.

b. Relation to Reality

What is the relation of the conditional statement to reality? This fits into the larger issue of the relation of language to reality: *language is essentially a **portrayal** of reality.* The portrayal is never a *complete* picture of reality. This does not necessarily mean that it is incorrect, but neither is the portrayal necessarily correct.

The implications of this for grammar in general and conditional clauses specifically are significant. By way of illustration, in Matt 18:8 the evangelist portrays the Lord as saying, "If your hand causes you to stumble, cut it off!" He uses the *first* class condition. But Mark, in the parallel passage (9:43), portrays the Lord as saying this in the *third* class condition. Now it is possible that one of the two writers got his information wrong. But it is equally likely that the semantic domains of first and third class conditions are not entirely distinct. Perhaps they are elastic enough that both of them can be used, at times, to speak of the same event.

c. Converse of the Condition (Semantically)

The converse of "If A, then B" is "If B, then A." The significance? Just that *the converse of a condition is not **necessarily** true*. For example, the converse of "If it is raining, there must be clouds in the sky" is "If there are clouds in the sky, it must be raining." The converse in this instance is patently false.

Applied to the biblical text, notice the following:

Rom 8:13   εἰ κατὰ σάρκα ζῆτε, μέλλετε ἀποθνῄσκειν.
             If you live according to the flesh, you are about to die.

> The converse of this is not necessarily true: "If you are about to die, you must have lived according to the flesh." There may be other reasons one is about to die besides living according to the flesh.

Gal 3:29   εἰ ὑμεῖς Χριστοῦ, ἄρα τοῦ Ἀβραὰμ σπέρμα ἐστέ
             If you belong to Christ, then you are Abraham's seed.

> The converse is not necessarily true: "If you are Abraham's seed, then you belong to Christ." There might be others who are Abraham's seed who do not belong to Christ. Whether the converse is true needs to be established on grounds *other than* the syntax of the condition.

d. Reverse of the Condition (Semantically)

By the reverse of the condition, I mean the opposite of the condition. The reverse of the condition, "If A happens, B happens" is "If A does *not* happen, B (still) happens." The significant point to remember is that *the reverse of the condition is not necessarily false*.[4]

- In the statement, "If you put your hand in the fire, you will get burned," the negation of this is not necessarily true. That is, "If you *don't* put your hand in the fire, you will not get burned"—for you could put your *foot* in the fire (or your hand in the oven, etc.).
- Or: "If I die, my wife will get $10,000." Negative: "If I don't die, my wife will *not* get $10,000." (This is not necessarily true: She could rob a bank....)

Biblically, consider the following examples.

1 Tim 3:1   εἴ τις ἐπισκοπῆς ὀρέγεται, καλοῦ ἔργου ἐπιθυμεῖ.
             If anyone aspires to the episcopate, he desires a noble work.

> Obviously, this does not mean that if someone does *not* aspire to the office, he does not desire a noble work.

---

[4] The *reason* for this is twofold: (1) Not all conditions are of the cause–effect type, and (2) even among the cause–effect type of condition, the stated cause does not have to be a necessary or exclusive condition. That is, if the condition is not fulfilled, this does not necessarily mean that the apodosis *cannot* come true.

Jas 2:9   εἰ προσωπολημπτεῖτε, ἁμαρτίαν ἐργάζεσθε
           If you show partiality, you commit sin.

> It is, of course, possible to sin in ways other than by showing partiality.

e. Summary

If the reverse of a condition is not necessarily false and the converse is not necessarily true, then what do conditions mean? The answer to this is related to *presentation*. *As far as it is **presented***, although sometimes the apodosis *may* be true without the protasis being true, the apodosis *must* be true when the protasis is true. That is to say, as far as portrayal is concerned, if the protasis is fulfilled, the apodosis is true. Thus, "If you put your hand in the fire, you will get burned" is saying that if you fulfill the condition, the consequence is true. All of this can be summarized as follows:

- Conditional statements refer to the portrayal of reality rather than to reality itself. However, within those parameters the following may be said:
- If A, then B ≠ if B, then A (the converse is not necessarily true).
- If A, then B ≠ if non-A, then non-B (the reverse is not necessarily false).
- If A, then B *does not deny* if C then B (the condition is not necessarily exclusive or condition not necessarily causal).

Conditional Sentences in Greek (Especially the NT)   *ExSyn 687–701*

Now that we have looked at the logical function of conditions, we are in a better position to interpret the various structures of Greek conditions.

1. Ways to Convey the Conditional Idea in Greek   *ExSyn 687–89*

Conditions may be conveyed *implicitly* (i.e., without the formal structural markers) or *explicitly* (i.e., with the formal structural markers).

a. Implicitly. Conditions may be implicitly indicated by (1) a circumstantial participle (e.g., Heb 2:3), (2) a substantival participle (e.g., Matt 5:6),[5] (3) an imperative (e.g., John 2:19), (4) a relative clause, especially involving an indefinite relative pronoun (e.g., Matt 5:39), or rarely (5) a question (e.g., Matt 26:15). Implicit conditions are normally equivalent to the third class condition semantically.

b. Explicitly. Explicit conditions are expressed with the *if* stated in the protasis. Greek has two words for *if* that are used most often—εἰ and ἐάν. The rest of this chapter will focus on these conditions.

---

[5] There is no *syntactical* category of "conditional substantival participle," but the notion of condition can still be implied with substantival participles. This often follows the formula ὁ + participle (+ participle) + future indicative.

2. Structural Categories of Conditional Sentences   *ExSyn* 689

Explicit conditional sentences follow four general structural patterns in the Greek NT.[6] Each pattern is known as a *class*; hence, first class, second class, third class, and fourth class.

Type	*Protasis ("if")*	*Apodosis ("then")*
First Class	εἰ + indicative mood any tense (negative: οὐ)	any mood any tense
Second Class	εἰ + indicative mood past tense aorist . . . imperfect . . . (negative: μή)	(ἄν) + indicative past tense . . . aorist (past time) . . . imperfect (present time)
Third Class	ἐάν + subjunctive mood any tense (negative: μή)	any mood any tense
Fourth Class	εἰ + optative mood present or aorist	ἄν + optative mood present or aorist

Table 10
The Structure of Conditions

3. Semantic Categories of Conditional Sentences   *ExSyn* 690–701

➡ ### a. First Class Condition
(Assumed True for Argument's Sake)   *ExSyn* 690–94

(1) DEFINITION. The first class condition indicates *the assumption of truth for the sake of argument*. The normal idea, then, is *if—and let us assume that this is true for the sake of argument—then.* . . . This class uses the particle εἰ with the indicative (in any tense) in the protasis. In the apodosis, any mood and any tense can occur. This is a frequent conditional clause, occurring about 300 times in the NT.

(2) AMPLIFICATION: PITFALLS TO AVOID. There are two views of the first class condition that need to be avoided. First is the error of saying too much about its meaning. The first class condition is popularly taken to mean the condition of

---

[6] We are here combining the third and fifth class condition because the fifth class is a subset of the third class structurally. If we were to distinguish them structurally, we should also distinguish the two types of second class condition structurally.

reality or the condition of truth. Many have heard this from the pulpit: "In the Greek this condition means *since*."[7]

This is saying too much about the first class condition. For one thing, this view assumes a direct correspondence between language and reality, to the effect that the indicative mood is the mood of fact. For another, this view is demonstrably false for conditional statements: (a) In apparently only 37% of the instances is there a correspondence to reality (to the effect that the condition could be translated *since*[8]). (b) Further, there are 36 instances of the first class condition in the NT that cannot possibly be translated *since*. This can be seen especially with two opposed conditional statements. Note the following illustrations.

> Mt 12:27–28 **εἰ** ἐγὼ ἐν Βεελζεβοὺλ ἐκβάλλω τὰ δαιμόνια, οἱ υἱοὶ ὑμῶν ἐν τίνι ἐκβάλλουσιν; . . .**εἰ** δὲ ἐν πνεύματι θεοῦ ἐγὼ ἐκβάλλω τὰ δαιμόνια, ἄρα ἔφθασεν ἐφ' ὑμᾶς ἡ βασιλεία τοῦ θεοῦ.
>
> **If** I cast out demons by Beelzebul, by whom do your sons cast them out? . . . But **if** I cast out demons by the Spirit of God, then the kingdom of God has come upon you.
>
>> Obviously it is illogical to translate both sentences as *since I cast out*, because the arguments are opposed to each other. Moreover, it would be inconsistent to translate the first particle *if* and the second *since*.

> 1 Cor 15:13   **εἰ** δὲ ἀνάστασις νεκρῶν οὐκ ἔστιν, οὐδὲ Χριστὸς ἐγήγερται
>
> But **if** there is no resurrection of the dead, then Christ has not been raised.

It is self-evident that the apostle Paul could not mean by the first class condition "*since* there is no resurrection"!

Second, because of the compelling evidence that the first class condition does not always correspond to reality, some scholars have assumed that it is just a simple condition. The first class condition, in this view, is sometimes called the "simple condition," "condition of logical connection," or "neutral condition." One might call this the "undefined condition" in that nothing can be said about the reality of the supposition.

But this view says too little.[9] Virtually all conditions can be said to make a logical connection between the two halves. This is the nature of conditions in general, not just the first class condition. The question is not how little the first class condition says, but how much. What are its distinctives?

---

[7] Grammarians such as Gildersleeve, Robertson, BDF, etc., have looked at conditions in light of the mood used and have argued that the indicative mood in first class conditions is significant. But their language has often been misunderstood: "assumption of truth" has been interpreted to mean "truth."

[8] We will argue that the first class condition should *never* be translated *since* (see the third section, "Assumed True for the Sake of Argument").

[9] At bottom, it assumes a *point* of meaning for a syntactical structure, ignores the mood used (the indicative means *something*), and makes no distinction between the various conditions.

(3) Assumed true for the sake of argument. The force of the indicative mood, when properly understood, lends itself to the notion of *presentation* of reality. In the first class condition the conditional particle turns such a presentation into a supposition. This does *not* mean that the condition is true or means *since*! But it does mean that as far as the portrayal is concerned, the point of the argument is based on the assumption of reality. Several examples will be provided to demonstrate this point. But three points need to be added.

- First, even in places where the argument is apparently believed by the speaker, *the particle* εἰ *should not be translated* **since**. Greek had several words for *since*, and the NT writers were not opposed to using them (e.g., ἐπεί, ἐπειδή). There is great rhetorical power in *if*. To translate εἰ as *since* is to turn an invitation to dialogue into a lecture.[10]
- Second, how can we tell whether a speaker would actually affirm the truth of the protasis? Context, of course, is the key, but a good rule of thumb is to note the apodosis: Does the logic cohere if both protasis and apodosis are true? Often when a question is asked in the apodosis, the author does not embrace the truth of the protasis. These are only simple guidelines. Where in doubt, check the broader context.
- Third, not infrequently conditional sentences are used rhetorically in a way that goes beyond the surface structure. Hence, on one level the structure might indicate one thing, but on another level, an entirely different meaning is in view. For example, suppose a mother says to her child, "If you put your hand in the fire, you'll get burned." The pragmatic meaning of the statement is, "Don't put your hand in the fire!" It is, in effect, a polite command, couched in indirect language.

Mt 12:27–28 εἰ ἐγὼ ἐν Βεελζεβοὺλ ἐκβάλλω τὰ δαιμόνια, οἱ υἱοὶ ὑμῶν ἐν τίνι ἐκβάλλουσιν; . . . εἰ δὲ ἐν πνεύματι θεοῦ ἐγὼ ἐκβάλλω τὰ δαιμόνια, ἄρα ἔφθασεν ἐφ᾽ ὑμᾶς ἡ βασιλεία τοῦ θεοῦ.
If I cast out demons by Beelzebul, by whom do your sons cast them out? . . . But **if** I cast out demons by the Spirit of God, then the kingdom of God has come upon you.

> We have already seen with this couplet that the particle cannot consistently be translated *since*. But leaving it as a mere simple condition is not saying enough. The force is "**If**—*and let's assume that it's true for the sake of argument*—I cast out demons by Beelzebul, then by whom do your sons cast them out? . . . But **if**—*assuming on the other hand that this is true*—I cast out demons by the Spirit of God, then the kingdom of God has come upon you." This yields satisfactory results for both halves.

---

[10] Often the idea seems to be an encouragement to respond, in which the author attempts to get his audience to come to the conclusion of the apodosis (since they already agree with him on the protasis). It thus functions as a tool of persuasion.

Luke 4:3   εἶπεν αὐτῷ ὁ διάβολος· **εἰ** υἱὸς εἶ τοῦ θεοῦ, εἰπὲ τῷ λίθῳ τούτῳ ἵνα γένηται ἄρτος.

The devil said to him, "**If** you are God's Son, tell this stone to become bread."

1 Thess 4:14   **εἰ** γὰρ πιστεύομεν ὅτι Ἰησοῦς ἀπέθανεν καὶ ἀνέστη, οὕτως καὶ ὁ θεὸς τοὺς κοιμηθέντας διὰ τοῦ Ἰησοῦ ἄξει σὺν αὐτῷ.

For **if** we believe that Jesus died and rose again, even so God will bring with him those who are asleep through Jesus.[11]

➡ **b. Second Class Condition (Contrary to Fact)**   *ExSyn* 694–96

(1) DEFINITION. The second class condition indicates *the assumption of an untruth (for the sake of argument)*.[12] For this reason it is appropriately called the "contrary to fact" condition (or the *unreal* condition). It might be better to call it *presumed* contrary to fact, however, since sometimes it presents a condition that is true, even though the speaker assumes it to be untrue (e.g., Luke 7:39). In the protasis the structure is εἰ + indicative mood with a secondary tense (imperfect or aorist usually). The apodosis usually has ἄν (though some examples lack this particle) and a secondary tense in the indicative mood. There are about 50 examples of the second class condition in the NT.

(2) AMPLIFICATION: PAST AND PRESENT CONTRARY-TO-FACT. There are two types of second class conditions: *present* contrary-to-fact and *past* contrary-to-fact.

The *present* contrary-to-fact condition uses the *imperfect* in both the protasis and apodosis. It refers to something that is not true in the present time (from the speaker's portrayal). A typical translation would be *If X were . . . then Y would be* (as in "If you were a good man, then you would not be here right now").

The *past* contrary-to-fact uses the *aorist* in both the protasis and apodosis. It refers to something that was not true in the past time (from the speaker's portrayal). A typical translation would be *If X had been . . . then Y would have been* (as in "If you had been here yesterday, you would have seen a great game").

(3) ILLUSTRATIONS

Luke 7:39   οὗτος **εἰ** ἦν προφήτης, ἐγίνωσκεν **ἂν** τίς καὶ ποταπὴ ἡ γυνὴ ἥτις ἅπτεται αὐτοῦ, ὅτι ἁμαρτωλός ἐστιν.

If this man *were* a prophet, *he would know* who and what sort of woman this is who is touching him, that she is a sinner.

John 5:46   **εἰ** ἐπιστεύετε Μωϋσεῖ, ἐπιστεύετε **ἂν** ἐμοί

If *you believed* Moses, *you would believe* me

The idea is "If you believed Moses—but you do not. . . . " This involves the imperfect tense, a present contrary-to-fact condition.

---

[11] For a discussion of this text, see *ExSyn* 694.

[12] For the NT, it is unnecessary to add "for the sake of argument" since the speaker/author of every second class condition in the NT apparently embraces the untruth of the protasis. But this is partially due to the paucity of examples.

1 Cor 2:8   εἰ ἔγνωσαν, οὐκ ἂν τὸν κύριον τῆς δόξης ἐσταύρωσαν
If *they had known, they would* not *have crucified* the Lord of glory.

➡   *c. Third Class Condition*   *ExSyn* 696–99

(1) DEFINITION. The third class condition often presents the condition as *uncertain of fulfillment, but still likely* (though there are many exceptions to this). It is difficult to give one semantic label to this structure, especially in Hellenistic Greek (note the discussion below). The structure of the protasis involves the particle ἐάν followed by a *subjunctive* mood in any tense. Both the particle (a combination of εἰ and the particle ἄν) and the subjunctive give the condition a sense of contingency. The apodosis can have any tense and any mood. This is a common category of conditional clauses, occurring nearly 300 times in the NT.

(2) CLARIFICATION AND SEMANTICS. The third class condition encompasses a broad semantic range from (a) a *logical connection* (if A, then B) in the present time (sometimes called *present general condition*), indicating nothing as to the fulfillment of the protasis; and (b) a mere *hypothetical* situation or one that probably will not be fulfilled; to (c) a *more probable future* occurrence.

Technically, the subjunctive is used in the ***third class condition*** as well as the ***fifth class condition***. Structurally, these two are virtually identical: The *fifth* class condition requires a present indicative in the apodosis, while the *third* class can take virtually any mood-tense combination, including the present indicative.

Semantically, their meaning is a bit different. The *third* class condition encompasses a broad range of potentialities in Koine Greek. It depicts what is *likely to occur* in the *future*, what could *possibly occur*, or even what is only *hypothetical* and will not occur. In classical Greek the third class condition was usually restricted to the first usage (known as *more probable future*), but with the subjunctive's encroaching on the domain of the optative in the Hellenistic era, this structural category has expanded accordingly.[13] The context will always be of the greatest help in determining an author's use of the third class condition.

The *fifth* class offers a condition the fulfillment of which is realized in the *present time*. This condition is known as the *present general condition*. For the most part this condition is a *simple* condition;[14] that is, the speaker gives no indication about the likelihood of its fulfillment. His presentation is neutral: "If A, then B."

Because of the broad range of the third class condition and the undefined nature of the fifth class, many conditional clauses are open to interpretation. But for the most part, the *present general condition* addresses a *generic* situation in the *present* time (broadly speaking), while the *more probable future* addresses a *specific* situation in the *future* time.

---

[13] See the discussion of this in the chapter on moods.

[14] Although many grammarians treat the first class condition as the "simple" condition, this label more appropriately belongs to the fifth class.

(3) ILLUSTRATIONS

Matt 4:9   ταῦτά σοι πάντα δώσω, **ἐὰν** πεσὼν *προσκυνήσῃς* μοι.
I will give you all these things, **if** *you will* fall down and *worship* me.
> This is a true third class since the apodosis involves a future indicative.

John 11:9   **ἐάν** τις *περιπατῇ* ἐν τῇ ἡμέρᾳ, οὐ *προσκόπτει*
If anyone *walks* in the day, *he does* not *stumble.*
> This is an example of the present general condition. There is no hint of uncertainty about this event occurring, nor is it something presented as an eventuality. This is a principle, a proverb. The subjunctive is used because the subject is undefined, not because the time is future.

1 Cor 14:8   **ἐὰν** ἄδηλον σάλπιγξ φωνὴν *δῷ,* τίς *παρασκευάσεται* εἰς πόλεμον;
If the trumpet *should give* an indistinct sound, who *will prepare* for battle?
> Although Paul puts his condition in the third class, he does not expect a bugler to play an inarticulate sound on the verge of battle! Due to the subjunctive's encroaching on the optative in Koine, it has come to cover a multitude of conditional situations.[15]

1 John 1:9   **ἐὰν** *ὁμολογῶμεν* τὰς ἁμαρτίας ἡμῶν, πιστός ἐστιν καὶ δίκαιος, ἵνα ἀφῇ ἡμῖν τὰς ἁμαρτίας καὶ καθαρίσῃ ἡμᾶς ἀπὸ πάσης ἀδικίας.
If *we confess* our sins, *he is* faithful and just to forgive us our sins and to cleanse us from all unrighteousness.
> This is probably a present general condition in which the subject is distributive ("if any of us"). The subjunctive is thus used because of the implicit uncertainty as to who is included in the *we.*[16]

d. Fourth Class Condition (Less Probable Future)   ExSyn 699–701

(1) DEFINITION. The fourth class condition indicates a *possible* condition in the future, usually a remote possibility (such as *if he could do something, if perhaps this should occur*). The protasis involves εἰ + the *optative* mood. The *optative* is also used in the apodosis along with ἄν (to indicate contingency). Because of the increasing use of the subjunctive and decreasing use of the optative in Hellenistic Greek, it should come as no surprise that *there are no complete fourth class conditions in the NT.*[17]

---

[15] The conditions in 1 Cor 13:1–3 are similar; see the discussion in *ExSyn* 698.

[16] For further discussion, see *ExSyn* 698–99.

[17] Sometimes the conditional clause is mixed, with a non-optative in the apodosis. On other occasions, there is an apodosis, but a verbless one. On still other occasions, no apodosis is to be supplied, the protasis functioning as a sort of stereotyped parenthesis.

(2) ILLUSTRATIONS. The first illustration includes just the protasis of the fourth class condition; the last two include just the apodosis.

1 Pet 3:14   εἰ καὶ *πάσχοιτε* διὰ δικαιοσύνην, μακάριοι.
Even **if** *you should suffer* for righteousness, [you would be] blessed.[18]

Luke 1:62   ἐνένευον τῷ πατρὶ αὐτοῦ τὸ τί *ἂν* **θέλοι** καλεῖσθαι αὐτό
they were making signs to his father as to what **he would want** to call him

> The implicit protasis is, "If he had his voice back so that he could call him some name." There is little expectation this will happen, however (note their reaction in v. 65 when this occurs).

Acts 17:18   τινες ἔλεγον· τί *ἂν* **θέλοι** ὁ σπερμολόγος οὗτος λέγειν;
Some [of the philosophers] were saying, "What **would** this babbler **say**?"

> The implicit protasis is, "If he could say anything that made sense!" It is evident that the philosophers do not think such is likely.

---

[18] For a discussion of this text, see *ExSyn* 700.

Volitional Clauses[1]
Overview of Commands and Prohibitions

Commands 316
  1. Future Indicative (Cohortative Indicative, Imperatival Future) 317
  2. Aorist Imperative. 317
    a. Ingressive. 317
    b. Constative 318
  3. Present Imperative 318
    a. Ingressive-Progressive. 318
    b. Customary 319
    c. Iterative 319
Prohibitions. 319
  1. Future Indicative (+ οὐ or sometimes μή) 320
  2. Aorist Subjunctive (+ μή) 320
  3. Present Imperative (+ μή) 320
    a. Cessation of Activity in Progress (Progressive) 320
    b. General Precept (Customary). 321

INTRODUCTION[2] *ExSyn 714–17*

The *basic* force of the aorist in commands/prohibitions is that it views the action *as a whole*, while the *basic* force of the present in commands/prohibitions is that it views the action *as ongoing process*. This basic meaning may, of course, be shaped in a given context to fit, say, an ingressive idea for the aorist. Thus if the conditions are right, the aorist prohibition may well have the force of "Do not start." This is an affected meaning or specific usage. But to call this the *essential* idea is not correct.[3]

SPECIFIC USES *ExSyn 718–25*

Commands *ExSyn 718–22*

Commands are normally expressed in one of three tenses in Greek (each having a different nuance): future, aorist, and present.

---

[1] See *ExSyn* 713–25.

[2] This chapter focuses on the tense-mood combination used in commands and prohibitions. It does not address modality in any detail. For a discussion of that, see the chapter on moods.

[3] Volitional clauses comprise a fascinating area of study in Greek grammar that has been retooled in recent years. Some breakthroughs on the use of the tenses in general, and the use of the present and aorist in imperatives in particular, have changed the way grammarians and exegetes have looked at commands and prohibitions in the NT. Without going into the history of the discussion, this chapter will simply reflect the current assessment of imperatives. For a discussion, see *ExSyn* 714–17.

1. Future Indicative (Cohortative Indicative, Imperatival Future) *ExSyn 718–19*

The future indicative is sometimes used for a command, almost always in OT quotations (the result of a literal translation of the Hebrew). Its force is emphatic, in keeping with the combined nature of the indicative mood and future tense. It tends to have a universal, timeless, or solemn force to it.

Matt 4:10   κύριον τὸν θεόν σου **προσκυνήσεις** καὶ αὐτῷ μόνῳ **λατρεύσεις**.
You shall worship the Lord your God and **serve** him only.

1 Pet 1:16   ἅγιοι **ἔσεσθε**, ὅτι ἐγὼ ἅγιός εἰμι.
You shall be holy, because I am holy.

2. Aorist Imperative *ExSyn 719–21*

The basic idea of the aorist imperative is a command in which the action is viewed as a whole, without regard for the internal make-up of the action. However, it occurs in various contexts in which its meaning has been affected especially by lexical or contextual features. Consequently, most aorist imperatives can be placed into one of two broad categories, ingressive or constative.

Further, the aorist is most frequently used for a *specific* command rather than a general precept (usually the domain of the present).

a. Ingressive

This is a command to *begin an action*. The stress is on the *urgency* of the action. This common usage may be broken down into two subcategories.

(1) MOMENTARY OR SINGLE ACT

Here a specific situation is usually in view rather than a general precept.

Mark 9:25   ἐγὼ ἐπιτάσσω σοι, **ἔξελθε** ἐξ αὐτοῦ
I order you, **come out** of him!

John 19:6   **σταύρωσον σταύρωσον**.
Crucify [him], **Crucify** [him]!
The stress is on the urgency of the action and is viewed as a single event—i.e., the part that *others* play in crucifying a man is a single event, while his hanging on the cross is durative.

(2) PURE INGRESSIVE

The stress is on the beginning of an action that the context usually makes clear is *not* a momentary action.

Rom 6:13   μηδὲ παριστάνετε τὰ μέλη ὑμῶν ὅπλα ἀδικίας τῇ ἁμαρτίᾳ, ἀλλὰ **παραστήσατε** ἑαυτοὺς τῷ θεῷ.
Do not present [present tense] your members as instruments of unrighteousness to sin, but **present** [aorist tense] yourselves to God.

Phil 4:5   τὸ ἐπιεικὲς ὑμῶν **γνωσθήτω** πᾶσιν ἀνθρώποις.
Let all men [come to] **know** your forbearance.

b. Constative

This is a solemn or categorical command. The stress is *not* "begin an action," nor "continue to act." Rather, the stress is on the *solemnity* and *urgency* of the action; thus "I solemnly charge you to act—and do it now!" This is the use of the aorist in general precepts. Although the aorist is here transgressing onto the present tense's turf, it adds a certain flavor. It is as if the author says, "Make this your top priority." As such, the aorist is often used to command an action that has been going on. In this case, both solemnity and a heightened urgency are its force.[4]

John 15:4   **μείνατε** ἐν ἐμοί, κἀγὼ ἐν ὑμῖν.
Remain in me, and I in you.

> Obviously the command is not ingressive: "Begin to remain in me." Nor is it momentary and specific. This is a general precept, but the force of the aorist is on urgency and priority.

2 Tim 4:2   **κήρυξον** τὸν λόγον   **Preach** the word!

> The idea here is hardly "**Begin** to preach the word," but, "I solemnly charge you to preach the word. Make this your priority!" (as the following context clearly indicates).

3. Present Imperative   *ExSyn* 721–22

The present imperative looks at the action from an internal viewpoint. It is used for the most part for general precepts—i.e., for habits that should characterize one's attitudes and behavior—rather than in specific situations.[5] The action may or may not have already begun. It may be progressive, iterative, or customary.

The present tense is also used at times for specific commands. In such contexts it is usually ingressive-progressive.

a. Ingressive-Progressive

The force here is *begin and continue*. It is different from the pure ingressive aorist in that it stresses both the inception and progress of an action commanded while the pure ingressive aorist imperative stresses only the inception, making no comment about the progress of the action.

Matt 8:22   **ἀκολούθει** μοι καὶ ἄφες τοὺς νεκροὺς θάψαι τοὺς ἑαυτῶν νεκρούς.
Follow me and leave the dead to bury their own dead.

> Here Jesus urges a would-be disciple to begin and continue following him.

---

[4] The difference between the aorist and the future indicative in such general precepts seems to be that the aorist is used for a sense of urgency while the future indicative does not stress this element.

[5] For a discussion of this and its differences with the aorist, see the previous section "Aorist Imperative."

John 5:8   ἆρον τὸν κράβατόν σου καὶ **περιπάτει**.
Take up your bed and **walk.**

> The momentary aorist is used, followed by an ingressive-progressive present. The force of this clause is, "Take up [right now] your bed and [begin and continue to] walk."

b. Customary

The force of the customary present imperative is simply *continue*. It is a command for action to be continued, action that may or may not have already been going on. It is often a character-building command to the effect of "make this your habit," "train yourself in this," etc. This is the use of the present imperative in general precepts.

Matt 6:9   οὕτως οὖν **προσεύχεσθε** ὑμεῖς
you should therefore **pray** as follows

> The focus is not on urgency, nor on a momentary act. This initial command at the beginning of the Lord's Prayer means, "Make it your habit to pray in the following manner."

Luke 6:35   **ἀγαπᾶτε** τοὺς ἐχθροὺς ὑμῶν καὶ **ἀγαθοποιεῖτε**
Love your enemies and **do good** [to them]

c. Iterative

The force of an iterative present imperative is *repeated action*. That is, "do it again and again." It is not continuous action that is commanded, but a repeated act. Normally, a good rule of thumb is that when an *attitude* is commanded, the force of the present imperative will either be *ingressive-progressive* or *customary*; when an *action* is commanded, the force of the present imperative will usually be *iterative*. It is, however, difficult to distinguish this usage from the customary present.

Matt 7:7   **Αἰτεῖτε** ... **ζητεῖτε** ... **κρούετε** ...
Ask ... **seek** ... **knock** ...

> The force of these commands is, "Keep on asking ... keep on seeking ... keep on knocking ..."

1 Cor 11:28   **δοκιμαζέτω** δὲ ἄνθρωπος ἑαυτὸν καὶ οὕτως ἐκ τοῦ ἄρτου **ἐσθιέτω** καὶ ἐκ τοῦ ποτηρίου **πινέτω**·
But **let** a person **examine** himself and thus **let him eat** from the bread and **drink** from the cup,

> The idea is that whenever the Lord's Supper is observed, this examination (and eating, drinking) needs to take place.

Prohibitions   *ExSyn 723–25*

Prohibitions, like commands, are normally expressed by one of three tenses in Greek: future, aorist, present.

1. **Future Indicative (+ οὐ or sometimes μή)**   *ExSyn* 723

This has the same force of the future indicative for commands, now put in the negative. It is typically solemn, universal, or timeless. (See the discussion above under "Commands.")

Matt 19:18   οὐ φονεύσεις, οὐ μοιχεύσεις, οὐ κλέψεις, οὐ ψευδομαρτυρήσεις
you shall not **murder**, you shall not **commit adultery**, you shall not **steal**, you shall not **bear false witness**

2. **Aorist Subjunctive (+ μή)**   *ExSyn* 723–24

The aorist in prohibitions is almost always in the subjunctive mood. With the second person, this is always the case.

The prohibitive aorist is normally used, like its positive counterpart, in specific situations. The force of the aorist is used to prohibit the action as a whole. Because of this, it sometimes has an *ingressive* flavor: *Do not start.*

But not all aorist prohibitions are used this way. Especially when used in general precepts, it seems to have the force of prohibiting an action *as a whole*. Yet even here, the ingressive notion may be part of the meaning. This is due to the fact that the prohibited action is normally not one yet engaged in, as the context shows.

The difficulty of deciding between these two notions is seen in the illustrations below. At bottom, the ingressive and summary perspectives of the aorist blend into one another at almost every turn.

Matt 6:13   μὴ εἰσενέγκῃς ἡμᾶς εἰς πειρασμόν.
Do not **lead** us into temptation.

2 Thess 3:13 μὴ ἐγκακήσητε καλοποιοῦντες.
Do not **become weary** in doing good.

3. **Present Imperative (+ μή)**   *ExSyn* 724–25

a. Cessation of Activity in Progress (Progressive)

Here the idea is frequently progressive and the prohibition is of the "cessation of some act that is already in progress."[6] It has the idea, *Stop continuing.* μὴ φοβοῦ is thus naturally used as the formula to quell someone's apprehensions.[7]

Matt 19:14 μὴ κωλύετε αὐτὰ ἐλθεῖν πρός με.
Stop preventing them from coming to me.
What indicates that the cessation of an activity is in view is the previous verse, where we read that the disciples were disturbed that some wanted to bring children to Jesus.

---

[6] Dana-Mantey, 302.

[7] Of the 50 instances of prohibition in the NT that use μή + imperative or subjunctive, 40 use the present imperative, while only ten use the aorist subjunctive.

Luke 1:30   εἶπεν ὁ ἄγγελος αὐτῇ· μὴ **φοβοῦ**, Μαριάμ. . . .
            The angel said to her, "**Do** not **be afraid**, Mary. . . . "

> The typical opening line of an angelic visitor is, "Do not fear."
> The sight is evidently sufficiently startling that the individual
> would already be moving in the direction of apprehensiveness.

Rev 5:5   εἷς ἐκ τῶν πρεσβυτέρων λέγει μοι· μὴ **κλαῖε**.
            One of the elders said to me, "Stop **weeping**."

b. General Precept (Customary)

The present prohibition can also have the force of a *general precept*. This kind of prohibition really makes no comment about whether the action is going on or not.

1 Cor 14:39   τὸ λαλεῖν μὴ **κωλύετε** γλώσσαις·
              Do not **forbid** the speaking in tongues.

Eph 6:4   οἱ πατέρες, μὴ **παροργίζετε** τὰ τέκνα ὑμῶν.
              Fathers, **do** not **provoke** your children **to wrath.**

In many of the NT letters the force of a particular present prohibition will not always be focused on the cessation of an activity in progress. It is *not*, then, safe to say that when an author uses the present prohibition the audience is being indicted for not heeding this command. Other factors—especially the overall context and *Sitz im Leben* of the book—must be taken into account.

SUBJECT INDEX / CHEAT SHEET

The *Exegetical Syntax* has two subject elements in the back of the book: "Cheat Sheet," which gives in list form all the major options a student needs to examine in order to determine how each grammatical form or word functions in a phrase or clause; and a "Subject Index," where all categories are discussed in alphabetical order (page numbers given).

This "Subject Index / Cheat Sheet" combines these two into one feature. While not in alphabetical order, you should be able to scan quickly the major headings in this listing to find what you are looking for, together with the page number on which discussion of the syntax of each category can be found. The categories that are in boldface type are those that occur with relative frequency in the New Testament

CASES

Nominative

Subject, 29–30
Predicate Nominative, 30–33
Nominative in Simple Apposition, 33
Nominative Absolute, 34
Nominativus Pendens (Pendent
    Nominative), 34–35
Parenthetic Nominative, 35
Nominative for Vocative, 35–36
Nominative of Exclamation, 36–37

Vocative

Simple Address, 39
Emphatic (or Emotional) Address,
    39–40
Apposition, 40

Genitive

Descriptive Genitive, 45–46
Possessive Genitive, 46–47
Genitive of Relationship, 47–48
Partitive Genitive ("Wholative"), 48
Attributive Genitive, 48–49
Attributed Genitive, 49–50
Genitive of Material, 50
Genitive of Content, 50–52
Genitive in Simple Apposition, 52–54

Genitive of Apposition
    (Epexegetical), 52–54
Predicate Genitive, 54
Genitive of Subordination, 54–55
Genitive of Separation, 55
Genitive of Source (or Origin), 56
Genitive of Comparison, 56
Subjective Genitive, 57–58
Objective Genitive, 58–59
Plenary Genitive, 59
Genitive of Time (kind of time), 60
Genitive of Means, 61
Genitive of Agency, 61
Genitive Absolute, 284–85
Genitive of Reference, 61–62
Genitive of Association, 62
**Genitive After Certain Verbs (as
    Direct Object)**, 63–64
Genitive After Certain Adjectives, 64
Genitive After Certain Prepositions, 64

Dative

Dative Indirect Object, 67–68
**Dative of Interest (including
    Advantage [*commodi*] and
    Disadvantage [*incommodi*])**,
    68–69
Dative of Reference/Respect, 69–70
Dative of Destination, 70

Dative of Possession, 70–71
Dative in Simple Apposition, 71
Dative of Sphere, 72
Dative of Time (when), 72–73
Dative of Association/Accompaniment, 73–74
Dative of Manner (or Adverbial Dative), 74–75
Dative of Means/Instrument, 75
Dative of Agency, 75–76
Dative of Measure/Degree of Difference, 76–77
Dative of Cause, 77
Cognate Dative, 77–78
Dative Direct Object, 78–79
Dative After Certain Nouns, 79
Dative After Certain Adjectives, 79
Dative After Certain Prepositions, 80

Accusative
Accusative Direct Object, 83
Double Accusative: Person-Thing, 83–84
Double Accusative: Object-Complement, 84–86
Predicate Accusative, 86–87
Accusative Subject of Infinitive, 87–88
Accusative of Retained Object, 88
Accusative in Simple Apposition, 89
Adverbial Accusative (Accusative of Manner), 89–90
Accusative of Measure (or Extent of Space or **Time**), 90–91
Accusative of Respect or (General) Reference, 91
Accusative After Certain Prepositions, 92

ARTICLE
Regular Uses
As a Pronoun ([Partially] Independent Use)
    Personal Pronoun, 95
    Relative Pronoun, 96
    Possessive Pronoun, 96–96

With Substantives (Dependent or Modifying Use)
    Individualizing Article
        Simple Identification, 97
        Anaphoric (Previous Reference), 98
        Deictic ("Pointing" Article), 99
        Par Excellence, 99
        Monadic ("One of a Kind" or "Unique" Article), 100
        Well-Known ("Celebrity" or "Familiar" Article), 100
        Abstract (i.e., the Article with Abstract Nouns), 100–101
    Generic Article (Categorical Article), 101–3
As a Substantiver, 103–6
As a Function Marker, 106–8

Absence of the Article
Indefinite, 108–9
Qualitative, 109–10
Definite, 110–12

Special Uses and Non-Uses of the Article
Anarthrous Preverbal Predicate Nominatives (Involving Colwell's Rule), 114–20
Article with Multiple Substantives Connected by καί (Granville Sharp Rule and Related Constructions), 120–28

ADJECTIVES
"Non-Adjectival" Uses of Adjective
Adverbial Use, 130
Independent or Substantival Use, 130–31

Positive, Comparative, Superlative
Positive
    Normal Usage, 131–32
    Positive for Comparative, 132
    Positive for Superlative, 132

Comparative
  Normal Usage, 132
  Comparative for Superlative, 132–33
  Comparative for Elative, 133
Superlative
  "Normal" Usage, 133–34
  Superlative for Elative, 134
  Superlative for Comparative,
    134–35

Relation of Adjective to Noun

Attributive Positions
  First Attributive, 135
  Second Attributive, 135–136
  Third Attributive, 136
Predicate Positions
  First Predicate, 136
  Second Predicate, 136–37
**Anarthrous Adjective-Noun / Noun-
  Adjective Constructionst**, 137–39

PRONOUNS

Personal Pronouns
  Nominative Case, 142–44
  Oblique Cases, 144
Demonstrative Pronouns
  Regular Uses (as Demonstratives),
    145–46
  For Personal Pronouns, 146
  Pleonastic (Redundant, Resumptive),
    147
  **Conceptual Antecedent/
    Postcedent**, 149
Relative Pronouns
  ὅς, 150–52
  ὅστις (called **Indefinite; better:
    Generic or Qualitative**), 153
Interrogative Pronouns
  τίς and τί, 153–54
  ποῖος and πόσος, 154
Indefinite Pronoun
  Substantival, 154
  Adjectival, 154
**Possessive "Pronouns" (=
  Adjectives)**, 154–55

Intensive Pronoun
  αὐτός as intensive pronoun, 155
  αὐτός as identifying adjective,
    155–56
Reflexive Pronoun, 156
Reciprocal Pronoun, 156

PREPOSITIONS
Nature and meaning, 160–73

PERSON AND NUMBER
Person
Editorial "We" (Epistolary Plural),
  175–76
Inclusive "We" (Literary Plural),
  176
Exclusive "We," 176–77

NUMBER
**Neuter Plural Subject with
  Singular Verb**, 177
**Compound Subject with
  Singular Verb**, 178
Indefinite Plural, 178

VOICE
Active
Simple Active, 181
Causative Active, 181
Stative Active, 181–82
Reflexive Active, 182

Middle
Direct Middle (Reflexive or Direct
  Reflexive), 183
**Indirect Middle (Indirect Reflexive,
  Benefactive, Intensive,
  Dramatic)**, 184
Permissive Middle, 185
Deponent Middle, 185–86

Passive
Simple Passive, 186–91
Causative / Permissive Passive, 189–90
Deponent Passive, 191

MOODS

Indicative

Declarative Indicative, 195
Interrogative Indicative, 195
Conditional Indicative, 195–96
Potential Indicative, 196
Cohortative (Command, Volitive)
  Indicative, 197
Indicative with ὅτι, 197–201

Subjunctive

In Independent Clauses
  Hortatory Subjunctive (Volitive),
    202
  Deliberative Subjunctive
    (Dubitative), 202–4
  Emphatic Negation Subjunctive,
    204
  Prohibitive Subjunctive, 204–5
In Dependent (Subordinate) Clauses
  Subjunctive in Conditional
    Sentences, 205–6
  ἵνα plus Subjunctive
    Purpose ἵνα Clause (Final or
      Telic), 206
    Purpose-Result ἵνα, 206–7
    Substantival ἵνα Clause
      (Sub-Final Clause), 207
  Complementary ἵνα Clause, 207–8
Subjunctive with Verbs of Fearing, 208
Subjunctive in Indirect Questions, 208
Subjunctive in Indefinite Relative
  Clause, 208–9
Subjunctive in Indefinite Temporal
  Clause, 209

Optative

Voluntative Optative (Obtainable
  Wish, Volitive Optative), 209–10

Imperative

Command, 210
Prohibition, 211
Request (Entreaty, Polite
  Command), 211
Conditional Imperative, 211–12

TENSE

Present

Instantaneous Present (Aoristic or
  Punctiliar Present), 221
Progressive Present (Descriptive
  Present), 222
Extending-From-Past Present, 222–23
Iterative Present, 223
Customary (Habitual or General)
  Present, 224
Gnomic Present, 224–225
Historical Present (Dramatic
  Present), 226–27
Perfective Present, 227–28
Conative (Tendential, Conative)
  Present, 228–29
Futuristic Present, 229–230
Present Retained in Indirect
  Discourse, 230–31

Imperfect

Progressive (Descriptive) Imperfect,
  233
Ingressive (Inchoative, Inceptive)
  Imperfect, 233–34
Interative Imperfect, 234–35
Customary (Habitual or General)
  Imperfect, 235–36
Conative (Voluntive, Tendential)
  Imperfect, 236–37
Imperfect Retained in Indirect
  Discourse, 237–38

Aorist

Constative (Complexive, Punctiliar,
  Comprehensive, Global) Aorist,
  241
Ingressive (Inceptive, Inchoative)
  Aorist, 241
Consummative (Culminative,
  Ecbatic, Effective) Aorist, 241–42
Epistolary Aorist, 242
Proleptic (Futuristic) Aorist, 242
Immediate Past Aorist / Dramatic
  Aorist, 242–43

Future

Predictive Future, 244–45
Imperatival Futures, 245
Deliberative Future, 245

Perfect

Intensive Perfect (Resultative Perfect), 247–48
Extensive Perfect (Consummative Perfect), 248–49
Aoristic (Dramatic, Historical) Perfect, 249
Perfect with a Present Force, 249–50

Pluperfect

Intensive (Resultative) Pluperfect, 251–52
Extensive (Consummative) Pluperfect, 252
Pluperfect with a Simple Past Force, 252–53

INFINITIVE

Adverbial Uses

Purpose, 256–57
Result, 257–58
Time, 258–59
Cause, 259
Complementary (Supplementary), 259–60

Substantival

Subject, 260–61
Direct Object, 261
Indirect Discourse, 261–62
Appositional, 262–63
Epexegetical , 263

PARTICIPLE

Adjectival Participles

Adjectival Proper (Dependent), 270
Substantival (Independent), 270–71

Verbal Participles

Dependent Verbal Participles
  Adverbial (or Circumstantial)
    Temporal, 272–73
    Manner, 274

Means, 274–75
Cause, 275–76
Condition, 276
Concession, 277
Purpose, 277–78
Result, 278–79
Attendant Circumstance, 279–81
Indirect Discourse, 281
Periphrastic, 281–82
Redundant (Pleonastic), 282–83
Independent Verbal Participles
  As an Imperative (Imperatival), 283

Participle Absolute

Nominative Absolute, 283–84
Genitive Absolute, 284–85

CLAUSES

Independent Clauses, 286
Dependent Clauses, 286–92
  Substantival Clause, 288–89
  Adjectival Clause, 289–90
  Adverbial Clause, 290–91

CONJUNCTIONS

Logical Functions

Ascensive, 296
Connective (Continuative, Coordinate), 296
Contrastive (Adversative), 297
Correlative, 297
Disjunctive (Alternative), 298
Emphatic, 298
Explanatory, 298
Inferential, 298–99
Transitional, 299

Adverbial Functions

Causal, 299
Comparative (Manner), 299–30
Conditional, 300
Local (Sphere), 300
Purpose, 301
Result, 301
Temporal, 301

Substantival Functions

Content, 302
Epexegetical, 302

CONDITIONAL SENTENCES

First Class Condition, 309–12
Second Class Condition, 312–13
Third Class Condition, 313–14
Fourth Class Condition, 314–15

VOLITIONAL CLAUSES

Commands

Future Indicative, 317

Aorist Imperative
   Ingressive (Momentary or Single
     Act; and Pure Ingressive),
     317–18
   Constative, 318
Present Imperative
   Ingressive-Progressive, 318–19
   Customary, 319
   Iterative, 319

Prohibitions

Future Indicative (+ οὐ or sometimes
   μή), 320
Aorist Subjunctive (+ μή), 320
Present Imperative (+ μή), 320–21

SCRIPTURE INDEX

DEUTERONOMY

18:15 98–99

PSALMS

68:18........................106

MATTHEW

1:16............................150
1:18............................299
1:19............................276
1:22......................75, 188
2:6.............................143
2:7.............................270
2:11.............................54
2:12............................189
2:16............................198
2:23....................104, 189
3:1...............................33
3:6.............................235
3:7.............................124
3:14............................236
3:15............................113
3:16....................107, 112
3:17.............................32
4:1.............................100
4:2......................90. 273
4:5.............................135
4:6.............................156
4:9......................205, 314
4:10............................317
5:3–11 287
5:3.......................72, 201
5:4.............................189
5:5.............................104
5:6.............................308
5:9.............................136
5:11............................209
5:17..................199, 257,
            297, 289, 298
5:21............................189
5:28............................268
5:32............................225
5:36............................298
5:39............................308

5:45............................181
5:46.............................83
6:4.............................270
6:8......................259, 291
6:9..............................96
6:10–11 211
6:13............104, 131, 320
6:19............................300
6:24............................260
6:25.............................56
6:31............................203
6:33.............................90
7:7..............212, 223, 319
7:15............................153
7:16............................178
7:29............................282
8:3.............................241
8:22............................318
8:24............................233
8:27....................145, 302
8:34.............................79
9:11....................125, 287
9:18....................243, 284
9:22.............................39
9:27............................241
9:34.............................54
9:36............................251
9:37............................297
10:3............................105
10:8.............................90
11:14............................32
11:25............................283
12:6............................132
12:8............................108
12:16............................289
12:27–28..............310–11
12:27............................196
12:31.............................59
12:43............................297
13:4............................258
13:11............................145
13:12............................289
13:13............................287
13:31.............................79
13:32............................133

13:38............................177
13:55....................32, 178
13:57............................139
14:15.............................99
15:26–27 95
15:28.............................39
15:32............................208
16:18............................108
16:21............................124
16:23............................105
16:24............................154
17:1............................123
17:15............................223
17:23.............................73
18:8....................132, 306
18:12.............................71
18:17............................102
19:1............................291
19:5–6 33
19:14............................320
19:18..........197, 245, 320
19:22............................274
20:4............................288
20:27............................288
20:28............................172
21:5.............................70
21:18, 23......................291
21:21.............................62
21:22............................276
21:28............................134
21:41............................291
22:3.............................88
22:7............................241
22:38............................132
22:43.............................86
23:31.............................69
24:15.............................35
24:20.............................73
24:27.............................57
24:50............................151
26:15............................308
26:32............................258
26:40............................227
26:51.............................47
26:65............................243

26:66..............................64
27:4..............................275
27:5..............................183
27:11............................195
27:12............................184
27:42............................117
27:49............................278
28:8..............................230
28:19–20 280

MARK

1:8..................26, 138, 168
1:15..............................162
1:34..............................253
1:37..............................222
1:41......................106, 227
2:1........................199, 231
2:5..............................189
2:14......................210, 273
2:16..............................125
2:17................................83
2:19..............................291
2:21................................50
2:28................................32
3:21..............................178
4:1..............................134
4:2..............................181
4:3..............................195
4:5..............................291
4:6..............................259
4:35..............................202
5:2................................79
5:30..............................156
5:36..............................211
5:39..............................242
5:41................................63
6:3..............................121
6:22................................84
6:37......................203, 245
8:27..............................154
8:29..............................143
8:37..............................204
9:5..............................260
9:7..............................278
9:15..............................273
9:20..............................234
9:21................................60
9:25..............................317
9:43..............................306

9:50..............................156
10:8................................33
10:13..............................30
10:19..............................250
10:29..............................288
10:33..............................230
10:45..............................172
11:28..............................154
12:10..............................151
12:18..............................262
12:31..............................138
12:36..............................155
12:41..............................217
12:44..............................217
13:24..............................100
13:25..............................282
14:4..............................287
14:59................................58
14:68..............................297
15:23..............................236
15:25..............................111
15:30..............................182
15:32................................54
15:46..............................252
16:1................................48

LUKE

1:18..............................287
1:30..............................321
1:34..............................299
1:35..............................111
1:45..............................271
1:47................................71
1:59..............................237
1:62..............................315
1:68..............................107
2:2..............................134
2:27................................88
2:41..............................236
3:5..............................113
3:16..............................223
3:21..............................259
4:2..............................189
4:3......................207, 312
4:15..............................279
4:20................................97
4:29..............................252
4:41................................87
4:43..............................287

5:1..............................143
5:5..............................113
5:7..............................258
5:20..............................248
5:33................................95
6:9..............................296
6:17..............................129
6:21..............................107
6:31......................207, 291
6:35..............................319
7:6..............................302
7:29..............................190
7:32................................96
7:39..............................312
7:44..............................108
8:25......................200, 290
8:54................................36
9:30..............................153
9:48..............................132
9:58..............................208
10:7..............................102
10:19..............................263
10:20......................200, 289
10:35................................63
11:6..............................289
11:7..............................108
11:8..............................290
11:30..............................32
11:42................................59
12:1..............................152
12:3..............................151
12:17..............................283
12:20..............................178
13:6..............................281
14:18..............................281
14:20..............................149
14:27..............................153
15:22..............................136
15:25................................70
15:29..............................223
16:6..............................280
16:7..............................154
18:2..............................113
18:12......................60, 224
18:13................................99
18:31................................70
19:8................................48
19:9..............................112
19:17..............................138

19:20......................281
19:47......................259
21:8........................208
21:12......................127
21:24......................301
21:25......................111
22:15........................78
22:25........................64
23:15........................76
23:40......................156
24:10........................48
24:18......................143
24:20......................297
24:23......................289

John

1:1..................111, 115,
        119–20, 182, 294
1:3........................188
1:6..........................35
1:7........................181
1:12........................47
1:14......................118
1:18................136, 165
1:19......................228
1:21....................98, 99
1:23........................30
1:26................150, 250
1:29......................100
1:33......................257
1:34......................248
1:38......................195
1:41......................130
1:45......................110
1:46................163, 211
1:49................115, 118
2:2........................178
2:11......................107
2:16........................46
2:19..................59, 308
2:20......................242
2:21..................53, 59
2:22......................238
2:24................144, 155
2:25......................290
3:2..........................60
3:3........................221
3:7........................205
3:8........................225

3:15......................162
3:16............30, 138, 206,
        224, 271, 294–95,
        298, 301
3:18......................289
3:23......................189
3:33......................289
4:1............199, 231, 289
4:6........................276
4:7................108, 144
4:8........................298
4:10........................68
4:11................107, 270
4:14......................209
4:17................198, 302
4:18................130, 151
4:19................119, 302
4:22......................101
4:24........................32
4:25......................270
4:26......................289
4:27......................110
4:30......................234
4:34................207, 289
4:35......................234
4:40, 43..................98
4:46........................86
4:50........................98
4:51........................79
4:54..................86, 107
5:2........................227
5:6........................146
5:8........................319
5:10......................299
5:11......................147
5:18.....108, 111, 278, 291
5:23......................119
5:27......................299
5:31................205, 300
5:34......................301
5:42........................59
5:46......................312
6:13........................52
6:19........................90
6:24................144, 301
6:39......................271
6:42......................198
6:66......................287
6:70......................111

7:26........................75
7:38......................284
8:56......................291
8:58................119, 227
9:2........................301
9:18......................238
9:22......................252
10:18......................59
10:27......................177
10:28................204, 206
10:30......................119
10:32......................229
10:34......................121
11:2........................75
11:9......................314
11:24......................134
11:26......................206
11:29......................146
11:38......................276
11:50......................173
12:33......................278
13:34......................156
14:17......................224
14:26................84, 148
15:1........................32
15:4......................318
15:16......................297
15:26......................148
16:13–14..................148
17:3................207, 289
18:16........................61
19:1........................181
19:3......................235
19:5........................99
19:6......................317
20:4......................134
20:17......................121
20:28............36, 47, 119
20:29......................126
21:8........................51
21:15........................48

Acts

1:1..................40, 134
1:11............154, 244, 291
1:24........................40
1:25......................128
2:4........................52
2:15........................32

2:23................................128
2:33................................131
2:38................................166
3:2................................233
3:14................................122
3:26........................278, 291
4:10................................150
4:11........................33, 145
4:12................................196
5:5................................280
5:41................................274
7:12........................281, 289
7:35................................249
7:40................................35
7:58................................54
8:10................................147
8:21................................71
9:7................................73
9:20................................32
9:22................................275
9:24................................301
9:34................................221
10:9................................97
10:13................................280
11:15................................136
11:2................................105
12:21................................183
13:2................................123
13:10................................40
13:31................................133
15:1................................96
16:12................................153
16:16................................291
16:17................................134
16:30................................206
16:31........................89, 178
17:18................................315
17:22................................133
18:6................................104
18:14................................40
19:2................................139
19:13................................110
20:21................................128
21:11................................181
21:29................................282
22:16................................185
23:3................................38
24:24................................71
26:12................................152

26:13................................107
27:20................................105
27:21................................40
27:32................................144
28:6........................85, 88

ROMANS

1:1................................34
1:4................................111
1:5................................176
1:12................................289
1:13........................36, 189
1:15................................290
1:18................................112
1:30................................79
2:12................................291
2:14................................147
3:3–4................................210
3:10................................248
3:21................................195
3:22................................58
3:23................................218
3:25........................58, 86
3:28........................75, 190, 188
4:11........................54, 61
4:15........................291, 300
4:20................................77
5:1........176, 191, 202, 290
5:5................................249
5:8........................54, 156, 200
5:12................................152
5:14................................241
6:2........................69, 72, 290
6:4................................30
6:6........................49, 149, 200
6:9................................230
6:11........................70, 86
6:12................................211
6:13................................317
6:17................................236
6:21................................236
7:3........................71, 285
7:7–25................................174
7:8................................139
7:12................................132
7:14–24................................227
7:18................................105
7:24................................37
7:25................................97

8:13................................307
8:14................................75
8:16................................74
8:17........................59, 305
8:21................................49
8:28................................83
8:30........................147, 242
8:32................................298
8:33................................61
8:35................................42
9:1................................222
9:3........................172, 237
9:22................................183
10:3................................56
10:5................................91
10:9........................86, 162
10:14................................204
11:11................................291
11:33................................37
12:1................................299
12:9........................101, 283
13:9................................106
15:7................................299
15:26................................48
15:32................................188

1 CORINTHIANS

1:1................................188
1:9................................188
1:13................................189
1:18........................31, 96
2:8........................196, 300, 313
2:10................................296
2:11................................300
2:13................................88
3:9................................62
3:13................................99
4:2................................289
4:3................................134
4:10................................177
4:14................................291
5:9................................287
5:10................................125
6:13................................69
7:23................................190
7:39................................263
10:2................................185
10:7................................177
10:30................................75

11:7.............................113
11:18...........................289
11:26...........................209
11:28...........................319
11:29.............................69
12:13............. 26, 88, 168,
                        188–90
13:1–3 314
13:2............................258
13:4............................182
13:8....................184, 186
13:9–10 105
13:10...........................131
13:13...........................133
14:5............................208
14:8............................314
14:15.............................96
14:39...........................321
15:3............................302
15:4............................248
15:10...........................150
15:13...........................310
15:32...........................202
15:44...........................305
16:15.............................74

2 CORINTHIANS

1:1.....................47, 188
3:3.......................56, 290
5:13.............................69
5:14 ....59, 172–73
5:17...........................177
5:20...........................211
6:2.............................46
6:14.............................74
8:5............................188
8:11...........................261
9:7............................225
10:11, 13.....................176
12:7.............................68
12:21...........................128

GALATIANS

1:1............................188
1:12.............................57
3:1.............................36
3:6.............................79
3:11...........................289
3:13...........................173

3:29...........................307
4:7............................188
4:22...........................100
5:4............................229
5:7............................291
5:10...........................209
5:16.............................76
6:9............................276
6:11...........................242
6:12.............................77

EPHESIANS

1:1.....................126, 188
1:2.............................54
1:3............................296
1:4............................184
1:7.............................89
1:13–14 148
2:1..................72, 87, 277
2:2.............................55
2:5....................112, 190
2:8..............112, 149, 282
2:12.............................55
2:14...........................122
2:15...................144, 279
2:19.............................62
2:20...................127, 285
3:1.............................47
3:8............................134
3:18...........................127
4:1–3 283
4:9............................106
4:11...........................126
4:21–22 262
4:25.............156, 201, 290
4:26...........................212
4:32...................290, 300
5:3............................296
5:16...........................184
5:18...................96, 168
5:19–21 ....279, 283
5:21–22 287
5:25...................97, 102
6:4............................321
6:17...........................290

PHILIPPIANS

1:5.....................60, 245
1:7 87–88

1:12...........................260
1:21 260–61
1:22.............................50
1:27....................64, 105
1:29...................105, 263
2:1............................154
2:3............................281
2:6–11 151
2:6................98, 277, 290
2:7............................275
2:9–11 207
2:12.............................77
2:13...........................261
2:25...........................122
2:28...........................242
3:1............................130
3:8............................298
3:17...........................289
4:5............................318

COLOSSIANS

1:1............................188
1:6............................282
1:9............................291
1:15–20 151
1:15.............................55
2:3.............................51
3:2............................104
4:10.............................62

1 THESSALONIANS

1:7............................162
3:11...........................210
4:14...........................312
5:15–22 287

2 THESSALONIANS

2:1....................128, 177
2:6–7 148
2:15.............................88
3:11...........................289
3:13...........................320

1 TIMOTHY

1:15...........................291
2:6............................173
2:8....................196, 289
2:11...........................113
2:12...........................225

3:1.....................307
3:2.....................102
3:16..............75, 151, 162
5:18.....................228
6:10.....................118

2 TIMOTHY

1:1.....................188
1:16.....................210
2:26.....................146
3:15–16.....................287
3:16.....................139
4:2.....................318

TITUS

2:10.....................86, 139
2:13.....................122

PHILEMON

10.....................150
13.....................172

HEBREWS

1:2.....................109–10
1:3–4.....................151
1:4–14.....................77
1:4.....................56, 77
1:6.....................76
1:8.....................36
1:9.....................84
1:10.....................39
2:3.....................245, 290, 308
3:1.....................122
3:4.....................154, 191
3:12.....................62
4:1.....................208
4:12.....................132, 270
5:8.....................151
6:4–6.....................276
6:4.....................136
7:5.....................47
7:24.....................259
8:3.....................291
9:3.....................132
10:31.....................289
11:23.....................188

12:10.....................63
13:5.....................204

JAMES

1:1.....................100
1:5.....................210
1:12.....................138
1:13.....................61, 143, 188
1:27.....................263, 289
2:4.....................49
2:9.....................308
2:11.....................305
2:14.....................98, 262
2:15.....................270
2:20.....................40
2:26.....................137
3:2.....................176
3:7.....................76
3:10.....................156
4:2.....................290
4:7.....................212
4:13–14.....................290
4:15.....................146
5:17.....................32, 78

1 PETER

1:3.....................122
1:6.....................151
1:7.....................50
1:8.....................78, 277
1:16.....................197, 245, 317
1:25.....................145
2:12.....................137
2:18.....................283
3:14.....................315
3:19.....................152
3:21.....................59
4:1.....................55
5:6–7.....................275

2 PETER

1:1.....................122–23
1:17.....................143
1:19.....................138
2:20.....................122–23
3:18.....................122–23

1 JOHN

1:9.....................314
2:1.....................206
2:7.....................290
3:6.....................104, 225
3:8.....................223
3:9.....................225
3:10.....................136
3:16.....................291
4:8.....................109, 118
4:18.....................135
5:7.....................148
5:20.....................145, 228

2 JOHN

7.....................148, 281
9.....................147

3 JOHN

4.....................148

REVELATION

1:1.....................34
1:3.....................126
1:4.....................105
1:5.....................33
1:20.....................91
2:18.....................146
3:12.....................35
3:20.....................171
3:21.....................284
5:5.....................242, 321
5:11–12.....................78
7:1.....................287
7:11.....................253
9:1.....................46
9:15.....................128
13:18.....................113
18:12.....................50
19:7.....................182
20:2.....................132
21:8.....................124
22:8.....................122
22:10.....................205
22:20.....................40, 230

We want to hear from you. Please send your comments about this book to us in care of zreview@zondervan.com. Thank you.